Alexander Bergs and Laurel J. Brinton (Eds.)
The History of English
Volume 4

The History of English

Volume 4: Early Modern English

Edited by
Alexander Bergs and Laurel J. Brinton

ISBN 978-3-11-052277-8
e-ISBN (PDF) 978-3-11-052506-9
e-ISBN (EPUB) 978-3-11-052291-4

Library of Congress Cataloging-in-Publication Data
A CIP catalog record for this book has been applied for at the Library of Congress.

Bibliographic information published by the Deutsche Nationalbibliothek
The Deutsche Nationalbibliothek lists this publication in the Deutsche Nationalbibliografie;
detailed bibliographic data are available on the Internet at: http://dnb.dnb.de.

© 2017 Walter de Gruyter GmbH, Berlin/Boston
Cover image: Ladiras/iStock/Thinkstock
Typesetting: jürgen ullrich typosatz, Nördlingen
Printing: CPI Books GmbH; Leck
♾ Printed on acid-free paper
Printed in Germany

www.degruyter.com

Table of Contents

Abbreviations —— VII

Laurel J. Brinton and Alexander Bergs
Chapter 1: Introduction —— 1

Arja Nurmi
Chapter 2: Early Modern English: Overview —— 8

Julia Schlüter
Chapter 3: Phonology —— 27

Claire Cowie
Chapter 4: Morphology —— 47

Elena Seoane
Chapter 5: Syntax —— 68

Ian Lancashire
Chapter 6: Lexicon and semantics —— 89

Dawn Archer
Chapter 7: Pragmatics and discourse —— 108

Anneli Meurman-Solin
Chapter 8: Dialects —— 128

Laura Wright
Chapter 9: Language contact —— 150

Lilo Moessner
Chapter 10: Standardization —— 167

Helena Raumolin-Brunberg
Chapter 11: Sociolinguistics —— 188

Ulrich Busse
Chapter 12: Pronouns —— 209

Anthony Warner
Chapter 13: Periphrastic DO —— **224**

Manfred Krug
Chapter 14: The Great Vowel Shift —— 241

Christine Johansson
Chapter 15: Relativization —— 267

Colette Moore
Chapter 16: Literary language —— 287

Ulrich Busse and Beatrix Busse
Chapter 17: The language of Shakespeare —— 309

Index —— 333

Abbreviations

ACC	accusative case
ACT	active
ADJ	adjective
ADV	adverb
AN	Anglo-Norman
Angl.	Anglian
AUX	auxiliary
C	consonant
COMPR	comparative
DAT	dative case
DEM	demonstrative
DU	dual
EModE	Early Modern English
EWSax.	Early West Saxon
FEM	feminine
Fr.	French
GEN	genitive case
Ger.	German
Gk.	Greek
Go.	Gothic
Grmc.	Germanic
IE	Indo-European
IMP	imperative
IND	indicative
INF	infinitive
INFL	inflected
INSTR	instrumental case
Kent.	Kentish
LAEME	*A Linguistic Atlas of Early Middle English*
LALME	*A Linguistic Atlas of Late Mediaeval English*
Lt.	Latin
LModE	Late Modern English
LWSax.	Late West Saxon
MASC	masculine
ME	Middle English
MED	*Middle English Dictionary*
ModE	Modern English
NEG	negative

NEUT	neuter
N	noun
NOM	nominative case
NP	noun phrase
O	object
OBJ	objective case
OE	Old English
OED	*Oxford English Dictionary*
OFr.	Old French
OHG	Old High German
ON	Old Norse
P	person
PASS	passive
PAST	past tense
PDE	Present-day English
PGrmc.	Proto-Germanic
PIE	Proto-Indo-European
PL	plural
PREP	preposition
PRON	pronoun
PRTC	participle
PRES	present tense
PRET	preterit
S	subject
SG	singular
SUBJ	subjunctive mood
SUP	superlative
SOV	subject-object-verb word order
SVO	subject-verb-object word order
T	tense
V	verb
V2	verb second
V	vowel
VO	verb-object word order
VP	verb phrase
WGrmc.	West Germanic
WSax.	West Saxon
>	changes to, becomes
<	derives from

Ø	no ending
*	reconstructed form, ungrammatical form
< >	spelling

Laurel J. Brinton and Alexander Bergs
Chapter 1: Introduction

1 English Language Studies —— 1
2 Description of the Series —— 2
3 Description of this Volume —— 4
4 References —— 7

1 English Language Studies

The study of the English language has a lengthy history. The second half of the 18th century saw a phenomenal increase in the number of published grammars of the vernacular language, while the field of comparative linguistics arising in the 19th century was concerned in large part with the Germanic languages, including English. Moreover, in the field of theoretical linguistics that English has played a truly central role. While there are no reliable statistics, it seems safe to say that the majority of studies in contemporary linguistics deal at least in part with English, and are also written in English.

During the 20th century, monumental works concerned with the English language, both synchronic and diachronic, were produced, following historical/comparative and more contemporary linguistic approaches. In keeping with developments on the field of general linguistics, today it is possible to find descriptions and analyses of the history and development of English from virtually any linguistic perspective: external, internal, generative, functional, sociolinguistic, pragmatic, comparative, phonological, morphological, syntactic, lexical, semantic. There are numerous "Histories of English" to cater to just about every (theoretical) taste, as well as detailed descriptions of historical periods, language levels, or theoretical frameworks of English and specialized studies of individual topics in the development of the language.

Work on the history of English has culminated most recently in the a series of edited handbooks and histories of English: the six-volume *Cambridge History of the English Language,* edited by Richard M. Hogg (1992–2001), *The Handbook of the History of English,* edited by Ans van Kemenade and Bettelou Los (2006), *The*

Laurel J. Brinton: Vancouver (Canada)
Alexander Bergs: Osnabrück (Germany)

Oxford History of English, edited by Lynda Mugglestone (2012 [2006]), *The Oxford Handbook of the History of English*, edited by Elizabeth Closs Traugott and Terttu Nevalainen (2012), the two-volume *English Historical Linguistics: An International Handbook*, edited by Alexander Bergs and Laurel J. Brinton (2012), and most recently *The Cambridge Handbook of English Historical Linguistics*, edited by Päiva Pahta and Merja Kytö (2015).

While study of the history of any language begins with texts, increasingly scholars are turning to dictionaries and corpora of English that are available online or electronically. The third edition of the *Oxford English Dictionary* online, while still undergoing revision, is now fully integrated with the *Historical Thesaurus*. The *Middle English Dictionary*, completed in 2001, is freely available online along with the *Corpus of Middle English Prose and Verse*. The pioneer historical corpus of English, *The Helsinki Corpus of English Texts*, was first released to scholars in 1991. The *Dictionary of Old English Web Corpus*, containing all Old English texts, is searchable online. ARCHER, *A Representative Corpus of English Registers 1650–1900*, accessible at a number of universities, provides a balanced selection of historical texts in electronic form. COHA, a 400-million-word, balanced *Corpus of Historical American English 1810–2009*, was launched online in 2010. Smaller corpora, such as the *Corpus of English Dialogues 1560–1760*, the *Lampeter Corpus of Early Modern English Tracts*, the *Corpus of Early English Correspondence*, the *Corpus of Early English Medical Writing*, the *Corpus of Late Modern English 3.0*, and the newly expanded *Old Bailey Corpus*, have made more specialized corpora – covering more periods and more text types – available to scholars. Archives of historical newspapers online, including the *Zurich English Newspaper Corpus* and the *Rostock Newspaper Corpus*, provide another source of electronic data. Finally, syntactically annotated corpora for historical stages of English are being produced, including *The York-Helsinki Parsed Corpus of Old English Poetry*, *The York-Toronto-Helsinki Parsed Corpus of Old English Prose*, *The Penn-Helsinki Parsed Corpus of Middle English*, and *The Penn-Helsinki Parsed Corpus of Early Modern English*. (For information on all of the corpora listed here, see http://www.helsinki.fi/varieng/CoRD/corpora/).

2 Description of the Series

The two-volume *English Historical Linguistics: An International Handbook* (Bergs and Brinton 2012) serves as the textual basis for the current five-volume reader series *The History of English*. The aim of this series is to make selected papers from this important handbook accessible and affordable for a wider audience, and in particular for younger scholars and students, and to allow their use in the classroom. Each chapter is written by a recognized specialist in the topic and includes an extensive bibliography suitable for a range of levels and interests.

While conventional histories of English (e.g., Brinton and Arnovick 2016) are almost universally organized chronologically, the six-volume *Cambridge History of English* (Hogg 1992–2001) is organized by linguistic level, as is the shortened version (Hogg and Denison 2006) and to a lesser extent *The Handbook of the History of English* (van Kemanade and Los 2006). Volumes 1 to 4 of this series likewise follow this pattern:

Volume 1: The History of English: Historical Outlines from Sound to Text provides a comprehensive overview of the history of English and explores key questions and debates. The volume begins with a re-evaluation of the concept of periodization in the history of English. This is followed by overviews of changes in the traditional areas of phonology, morphology, syntax, and semantics as well as chapters covering areas less often treated in histories of English, including prosody, idioms and fixed expressions, pragmatics and discourse, onomastics, orthography, style/register/text types, and standardization.

Volume 2: The History of English: Old English provides an in-depth account of Old English. Individual chapters review the state of the art in phonological, morphological, syntactic, and semantic studies of Old English. Key areas of debate, including dialectology, language contact, standardization, and literary language, are also explored. The volume sets the scene with a chapter on pre-Old English and ends with a chapter discussing textual resources available for the study of earlier English.

Volume 3: The History of English: Middle English provides a wide-ranging account of Middle English. Not only are the traditional areas of linguistic study explored in state-of-the-art chapters on Middle English phonology morphology, syntax, and semantics, but the volume also covers less traditional areas of study, including Middle English creolization, sociolinguistics, literary language (including the language of Chaucer), pragmatics and discourse, dialectology, standardization, language contact, and multilingualism.

Volume 4: The History of English: Early Modern English provides a comprehensive account of Early Modern English. In seventeen chapters, this volume not only presents detailed outlines of the traditional language levels, such as phonology, morphology, syntax, semantics and pragmatics, but it also explores key questions and debates, such as *do*-periphrasis, the Great Vowel Shift, pronouns and relativization, literary language (including the language of Shakespeare), and sociolinguistics, including contact and standardization.

The last volume in the series turns its attention to the spread of English worldwide. **Volume 5: The History of English: Varieties of English** is one of the first detailed expositions of the history of different varieties of English. It explores language variation and varieties of English from an historical perspective, covering theoretical topics such as diffusion and supra-regionalization as well as concrete descriptions of the internal and external historical developments of more than a dozen varieties of English including American English, African American Vernacular English, Received Pronunciation, Estuary English, and English in Canada, Africa, India, Wales, among many others.

Taking into account the important developments in the study of English effected by the availability of electronic corpora, this series of readers on *The History of English* offers a comprehensive, interdisciplinary, and theory-neutral synopsis of the field. It is meant to facilitate both research and teaching by offering up-to-date overviews of all the relevant aspects of the historical linguistics of English and by referring scholars, teachers, and students to more in-depth coverage. To that end, many articles have been updated from the 2012 edition to include more recent publications.

3 Description of this volume

This volume provides a comprehensive and wide-ranging treatment of Early Modern English, covering the standard topics included in traditional histories of English (such as Early Modern English phonology, morphology, and syntax) as well as a range of topics usually reserved for more specialized texts (such as the development of *do*-periphrasis and pronouns, the Great Vowel Shift, standardization, and literary language).

The first chapter on "Early Modern English: Overview" by **Arja Nurmi** provides a general introduction to this period of the English language by discussing major social, political and cultural changes. She describes the role of the printing press and of increased mobility in the process of vernacularization and the spread of new linguistic forms.

The next four chapters cover the traditional components of linguistic study: phonology, morphology, syntax, and semantics/lexicon. **Julia Schlüter** in her chapter on Early Modern English "Phonology" points out that English saw some fundamental changes in all its phonological subsystems during the Early Modern period. After an extensive discussion of suprasegmental aspects, such as word stress and syllable reduction, she concentrates on changes in both the consonantal and vowel inventories. Her treatment of qualitative changes in the vowel system excludes the Great Vowel Shift (for which see Krug, Chapter 14), and instead focuses on monophthongization of Middle English diphthongs, the development of short vowels, and the interplay of vowels and consonants in particular environments. **Claire Cowie** presents the effects of the shift from synthetic Old

English to analytic Modern English in her chapter on "Morphology". She shows that, while the inflectional systems of Early Modern English are more or less those of Modern English, the derivational morphology of the period shows some radically new phenomena, including the reanalysis of Latin affixes from borrowed terms. The rate of change, however, is very variable, and one of the major aims of the chapter is to capture this dynamicity. In her chapter on "Syntax", **Elena Seoane Posse** begins by stressing that abundant, heterogeneous data make the study of syntax for this period particularly interesting and rewarding, especially since sociolinguistic and stylistic factors can also be systematically included. The chapter presents six core areas of morphosyntactic change: the genitive, the loss of impersonal constructions, changes in verbal periphrases and in the complementation system as well as negation and the fixation of word order. **Ian Lancashire** points out that modern digital resources (such as the Online OED, Early English Books Online, or the Textbase of Early Tudor English) are radically changing the study of "Lexicon and semantics", just as printing technology itself changed the language in the Early Modern period. English as a language seems to have grown from only 10,000 words or so to a lexically rich language during this period – even though under the early Tudors it was still often seen as a vulgar and unsophisticated tongue.

Moving beyond the standard linguistic components, the remaining chapters discuss a variety of larger topics pertaining to Early Modern English. In "Pragmatics and discourse", **Dawn Archer** presents an overview of the most prominent phenomena from pragmatics and discourse, including speech acts, (im)politeness, address terms, discourse markers and discourse strategies. In particular, she suggests that researchers need to be aware of the relationship of individual, language and society when they discuss discourse or pragmatics. Early Modern English dialectology is a relatively under-researched field of study, **Anneli Meurman-Solin** concedes in her chapter on "Dialects", partly because there has been a lack of quantitative and qualitative digital data, but also because previous research often concentrated on language attitudes and prescriptivist traditions. Now, with the advent of comprehensive digital databases, there is a new line of research that focuses on inductively discovering inventories and features of linguistic subsystems in particular areas. "Language Contact" between English and other languages (and also between different dialects in Britain) is the topic of **Laura Wright**'s chapter. She argues that such contact not only led to lexical borrowings, but also implied grammatical changes and was probably part and parcel of the development of Standard English. Moreover, the chapter also explores the export of varieties of English beyond the British Isles, into the New World and the Southern Hemisphere. The reduction of variation and the elaboration of function are key concepts in **Lilo**

Moessner's chapter on "Standardization". During the Early Modern period, we see the reduction of variation on the level of morphology, syntax, and spelling, and, simultaneously, the spread of English into new functions, such as learned discourse, which was previously dominated by Latin. The development of vocabulary plays a central role in this process. **Helena Raumolin-Brunberg** focuses on "Sociolinguistics" and shows in her chapter that in the Early Modern English factors such as gender, social rank, region or register can be investigated in great detail and with important findings, especially for the diffusion of linguistic change. Three variables take center stage in this chapter: the replacement of *ye* by *you*, third person singular verb inflection with *-s/-th*, and multiple negation. All these variables show some significant interplay with the factors gender and region. Moreover, micro-sociolinguistic factors such as social networks also seem to play a role.

The following four chapters deal with phenomena which are more or less specific for Early Modern English and which warrant individual detailed treatment. **Ulrich Busse**'s chapter on "Pronouns" discusses the development of the third person plural pronoun *hem* vs. *them*, the third person singular neuter pronouns *his/its*, as well as *my/thy* versus *mine/thine* and of course the second person pronouns *ye/you* and *thou/you*. Busse suggests breaking down the Early Modern English period into three isolectal stages in order to show the variability of the individual forms and their development. **Anthony Warner**'s chapter deals with one of the most central developments of Early Modern English morphosyntax, the rise of "Periphrastic *do*". Warner studies the variability in the use of *do* and its evolution towards the modern pattern in the context of a number of parameters, including discourse/style, lexematic context or collocations, phonotactics, and clause types. While conceding that it is still unclear whether some of this variability reveals motivations for the development of *do*, or simply reflects speakers' choices, Warner points out that new digital corpora can help us shed some more light on this central problem of syntactic change. **Manfred Krug** tackles an equally old and big problem from phonology in his chapter on the "Great Vowel Shift". He presents a comprehensive survey of Great Vowel Shift theories and their main issues and tenets. He argues that many of the existing theories are actually very problematic or controversial, and that in fact we know very little about this important sound change. In conclusion, this chapter tries to develop some firm, factual ground for further discussion. "Relativization" in Early Modern English is the topic of **Christine Johannson**'s chapter. After *that* as the sole relativizer in the middle Middle English period, we see the rise and spread of the *wh*-relativizers in late Middle English and Early Modern English. In her study, Johannson focuses on speech-related material (drama and trials) and shows that *that* is the predominant form here. *Who* is rare and *which* is even declining in these genres. Instead, she finds zero (i.e. relativizer ellipsis) to be on the increase as a real competitor for *that*.

The final two chapters of this volume deal with literary language. **Colette Moore** in her chapter "Literary Language" takes a more general stance towards the matter and shows that many literary forms were actually influenced by classical models. This, and the desire to codify and organize become apparent not only in language, but also in literary styles and the abundant publication of rhetorical manuals. At the same time, we see the first efforts in the later Early Modern period to use English as a literary, elaborate language and English literary works in nation-building. **Ulrich Busse** and **Beatrix Busse** concentrate on one single author and discuss "The Language of Shakespeare". After a brief discussion of reference works and research tools, they describe Shakespeare's language in some detail on the level of phonology, vocabulary, and grammar before they turn more recent domains, such as pragmatics and sociolinguistics. In their conclusion, they emphasize that modern digital tools may help to shed further light on some open questions, and may also be helpful in the empirical investigation not only of syntactic features or Shakespeare's grammar, but also of speech acts or discourse markers in the Shakespeare corpus.

4 References

Brinton, Laurel J. and Leslie K. Arnovick. 2016. *The English Language: A Linguistic History*. 3rd edn. Toronto: Oxford University Press.

Hogg, Richard. 1992–2001. *The Cambridge History of the English Language*. 6 vols. Cambridge: Cambridge University Press.

Hogg, Richard and David Denison. 2006. *A History of the English Language*. Cambridge: Cambridge University Press.

Kemenade, Ans van and Bettelou Los. 2006. *The Handbook of the History of English*. Chichester: Wiley-Blackwell.

Kytö, Merja and Päiva Pahta. 2015. *The Cambridge Handbook of English Historical Linguistics*. Cambridge: Cambridge University Press.

Nevalainen, Terttu and Elizabeth Closs Traugott. 2012. *The Oxford Handbook of the History of English*. Oxford: Oxford University Press.

Mugglestone, Lynda. 2012. *The Oxford History of English*. Updated edn. Oxford: Oxford University Press. [First published 2006]

Arja Nurmi
Chapter 2:
Early Modern English: Overview

1 Introduction —— 8
2 Historical and social background —— 10
3 Printing and vernacularization —— 16
4 Resources for the study of Early Modern English —— 20
5 Changes in Early Modern English —— 22
6 References —— 24

Abstract: The two most notable changes in the Early Modern English period (1500–1700) were standardization and the growth of the lexicon. Changes in the cultural and political climate, such as the spread of printing and increasing availability of education and subsequent growing literacy among the population, were linked to these changes. The process of vernacularization in many areas (science, religion, law, government) produced new uses for English, and the Renaissance ideals of writing produced new styles and registers. Increased mobility, particularly towards London, contributed to the spread of linguistic innovations. The progressively more global trade brought contacts with new languages, and the spread of English world wide took its first steps in the colonialization of North America.

1 Introduction

Early Modern English is perhaps most commonly said to range from 1500 to 1700, but since language change is gradual rather than abrupt, such demarcation lines are naturally abstractions. Late Middle English during the 15th century increasingly shows features typical of Modern English, becoming more easily understandable even to the untrained present-day reader. The spread of the printing presses, one of the shaping forces on the development of Early Modern English, started towards the end of that century. Similarly, the cut-off date at 1700 marks the approximate time when most great changes during the Early Modern English period had run their course, and leaves the heyday of the prescriptive and normative tradition of the 18th century outside this stage in the development of the language.

Arja Nurmi: Tampere (Finland)

The social, political, and cultural changes associated with the Renaissance all influenced the development of the English language in the early modern period. These changes were in many ways interrelated, and reinforced each other. The preference for studying classical sources instead of the medieval authorities' commentaries on them (*Ad fontes*) led to an educational reform, benefiting from the new appreciation of learning. The new schools provided literacy for an increasingly large part of the population. The changes in the intellectual climate and educational opportunities were both tied to the advancement of science and the concomitant vernacularization process of scientific writing. The Reformation, with a gradual break from the Latin traditions of the Catholic Church and the vernacularization of religious life, showed a parallel trend in stressing the authority of the original source, the Bible, and the need for people to have the ability to study it first-hand. Similar trends of vernacularization can be found in other areas of life, such as politics and law. Finally, the Age of Discovery provided contacts with new cultures as well as the beginnings of colonialization and, on the linguistic front, the first stages of American English. Many changes had a direct impact on the daily lives of the population, and the printing press was instrumental in disseminating these trends to the reading public.

On the level of linguistic change, the two most notable processes are the standardization of written language and the vast increase in the lexicon. Much attention has been paid to the standardization process, which tends to provide an overly narrow view of the language as a whole, since dialects continued to be spoken (and in some cases written) by a vast majority of the population, even if this is disguised in the evidence remaining to us. While standardization of particularly printed sources tends to mask existing linguistic variation, there are also sources which give us a new perspective on the language. From the point of view of the linguist studying the period, the most important difference with earlier centuries is the wealth of new evidence on the linguistic practices of the population, providing us with English that was never written down before, or not in such quantity. Not only are there more types of texts (such as scientific and religious writing) being written in English, there are also more people than ever leaving written evidence concerning their lives. "Ego documents", such as letters, autobiographies, wills, and travelogues, all have first person singular in common, but they also all give first-hand evidence of the linguistic practices of people in often quite private and personal, informal circumstances. We are still at the mercy of what has been preserved, but because more texts of all kinds were produced, there are also more kinds of writing remaining.

There are few general descriptions of Early Modern English. The most extensive of these is the third volume of the *Cambridge History of English* (Lass 1999). There are also three book-length introductions aimed primarily at an undergraduate readership: Barber (1997), Görlach (1991), and Nevalainen (2006). Each represents a particular stage in the scholarship on Early Modern English, as can be most clearly seen in the evidence they use to support their description of the language. Barber illustrates his volume mostly through literary texts, following the tradition of stressing the importance of Shakespeare, and the value of drama as evidence of spoken language. Görlach includes an ample selection of texts from a number of genres, bringing a wider perspective by the inclusion of more formal, non-literary types of writing. Nevalainen is a representative of the present-day paradigm of corpus-based research and draws her examples from electronic corpora and databases (see Section 4 below). All approaches have their merits, and together they provide a fuller picture of what the English language was like. Together they also illustrate the varied approaches it is possible to take when studying the language of the early modern period.

This chapter has its main focus on the social, cultural, and political contexts in which Early Modern English was produced (Section 2) and on the production of English language texts (Section 3). A brief introduction to resources for the study of Early Modern English is provided in Section 4. The last section gives a brief overview of some of the changes in the language of the period, but leaves the more detailed discussion of all the linguistic aspects of Early Modern English to be found in the relevant chapters elsewhere in these volumes.

2 Historical and social background

Language variation and change never take place in isolation. The connections between language and society mean that historical events need to be taken into account also when discussing the overall developments of Early Modern English. While Lass (1999: 5) is certainly correct in asserting that "[t]he story of a language 'itself' must be carefully distinguished from the story of its changing uses, users and social context – just as the changes themselves (as results) must be distinguished from the mechanisms by which they came about (e.g. lexical and social diffusion)", it would still be remiss of us to overlook the influence of political and social changes taking place in the society where Early Modern English was being spoken and written. These changes required language users to adapt to new situations by creating new words and new styles of writing, they facilitated or hindered the dissemination of changes, and they influenced the variety of texts produced and preserved to us for study.

Arguably, the most significant political events in the history of the period (at least when looked at from a linguistic point of view) were probably the Reformation and the consequent dissolution of the monasteries in the 16th century and the Civil War in the 17th century. Both episodes led to increasingly loose network ties because of the increased mobility of the population, and these in turn sped up linguistic change for some variables (Milroy 1992; Raumolin-Brunberg 1998). Both also produced, directly or indirectly, new types of texts, which allowed English to be written down in ways unlike those of previous centuries.

The main development in social history relevant for language change was the advancement of educational opportunities for a wider range of social strata and the subsequent increased literacy rate of the population. This, in turn, gives us more linguistic first-hand evidence from a larger proportion of the population. The more widespread literacy also tied in with the advancement of printing, since there was a more extensive reading public than before. The availability of new genres for a lay audience and the growing vernacularization of genres such as science and religion, which had previously been mainly the province of Latin, were all part of the larger picture.

The population of England increased rapidly during the 16th century, followed by a time of stagnation before a further increase began in the 18th century (Coleman and Salt 1992: 2). Since there were no reliable statistics or census data created at the time, estimates of population size have been made based on such divergent data as muster rolls, lay subsidy rolls, ecclesiastical censuses, and parish registers. The reliability of population information increases when "a modernizing mercantilist state" required accurate information of resources and security, but also increasing literacy and numeracy and a more settled social and political order contributed to the development (Coleman and Salt 1992: 7). A summary of different population estimates suggests that the mid-16th-century population of England was somewhere around 2.8 million, rising to 4.1 million in the early 17th century, and showing a reasonably steady 5.0–5.2 million in the latter half of the 17th century (Coleman and Salt 1992: 5). The population of Scotland around 1600 has been estimated at one million, stagnating after that, while Ireland went from the same one-million population in 1600 to twice that in 1700; the North American English-speaking population started from a few thousand and reached quarter of a million by 1700 (Kishlansky 1996: 8). The population of London increased at a much more rapid pace than that of the country in general, from 50,000 in 1500 to 200,000 in 1600 and 575,000 in 1700 (Coleman and Salt 1992: 28). This shows the growing importance of the metropolis as a hub of government, commerce, and culture, and points to a special position also from the point of view of linguistic development.

Already in medieval Britain there was a fair amount of geographical mobility and a later age of marriage than seems to have been common elsewhere in Europe. This was due to a free market in land, labor, and food. During the early modern period the average household consisted of 4.7 people, who were members of the nuclear family, and only rarely were there three generations under one roof. Up to 30% of households included servants, i.e. resident household or farm workers, who were typically single, aged between 15 and 30, and both men and women. As many as three quarters of boys and half of girls were in service at some point of their life. The common practice of service increased the geographical mobility of the population even further. The average age of first marriage in the 17th century for men was around 28 and for women 26 (Coleman and Salt 1992: 7, 14–15). This pattern of population movement had an impact on linguistic change in promoting dialect contact.

As the population increased, there was even greater pressure for migration. While there was a great deal of subsistence migration by the unskilled and poor, particularly after 1650 there was also a large number of skilled people migrating to better themselves. Especially Scotland and Ireland produced a constant stream of migrants both to England and later to the New World (Kishlansky 1996: 13). We can only speculate how different the linguistic patterns of the mostly unlettered subsistence migrants and the at least minimally educated skilled migrants were, and how much influence either group would have had in the new location they settled at. The effect of social ambition on linguistic patterns has been established, so it is plausible that skilled workers would have more resources for linguistic adaptation.

The major population crises during the early modern period were epidemics of the sweating sickness in the mid-16th century and recurring plague. In London, over 15% of all deaths between 1580 and 1650 were caused by the plague. There were significant epidemics in 1563, 1593, and 1603, with minor outbreaks in 1578 and 1582 (Rappaport 1989: 72). The epidemics increased mobility among the population in two ways. On the one hand, the number of deaths meant there was more room for newcomers from all over the country. On the other hand, people fleeing London because of the danger probably took their new city ways, including any linguistic innovations, with them. In the 17th century, the Civil War had its own cost in loss of life: the estimated number of deaths was 80,000 in combat and 100,000 from disease (Coleman and Salt 1992: 24). Overall, the death rate in towns was higher than the birth rate, which made constant migration necessary for their growth. The continuous stream of migrants to London meant that English from all over the country could be heard in the streets, even if some areas (particularly North England) were over-represented (Coleman and Salt 1992: 27).

During the early modern period, unlike the medieval times, there was no major, linguistically significant, influx of immigrants from abroad, but there were foreign craftsmen who moved to England to stay. Many of these were Protestants escaping religious persecution on the continent, but also skilled craftsmen from various countries seeking a livelihood. Around 1500 one in ten craftsmen in

London were immigrants, and by 1540 they numbered one in six. In the rest of the country they were found in smaller numbers (Youings 1984: 128). Again, we can only speculate on the influence of these people, but arguably they would have had some influence on the professional language of their particular trade if nothing else.

In contrast to earlier periods, there was more emigration from England, Ireland, and Scotland. The colonization of North America began, and after the first wave of migrants the surplus population of Ireland and Scotland was overrepresented among those seeking opportunities in the New World. This obviously had an impact on how the new variety began to be shaped.

As a result of new trade routes being discovered, English merchants, such as the East India Company, could be found trading at far distant places from the late 16th century onwards. While the original intent was to trade mostly with the East Indies, the company founded trading posts all over the Asian coastline, including India and China, but also e.g. Japan. There were also other trading companies in the West Indies and West Africa, but none was quite as long-lived or influential. The trading contacts led not only to new vocabulary for previously unknown peoples, cultures, and merchandise, but also to yet another new genre of popular writing, the travelogue. Contact was maintained not only with the indigenous peoples but also with other European traders working in the same areas, which led to the creation of trading jargons, and numerous letters were sent home, describing conditions of trade.

2.1 Education

The humanist ideas of the Renaissance led to an increased appreciation of education. The aristocracy began to maintain the ideal of the well-rounded gentleman, which included learning. At the same time, education was increasingly seen as the means of providing the country with competent public servants. This was a trend that had already started in the 15th century, but it became increasingly important in the early modern period. Since the reorganization of the Tudor state and the expansion of government activities, as well as the increase in diplomacy and foreign trade, came with a concomitant need for voluminous correspondence and detailed record keeping, there was a constant demand for literate and learned civil servants (Briggs 1994: 97; Cressy 1975: 5).

Education was increasingly a secular business (Youings 1984: 17). While the dissolution of the monasteries had led to the end of schools in connection with monasteries, it provided the country with unemployed monks, who were often able to work as freelance school teachers in informal schools over the country.

At the same time, new secular schools were being founded. Henry VIII alone is linked to at least eighteen schools founded or re-established during his reign, and many of the nobility followed suit. Schoolmasters needed a license to teach, and before the Civil War these licenses were under ecclesiastical control, with the purpose of preventing Catholic and Puritan teaching. During the Commonwealth control was shifted to the Parliament, but the success of any authority on imposing their demands on individual teachers is likely to have been limited at best.

Education, like everything else in the society, depended on social status. The number of schools increased by at least 300 in 1500–1620, but the type of schools was extremely varied. At the one end, there were small private schools kept by a single master, at the other, grammar schools with wealthy patrons (Briggs 1994: 123). In 1647, educational reformer Samuel Hartlib envisioned four different types of education for the different social strata: one for the "vulgar, whose life is mechanical", another for the gentry, "who are to bear charges in the commonwealth". The third kind of school should be for scholars, who would go on to be teachers, and the fourth for the ministry (cited from Cressy 1975: 23). For the highest ranks of society, education was a value in itself, often initially received at home from tutors, while the lower ranks saw education as a means of social advancement, and were more typically educated at the various types of schools (Youings 1984: 119–120).

Apart from social rank, gender was another major influence on the type and breadth of education available for individual people. While there were exceptional women at any given time, highly educated and well-read, they were definitely in the minority. Women like Margaret Roper, Katherine Astley, Queen Elizabeth, Ann Conway, or Dorothy Osborne were the exception, not the rule. Formal education was mostly unavailable, although some girls attended petty schools, small elementary schools often run by a single teacher. With higher social status came the possibility of private tutoring, at times including even classical learning. Since women did not work outside the home in professions where literacy and learning were needed, teaching them anything beyond basic skills was not considered a priority. In 1581 Richard Mulcaster, when discussing the education of women, suggested that "[r]eading if for nothing else (…) is very needful for religion, to read that which they must know and ought to perform" (cited from Cressy 1975: 110). A century later, in 1673, Bathusa Makin started a private academy for young ladies at Tottenham, but was very conscious of the resistance she was likely to meet: "I expect to meet with many scoffs and taunts from inconsiderate and illiterate men, that prize their own lusts and pleasure more than your [= that of 'all ingenious and virtuous ladies'] profit and content" (cited from Cressy 1975: 113).

Increased educational opportunities appeared at all levels of schooling: the number of students attending universities rose, and new groups of people, such as parish priests, had a university degree. For lay people, universities were a means of social advancement in the administration, but many depended on a wealthy patron or a scholarship to pay for their expensive education. Legal training at the Inns of Court was almost entirely beyond people below the rank of gentry because of the prohibitive cost (Briggs 1994: 124).

In the end, sources describing the realities of education leave much for conjecture, and a great deal of what we know is based on estimations, but there is a body of writing on the theory. A great many handbooks describing the kind of education that was desirable were published, ranging from Elyot's *Book Named the Governor* (1531) to Ascham's *Schoolmaster* (1570) and Mulcaster's *Positions* (1581). What the existence of these books shows us is that the content of a suitable education was in general agreed upon. The handbooks range from the philosophical to the practical, discussing the education of all strata of society (Brink 2010: 31).

2.2 Literacy

At the beginning of the early modern period literacy in England was restricted to the elites of society, but the transition to mass literacy began during this time (Cressy 1980: 175). Around 1500, the estimated rate of illiteracy for men was approximately 90%, while for women it was still very close to 100%. The literate people belonged to the highest strata of the population, and literacy was, for talented young men lucky enough to find a patron to support their education, a way of social advancement. Around 1600, illiteracy had clearly decreased, close to 30% of men being literate, but still only 10% of women. By 1700, the change is remarkable, since nearly half of all men could read and write and a quarter of women as well (Cressy 1980: 177). It should be remembered that these statistics are based on estimates, and that some of the assumptions at the basis of them are not completely reliable. It may well be, for example, that a person may sign a document with a mark and yet be able to write. Particularly the literacy of gentlewomen may be underestimated. There were many occasions when it was vitally important for a woman de facto looking after the estates in the absence of her husband to be able to keep account of household matters, to oversee the work of scribes employed by the family and the like, and this could be achieved more reliably if the mistress of the house was herself literate. At the same time, when scribes were available, women may simply have preferred to make use of their services rather than writing themselves (Brink 2010: 28–29).

Literacy in early modern England was taught as two separate skills, reading and writing. This means that those who could read were not necessarily able to write. Reading was advocated by religious and secular writers alike. The ability to read the Bible was considered to be a spiritual benefit of great value to the general public. At the same time, education was seen as having both a moral and a civic value (Cressy 1980: 186).

As mentioned above, different strata of the population did not have equal access to education, which also leads to literacy being unequally represented among them. It should be remembered, however, that literacy was not necessarily learned at school, but could also be taught by a family member or employer. Boys apprenticed to craftsmen and merchants were usually expected to have an elementary command of literacy and numeracy (Youings 1984). They would then be further instructed by their masters in the skills specific to their trade. Letter writing, for example, was often learned by copying old letters. This transferred not only the spelling conventions of the writing community, but also the textual practices involved in that particular genre. In addition to factual literacy, being able to transfer one's thoughts to paper, it was often necessary to be familiar with genre conventions and the requirements of a particular author-audience relationship. While some social conventions of spoken language (such as forms of address) could be more or less directly transferred to written form, there were other practices in the areas of, for example, style shifting and deferential discourse which were probably more tied to the written expression of social relations. In addition, much depended on a writer's command of the "rules" of written language (see e.g. Palander-Collin 2009).

3 Printing and vernacularization

One of the greatest changes in the early modern period when compared to the Middle Ages was the proliferation of all kinds of writing in English. As mentioned above, this was linked to the cultural developments related to the Renaissance and to the greater number of literate readers as a lay audience for new genres. Both entertainment and information of all kinds were reaching their readership. This new proliferation of different types of texts was possible because there was a reading public willing to pay.

The mass-production of books, the increased literacy, and the relative affluence of middle ranks gave rise to a new audience for the more popular sorts of writing. Fiction of all kinds – prose, verse, and drama – was published in increasing amounts, ranging from broadside ballads to multivolume collections of plays. Pamphlets were produced to enlighten the public, to present political views, and to introduce new ideas and inventions. For example, sermons, the pros and cons of tobacco smoking, and new scientific discoveries were all topics suited for this form of publication. Handbooks providing instruction on many fields from medicine and culinary recipes to letter writing and proper conduct in polite society were increasingly made available to the lay readership.

For the linguist, there is also much more surviving data than from earlier centuries, probably because so much more was written, both for publication and for private audiences. Many examples of private writing, particularly ego documents such as private letters and journals, remain unedited in archives, but the wealth of edited data is significantly more varied than in previous centuries. On the one hand, English was being used in new kinds of written language, presenting us with registers which either did not exist in earlier centuries or were curtailed to spoken language. On the other hand, because of the increased proportion of literate people, we are gaining direct access to the language of an ever widening part of the population. We are no longer solely reliant on fiction for the language of the middle and even lower ranks, since they – or at least some of them – are able to put pen to paper themselves. Similarly, women's voices are more clearly heard during the early modern period than ever before. As the legal system increasingly functioned in English, court proceedings were also beginning to be recorded (and published) in that language, giving further voice to the previously silent. This means that our understanding of the full range of English in use is more complete than during earlier centuries. We are still far from actual spoken language, but we are getting a better idea of private and informal language from the actual speakers themselves.

Personal correspondence is one obvious genre, made necessary, for example, by the mobility of people, as they entered service, moved to London to find their fortunes, or married outside their own immediate locality. There are also more personal journals, commonplace books, and household accounts, which all reveal the more private and often informal side of people. On the more official side, the number of documents prepared by the growing number of civil servants increases notably during the period, and these documents are more typically written in English than during the Middle Ages, when they were more often written in Latin and Norman French. Because we have very little corresponding material from earlier periods, it is often difficult to estimate whether some words or forms of expression are new to the age or have simply never been written down before – or at least not in a form that has survived to us.

3.1 Printing

Printing was a way of disseminating ideas, but also a way of disseminating the emerging written standard language. Printed books had a wider circulation than manuscripts (and many genres still circulated largely in that form), but it is notoriously difficult to estimate how great a difference this made to the actual size of the reading public. Ownership of books was certainly fashionable, and a way of displaying wealth (Youings 1984: 194). The number of books printed each year increased steadily, and in addition to books, there were pamphlets and broadsheets (Briggs 1994: 123).

The book trade had its centre in London, but was by no means confined to it. Major towns had their established book sellers, and books were available at markets and fairs, by traveling peddlers along with other merchandise. During the third quarter of the 16th century nearly 4,000 books were published, and during the last quarter this nearly doubled. In the 17th century, nearly ten thousand books were published in each quarter century (O'Callaghan 2010: 165).

One of the consequences of the educational system becoming more regulated was a greater degree of shared background amongst the educated, and a widening of areas of interest. The ideal of the "Renaissance Man" included both literary culture and the visual arts, but also physical skills such as fencing, shooting, riding, and dancing (Briggs 1994: 124). This led to an interest in guides and handbooks in the various areas of expertise deemed necessary for the perfect courtier. Also other books, ostensibly aimed at a more common readership, were in actual fact aimed at the highest ranks. For example, Fitzherbert's *Book of Husbandry*, published in 1523, was quite expensive and had a small print run of a few hundred copies (Youings 1984).

There was also an increasing interest in news, which led to the publication of newsbooks from the early 1620s onwards. There were newsletters that readers could subscribe to, and these were often distributed in manuscript form, but printing was eventually the way for news as well. By the end of the 17th century, there were numerous news sheets being published, as well as twice- or thrice-weekly newspapers such as the *London Gazette* or the *British Mercury* (Briggs 1994: 165–166).

Cheap, popular writing of the era included ballads, chapbooks, almanacs, and jestbooks, as well as other types of fairly ephemeral writing, which has often been regarded as representing the literary tastes of the lower ranks of society (Barry 1995: 73). On the other hand, escapist literature in the form of chivalric romances continued to be quite popular, and it is more than likely that the readership of these books went far beyond the highest strata of literate society (Barry 1995: 74). Texts were translated, abridged, rewritten, and sampled for the benefit and pleasure of those not able to read them in the original (Barry 1995: 80). Snippets were published as unbound books and in newspapers and magazines, which made them available at a lower price. Texts would be shared by several people by reading aloud in places where people gathered, which further lowered the cost for each reader (Barry 1995: 81).

3.2 Vernacularization

Early modern England was no longer a multilingual country in the way medieval England was. While Celtic languages continued to be spoken in the west, the Norman French aristocracy had seemingly lost their language by the 16th century. Despite the loss of societal multilingualism, functional multilingualism continued in many ways. Latin was still the language of higher and upper-class education, and people would learn other languages according to the necessities of their trade. So, for example, merchants involved in foreign trade would know a variety of languages depending on the direction of trade. For trade with continental Europe, French, Dutch, and Italian could be useful, while the more far-reaching trade of the East India Company, for example, made it useful for traders to learn at least a smattering of the languages of people traded with, as well as trading languages and jargons.

The knowledge and use of languages other than English was reflected in the code-switching patterns of different genres. There was a greater variety of languages switched into than in medieval times (see Raumolin-Brunberg, Chapter 11), reflecting the changes in society and types of texts, but Latin was still the most frequently occurring language. Particularly scientific and religious texts show a high incidence of passages in languages other than English, especially when the intended audience was professional (Pahta and Nurmi 2006). This seems to indicate that there was still an expectation of Latin being known by the readers, even if the main body of the text was in English.

Code-switching in these two domains can be seen as a bridge phenomenon in one of the processes that had a great influence on the development of Early Modern English, vernacularization (see Wright, Chapter 9). This was a progression that could be seen in many types of texts. While scientific and religious writing are often cited as examples, the same development could also be seen in e.g. administrative documents. English was now being used in registers and domains which had previously been performed in another language, most typically Latin and French. Görlach (1999: 462) estimates that around 1500 legal texts were already mostly produced in English, although there were still remnants of Latin and French. In the realm of literature the rise of standard English is most evident, while some Latin and also dialects of English are still used. Scholarly texts are the area where Latin is still most frequently used. In Görlach's estimate, approximately half of scientific writing was in English at the beginning of the early modern period, the other half being mostly in Latin. The vernacularization process continued through the 16th and 17th centuries, and by the mid-17th century English was the primary language for scholarly texts in England.

The language of religion also went through a gradual change. With the Reformation, Bible translations were ever more widely spread, and the language of liturgy changed from Latin to English. Because of the constant tension between Anglicans and Catholics and later also the Puritans and other groups, not to mention the rising Quakerism and other minor groups, there was also a constant need of discussion and writing on religion, and this was carried out in English, outlining the particularly English context in which these debates were carried out.

The expansion of English into new registers placed requirements on the language, and the influences can be seen on many levels of language. Not only does the lexicon constantly expand to accommodate the expression of new ideas, but new rhetorical styles had their influence on ideals of writing. The fact that education was still very much on the pattern of classical Latin meant that "the English style used in many formal text types was apparently praised according to how close it came to Latin models" (Görlach 1999: 464). Even on the level of individual linguistic items the influence of education can be suspected. So, for example, epistemic uses of *may* and *must* spread first in the language of university-educated high-ranking men, which would suggest that the thought styles taught at Oxford and Cambridge included the use of epistemic modality (Nurmi 2003, 2009).

4 Resources for the study of Early Modern English

Because of the proliferation of different types of text, we are also able to benefit from a larger variety of electronic corpora as sources for studying Early Modern English. On the one hand, we have multi-genre general-purpose corpora, and on the other, there are also more specialized corpora of a single genre or domain of writing. Of the first type, the *Helsinki Corpus* (Rissanen et al. 1991) covers the years 1500–1710 and consists of 500,000 words in 18 genres. The ARCHER corpus (Biber and Finegan 1990–93/2002/2007/2010) focuses more on the late modern period, but it starts from 1650, and has 11 genres. Also, other varieties are covered: ARCHER includes a corresponding selection of both British and American English, and the *Helsinki Corpus of Older Scots* (Meurman-Solin 1995) brings a possibility of contrastive studies. With the digitization of more and more materials, large commercial databases offer an ever increasing selection of the early printed sources in massive archives, such as *Early English Books Online* (Chadwyck-Healey 2003–2011), with a full-text sample made recently available online (EEBO-TCP), and the *Literature Online* (Chadwyck-Healey 1996–2011) database.

The more specialized corpora focus on a single genre, topic domain, or publication type. A good example of the last is the *Lampeter Corpus* (Claridge et al. 1999). It contains tracts published between 1640 and 1740, and has six topic domains, which are represented for each decade of the timeperiod, numbering over a million words. The *Zurich English Newspaper Corpus* (ZEN) (Fries, Lehmann et al. 2004) covers early English newspapers between 1661–1791, giving access to 1.6 million words of whole newspaper issues with their varied content types. *Newdigate Newsletters* (Hines 1995) presents the precursor and competitor of the newspaper, written between 1674–1715 (750,000 words). The single-genre *Parsed Corpus of Early English Correspondence* (PCEEC) (Nevalainen et al. 2006) consists of personal letters written between 1410 and 1681, altogether 2.2 million words. There is also a short version containing a selection of the texts, the *Corpus of Early English Correspondence Sampler* (CEECS) (Keränen et al. 1998), with 450,000 words. A *Corpus of English Dialogues 1560–1760* (Kytö and Culpeper 2006) focuses on speech-based texts, containing both authentic dialogue in trial proceedings and witness depositions, and constructed dialogue in drama and prose fiction, again reaching over a million words. Another corpus presenting speech-based texts from the tail-end of the 17th century is the *Old Bailey Corpus* (Huber et al. 2016).

There are also corpora focusing on a special domain of writing. The *Corpus of Early English Medical Writing* (Taavitsainen et al. 1995–) presents various text categories aimed at both expert and lay readership and covering multiple types of writing from the purely academic to health guides for the general public. The *Corpus of English Religious Prose* (Kohnen et al. forthc.), with a one-million-word sampler available, tackles the domain of religion and the various genres of writing that are connected with it. New corpus projects arise all the time, and the variety of these projects and the types of corpora they aim to build are a testimony to the multiplicity of material available for scholars of Early Modern English.

5 Changes in Early Modern English

The two most striking changes taking place in the early modern period were the standardization, particularly of orthography, in published writing (with a gradual spread of similar spelling conventions to private texts as well) and the explosive growth of the lexicon. The early stages of descriptive and prescriptive writing on language were also seen during this period, even if the main developments only arrived in the 18th century. Many of the other linguistic developments of the age were continuations of long-term trends which had their origins in Middle and – in some cases – Old English.

Standardization is most often viewed on the level of orthography, and certainly the changes there were remarkable during the two centuries in question, but also other levels of language can be argued to have developed some form of standard. Printing and the growing and developing civil service spread the particular type of writing of literate people in London and at the universities to a more varied readership than before, and provided a model to aim towards. Many linguistic features which become an established part of the new general dialect did not necessarily spread to the spoken regional forms of language, but, since our remaining sources are written, they tend to obscure the richness of local variation which must have existed all through the centuries in order to have survived to the present day (see Moessner, Chapter 10).

The vocabulary of English was increasing as more types of texts were produced, and this led to hard word dictionaries being published. These often took the form of wordlists, which might contain words invented by the compiler of the lexicon, never seen outside these compilations, but they also presented many words which have since established their place in the English lexicon. Some dictionaries were aimed at translators, others specialized in a given field, such as legal or medical terminology or the language of thieves. The orthoepists discussed ways of improving the English spelling system and as an unintended side product gave us a clearer idea of how the language was pronounced. Early grammars were heavily based on the Latin model, and were often not very succesful in describing English in those terms. Because of the newly literate middle ranks of society, there was a welcoming readership for these works, although the age of the autodidact did not properly begin before the 18th century. How much influence any of these volumes had on the English actually used is an open question, but they give us an indication of the increasing interest in codifying, analyzing and teaching English.

The English lexicon increased in size in several ways and for several reasons. New words were borrowed for new concepts, both scientific and cultural, from any number of languages. While Latin was the most influential source, the influx of new words from both European and world languages is notable. As the English became more familiar with the world, they introduced new words to describe the flora and fauna, the artefacts and merchandise, the peoples and cultures they encountered. At the same time, the Renaissance ideal of expressing an idea in as many ways as possible contributed to the borrowing of Latin words in order to introduce variety. New words did not come solely from borrowing: also word formation through prefixes and suffixes, as well as compounding, was frequent. Many of the elements included in these processes were borrowed themselves, but there was eventually also mixing of native and borrowed elements. Many near synonyms were introduced, but only a selection of those has survived (see Lancashire, Chapter 6).

On the level of morphology, the loss of nominal case endings that had been going on for a long time reached its culmination, with only the genitive -s remaining in the nominal system. The use of apostrophes to signify the genitive as distinguished from plural (or to distinguish genitive singular and plural) arose only gradually, and did not reach present usage before the 18th century.

In the case of personal pronouns the most notable changes appeared with regard to second person. The singular pronoun *thou* became increasingly marked, and was used less and less except for highly specific contexts (intimacy, status difference, religious language). As *thou* disappeared, the corresponding verbal inflection disappeared as well. In the plural, the object form *you* replaced the old subject form *ye*. In the case of relative pronouns, subject pronoun *who* became established in human reference (see Busse, Chapter 12).

Adjectives and adverbs showed more variation in the formation of comparative and superlative forms than Present-day English, and the rules governing the use of inflections or the periphrastic forms were still in flux, leaving room for double forms (*most happiest*). Adverbs had variant forms without the suffix *-ly*, so that *smooth/smoothly* could be used interchangeably.

The verbal system saw a rise of auxiliaries. Periphrastic *do* established itself in questions and negative statements. For a while, it seemed that *do* was also making inroads in affirmative statements, but this development was cut short (see Warner, Chapter 13). Verbal inflections followed a similar trend as nominal case endings, and the early modern period saw the loss of all but the third-person singular suffix, which changed from the earlier *-th* to *-s*. Since the loss of inflections made the subjunctive scarcer, modal auxiliaries took some of its functions. The meanings of modal auxiliaries shifted more towards the present model with the increasing frequency of epistemic meanings. The progressive *be* + *-ing* form started increasing, although the real development of this construction took place in the 18th and 19th centuries.

As for word order, the long-term change towards a fixed pattern of subject-verb-object in declarative statements saw the last stages of formalization. Sentence-initial adverbs could still cause subject-verb inversion in the early modern period, but, apart from the greater liberties taken by verse, this pattern was notably less frequent by 1700. Many syntactic patterns typical of Latin could be seen in high styles of writing, whether legalese or ornate literature (see Seoane, Chapter 5).

On the level of pronunciation, the Great Vowel Shift was perhaps the most notable development. The raising of long vowels took place over three centuries, and was a series of local developments (see Krug, Chapter 14). All parts of the shift did not run their course in all dialects, and there was variation in how individual words were affected. Local dialects continued as the main spoken form, but the beginnings of Received Pronunciation appeared in the cultural hub that was London.

All in all, developments in Early Modern English levelled much of the earlier variation as the new standard language was formed. The place for standard was in official, published and formal kinds of writing, but private, unpublished, and informal language continued to show much more regional and stylistic variation. Being able to command the standard register was one of the requirements of inclusion in the elites of the country, but large parts of the population could lead successful lives without the requirements of shaping their language to this new pattern.

6 References

6.1 Online resources

Biber, Douglas and Edward Finegan. 1990–93/2002/2007/2010. *A Representative Corpus of Historical English Registers* (ARCHER). Version 3.1 http://www.llc.manchester.ac.uk/research/projects/archer/; last accessed 14 April 2017.

Chadwyck-Healey. 2003–2011. *Early English Books Online, 1475–1700* (EEBO). Ann Arbor: ProQuest. http://eebo.chadwyck.com/home; last accessed 14 April 2017.

Chadwyck-Healey. 1996–2011. *Literature Online* (LION). http://lion.chadwyck.com/; last accessed 14 April 2017.

Claridge, Claudia, Josef Schmied, and Rainer Siemund. 1999. *The Lampeter Corpus of Early Modern English Tracts*. Available at: https://www.tu-chemnitz.de/phil/english/sections/linguist/real/independent/lampeter/lamphome.htm; last accessed 14 April 2017.

EEBO-TCP. Early English Books Online Text Creation Partnership. http://www.textcreationpartnership.org/tcp-eebo/; last accessed 14 April 2017.

Fries, Udo, Hans Martin Lehmann. 2004. *Zurich English Newspaper Corpus* (ZEN). Version 1.0. Zürich: University of Zürich. http://www.es.uzh.ch/en/Subsites/Projects/zencorpus.html; last accessed 14 April 2017.

Hickey, Raymond 2003. *A Corpus of Irish English 14th–20th c.* (CIE). https://www.uni-due.de/ IERC/CIE.htm; last accessed 14 April 2017.

Hines, Philip, Jr. 1995. *Newdigate Newsletters*. In: *ICAME Collection of English Language Corpora (CD-ROM)*, 2nd edn., Knut Hofland, Anne Lindebjerg, and Jørn Thunestvedt (eds.), The HIT Centre, University of Bergen, Norway. For manual see http://icame.uib.no/newdigateeks.html; last accessed 14 April 2017.

Keränen, Jukka, Minna Nevala, Terttu Nevalainen, Arja Nurmi, Minna Palander-Collin and Helena Raumolin-Brunberg. 1998. *Corpus of Early English Correspondence Sampler* (CEECS). In: *ICAME Collection of English Language Corpora (CD-ROM)*, 2nd edn., Knut Hofland, Anne Lindebjerg, and Jørn Thunestvedt (eds.), The HIT Centre, University of Bergen, Norway. For manual see http://clu.uni.no/icame/manuals/; last accessed 14 April 2017.

Kohnen, Thomas, Sandra Boggel, Tanja Rütten, Dorothee Groeger, Ingvilt Marcoe, and Kirsten Gather. forthc. *Corpus of English Religious Prose* (COERP). http://coerp.uni-koeln.de/; last accessed 14 April 2017.

Kytö, Merja and Jonathan Culpeper. 2006. *A Corpus of English Dialogues 1560–1760*. With the assistance of Terry Walker and Dawn Archer. Uppsala University and Lancaster University. http://www.helsinki.fi/varieng/CoRD/corpora/CED/index.html; last accessed 14 April 2017.

Magnus Huber, Magnus Nissel and Karin Puga 2016. *Old Bailey Corpus 2.0*. hdl:11858/00-246C-0000-0023-8CFB-2

Meurman-Solin, Anneli. 1995. *Helsinki Corpus of Older Scots*. Department of English, University of Helsinki. http://www.helsinki.fi/varieng/CoRD/corpora/HCOS/index.html; last accessed 14 April 2017.

Nevalainen, Terttu, Helena Raumolin-Brunberg, Jukka Keränen, Minna Nevala, Arja Nurmi, and Minna Palander-Collin. 2006. *Parsed Corpus of Early English Correspondence* (PCEEC). Annotated by Ann Taylor, Arja Nurmi, Anthony Warner, Susan Pintzuk, and Terttu Nevalainen. Helsinki: University of Helsinki and York: University of York. Distributed through the *Oxford Text Archive*.

Rissanen, Matti, Merja Kytö, Leena Kahlas-Tarkka, Matti Kilpiö, Saara Nevanlinna, Irma Taavitsainen, Terttu Nevalainen, and Helena Raumolin-Brunberg. 1991. *The Helsinki Corpus of English Texts*. In: *ICAME Collection of English Language Corpora (CD-ROM)*, 2nd edn., Knut Hofland, Anne Lindebjerg, and Jørn Thunestvedt (eds.), The HIT Centre, University of Bergen, Norway. For manual, see http://clu.uni.no/icame/manuals/; last accessed 14 April 2017.

Taavitsainen, Irma, Päivi Pahta, Martti Mäkinen, Turo Hiltunen, Ville Marttila, Maura Ratia, Carla Suhr, and Jukka Tyrkkö. 1995–. *Corpus of Early English Medical Writing* (CEEM). University of Helsinki. http://www.helsinki.fi/varieng/CoRD/corpora/CEEM/index.html; last accessed 14 April 2017.

6.2 Printed resources

Barber, Charles. 1997. *Early Modern English*. 2nd edn. Edinburgh: Edinburgh University Press.

Barry, Jonathan. 1995. Literacy and literature in popular culture: Reading and writing in historical perspective. In: Tim Harris (ed.), *Popular Culture in England, c. 1500–1850*, 69–94. London: Macmillan.

Briggs, Asa. 1994. *A Social History of England: From the Ice Age to the Channel Tunnel*. 2nd edn. London: Weidenfeld and Nicolson.
Brink, Jean R. 2010. Literacy and education. In: Hattaway (ed.), Vol. 1, 27–37.
Coleman, David and John Salt. 1992. *The British Population: Patterns, Trends, and Processes*. Oxford: Oxford University Press.
Cressy, David. 1975. *Education in Tudor and Stuart England*. London: Arnold.
Cressy, David. 1980. *Literacy and the Social Order: Reading and Writing in Tudor and Stuart England*. Cambridge: Cambridge University Press.
Görlach, Manfred. 1991. *Introduction to Early Modern English*. Cambridge: Cambridge University Press.
Görlach, Manfred. 1999. Regional and social variation. In: Lass (ed.), 459–538.
Hattaway, Michael (ed.). 2010. *A New Companion to English Renaissance Literature and Culture*. Vols. 1–2. Oxford: Wiley-Blackwell.
Kishlansky, Mark. 1996. *A Monarchy Transformed: Britain 1603–1714*. London: Penguin.
Lass, Roger. 1999. Introduction. In: Lass (ed.), 1–12.
Lass, Roger (ed.). 1999. *The Cambridge History of the English Language*. Vol. III. *1476–1776*. Cambridge: Cambridge University Press.
Milroy, James. 1992. *Linguistic Variation and Change*. Oxford: Blackwell.
Nevalainen, Terttu. 2006. *Introduction to Early Modern English*. Edinburgh: Edinburgh University Press.
Nurmi, Arja. 2003. The role of gender in the use of MUST in Early Modern English. In: Sylviane Granger and Stephanie Petch-Tyson (eds.), *Extending the Scope of Corpus-based Research: New Applications, New Challenges*, 111–120. Amsterdam/Atlanta: Rodopi.
Nurmi, Arja. 2009. *May*: The social history of an auxiliary. In: Andreas H. Jucker, Daniel Schreier, and Marianne Hundt (eds.), *Corpora: Pragmatics and Discourse. Papers from the 29th International Conference on English Language Research on Computerized Corpora (ICAME 29). Ascona, Switzerland, 14–18 May 2008*, 321–342. Amsterdam/Atlanta: Rodopi.
O'Callaghan, Michelle. 2010. Publication: Print and manuscript. In: Hattaway (ed.), Vol. 1, 160–176.
Pahta, Päivi and Arja Nurmi. 2006. Code-switching in the Helsinki Corpus: A thousand years of multilingual practices. In: Nikolaus Ritt, Herbert Schendl, Christiane Dalton-Puffer, and Dieter Kastovsky (eds.), *Medieval English and its Heritage: Structure, Meaning and Mechanisms of Change*, 203–220. Frankfurt: Peter Lang.
Palander-Collin, Minna. 2009. Patterns of interaction: Self-mention and addressee inclusion in the letters of Nathaniel Bacon and his correspondents. In: Arja Nurmi, Minna Nevala, and Minna Palander-Collin (eds.), *The Language of Daily Life in England (1400–1800)*, 53–74. Amsterdam/Philadelphia: John Benjamins.
Rappaport, Steve. 1989. *Worlds within Worlds: Structures of Life in Sixteenth-century London*. Cambridge: Cambridge University Press.
Raumolin-Brunberg, Helena. 1998. Social factors and pronominal change in the seventeenth century: The Civil-War effect? In: Jacek Fisiak and Marcin Krygier (eds.), *Advances in English Historical Linguistics (1996)*, 361–388. Berlin: Mouton de Gruyter.
Youings, Joyce. 1984. *Sixteenth-century England*. London: Penguin.

Julia Schlüter
Chapter 3:
Phonology

1 Introduction —— 28
2 Word stress —— 29
3 Syllable reduction —— 30
4 Consonants —— 31
5 Vowels —— 34
6 Summary —— 44
7 References —— 45

Abstract: In the Early Modern English period, English underwent a number of substantial changes in all phonological subsystems, which transformed the Middle English system into a distinctly modern one. The present chapter highlights in turn changes in lexical stress patterns, the reduction of unstressed syllables, changes in the distribution of certain consonants and their allophones (in particular /h/, [ç], [x], /r/), the reduction of consonant clusters (including the emergence of the novel /ʒ/ and /ŋ/ phonemes), and changes in the vowel system. A large part of the chapter is devoted to the important shifts undergone by the latter category of sounds in the Early Modern era; yet it excludes the massive turnover known as the Great Vowel Shift (which is treated in Krug, Chapter 14). The vowel changes are, for expository purposes, subdivided into unconditioned and conditioned changes; the subsystems of long vowels, diphthongs, and short vowels are treated separately. The chapter describes the most important qualitative changes in long vowels (beyond the Great Vowel Shift), the monophthongization of many ME diphthongs, the development of some of the short vowels, and the interfering effect of certain consonantal environments, partly leading to phonemic splits.

Julia Schlüter: Bamberg (Germany)

1 Introduction

In the Early Modern English (EModE) period, English underwent a number of substantial changes in all phonological subsystems. As a result, by the end of the period, English had evolved from the distinctly old-fashioned state of affairs preserved in Middle English (ME) to a system largely representing Present-day English (PdE). The language manifested shifts in the location of lexical stresses (see Section 2); it had cemented the phonological contrast between stressed and unstressed syllables (see Section 3); some distributional changes, a few new acquisitions as well as cluster reductions had yielded the present-day consonant system (see Section 4); and the vowel system had changed almost beyond recognition, now being characterized by an asymmetric relationship between long and short vowels and an almost complete renewal of the set of diphthongs (see Section 5). Yet further changes were to follow before the vowel system reached its present-day state. All of these aspects will in turn be highlighted in the following sections.

However, what makes the descriptive task undertaken in this article easier than, for instance, a comprehensive outline of the phonology of Middle English, is the fact that Early Modern English was also a time of standardization: after an era of dispersion and dialectal diversity, the English language had regained most of the functions taken over by French in the centuries following the Norman Conquest. From the EModE era date numerous grammars, proposals for spelling reforms, rhyming dictionaries, shorthand guides and materials developed for teaching English, all of which provide useful sources for the reconstruction of EModE phonology (see the monumental work by Dobson 1968, drawing together much of this evidence). As a consequence of the generalized use of English for official purposes, the standardization of spelling, begun by the Chancery in the 15th century, continued at increasing speed, making written texts difficult to assign to any particular region. Of course, the standardization of written usage went considerably further than that of spoken dialects, which varied as a function of the social status of the speaker. In an often-quoted passage defining the origin of the newly risen English standard, Puttenham (1589) recommends

> the vsuall speach of the Court, and that of London and the shires lying about London within lx. myles, and not much aboue. I say not this but that in euery shyre there be gentlemen and others that speake but specially write as good Southerne as we of Middlesex or Surrey do, but not the common people of euery shire ... (Puttenham 1589: 120–121).

Not surprisingly, it was thus the variety used in the political, cultural, and economic centre that set the norm to which other dialects were attracted, while differences persisted particularly in spoken usage.

Possibly as part of this standardization process, the phonological makeup of many high-frequency words stabilized in one way or the other. While Middle English had been an era characterized by an unprecedented flexibility in terms of the presence or absence of variable segments, Early Modern English had lost these options. A word-final <e> was no longer pronounceable as [ə]; vowel-final and consonant-final forms of the possessives *my/mine, thy/thine*, and of the negative *no/none* were increasingly limited to determiner vs. pronoun function, respectively; formerly omissible final consonants of the prepositions *of, on*, and *in* became obligatory, and the distribution of final /n/ in verbs was eventually settled (e.g. infinitive *see* vs. past participle *seen*). In ME times, this kind of variability had been exploited to optimize syllable contact at word boundaries by avoiding hiatuses and consonant clusters (e.g. *my leg* but *min arm, i þe hous* but *in an hous, to see me* but *to seen it*). The increasing fixation of word forms in Early Modern English came at the expense of phonotactic adaptability, but reduced the amount of allomorphy; in other words, phonological constraints were increasingly outweighed by morphological ones (cf. Schlüter 2009b).

2 Word stress

Stress assignment has since ME times been a hybrid of two conflicting systems of different origins. Throughout the history of English, native Germanic lexemes have as a rule had their stress on the first syllable from the beginning (unless they carried a stressless prefix). In contrast, Latin and French loanwords arrived with a stress system that counted syllables from the end and assigned stress to the first stressable (or heavy) syllable from there, with the final syllable as a rule being skipped in Latin. Predictably, Early Modern English, which contained and continued to adopt vast numbers of Romance loanwords, was characterized by a considerable vacillation with regard to the location of main accents.

Application of the French stress rule led to accent on final syllables, e.g. *parént, precépt, colléague*, where Present-day English has in many cases developed initial stress. Overall, educated speakers can be expected to have stuck to this rule longer than the less educated part of the population, who commonly generalized the initial stress rule, e.g. *párent, précept, cólleague*. In some cases, the initial stress rule was extended to items where it did not eventually become established, giving pronunciations like *cónvenient, défective, pérspective,* and *súggestion* (examples from Levins 1570). The aphesis of unstressed initial vowels attested in EModE loans like *lárum* (< *alárum*) and *spáragus* (< *aspáragus*) seems likewise due to an overextension of Germanic initial stress. Alongside these Romance stress rules on the one hand and fully anglicized stress patterns on the other, the EModE system contained numerous exceptions. Thus, stressable final syllables and word-initial syllables in some cases remained unstressed, while word-medial syllables received the main accent, e.g. *demónstrate*, *embássage*, *illústrate*, *retínue*, *sonórous*. In the course of the later history of the language, the variability in terms of word accent that characterized the 16th and 17th centuries largely subsided in favor of stable patterns that were often a result of the history of individual words.

Furthermore, for much of the Early Modern period, lexemes of three or more syllables tended to carry a relatively prominent secondary stress, separated by at least one syllable from the primary one (indicated here by grave accents). As a consequence, speakers tended to alternate between realizations like *ádvertìze* and *àdvertíze*, *állegòrical* and *àllegórical*, *áccessòry* and *àccessóry*, *páramòunt* and *pàramóunt*, *partícipàte* and *partícipáte*. It is only in the 17th century that pronunciations that had lost the secondary stress began to compete with those that preserved it. In British English, the innovative variants ousted the older ones in subsequent centuries, while in American English secondary stress survives in many lexemes.

3 Syllable reduction

Since the period under discussion, the presence or absence of stress has had important consequences for the phonological makeup of a syllable, in particular of its nuclear vowel. As early as Middle English, there had been a tendency for unstressed vowels to be reduced (which had gone to completion in final syllables), but the trend only gained considerable momentum in Early Modern English. At that time, vowels in non-primary stressed syllables could be of at least three kinds, corresponding to different degrees of reduction. In realizations that preserved secondary stress, long vowels and diphthongs were retained, e.g. *púrpòse* /oː/, *ópenlỳ* /əɪ/, *hístorỳ* /əɪ/, *glóriòus* /əʊ/, *émperòur* /əʊ/, *cértàin* /ɛɪ/, *cáptàin* /ɛɪ/. Even when short and stressless, vowels remained clearly distinct in careful speaking styles, e.g. *cóuntenance* /a ~ æ/, *víllage* /a ~ æ/, *kíngdom* /u/, *séldom* /u/, *cáptain* /e ~ ɛ/, *ópenly* /i/, *émperour* /u/. In less conscious styles, however, all vowels merged under one or two realizations, a centralized vowel /ə/ or /ʌ/, and a slightly higher /ɪ/, depending on the variety, the segmental context, and the lexeme. In appropriate contexts, unstressed vowels could be dropped completely (as is still the case in Present-day English): For one thing, in combinations with nasals or liquids, vowels could disappear in favor of a syllabic quality of the consonant, e.g. in *bottom*, *garden*, *bottle*, *double*, *acre*, and *slender*. For another, they could disappear in medial position of initially stressed words (which was in some cases indicated by the spelling), e.g. *evry ~ every*, *sentry* (< *century*), *curtsy* (< *courtesy*), *fancy* (< *phantasy*). (Note that these examples present a mixed set: While *evry* is a purely orthographical indication of syncope, the other three are instances of a beginning orthographic differentiation of a polysemous word, eventually resulting in a meaning split.)

Phonological reduction up to and including the loss of unstressed vowels has since EModE times also characterized function words (prepositions, pronouns, auxiliaries etc.). Depending on factors such as speaking rate, formality, prosodic prominence, and syntactic independence, speakers had strong and weak forms at their disposal, e.g. *and* [and/ən], *have* [hɛːv/əv], *would* [wəʊld/wʊd], *my* [maɪ/mɪ], *through* [θrəʊx/θrʊ], *you* [jəʊ/jʊ]. Moreover, in high-frequency collocations, two function words could be contracted, leading to the loss of either the first (e.g. *'tis, 'twas, 'twill*) or the second vowel (e.g. *they're, we'll, you've, can't*). While the phenomenon is not unknown in Old and Middle English (e.g. *cham* < *ich am, het* < *he it, nabban* < *ne habban, nas* < *ne was*), its currency increased considerably in the Early Modern period, and it is obvious from the examples given that the inventory of possible contractions underwent considerable change.

4 Consonants

Compared to the vowel system, the consonant system remained fairly constant in the EModE period. The distribution of one or two consonants changed significantly, two phonemes were newly formed, and several initial and final clusters were simplified.

4.1 Distributional changes

Initial /h/ had always been part of the English system, but had almost become extinct in ME times, with the exception of East Anglia and the Northeast. Thus, most early ME varieties spoken in England and Wales were completely /h/-less, not only in unstressed function words (where standard Present-day English still drops the /h/, e.g. *he, his, him, her, has, have, had,* etc.), but also in initial position of content words of Germanic origin (e.g. *hand, heart, hair, house, husband,* etc.). While the weakening of initial /h/ had been a natural continuation of its OE demise in less prominent positions, and the arrival of French loanwords with mute <h> (e.g. *habit, hazard, heir, history, horror*) played at most an auxiliary role, a reversal of the trend is traceable to later Middle English (from about 1350 onwards) and gained considerable momentum in the EModE era (cf. Schlüter

2006, 2009a). The comeback of initial /h/ in Germanic as well as Romance words – spanning the 14th to 20th centuries – was certainly helped by the consistent preservation of ⟨h⟩ in the spelling. In large part, it was however a naturally occurring process whose functional motivation may be seen in the restitution of a consonantal syllable onset (which is universally preferred to vowel-initial syllables). The reinforcement of /h/ was retarded by factors such as the Romance origin of the lexeme, a high token frequency, and the absence of stress on its initial syllable, and it was speeded up by its native Germanic origin, a low frequency, and a primary stress on the first syllable (cf. Schlüter 2009a). Throughout the Early Modern period, the realization of /h/ thus remained highly variable; witness numerous spellings like *an hundred*, *myn husband*, *thyn humble servant*, *non history*, etc., but it strengthened continuously long before /h/-dropping became stigmatized in the 18th century.

In contrast, /h/'s allophones [ç] (following front vowels) and [x] (following back vowels), which occurred in word-final position and before /t/, were lost in all southern English dialects in the course of the EModE era. The palatal variant [ç] possibly disappeared somewhat earlier (15th to 17th centuries) than the velar one. It was vocalized and thus led to a compensatory lengthening of a preceding short vowel (e.g. *high*, *night*, *thigh*). Velar [x] was from the 14th century in some dialects replaced by the acoustically related consonant /f/, most typically when following /u/. For a while, /f/ had a wider spread in standard English than today, occurring for instance in *daughter*, *bought*, *naught*, *taught*, etc. By the mid-18th century, the modern distribution had been reached (*cough*, *enough*, *laugh*, *rough*, *tough*, *trough*, *draught*, and *laughter*).

A distributional change that was to have important repercussions in the vowel system was the weakening of /r/ in non-prevocalic contexts. The process affected the southern British English standard and related dialects, but did not occur in Scotland, Ireland, most of the United States or Canada, which remained /r/-pronouncing (rhotic). It is assumed that the phonetic weakening of /r/ proceeded from an original trill or flap via an approximant stage to a complete loss of the consonantal closure. The first sporadic spellings testifying to /r/-loss occur in late Middle English of the 15th century, further evidence comes from EModE private writings, but the main changeover happened only in the 18th century, that is, after the end of the period focussed on here (cf. Lass 1999: 114–116). While Early Modern English was thus mostly rhotic, /r/-loss nevertheless deserves to be mentioned here because when following a stressed vowel, the weakening /r/ vocalized to produce a transitional /ə/ or led to a compensatory lengthening of the vowel as early as the 16th and 17th centuries. In addition, a following /r/ interfered significantly with the major reshuffling of the vowel system known as the Great Vowel Shift (see Section 5.2.1).

Further consonantal changes concerned phonotactics, i.e. the ways in which consonants could be combined into consonant clusters. Cluster reduction, in particular, led to the creation of two new members of the consonant system, /ʒ/ and /ŋ/, which are therefore treated in Section 4.2.

4.2 Cluster reduction

The reduction of onset clusters pursued the road already taken in Middle English. The consonant clusters /hr/, /hl/, /hn/, and /wl/ had shed their first members in early Middle English. The combination /hw/, with its first member weakening, continued to be distinguished from /w/ in general usage (though no longer in the southern dialects), so that *which* and *witch*, *whine* and *wine* were kept apart up to the 18th century (and continue to be in certain dialects, including Scottish and Irish English as well as a few American and Canadian accents). The reduction of the /wr/-cluster in items like *write*, *wrong*, and *wrist* began in the 15th and 16th centuries and was completed in the 17th. The clusters /gn/ in *gnash*, *gnat*, *gnaw* and /kn/ in *knee*, *knit*, *know* persisted somewhat longer, possibly in the form of assimilated /dn/ or /ŋn/ for /gn/ and /tn/ for /kn/. The simplification to /n/ began in the 17th century and was generally accepted in the South of England only in the early 18th century.

An addition to the consonant inventory of Early Modern English resulted from an assimilation of the consonant sequence /zj/, occurring in medial position of French loanwords like *vision*, *occasion*, and *leisure*. In the 16th century, the two components assimilated to form a new consonant /ʒ/. Comparable assimilatory simplifications affected the clusters /sj/, /tj/, and /dj/ in unstressed syllables. Rather than producing novel consonant phonemes, these added to the numbers of the existing /ʃ/-, /tʃ/-, and /dʒ/-phonemes, respectively. The 15th century saw the appearance of /ʃ/ in words like *session*, *obligation*, and *mathematician*, and the 17th century the rise of /tʃ/ in words like *Christian*, *creature*, and *mutual* and that of /dʒ/ in words like *soldier*, *Indian*, and *grandeur*. All of these new realizations, in particular the new /ʒ/-phoneme, took a long time to become accepted into the standard, and in some cases variation between consonant clusters and assimilated pronunciations persists to the present day.

Further phonotactic changes concerned the reduction of final consonant clusters, which did not, however, become ubiquitous. Word-final /mb/ had already been reduced to /m/ in Middle English in items like *bomb*, *dumb*, *lamb*, *plumb*, *tomb*, etc. In the late 16th and 17th centuries, /g/ was deleted after the velar allophone of /n/, making /ŋ/ phonemic. This loss occurred first in word-final position (e.g. *sing*, *ring*, *strong*, *long*) and then also in morpheme-final position (e.g. *singer*, *ringing*) except before adjectival inflections (e.g. *stronger*, *longest*). In the unstressed present participle ending *-ing*, /ɪŋ/ was further changed to /ɪn/ in many standard dialects. However, in later centuries, the /ɪŋ/-realization was enforced in standard usage and /ɪn/ restricted to rapid or colloquial speech.

Finally, a minor consonantal change limited to a certain number of lexemes and dating to Early Modern English is the disappearance of /w/ when following another consonant and preceding a rounded back vowel, e.g. in *sword*, *two*, and *who*, and somewhat more systematically in unstressed syllables, e.g. *Southwark*, *conquer*, *answer*. In some further items, e.g. *swollen*, *swoon*, *swore*, *awkward*, *boatswain*, *forward*, *housewife*, and *pennyworth*, /w/ was later restored on the basis of the spelling or of related words.

After the re-establishment of initial /h/, the loss of its allophones [ç] and [x], and the introduction of /ʒ/ and /ŋ/, the EModE inventory of consonants was practically identical with the present-day one. All in all, the consonantal system of English has, however, remained relatively stable, in particular when compared to the fundamental turnover undergone by vowels in the same period of time.

5 Vowels

The vowel system Early Modern English inherited from Middle English was very much unlike that of Present-day English. In EModE times, many changes happened that gave rise to a much more "modern" system. At the beginning of the period, the system was largely based on quantity contrasts that were inherited from Old and Middle English: many monophthongs occurred in pairs of long and short members, and the lengthenings and shortenings created by ME sound changes persisted, even within individual paradigms or word families, e.g. *keep* : *kept*, *child* : *children*, *holy* : *holiday*, *wise* : *wisdom*, *wild* : *wilderness*. The short vowels distinguished three and the long vowels four heights (both front and back). In addition, Middle English had a few closing diphthongs, whose second element was either /ɪ/ or /ʊ/. In the course of the Early Modern period, long and short vowels developed in different ways, giving rise to quality differences in addition to the quantity differences. Many of the former diphthongs monophthongized, thus giving the English vowel system a less diphthongal character than it had either before or after Early Modern English. Some instances of the monophthongs, in particular ME /ɛː/ and /oː/ (corresponding to EModE /eː/ and /uː/), shortened, which accounts for those cases where the Present-day English spellings indicate length, but the vowels are pronounced short, e.g. *bread*, *flood*. In addition, many vowels underwent conditioned sound changes in specific phonological contexts, above all before /r/ and /l/. The most important changes will be discussed in what follows. The sections focus on unconditioned and conditioned changes, respectively, and treat long monophthongs, diphthongs, and short monophthongs in turn, but since these classes are to some extent interconnected through sound changes, this separation serves only expository purposes and will be deviated from in some places.

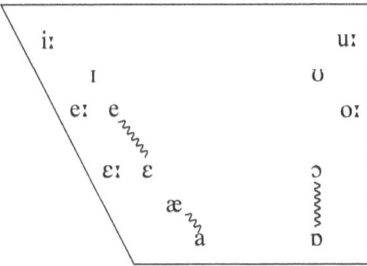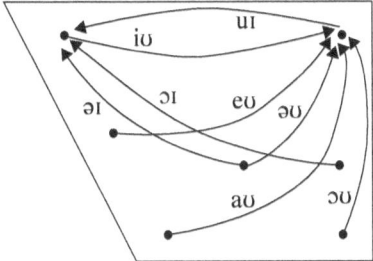

Figure 3.1: Early Modern English stressed monophthongs and diphthongs around 1600 (adapted from Görlach 1994: 53)

Figure 3.1 depicts the location of monophthongs and diphthongs in the vowel chart around the middle of the EModE period. Some of the changes mentioned had already taken place at this time; some others were yet to come. Wavy lines in the diagram on the left show changes under way at the turn of the century; arrows in the diagram on the right indicate the starting points and targets of diphthongal realizations (but not the directions of diachronic changes).

5.1 Unconditioned changes

The most momentous unconditioned change affecting all the long monophthongs in the Early Modern period is the Great Vowel Shift (GVS). The GVS raised ME /aː/, /ɛː/, /eː/, /ɔː/, and /oː/ by one step each, and the two ME vowels that were already maximally close, namely /iː/ and /uː/, diphthongized. Since the changes are assumed to be causally connected, the GVS represents a showcase example of a chain shift. While the initial signs of the shift go back at least to the 15th century, the first stage was completed in the 16th century. The results of this systematic shift can be seen in Figure 3.1, illustrating the status quo around the year 1600. Despite its systematic character and reasonably detailed documentation in contemporary orthoepic descriptions, the precise mechanics continue to be debated among linguists. Since the present volume contains a chapter expressly devoted to the GVS, this important part of EModE phonology will be omitted here (see Krug, Chapter 14).

5.1.1 Long vowels

Depending on what is included under the concept of the GVS, the end point of the shift is also open to discussion (cf. Lass 1999: 80–85). After 1600, the long vowels continued to evolve, and the focus of the present discussion will be on these subsequent changes of the second half of the EModE period.

While no mergers happened as part of the GVS chain shift, /i:/ (going back to ME /e:/) and /e:/ (going back to ME /ɛ:/) fell together in /i:/ around the year 1700, though variation continued during the 18th century. This merger eliminated the opposition between items like *see* : *sea* and *meet* : *meat*.

Another partial merger resulted from the further evolution of /ɛ:/ (going back to ME /a:/) as in *make*, *ale*, *ape*, *bake*, *drake*, *hate*, *knave*, etc.: the sound raised to /e:/ in the 17th century and diphthongized to /eɪ/ around 1800. At the same time, not all instances of /e:/ (going back to ME /ɛ:/) had in all dialects completed the rise to /i:/, so that they merged with items from the /ɛ:/ class. In the 18th century, this merger became limited to a few lexemes in standard pronunciation, in particular *grate* : *great* and *brake* : *break*, while raised realizations came to prevail for other members of the /e:/ class, e.g. *reach*, *leaf*, *clean* (unless they had previously been shortened; see Section 5.2.1).

ME /ɔ:/ as in *boat* or *no* had, by virtue of the GVS, moved to /o:/. In the late 16th and 17th centuries, it was joined by ME /ɔu/ as in *blow* or *know*. Whether the vowel resulting from this merger was monophthongal or diphthongal is debatable and without doubt varied from one dialect to another (see Section 5.1.2). From the 18th century onwards, the diphthongal realization /oʊ/ prevailed in the standard (and became Received Pronunciation /əʊ/ around 1920).

The ME monopthongs /i:/ and /u:/, which had diphthongized under the GVS, provide a transition to the field of the EModE diphthongs. The exact quality of the sounds resulting from the diphthongization is controversial. The versions with a centered initial element given in Figure 3.1, namely /əɪ/ and /əʊ/, represent the time-honored view still adhered to by most linguists, which has however been challenged by others – see, for instance, Faiß (1989) and Lass (1999), who reconstruct /ɛɪ/ and /ɔʊ/ (for further discussion, see Krug, Chapter 14). Be that as it may, in the second half of the EModE period, the new diphthongs continued to develop in a way to widen the distance between their first and second components. The modern situation, with /aɪ/ for the front diphthong and /aʊ/ for the back one was reached in standard British English in the 18th century.

5.1.2 Diphthongs

Many of the diphthongs inherited from Middle English changed into monophthongs in the Early Modern era. The only two that remained were /ɔɪ/ and /ʊɪ/, which merged into /ɔɪ/ by the end of the period. The diphthong /ɔɪ/ occurred mostly in loanwords from Old French such as *choice, joy, noise, toy,* while /ʊɪ/ was typical of the Anglo-Norman dialect of French that brought words like *join, boil, coin, point, poison,* and *toil* into Middle English. EModE texts show some variation between ⟨oi⟩ and ⟨ui⟩ forms (e.g. *point/puint, poison/puison*), but the latter were less frequently used than the former and were eventually given up around the end of the 17th century. In a transitional phase, some members of the /ʊɪ/ group apparently merged with the reflexes of ME /iː/, when the latter reached the /əɪ ~ ʌɪ/ stage. Thus, *loin* : *line* and *point* : *pint* became homophones. This realization was however stigmatized as a provincialism and given up in favor of /ɔɪ/ in the 19th century.

As already mentioned, all the other ME diphthongs are in standard accounts assumed to have turned into monophthongs in the EModE era, though in some cases, new diphthongs were established in the later evolution (cf. Barber 1997: 114–115; Görlach 1994: 55–56; Lass 1999: 91–94; Nevalainen 2006: 123–124). (Note, however, that there is no consensus among historical linguists concerning the evidence for the assumed monophthongizations of /ɔu/ to /ɔː/ and of /aɪ/ to /ɛː/ and their subsequent re-diphthongizations. It is probably more judicious to assume that the monophthongizations were only completed in some dialects, while others preserved more or less markedly diphthongal realizations and played a role in their establishment in the LModE standard.)

To start with, /aʊ/ became /ɒː/ in the mid-17th century, thus filling the gap in the open back corner of the long vowel system (Figure 3.1), and later changed into /ɔː/, e.g. in *cause, law,* and *taught*. Second, /ɔʊ/ monophthongized in the second half of the 16th and first half of the 17th century to /ɔː/ and took part in the GVS-conditioned raising to /oː/ (which became /oʊ/ in Late Modern English), e.g. in *bowl, flow, know, low,* and *soul*. Third, the ME /aɪ/ diphthong narrowed to /ɛɪ/ and subsequently monophthongized to /ɛː/, which joined the GVS raising to /eː/. As a result of this merger with former /aː/ as in *make*, a large number of homophones were created in the mid-17th century, e.g. *days* : *daze*, *hail* : *hale*, *raise* : *raze*, *tail* : *tale*. In Late Modern English, the monophthong developed into a new diphthong /eɪ/, representing the modern state of affairs.

In addition, Middle English had two diphthongs, /eʊ/ (occurring in words like *beauty, dew, few, hew,* and *newt*) and /iʊ/ (occurring in words like *chew, due, hue, new,* and *true*), that eventually collapsed under /juː/. Phonetically, the change proceeded by a raising of the first component of /eʊ/ to /i/ and a shift of the vocalic centre of the diphthong from the first to the second component. As a result, /i/ was reanalyzed as the glide /j/ and assigned to the onset, while /ʊ/ lengthened to compensate for the loss of vowel quantity. The chronology of the merger of /eʊ/ and /iʊ/ on the one hand and the development from diphthong to glide plus long monophthong on the other is somewhat disputed. In Lass's (1999: 99–100) account, the merger and the development of /juː/ coincided in the second half of the 17th century. In contrast, Dobson's evidence indicates that the development of the glide began as early as the late 16th century, while the loss of the distinction between /eʊ/ and /iʊ/ proceeded slowly south- and westwards and was completed in the standard by the last third of the 17th century. According to this chronology, the realization /juː/ must have appeared earlier for the /iʊ/ words than for the /eʊ/ words, but the difference should have been neutralized by the late 17th century (cf. Dobson 1968: 700–713, 798–799). On the basis of the corpus study provided in Schlüter (2006), both datings of the relevant changes stand in need of revision. For one thing, the emergence of the glide in the reflex of ME /iʊ/ can be traced back at least to the late 16th century (confirming Dobson thus far). For another, former /eʊ/ words show the first signs of an emerging glide only in the late 18th century and keep lagging behind /iʊ/ words as late as the end of the 19th century. This suggests, *pace* Lass and Dobson, that the merger was not completed until the 20th century. Furthermore, it indicates that while the evolution of the /j/ onset in /iʊ/ words is properly part of an account of EModE phonology, the merger of (former) /iʊ/ and /eʊ/ as well as the adoption of /j/ by the latter belongs to later chapters of the history of English. The same is true of the dropping of /j/ that later reduced /juː/ to /uː/ in certain environments. The reduction occurred early after /r/, /dʒ/, and /tʃ/, as in *rude*, *June*, and *chew*, at the beginning of the 18th century extended to /l/ and /s/ as in *clue* and *suit*, and in American English further to /t/, /d/, and /n/ as in *tube*, *due*, and *new*.

5.1.3 Short vowels

Turning to the set of short vowels, the spontaneous, unconditioned changes that occurred in the EModE era were much less dramatic than the GVS or the large-scale reduction of diphthongs to monophthongs. Among the three short front vowels, we find a moderate degree of variation with regard to height. There is some disagreement in the literature on whether the close vowel /i/ as in *bit*, *thin*, and *give* was the first or the last one to move. Many authors hold that it lowered and centralized to /ɪ/ as early as Middle English (Faiß 1989: 33–34; Nevalainen 2006: 124; Stockwell and Minkova 1990, 2002), while Lass (1999: 88) concludes from contemporary descriptions that the change occurred only towards the end of the Early Modern era. In some dialects, including London, /ɪ/ lowered even further, leading to spellings like *menysters* 'ministers' and *cete* 'city', but these variants were not adopted into the standard. Similarly, the precise quality of the vowel of *bed, set,* and *rest,* occupying the middle height, is somewhat unclear. Opinions diverge on whether the ME vowel was /e/, which lowered to /ɛ/, or conversely, /ɛ/, which raised to /e/ in the first half of the EModE period (cf. Lass 1999: 87 vs. Barber 1997: 109 and Nevalainen 2006: 124, respectively). Concerning the lowest among the ME short vowels, instantiated in *bad, man,* and *rap,* linguists disagree about its history before the present-day state of /æ/ was reached in the mid-17th century. The widespread view according to which ME /a/ raised to /æ/ in the early 17th century (Faiß 1989: 36; Lass 1999: 85; Nevalainen 2006: 124) is contested by Minkova (2001: 85), who concludes from scribal and rhyme evidence that a higher /æ/ vowel survived from Old English in southern dialects of Middle English.

Both of the short back vowels became more open in Early Modern English. The mid-low /ɔ/ as in *dog, hot,* and *rob* lowered further to /ɒ/, which was well established by 1670. Occasionally, it merged with the more front /a ~ æ/ in fashionable realizations of the second half of the 17th century (cf. contemporary spellings like *plat* 'plot' and *Gad* 'God'). In most Northern American dialects, /ɒ/ pursued a different path: it lengthened and unrounded to /ɑː/ in the late 17th or early 18th century. Finally, as in the case of /i/ > /ɪ/, the change of the high back vowel from /u/ to /ʊ/, which is generally dated to (late) Middle English (Faiß 1989: 39; Stockwell and Minkova 1990), is argued by Lass (1999: 88) to have occurred only towards the end of the 17th century. As a rule /ʊ/ lowered and unrounded to /ʌ/ not long after the year 1600 in the standard dialect (though not in the Midlands and the North of England). In certain conservative environments, however, it remained as /ʊ/. (The specific environments concerned and the resulting phonemic split will be discussed at the end of Section 5.2.2.)

As is obvious from the above discussion, it is virtually impossible to assign to the short vowels of Early Modern English a precise location in the vowel chart. While it can be considered certain that short vowels were more lax than long vowels at the end of the period, it is unclear if and to what extent the same was already true at its beginning. The many controversies revolving around the issue are doubtless due to the fact that by their very nature, short vowels tend to have less extreme realizations than long ones and are therefore harder to describe, a problem that is exacerbated by the fact that the short-long pairings of vowels, characteristic of earlier stages of the language, were lost by virtue of the outcomes of the GVS.

5.2 Conditioned changes

In addition to the general trends outlined in Section 5.1, both long and short vowels were implicated in a large number of conditioned sound changes. The present section concentrates on the most important sound changes conditioned by specific phonological environments.

5.2.1 Long vowels

While unconditioned changes generally left vowel quantities intact, conditioned (or combinative) changes could involve quantities, qualities, or both. In many cases where the modern spelling with a double vowel grapheme indicates a long vowel but the vowel is pronounced short, it was shortened after 1400, which is about the time when major grapheme-phoneme correspondences were fixed. In the EModE era, shortenings concerned, above all, the vowels /eː/ and /uː/ and occurred in monosyllabic words ending in /d/, /t/, /θ/, /f/, /k/, or /v/. Examples of the reduction of /eː/ to /e ~ ɛ/ include *bread*, *dead*, *lead* (N), *sweat*, *death*, *breath*, and *deaf*; examples illustrating the reduction of /uː/ to /u ~ ʊ/ are *good*, *stood*, *hood*, *foot*, *book*, *took*, and *look*. The reduction process was not a monolithic one, but reached individual lexemes at different points in time. This becomes evident when it is seen against the background of the unconditioned change from /u/ to /ʊ/, which has been dated in Section 5.1.3 to a time shortly after the turn of the 17th century: Consequently, the items *flood*, *blood*, and *glove* must have been shortened by the early 17th century to take part in the change to /ʌ/; the items mentioned above (*good*, *stood*, *hood*, etc.) were shortened later than that and therefore failed to undergo lowering and unrounding; finally, items retaining long /uː/, like *mood*, *food*, *rood*, and *shoot* resisted the reduction to /u ~ ʊ/.

As mentioned in Section 4.1 above, the presence of a following /r/ often interfered with the regular evolution of long vowels under the GVS. While rhoticity was largely preserved throughout the EModE period, the /r/ had a variety of effects on the preceding vowel. First, as early as the 15th century an additional [ə] appears to have been inserted between a vowel and the /r/. This has eventually resulted in the modern centring diphthongs, e.g. /ɪə/ in *dear*, /ɛə/ in *bear*, and /ʊə/ in *poor*. Second, due to the complex articulatory movements involved in the production of /r/ – Lass (1999: 108) describes it as an alveolar or post-alveolar approximant with a velar plus a pharyngeal secondary articulation – it often exerted a lowering and rounding influence on the preceding vowel, but in some cases it also had a raising effect.

The lowering effect of postvocalic /r/ in particular had the potential to counteract the raising of vowels under the GVS. Developments in the rows of front and back vowels will be treated in turn here since shifts in vowel height often led to (partial) mergers within these rows. For instance, /eːr/ was partly lowered to /ɛːr/ in the 15th and 16th centuries. Therefore, instead of the expected spellings *deer* and *heer* for the reflexes of OE *dēore* and *hēran*, we find *dear* and *hear* today, bearing witness to the lowered realization. In the examples given, the normal development to /iːr/ and later /ɪə/ has eventually prevailed. In contrast, lexemes containing /ɛːr/ did not in general undergo raising under the GVS and thus did not merge with the former class. They preserve unraised /ɛə/ to the present day, e.g. *bear*, *pear*, *swear*, *wear*. There are however a few lexeme-specific exceptions to this rule, including *shear*, *spear*, *fear*, *ear*, whose vowels did raise and merge with /eːr/ in Early Modern English, giving PDE /ɪə/. The /ɛːr/ (> PDE /ɛə/) group was partly joined by the reflexes of ME /aːr/, which closed to /æːr/ and /ɛːr/ under the GVS, involving examples like *bare*, *fare*, *hare*, *pare*, and *share*. Thus, while ME /ɛː/ as a rule merged with higher /eː/ (the merger of *sea* and *see*; cf. Section 5.1.1), before /r/ it collided with the next lower ME vowel /aː/.

The changes undergone by the row of back vowels under the influence of a following /r/ were even more unpredictable. Starting from the lowest member, ME /ɔːr/ raised temporarily, approximately between 1650 and 1750, to /oːr/, only to lower again to /ɔːr/, where it stayed, evolving into PDE /ɔə/ around 1800, e.g. *oar*, *lore*, and *more*. At the same time, some instances of ME /oːr/ raised to and merged with /uːr/ around the year 1650, giving PDE /ʊə/, as in *poor* and *moor*. Most members of both the raised and the unraised groups later, around the year 1700, lowered to and merged with /ɔːr/, thus also ending up as /ɔə/, e.g. *door*, *floor*, *whore* and the alternative pronunciation of *poor*. Finally, ME /uːr/ developed regularly to /aʊr/ and then /aʊə/, as in *flower*, *shower*, and *our*. However, when followed by another consonant, it lowered and merged with /oːr/ and then /ɔːr/ as in *court*, *mourn*, and *source*.

A last combinative change interfering with the regular development of a long vowel concerns ME long /uː/. After the glides /w/ and /j/ and in the context of labial consonants, it did not diphthongize, as would have been normal in the Early Modern period, but remained /uː/ instead. Examples include *you*, *youth*, *wound*, *swoon*, *room*, *stoop*, *droop*, *loop,* and *tomb*. This arrest of the regular development can be clearly attributed to functional constraints opposing a dissimilation of articulatory gestures.

5.2.2 Short vowels

This section surveys conditioned changes in the area of short vowels, which again involved quantitative as well as qualitative changes that were frequently interconnected. What is more, in a few cases the changes led to the creation of new phonemes out of conditioned allophones, in particular when the conditioning environment was lost or one or the other set of allophones was augmented by additional members as a result of an independent sound change.

Once again, a following /r/ played an important role as a factor interfering with regular developments. For instance, the short vowels /ɪ/, /ʊ/, and /e ~ ɛ/ became indistinct before an /r/ in final position or followed by another consonant, e.g. in *bird*, *firm*, *sir*, *murder*, *hurt*, and *curb*. The three vowels collapsed under a mid-central /ʌ/ or /ə/, which after the loss of rhoticity evolved into /ɜː/, and thus added a new phoneme to the set of long vowels. This change first affected /ɪ/ and /ʊ/ and only later reached /e ~ ɛ/; it started in the North and East in the 16th century, reached London by the 17th century and was complete only by the turn of the 19th century. However, in some items, /e ~ ɛ/ had been lowered to /a/ in the 15th century and thereby escaped this change (if only temporarily). Typical spellings from the long period of vacillation that indicate this realization include *clark*, *dark*, *far*, *harvest*, *heart*, *starre*, *saruant*, *sarvice*, and *marcy*. As can be inferred from these examples, the lowered realization was generally retained in Germanic words, whereas /e ~ ɛ/ was reintroduced (along with the elimination of spelling variants with ⟨a⟩) in most loanwords, where it eventually merged with /ɜː/.

The remaining two short vowels, /a ~ æ/ and /ɔ ~ ɒ/ did not change to the same extent. Their lower allophones were favored in the context of a following /r/ and were lengthened to EModE /aː/ and /ɒː/, respectively. Around 1800, the front /aːr/ changed into /aːə/, which was then reduced to /ɑː/, as in *arm*, *bar*, *cart*, *garden*, *harm*, *mark*, and *sharp*. Similarly, the back /ɒːr/ evolved into /ɒːə/ and was reduced to /ɔː/ at the beginning of the 19th century, e.g. *border*, *corn*, *for*, *horse*, and *north*.

Apart from /r/, the other liquid /l/ in the English consonantal system had comparable, though less pervasive effects on preceding vowels, in particular on /a ~ æ/ and /ɔ ~ ɒ/. When /l/ was followed by a word boundary or another consonant, an additional /ʊ/ glide was inserted between it and the preceding /a/ or /ɒ/ in the 16th century, resulting in the formation of the closing diphthongs /aʊ/ and /ɒʊ/. Where the /l/ was followed by another consonant, it was in addition totally assimilated to the /ʊ/; in other words, it vocalized. Subsequently, the new diphthongs were variably reduced to monophthongs, alternated with them throughout the 17th century and were ousted by them after the end of the Early Modern period. More precisely, /aʊ/ became /aː/ when it preceded (assimilated /l/ and) a labial consonant as in *alms, balm, calf, calm, half,* and *palm,* and it became /ɔː/ elsewhere, e.g. in *all, ball, call, balk, chalk, stalk, talk,* and *walk*. On the other hand, /ɒʊ/ became /oː/, which joined the regular post-GVS diphthongization, turning into /oʊ/ and later /əʊ/, as in *roll, toll, colt, folk, holm,* and *yolk*.

A further combinative sound change concerned the evolution of /a ~ æ/ after /w/. Where /a/ followed /w/ and did not precede a velar plosive (/k/ or /g/), it did not raise to /æ/, but backed and rounded to /ɔ/ in the course of the 17th century, e.g. in *what, warm, wand,* but not in *whack* and *wag*. Like the lack of diphthongization of long /uː/, mentioned above, the velarizing effect of /w/ is explained by the velar articulation of the glide itself.

Turning now to some further changes conditioned by specific phonological contexts, we witness the creation of two new vowel phonemes, one short and one long. First, as already pointed out in Section 5.1.3, short /ʊ/ lowered and unrounded to /ʌ/ in an unconditioned change taking place at the beginning of the 17th century. However, /ʊ/ remained in many cases after labial consonants (/p/, /b/, /f/, and /w/) and before /l/ or /ʃ/, though this arrest of the change did not apply across the board. For instance, /ʊ/ was preserved in *bull, full, bush, put,* and *wolf,* but /ʌ/ established itself in *but, buff* and *fuss*. In addition, as mentioned above, lexemes containing shortened /uː/ increased the numbers of both /ʊ/ (e.g. *good, stood, hood,* etc.) and /ʌ/ (e.g. *flood, blood* and *glove*). As a result, the former short /ʊ/ phoneme split in two, namely /ʊ/ and /ʌ/, contrasting, for instance, in *look* and *luck*.

Second, the short /a ~ æ/ was lengthened in the South in the 17th century where it preceded one of the voiceless fricatives /s/, /f/, or /θ/ (but not /ʃ/) or the clusters /ns/ or /nt/, for instance in *glass, pass, castle, last, chaff, staff, bath, path, dance,* and *plant*. This produced a new low front phoneme /aː ~ æː/ in a slot that had been vacated as a result of the GVS. The lengthened realization was stigmatized to some extent, so that it retracted in some lexemes, but became established in others. In 18th-century British English, the novel phoneme backed to /ɑː/, where it was later joined by instances of /a ~ æ/ that had lengthened before /r/ (*arm, bar, cart, garden,* etc., discussed above). This change did not happen in American English, which preserves /æ(ː)/ to the present day.

A related change affected short /ɔ ~ ɒ/, which was lengthened at the same time and in the same environments as /a ~ æ/, i.e. before voiceless fricatives. Examples include *loss, off,* and *cloth*. Rather than creating a new phoneme, in the late 17th century the sound merged with /ɒː/ (which resulted from the monophthongization of ME /aʊ/ in the middle of that century). For a while, long and short versions coexisted side by side, but again the long ones were partly stigmatized. In contrast to the lengthened /a ~ æ/, short /ɒ/ was eventually restored before voiceless fricatives (except for some speakers of southern dialects).

Summing up Section 5.2, it turns out that, compared to the set of long vowels, short vowels were considerably more liable to conditioned changes. While phonotactic contexts mainly interfered with GVS-related raisings in long vowels, their influence on short vowels did not remain as limited: they led to important qualitative and quantitative changes, a large-scale merger before /r/ and a phonemicization of two (and after the EModE era, three) allophonic contrasts, namely /u ~ ʊ/ vs. /ʌ/ and /a ~ æ/ vs. /aː ~ æː/ (and later /ɪ/, /ʊ/, and /e ~ ɛ/ vs. /ɜː/). The functional reason for the greater liability of short vowels to conditioned changes can be found in the fact that their articulatory targets are not as clearly defined as those of long vowels.

6 Summary

To sum up, Early Modern English has revealed itself to be a period of massive changes, even discounting those subsumed under the Great Vowel Shift (Krug, Chapter 14). For one thing, the considerable variability in the domain of lexical stress patterns was limited in favor of one or the other pattern along the lines of either Germanic or Romance stress rules. For another, syllables not carrying the word accent were increasingly reduced, giving English the stress-timed rhythm that characterizes it today. And for another, the inventory of consonants acquired its present structure, albeit without undergoing any massive changes. The loss of the palatal and velar allophones of /h/, [ç] and [x], is counterbalanced by the establishment of the phonemes /ʒ/ and /ŋ/. In addition to many consonant clusters given up in Middle English, a few further combinations were simplified by dropping their first or second member, in particular /wr/, /gn/, /kn/, and /ŋg/, or by assimilating both into a single consonant, as in the case of /zj/, /sj/, /tj/, and /dj/.

The area that underwent the most dramatic changes in EModE phonology were the vowels. Among the short vowels, there was a limited amount of variation and change. But even beyond the GVS, the long monophthongs continued to change, which gave rise to noticeable qualitative differences between short and long vowels: both /eː/ and /ɛː/ raised further, in the first case leading to the *see : sea* merger, and the trajectory of the newly formed diphthongs /əɪ/ and /əʊ/ (or /ɛɪ/ and /ɔʊ/) widened to /aɪ/ and /aʊ/. Most of the ME diphthongs monophthongized, with the exception of /ɔɪ/ (< /ɔɪ/ and /ʊɪ/). Last but not least, an important number of conditioned vowel changes took place in the Early Modern era, involving certain shortenings and lengthenings in addition to qualitative changes (or the arrest of such changes). The contexts responsible for these combinative changes were, above all, a following weakening /r/, but also a following /l/, a preceding /w/, a preceding labial consonant, or a following voiceless fricative, plus some further segmental environments. What were allophonic differences at the outset evolved into novel phonemes in the cases of /aː ~ æː/ and /ʌ/ (and, after the loss of non-prevocalic /r/, also /ɜː/).

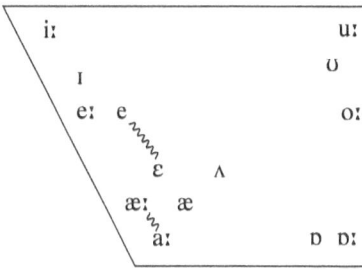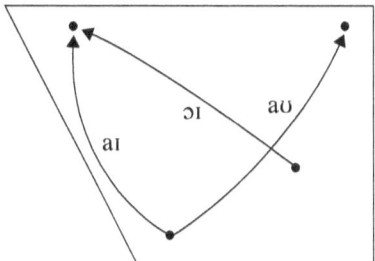

Figure 3.2: Early Modern English stressed monophthongs and diphthongs around 1700

Despite these massive changes, the vowel system at the end of the period, represented in Figure 3.2, was still markedly different from the Present-day English one. It remained for later periods to develop the strongly diphthongal ring that characterizes English vowels today.

7 References

Barber, Charles. 1997. *Early Modern English*. 2nd edn. Edinburgh: Edinburgh University Press.
Dobson, Eric J. 1968. *English Pronunciation 1500–1700*. 2 vols. 2nd edn. Oxford: Clarendon.
Early English Books Online. 1999. Ann Arbor: Proquest Information and Learning. http://eebo.chadwyck.com/home/; last accessed 14 April 2017.
Faiß, Klaus. 1989. *Englische Sprachgeschichte*. Tübingen: Francke.
Görlach, Manfred. 1994. *Einführung ins Frühneuenglische*. 2nd edn. Heidelberg: Winter.
Lass, Roger. 1999. Phonology and morphology. In: Roger Lass (ed.), *The Cambridge History of the English Language*. Vol. III. *1476–1776*, 56–186. Cambridge: Cambridge University Press.
Levins, Peter. 1570. *Manipulus Vocabulorum*. London: Henrie Bynneman. (Source: *Early English Books Online*.)
Minkova, Donka. 2001. Review of Lass, Roger (ed.). 1999. The Cambridge History of the English Language *Vol. III. 1476–1776*. *Journal of English Linguistics* 29: 83–92.
Nevalainen, Terttu. 2006. *An Introduction to Early Modern English*. Edinburgh: Edinburgh University Press.
Puttenham, George. 1589. *The Arte of English Poesie*. London: Richard Field. (Source: *Early English Books Online*.)
Schlüter, Julia. 2006. A small word of great interest: The allomorphy of the indefinite article as a diagnostic of sound change from the sixteenth to nineteenth centuries. In: Nikolaus Ritt,

Herbert Schendl, Christiane Dalton-Puffer, and Dieter Kastovsky (eds.), *Medieval English and its Heritage: Structure, Meaning and Mechanisms of Change*, 37–59. Frankfurt: Lang.

Schlüter, Julia. 2009a. Consonant or "vowel"? A diachronic study of initial ⟨h⟩ from early Middle English to nineteenth-century English. In: Donka Minkova (ed.), *Phonological Weakness in English: From Old to Present-Day English*, 168–196. Houndsmills, Basingstoke/Hampshire/New York: Palgrave Macmillan.

Schlüter, Julia. 2009b. Weak segments and syllable structure in Middle English. In: Donka Minkova (ed.), *Phonological Weakness in English: From Old to Present-Day English*, 199–236. Houndsmills, Basingstoke/Hampshire/New York: Palgrave Macmillan.

Stockwell, Robert and Donka Minkova. 1990. Early Modern English vowels, more o'Lass. *Diachronica* 7: 199–215.

Stockwell, Robert and Donka Minkova. 2002. Interpreting the Old and Middle English close vowels. *Language Sciences* 24: 447–457.

Claire Cowie
Chapter 4: Morphology

1 Nominal inflectional morphology —— 47
2 Verb morphology —— 51
3 Derivational morphology —— 54
4 References —— 65

Abstract: By the end of the Middle English period there is already considerable loss of inflectional morphology, and in Early Modern English we see the last reflexes of a shift from synthetic Old English to analytic Modern English (Lass 1999: 139). In fact, the inflectional system of Early Modern English is not very different from what we have today (Görlach 1991: 79). The changes in inflection which do take place between 1500 and 1700 show marked sociolinguistic differentiation and are the subject of well-known case studies in sociohistorical linguistics. The derivational morphology of Early Modern English, on the other hand, is considered to demonstrate much more wholesale and radical change in the form of new Latin prefixes and suffixes reanalyzed from borrowed lexis. The rate of integration of these word-formation processes is not, however, very uniform, and capturing this diversity is a major aim of this survey.

1 Nominal inflectional morphology

1.1 Nouns

Gender marking on nouns was already lost by late Middle English. The only case marking left by 1500 is the genitive -*s* with the same allomorphs (/ɪz/, /s/, and /z/) as the plural morpheme (Barber 1997: 145). The use of the apostrophe *s* ('s) for the spelling of the possessive singular is not common until the late 17th century, and the *s* apostrophe (*s*') for the possessive plural is not common until the late 18th century (Barber 1997: 143; Görlach 1991: 82). The analytic variant, the *of* genitive, is available from late Middle English but becomes markedly more popular over the Early Modern period. The -*s* genitive tends to occur with human nouns and on

Claire Cowie: Edinburgh (UK)

modifiers in subjective relation to the head (*the boy's arrival*) and the *of* genitive tends to occur with inanimate nouns and on modifiers in objective relation to the head (*the release of the boy*). This pattern remains quite consistent in the 17th century. At this time the *-s* genitive is regarded as somewhat more informal (Altenberg 1982; Rissanen 1999: 201–202).

A much discussed construction associated with Early Modern English is the "*his* genitive" (*the Kinge his fool*). This is widespread in the 16th and 17th centuries, but in fact arose earlier (12th century) due to the homophony of the genitive morpheme and weak forms of *his* with /h/ deletion (Barber 1997: 146; Lass 1999: 146). It may have been a popular feature which then in the 16th century made its way into "respectable" prose (Görlach 1991: 81). An oft-cited example from Shakespeare is *the Count his gallies* (*Twelfth Night*). The construction was extended to feminines in the 16th century, as in Lyly's *Juno hir bed,* and apparently to plurals, as in *the vtopians their creditors* (Robinson's translation of More's *Utopia* 1551). However Allen (2008) has shown some well-known examples such as the latter, which is cited in the OED, to be misanalyzed cases of apposition. Typically the construction is restricted to proper names ending in sibilants which would otherwise have no formal marker of possession as in Glanvill's *Democritus his Well* and *Hercules his Pillars* (Barber 1997: 146; Görlach 1991: 81).

Number marking with inflectional *-s* is highly regularized in Early Modern English. In Middle English the unstressed schwa of [əz] was lost except after sibilants, and this was followed by assimilation to preceding voiceless consonants, giving three allomorphs /ɪz/, /s/, and /z/. This allomorphy is more or less established by the 15th century, but unexpected forms in Hart's transcriptions of 1569 such as *birds, prinses,* and *faultz* show that the system is not stabilized until about 1600 (Barber 1997: 144; Lass 1999: 141–142).

Some of the mass nouns of Modern English are count nouns in Early Modern English (*salmons, trouts*). Conversely some nouns that today have an *-s* plural today could take a zero plural in Early Modern English (*board, brick*). *Horse, winter, year,* and *lamb* in Early Modern English are variable. Umlaut plurals (*mice, geese*) are in decline by Middle English and the older Old English plural in *-en* (as in *oxen* and *children*) is used only for deliberate archaism such as Spenser's *eyen, foen, skyen* (Lass 1999: 141; Barber 1997: 145; Görlach 1991: 80).

1.2 Pronouns

Unlike nouns, pronouns in Early Modern English are still marked for person and gender as well as number and case. The EModE paradigm in Table 4.1 shows that as per the ME development, gender is marked in the third person only.

Although the /h-/ of neuter *hit* was lost in Middle English, some claim that *hit* was still in use in the 16th century (Barber 1997: 150). In the late 16th century, *its* emerges as the neuter possessive pronoun, replacing *his* (Lass 1999: 148; Görlach 1991: 85–86). *His* can still be observed in the Authorized Version, as in (1):

(1) *if the salt haue lost **his** savour, wherewith shall **it** be salted?* (1611 *King James Bible* Matthew 5:13; Barber 1997: 150)

Mine and *thine* as determiners are common before vowels and /h/ in the 16th century, but by the 17th century attributive /-n/ forms are rare (Barber 1997: 152; Görlach 1991: 85). Changes in the neuter third person pronoun and the system of second person pronouns are shown with arrows.

Table 4.1: Early Modern English personal pronouns (Nevalainen 2006: 77)

Person/ number	Subjective	Objective	Possessive determiner	Possessive
1P SG	I	me	my/mine	mine
1P PL	we	us	our	ours
2P SG	thou ~ ye → you	thee ~ you	thy/thine → thy ~ your	thine ~ yours
2P PL	ye → you	you	your	yours
3P SG personal	he, she	him, her	his, her	his, hers
3P SG non-personal	(h)it → it	him, (h)it → it	his → its (of it)	(his > its)
3P PL	they	them	their	theirs

One of the most remarkable developments in the pronoun system of Early Modern English is the emergence and then decline of social deixis in the second person. *You*, historically the plural form, became used in Middle English, under courtly French influence, as a polite or deferential singular (Barber 1997: 153; Görlach 1991: 85). In a parallel change, nominative *ye* ceases to be an alternative to *you* (complete by 1600) and *you* becomes the form for the nominative and the accusative. Yet English did not develop a typically European T/V system (Brown and Gilman 1960) with reciprocal *thou* (T) encoding intimacy and solidarity and non-reciprocal T/V encoding asymmetry in power or status (Brown and Gilman 1989: 177; Lass 1999: 149; Wales 1983). In the middle of the Early Modern period, *you* is the polite form used by inferiors to superiors, but it is also a neutral and unmarked form among the upper classes. The general use of *you* spread down the social hierarchy and "by 1600, *you* was the normal unmarked form for all speakers with any pretension to politeness" (Barber 1997: 155). *Thou* was retained to occasionally mark asymmetrical relationships; mostly it had an "emotional" use to convey intimacy and affection, sometimes contempt.

These affective shifts are reflected in the switching of pronouns by the same interlocutors even within the same text. Some evidence comes from dramatic dialogue: In *Macbeth*, Malcolm addresses Macduff with *you*, a proper form for a Scottish thane, until Malcolm's emotional statement "but God above deal between me and thee" (IV.iii.120–121; Brown and Gilman 1989: 177). There are also abundant examples from private letters. Sir Thomas More, who otherwise addresses his daughter as *you*, says "Surely Megge a fainter hearte than thy fraile father hath, canst you not haue" with the concord for *thou* applied to *you* (Lass 1999: 151). *Thou* becomes increasingly restricted to high registers by the end of the 17th century, although it is also associated with regional use (Nevalainen 2006: 18) (see Busse, Chapter 12).

1.3 Adjectival comparison

In Early Modern English the only morphological marking on adjectives is the comparative and superlative degrees of comparison (*-er, -est*). The periphrastic expression of gradation (*more, most*) had already become common in Middle English, providing two systems. In the modern system periphrasis is in complementary distribution with suffixes: monosyllabic bases take suffixes (*bigger, biggest*), disyllables prefer suffixes, but can take periphrasis (*hairier, more hairy*); trisyllabic and longer forms take periphrasis (**beautiful-er*). This situation is not completely established in Early Modern English, however. We find forms like *easilier* and *more brief* in John Hart's *Orthographie* of 1569, *famousest* and *difficultest* in Milton, *learneder* in Johnson, and *ragingest* in Nash. Double comparison was more common in the 16th and 17th centuries, illustrated by Shakespeare's "this was the most unkindest cut of all" (*Julius Caesar*) and *"more nearer"* (*Hamlet*). There is also apparently more free variation: Ben Jonson uses both *fitter* and *more fit*, Shakespeare uses *sweeter* and *more sweet* (Lass 1999: 156–158; Barber 1997: 136–147).

Görlach (1991: 83–84) believes that the periphrastic form was more associated with written or educated language and that much of the loss of the inflected form for disyllabics was due to prescriptivism. However, studies of the Helsinki and ARCHER corpora (Kytö 1996; Kytö and Romaine 1997) suggest that the inflectional forms reassert themselves after 1700.

2 Verb morphology

2.1 Person and number

The second person continues to be marked in Early Modern English in concord with the pronoun *thou*, but falls into disuse along with *thou* in the 17th century (Barber 1997: 164–165; Görlach 1991: 88; Lass 1999: 139). The second person marker *-st* appears on the present (*bearest, giuest, walkest*) and the past (*barest, gauest, walkedst*). Third person plural is marked in the present by the Midlands variant *-en* in 15th century texts, as in (2):

(2) *Southern western & northern men* **speken** *frenssh all lyke in soune & speche* (1480 *The Description of Britain* [Caxton edn.]; Görlach 1991: 89)

The marker falls away quickly in the 17th century from the standard language. The normal plural for Early Modern English is the uninflected form (Barber 1997: 170–171).

Although there is only one marker of third person singular in Modern English, *-s* is in competition with *-eth* throughout the Early Modern English period. The *-s* form was originally northern and had spread to the East Midland system by the 15th century. The original southern *-eth* form became the standard written form when the new standard literary language took shape. Yet *-s* continued to move southwards and in 1500 was probably common in southern speech. The use of *-s* increases and over the 16th century it becomes the normal spoken form (Barber 1997: 166–167; Lass 1999: 162–164; Nevalainen 2006: 17). More precisely, variation in the early stages is between *-eth* and *-es* (as in *comyth* and *makys*) rather than the contracted *-s* and the syllabic *-eth* which we find in the 17th century (Nevalainen and Raumolin-Brunberg 2003: 67–68).

Yet it would be simplistic to think in terms of a spoken variant and a written variant. Rather, *-eth* is associated with more formal text types, namely official documents, poetry, sermons, and biblical translations (such as the Authorized Version of 1611); and *-s* appears in journalistic prose, drama, private letters, and diaries (Barber 1997: 166–168; Görlach 1991: 88; Nevalainen and Raumolin-Brunberg 2003: 81). Studies of the variation in Shakespeare's plays reveal rapid change over a short critical period (Taylor 1976; Stein 1988). More longitudinal research using the *Corpus of Early English Correspondence* (CEEC) shows two waves of change. In the "first wave" in the latter half of the 15th century, the change to *-s* is led socially by the "lowest literate ranks". In the second wave, around 1600, the middle or upwardly mobile ranks lead this change, especially women in these ranks (Nevalainen and Raumolin-Brunberg 2003: 121–122, 140, 144, 178–179).

The (present) inflected forms of HAVE and DO (*hath* and *doth*) retain the older form for much longer, but it may be that these continued to be used as written forms after the spoken use of *has* and *does* (Lass 1999: 163–165; Barber 1997: 168). Modal auxiliaries were normally not inflected for the third person singular (unless they are also still lexical verbs as in *he dares* and *he willeth*), but they do have the second person singular inflection (*thou canst*). The second person singular forms of *shall* and *will* are *shalt* and *wilt* (Barber 1997; Görlach 1991: 89).

2.2 Tense, mood, and aspect

All weak verbs in Early Modern English as today are marked in the past tense. The Modern English system of allomorphy of the past tense marker *-ed* was not established until 1600: /əd/ after /t/ or /d/ (*waited, heeded*), /d/ after a vowel or voiced consonant (*died, begged*) and /t/ after a voiceless consonant (*looked, wished*) (Barber 1997: 174). There was considerable variation into the 18th century (Lass 1999: 172), and the /əd/ pronunciation with the schwa vowel, which began to be lost in the 16th century (Görlach 1991: 92) could be used in more positions than is possible today. Syncope is indicated around 1600 by spelling (*begd, lookte, placst*); there is a 17th century tendency to standardize spelling as *-ed*, but syncope is indicated in poetry e.g. Dryden's *confess'd* (Barber 1997: 175; Nevalainen 2006: 6).

Certain Old English strong verbs developed a regular past tense, but both forms remained available in Early Modern English; for example, the past tense of *help* could be *holp* or *helped*, with past participle as either weak *holped/helped* or strong *holp/holpen* (with original strong past participle ending *-en*). Not all strong verbs which developed this past tense variation in Early Modern English (e.g. *shake* could be *shaked* or *shook*) retained the regular form in Modern English (Barber 1997: 174). Some historically weak verbs had strong forms in Early Modern English e.g. *snow, snew*. Some weak verbs even changed over to the strong class on the basis of analogy e.g. *spit* and *stick* (Görlach 1991: 91).

Tense marking on strong verbs in Early Modern English often had a different pattern for the form of the preterit and the past participle to both Middle English and Modern English. Different verbs go through different patterns, taking some time to stabilize (Nevalainen 2006: 20). As Lass says "it seems as if each verb has its own history" (1999: 168–170), which can be illustrated by changes in the paradigm for DRINK:

late 15th	drink, drank, drunk
end of 16th to 19th	drink, drunk, drunk
17th to 19th	drink, drank, drank

The periphrastic expression of the future with auxiliaries *shall* and *will* goes back to Old English. By the early 16th century both auxiliaries had lost much of their modal meaning of obligation and volition and could express pure future.

Perfect and pluperfect aspect has been expressed through auxiliaries HAVE and BE since Old English (Rissanen 1997: 213); the expression of progressive aspect by means of the BE + present participle construction can also be found in Old English. However, after its growth in Middle English the progressive can only be said to be grammaticalized by 1700, and according to Rissanen, "the set of progressive forms in all tenses, active and passive, is fully developed around the end of the eighteenth century" (1997: 216). He shows how Polonius in *Hamlet* (II.ii) asks "What do you read my lord?" but in *Troilus and Cressida* (III.iii) Achilles uses "What are you reading?". (See further Seoane, Chapter 5.)

As always in English, the base form of the verb in Early Modern English serves as the imperative mood. Although in Middle English already there is no distinct plural form of the subjunctive mood, the subjunctive is far more in evidence in Early Modern English than it is in Modern English. This is due in part to the contrast of zero-marked to inflected verb forms in the singular. The subjunctive is typically found in subordinate clauses following a conditional conjunction. In the present, we find the base form of the verb used with the second and third person instead of the inflected forms (*-st*, *-s*, *-eth*). The subjunctive form of BE is invariable *be* in the present tense (*I be, you/thou be, s/he be*), and plural *were* with the singular in the past tense (*I were, thou were*). This passage (3) from Tyndale illustrates both regular verbs in the subjunctive and BE:

(3) *Agre with thyne adversary quicklie / whyles thou arte in the waye with him / lest that adversary **deliver** the to the iudge / and the iudge **delivre** the to the minister / and then thou **be** cast into preson* (1526 Tyndale, *Bible*; Barber 1997: 171)

In modern English traces of the subjunctive remain in phrases such as "long live ...", "if need be" and "if he were". Through drama especially, it is evident that the subjunctive is not elevated language in Early Modern English, but "comes regularly from the lips of tradesmen, apprentices, artisans, peasants, people with no social pretensions" (Barber 1997: 173). Auxiliaries have been important in the expression of modality since Old English, but the loss of distinctive verb endings almost certainly speeded up the replacement of subjunctive forms by auxiliary periphrasis (Rissanen 1999: 228–230; Nevalainen 2006: 96). For example, we find *may* used for the optative subjunctive (*in heauen may you finde it*) and *let* for hortative subjunctive (*let him love his wife even as himself*). The preterit subjunctive (*were*) is replaced by *would* or *should*, (4):

(4) if any body **should** ask me ... I should say, I heard so; and it **would** be very good Evidence, unless someone else were produc'ed (1685 Trial of Titus Oates; Nevalainen 2006: 97)

3 Derivational morphology

Both popular and scholarly accounts hold that not only did non-native derivational morphology became productive in the course of the 16th century, but the period showed intensified productivity and creative word-formation with native morphology too. Indeed, it is often remarked that the exploitation of lexical resources in the Renaissance has never been surpassed (Hughes 2000: 162). George Gordon writes of the "genuine and widespread feeling for word-creation" of the Elizabethans and "the fertility and happy-go-luckiness of Elizabethan English" (1928: 262, 269). Shakespeare's experiments in word-formation are, for Gordon, the emblem of these Elizabethan tendencies. Scholarly debate has swung between the Victorians who characterized Shakespeare as a Saxonist "lack Latin" who drew mainly on his native vocabulary, and later 20th century critics who claimed that Shakespeare coined thousands of Latinate words. More considered analyses reveal that Shakespeare made extensive use of Latinate prefixes and suffixes, although not always according to the rules of Latin word-formation, for instance in the way that he prefixes the noun *moment* with *in-* to form the adjective *immoment* "unimportant", or the way that he combines native and non-native elements in hybrids like *bi-fold* and *fore-recited* (Garner 1987: 215; Schäfer 1973; Schäfer 1980).

The integration of non-native elements into the English word-formation system began in Middle English, predominantly through the attachment of native suffixes to Fr. bases, for example *chasteness* (1386). Much less common, and typically later, is the attachment of non-native suffixes to native bases, as in *allowment* (1579) (Gadde 1910; Nevalainen 1999: 357). Despite their rarity, these hybrid forms are often taken as an indication that lexemes containing the non-native suffix are analyzable for speakers of Early Modern English and that the suffix is thus in some qualitative sense productive (Dalton-Puffer 1996). As most of the new borrowed affixes were in fact limited to Romance and classical bases, it makes sense to speak of a "quantitative shift towards a non-native basis of coining new words in Early Modern English" (Nevalainen 1999: 378).

This picture of emerging productivity in non-native affixes in Early Modern English is supported by research following the publication of the *Chronological English Dictionary* (CED) (Finkenstaedt et al. 1970). With this new tool, Finkenstaedt, Leisi, and Wolff, followed by scholars like Richard Wermser, were able to show how French and Latin loans were the greatest source of new vocabulary between 1600 and 1700 (Finkenstaedt et al. 1973: 118–119; Wermser 1976: 45; Görlach 1991: 166; Nevalainen 1999: 364; Hughes 2000: 152–153). Subsequently it has become clearer that the apparently dramatic peak of Latinate vocabulary observable at the turn of the 16th century is an effect of the OED's extensive sampling of this period relative to the 18th century (Schäfer 1980; Brewer 2006), and in particular the sampling of hard word dictionaries (Osselton 1958; Starnes and Noyes 1946; Barber 1997: 169) (see Lancashire, Chapter 6).

Wermser further aimed to show on the basis of the CED how affixation increased in relation to loanwords. Coined words outnumber loans by 58.3% to 37.6% by the 18th century, after two centuries of the two processes being roughly even (Wermser 1976: 40; Nevalainen 1999: 350; Görlach 1991: 138). This proportion is later confirmed by Barber's 2% sample of the OED (Barber 1997: 221). The relative frequency of nonnative affixes to native affixes in coined words rises from 20% at the beginning of the Early Modern English period to 70% at the end of it (Wermser 1976: 64; Nevalainen 1999: 352). The proportion of Germanic to French and Latin bases in new coinages falls from about 32% at the beginning of the Early Modern period to some 13% at the end (Wermser 1976: 64, 67; Nevalainen 1999: 378). Together these measures confirm the emergence of non-native affixes as independent English morphemes over the Early Modern period. They also seem to contradict claims that the native affixes in Early Modern English are just as, if not more productive, than ever (Barber 1976: 185–188; Nevalainen 1999: 391), although it is always less likely that words coined with native affixes would be recorded in a dictionary, especially the Shorter OED, on which the CED is based.

We cannot be sure how Wermser was interpreting the etymologies of OED entries – the OED etymologies frequently equivocate, sometimes providing the source of a loan *and* showing how it could be formed through affixation. For any historical period, it is hard to ascertain whether a given word with a non-native base and a non-native affix is a loan or a coined word, in the "language", as well as in the mental lexicons of individual speakers. Accounts of Early Modern English word-formation rely on the idea that non-native suffixes become productive over this period, but this is not always based on extensive evidence, and substantial differences in the productivity of processes can be obscured. Thomason and Kaufman (1988) are less persuaded of a new integrated word-formation system emerging in Early Modern English. With the exception of some suffixes like adjective-forming *-able* (first seen on Middle English loans from French), they consider the derivational phenomena emerging from Latin lexical influence in English post-1450 as "productive for uncultivated speakers to a limited extent only" (Thomason and Kaufman 1988: 308; 1988: 329).

Detailed overviews of native and non-native individual prefixes and suffixes can be found in works such as Marchand (1969) and Nevalainen (1999). Like these, the summaries below rely extensively on the OED (Simpson [ed.] 2000–) articles for individual prefixes and suffixes. Here the focus is on affixes emerging in Early Modern English. Sometimes the OED article offers an explicit comment on the stage at which the form is considered to be an independent affix; sometimes this trajectory, where there is one, must be inferred from the dates of coined words. Emphasis is placed on the loanword models for words coined with the new affixes, most commonly on non-native bases. Where non-native affixes do appear on native bases this may be indicative of greater productivity, but not necessarily.

3.1 Prefixation

The new negative prefixes, with their general semantics, probably have the greatest impact on the word-formation system of all the new prefixes. *Non-* is adopted early (late 14th century) through Old French loans which in turn came from Law Latin (*nonsense, nonchalant*). The prefix first coined words on native and non-native nouns (*non-truth; non-activity*), but the input range broadened in the 17th century to adjective bases (*non-harmonious*), including some participles (*non-preaching*) (Nevalainen 1999: 380) although native adjectival bases (*non-bookish, non-English*) tend to be 19th century. There are rare examples of *non-* prefixed to native and non-native verbs (*non-act; non-licentiate*). *In-* with its allomorphs *il-* and *im-* appears later in the form of Latin (*innocens, illiteratus, immensus*) as well as Fr. loans (*incompetent, inexpressive*). From the 16th century we find *in-* on primarily non-native adjectives (*incautious, inarguable, inexpedient; infit*). Reversative and privative *dis-* is also a later addition appearing in Lt. loans such as *dispute* from *disputare* even though *dis-* is not a separable prefix in Latin (Garner 1987: 215). *Dis-* is described as a "living prefix" after 1600 by the OED, used to form new verbs on existing native and non-native verb bases (*disown, disangularise; disrank*) and even some noun (*discharacter, diseye*) and adjective bases (*disgood, disrespectful dishonest*).

All three imported negatives parallel native *un-*, which appears on all classes of base (*unfortunate, unhouse, unnerve*), and remains the most common negative prefix in Early Modern English (Nevalainen 1999: 380–382). There is ample evidence of alternation between *un-* and *in-* on adjectival bases before the 16th century. The OED indicates that both could appear before the adjectives *cautious, ceremonious, certain, communicative, devout,* and *distinguishable*. The practice in the 16th and 17th centuries was to prefer the form with *in-*, as in *inaidable, inarguable,* and *inavailable,* but items with Latinate bases were later revised to *in-*, with other bases taking *un-* (*unavailing, uncertain, undevout, unexpected*). Matthews has described a kind of cyclic process whereby negative prefixes lexicalize with evaluative meanings as in *improper,* and the alternate prefix remains neutral. Compare *unnatural* and *non-natural, immeasurable* and *unmeasurable, immoral* and *amoral* (Matthews 1991: 72–74). Words prefixed with *in-* are probably more inclined to lexicalize in this way given their strong link to Latin lexis. *De-* and *dis-* overlap on verb bases as in the oft-cited *disthronize, disthrone, dethrone, unthrone, dethronize* (Görlach 1991: 80). The prefix *de-* is only found in the 18th century, although there are some "tentative" 17th century examples like *detomb* 1607 (Nevalainen 1999: 383).

Whilst some suffixes are assimilated relatively early through French, the numerous new prefixes are, by contrast, typically borrowed later from Latin (Burnley 1992: 446–449). They tend on the whole to be restricted to certain technical registers, or at least, to form exclusively technical terms. Typical examples from the set of locatives would be *sub-* emerging from French loans such as *subsequent, subsection,* and forming words on all classes of base, as in *subtrench, subconsulary, subrenal,* and *subdecimate*; *trans-*, also from Fr. loans like *trespasser* and Lt. *transferre,* forming verbs on verb bases (*transplace*) and some noun bases (*transfashion*); and *circum-*, from Lt. *circuminvolvere* and *circonscrire*, appearing on native and non-native verbs (*circumbind, circumgyre, circumclose*). The intensifying prefix *hyper-* appears in *hyperconformist, hyper-angelical,* and *hyper-magnetic* on analogy of Gk. words like *hyperbole, hyperborean*. The quantitative prefixes are late 16th or 17th century: *multi-*, from Lt. *multiplex, multifarious* and Fr. *multiply, multitude,* is applied to noun and adjective bases to form *multivariety, multilateral; mono-*, from Fr. (*monarch, monosyllable*) and Gk. (*monoculus, monoxylon*) loans, forms *monoptic, monopyrenous; uni-*, from Lt. *universitas, unicornus,* forms *univalve, unifoil, unipresence* (from which *unipresent* is then back-derived); *bi-*, on the analogy of loans *hicome, biennium* appears principally on non-native adjectives such as *bicapsular; tri-* appears on noun and adjective bases *trigram, tricentrall*; Lt. compounds such as *semicirculus* are imitated to form *semi-quaver, semi-riddle, semi-cubit, semi-Atheist. Demi-* in fact is somewhat earlier than *semi-*, appearing in 15th century heraldic loan translations (*demigod, demi-angel, demi-lion*).

A number of the prefixes with productivity restricted by register only show a substantial increase in frequency *after* the Early Modern period. For example, types like *transapical, circumcorneal, postcerebellar, pre-chemical* are all 19th century and later. The prefixes *pan-* (from Gk. *pandemic, panoply*) and *poly-* (from Gk. *Polygamia*) do form words in Early Modern English (*panpharmacon, pantheology, Panglyphic; Polyacoustic*) but this is rare, and most examples are 19th century and later. Although *pseudo-* occurs in borrowed words in Early Modern English (*pseudo-christ* from Gk. *pseudochristus*) it is rarely a "living prefix" in English before 1800 (*pseudo-religious* 1672) (Marchand 1969: 188; Nevalainen 1999: 388).

Some of the new prefixes extend beyond technical terms, and these are often processes that are borrowed earlier. So locative *en-* became productive in the 15th century and is widely used in the 16th century on native and non-native bases (Nevalainen 1999: 389) to form verbs such as *endanger, embody, encamp, ennoble*; *super-*, from Fr. loans *superlative, superstition*, also takes off in the 15th century and is frequent in Elizabethan times, appearing on nouns (*superstructure*), adjectives (*super-aerial*) and verbs (*superinvest*); *inter-*, from Lt. (*intercedere, intermedius, interregnum*) and Fr. (*enterfere, entercourse*) loans, leads to formations on native and non-native noun bases (*interdispensation, intermatch*); native and non-native verb bases (*intermention, intertwine*) and adjective bases (*interconciliary*).

Temporal prefixes tend to be introduced earlier and found more widely. *Re-*, from Fr. verbs *redress, regard* and Lt. *reducere* (and in contemporary lexicographers' renderings of Italian words such as *ristoppare*), becomes "freely prefixed" (OED, Simpson [ed.] 2000–) towards the end of the 16th century, primarily on non-native verbs (*re-elect*) but also native verbs (*regreet*). *Pre-*, from Lt. *preambulare*, already coins words in late Middle English; these are "numerous" from the 16th century onwards and include *pre-petition, pre-excellence* on nouns, and on verbs *preconceive, pre-close, pre-ordinate, pre-sift*. Formations after Lt. loans like *postponere* and Fr. *postcommunion, postposer* first appear in English in the late 14th century: examples on nouns include *post-accession, post-argument, post-pardon* and on verbs include *postcribrate, post-place*.

"Attitudinal" prefixes (Nevalainen 1999) tend not to be restricted to technical terms. *Counter-*, from Fr. *counterbalance, countersign*, prefixes native and non-native nouns (*counterplot, countermotion*) and native and non-native verbs (*counterhit, counterfix*). The Latin version (*contraponere*) can be found on *contraproposal, contra-civil* and *contra-distinguish*. *Anti-*, from Gk. (*antithesis*), appeared exclusively in loan translations such as *antipope, antichrist* before 1600, but after that was generalized to other noun bases to produce *antideity, antiface, antihemisphere, anti-romance* and adjectival bases to produce *anticreative, antiliturgical*.

3.2 Suffixation

3.2.1 Noun suffixes

None of the new suffixes forming concrete nouns managed to usurp the ubiquitous native agentive *-er* suffix (Nevalainen 1999: 392; Görlach 1991: 172). They tend on the whole to be both semantically and formally restricted. *-ician* is added to arts or sciences in Lt. *-ica*, Fr. *-ique* or Eng. *-ic, -ics* to denote a person skilled in the art or science. *Musician* and *physician* are loans but in some cases it is not possible to tell if a word (e.g. *magician*) is formed in English. Some words like *geometrician* are formed by analogy on names not even ending in *-ic* (although there may be an adjective in *-ic*). *-eer* is added to English nouns in the early 17th century to form designations of persons (*pamphleteer, auctioneer, pulpiteer*) in imitation of earlier Fr. loans like *canonnier* (> *cannoneer*) with the Fr. agent suffix *-ier* (still evident in *bombardier*). It hardly appears on native bases, and when it does (as in *waistcoateer* 'a prostitute') it is not transparent. Concrete nouns ending in *-ant* may be Fr. participles borrowed before 1500 (*attendant, dependant*) later refashioned as Lt. *-ent* (*dependent*), or participles borrowed directly from Lt. (*stimulant* 1728). There are some analogical formations (*anaesthesiant* 1879), but not many, in Early Modern English.

Nouns such as *curate, senate* are English renderings of Lt. nouns *curatus, senatus* (including medieval Lt. nouns *aldermannatus > aldermanate*) and this pattern is used to generate words in English on other Lt. nominal stems (*syndicate* 1624, *electorate* 1675). Perhaps the most interesting development in this group of noun suffixes is the passive benefactive suffix *-ee*, for which there is no native equivalent. The first examples are from Anglo-French participles (*appellee, refugee*) but later words are coined with the suffix in English (*referee* 1549, *vendee* 1547). Many subsequent formations in English (*laughee* 1829) are listed as "nonce-words" but the suffix certainly seems to be alive in Present-day English (Mühleisen 2010).

Borrowed abstract noun suffixes are without doubt the most noticeable elements of the new "layer" of derivational morphology. This is due in part to the sheer numbers of complex nouns borrowed, resulting in a wide range of possible noun endings some of which are semantically general. There was already a choice of native abstract-noun forming suffixes in Middle English, particularly for the description of states or qualities as in *hethenness, hethenhood, hethenship* (Dalton-Puffer 1996: 126).

Gerundial *-ing* is the deverbal noun-forming suffix of choice in Middle English (on native and non-native bases), and the suffix continues to have near inflectional levels of productivity in Early Modern English (Görlach 1991: 172). It is rivalled by the new deverbal suffix -*ation*, and to a lesser extent -*ment* (Bauer 2001: 184); other suffixes forming abstract nouns on verbs are more restricted: -*ance*/-*ence* became "to a certain extent a living formative" (OED, Simpson [ed.] 2000–) after appearing in Fr. (*nuisance, parlance*) and Latin or refashioned-as-Latin loans (*providence, prudence*) and even coins some nouns on native bases (*clearance* 1563, *hindrance* 1436, *furtherance* 1440); -*ance* nouns could be refashioned as -*ancy* if the state/condition meaning was more prominent than the action/process: cf. *temperancy* 1526 vs. *temperance* 1340.

The suffix -*ure* (Fr. *scripture*, Lt. *aperture*) became "mildly productive" in Early Modern English on verbs ending in -*s* and -*t* (Nevalainen 1999: 398) as in *exposure* 1605; from the 17th century onwards -*al* from Lt. suffix -*alia* (via loans like *arrival* > Anglo-French *arrivaille*) coins words such as *denial* 1528. Derivations on native bases (*bestowal, betrothal, beheadal*) are all 19th century.

Already in the 15th century, -*ment* is used to coin words denoting the result or product of action or the action itself: *chastisement* 1340 may be a coined word, and items on Germanic bases like *hangment* 1440 certainly are. These are modelled on Fr. loans *garment, accomplishment* and Lt. loans *fragment* < *fragmentum*. Later EModE examples include *banishment* 1507 and *enhancement* 1577 on Romance bases and *amazement* 1595 and *atonement* 1513 on Germanic bases. Some of the latter are also prefixed with *em-*, *en-* and *be-* (*enlightenment* 1669, *bereavement* 1731). There are even some formations on adjectives (*merriment* 1574).

The borrowed suffix -*ation*, however, is considered the most productive deverbal noun-forming suffix after -*ing* and one of the most productive new suffixes from the Early Modern period. We will examine this suffix more closely to consider what it means to develop productivity in Early Modern English. The productivity of -*ation* is often attributed to the fact that it is "the only alternative available for verbs ending in -*ise*, -*ate*, and -*ify*" (Nevalainen 1999: 397). Yet some caution is required in treating Early Modern words in -*ation*, even ones on base verbs ending in -*ize*, -*ate* and -*ify*, as confirmation of the emerging productivity of this suffix.

English formatives in -*ation* are considered to "show productivity from the beginning of the 17th century through to the 20th century, but always on Latin or French bases" (Bauer 2001: 181-182) with some well-known exceptions such as *starvation*. Synchronic morphologists (Kastovsky 1986: 589, 1992: 291) routinely distinguish between -*ation* words which are recognizable loans such as *communion, opinion, protection* where -*io*/-*io-n-em* has been added in Latin to the stem of a noun (*communis*), verb (*opinari*) or participle (*protegere*), and the more transparent cases, where Lt. loans such as *qualification* are formations on the past participial stem of verbs in -*are* (*qualificat*- from *qualificare*). The latter are often treated as English derivations. The general attachment of -*ation* to non-native bases makes it impossible to tell whether forms which contain the string -*ation* such as *recommendation* (a Fr. loan) are the result of borrowing or deverbal derivation in Early Modern English (Nevalainen 1999: 397).

Marchand (1969: 259) would like for convenience to treat all items on verb bases in *-ate* from 1500 as English derivations. So *education* 1540 would be treated as a derivation even though the OED shows this is a Latin loan. For many of these items the verb is back-derived from the borrowed abstract noun (see verb suffixes below). Sometimes there is not even a back-formed verb to hint at transparency for users as in *constellation, duration, ovation* (OED *-ation* article, cited by Marchand 1969: 261). Similarly, Marchand would like to classify *-ize + ation* words, many of which are Lt. nominalizations, either of Gk. verbs in *-ize* (*baptization*) or Lt. verbs in *-ize* (*moralization*) or Fr. verbs in *-iser* (*civilization*), as English derivations after 1600. We still find loans after 1600 though, such as *sacrification* 1694. The cut-off of 1600 seems to fit better for *-ify + -ation*: *amplification* 1546, *modification* 1492 and *verification* 1523 are Latin loans but *identification* 1644 and *beautification* 1640 are derivations on verbs in *-ify*. Interestingly, some early items previously presented by the OED as derivations are now shown as loans for example *pontification* 1500. More such cases are coming to light in the OED's latest revisions with the benefit of new resources (Durkin 2002).

Finally, there is the question of how we should treat "Latinate coining", where a noun such as *fecundation* is in fact formed in English, but on a verb base that exists only in Latin (*fecundare*). This is a well-known practice in Early Modern English, yet its extent has not been measured. In sum, the suffix *-ation* may not be as productive in Early Modern English as is commonly assumed. It might even be argued that this suffix never developed productivity in a quantitative sense. Bauer reflects that recent formations such as *lambadazation* and *electronification* must be analogical formations (Bauer 2001: 80–81, 96). The OED in fact indicates that a subset of scientific words including *ossification* 1671 do not have a pre-existing English verb base. Tellingly, *-ization* and *-(i)fication* are listed as complex suffixes alongside *-ation*.

Similar considerations apply to borrowed noun-forming suffix *-ity*, typically found on non-native adjectival bases in *-able/-ible, -ic, -al* and *-ar* and rarely found on native bases (Nevalainen 1999: 398): *oddity*, the classic exception, is as late as 1713. Unsurprisingly, many of the Early Modern examples turn out to be direct loans from Latin such as *implacability* 1531, and not a formation from *implacable* (1552) (Marchand 1969). Lt. nouns in *-itas* are Englished to *-ity* often via Fr. *-ite*. Here too there is Latinate coining (*carneity* 1691 is coined in English but the adjectival base *carneus* does not exist in English) and here too there may be a case for complex suffixes (*-ability, -icity*) rather than a single *-ity* suffix.

The appearance of native suffix *-ness* on non-native bases and the consequent appearance of doublets such as *sincereness/sincerity; singularness/singu-*

larity, fatalness/fatality (Marchand 1969: 335) is often used to draw attention to affix rivalry in Early Modern English (Nevalainen 1999: 398; Görlach 1991: 137; Romaine 1985; Riddle 1985). Sometimes the increasing productivity of *-ity* in Early Modern English is presented as claiming territory from *-ness* (Aronoff and Anshen 1998) but this is based on treating all *-ity* items as derivations, when in fact many of the rival Early Modern pairs concern an *-ity* loanword as in *absurdity* 1529 *absurdness* 1587 and *penetrability* 1609 *penetrableness* 1684.

Classical Latin words in *-acia* (*fallacia* > *fallacy*) or medieval Latin words in *-atia* (*legatia* > *legacy*) are Englished as words ending in *-acy*. The form is added to Lt. words in *-atus* (*advocatus* > *advocacy* 1413) or English adjectives in *-ate* (*accuracy* 1662, *privacy* 1534) from the 14th century already but is only "generalised" in the 16th century (Nevalainen 1999: 399).

The two best known non-native Early Modern English suffixes for forming abstract nouns with a condition /state/ collectivity meaning are *-age* (from loans such as *voyage, umbrage, plumage*) and *-ery* (from loans such as *pottery, bravery, machinery*). We see *-age* appear on non-native bases in *clientage* 1633, *orphanage* 1538 and non-native bases in *leafage* 1599, and *-ery* appears on non-native bases (*confectionery* 1545) and native bases (*brewery* 1658).

The suffix *-ism* is striking in that it comes from Gk. loans via Latin (*baptism, Atticism, Judaism*). From the 16th century it can be found on non-native bases (*modernism* 1737, *magnetism* 1616) and native bases (*truism* 1708). It can simply derive nouns of action (*plagiarism* 1621) but its primary uses are semantically narrower: it can denote the conduct of a class of persons (*patriotism* 1716*)*, a system of theory or practice (*Quakerism* 1656), a doctrine or principle (*libertinism* 1641), or a peculiarity or characteristic (*witticism* 1677).

3.2.2 Adjectival suffixes

As with nouns, numerous adjectives were added to Early Modern English through morphological Anglicization. In many cases an inflectional ending is simply dropped (*content* < *content-us*). In others, a set of adjectival loanwords becomes associated with a modified Latinate ending. For example *-ary*, in Early Modern English appears predominantly in loans such as *voluntary* and *contrary* from Fr. *voluntaire* and Latin *contrarius* and very infrequently in a word coined in English (*complementary* 1628).

Especially prominent are adjectives in *-ate* formed from Lt. participles (*desolate* < *desolatus*, *separate* < *separatus*). Fr. adjectives can be adapted with this ending (*affectionate* < *affectionnè*) and so can other Lt. stems (*roseate* 1589 is from Lt. *roseus*); thus *-ate* cannot be considered a productive adjectival suffix.

The non-native adjectival suffixes that are productive in Early Modern English, and later, tend to have gotten off the ground in Middle English. Following Fr. loans such as *capable, agreeable,* deverbal *-able* (as noted earlier), which is highly general in meaning, occurs on native (*takeable* 1449, *breakable* 1570) as well as non-native bases (*praisable* 1350). Whilst new words are coined in this process in Early Modern English, borrowing continues. The suffix is attached to nouns from the 16th century: *marriageable* 1575; but in some cases the base may be the noun or verb e.g. *rateable* 1503.

Deverbal *-ive* from Fr. (*adoptif*) and Lt. (*nativus*) loans is productively added to Fr. or Lt. verbs, but is formally restricted to those ending in *-s* or *-t* (*conducive* 1646, *depressive* 1620). These products are essentially analogical formations (Nevalainen 1999: 405); "ative" does become a "living form" as in *talkative* (1432) but there are few such examples. Denominal *-ous* (Fr. *dangerous*; Lt. *famosus, obliviosus*) is already used to coin words in English from the 14th century (*leguminous* 1656) although seldom on native bases (*timeous* 1470), possibly because denominal native adjectival suffixes (*muscled, heathery*) are widely used in Early Modern English (Nevalainen 1999: 400; Barber 1997: 234).

Lt. adjectives in *-alem* (*mortalem*) were borrowed early through French with *-el* (*mortel*) later refashioned to *-al* (*mortal*). The number of Lt. adjectives in *-alis* increased dramatically in medieval and modern Lt. (*cordialis*) also producing a suffix *-al* which could be added to any noun (*longitudinal* 1706; *constitutional* 1682). The *-al* ending could also be added to Lt. adjectives with endings such as *-eus* "to give them a more distinctively adjectival form" (OED, Simpson [ed.] 2000–); e.g. *funere-al* 1725. In late Lt. *-alis* nouns (*grammaticalis*) are formed on adjectives in *-ic-us* (*grammaticus*) hence the English *grammatical*, and so also *clerical, medical*. Somewhat later Lt. adjectives in *-icus* are rendered in English with an *-ic* ending (*poetic* < *poeticus*). Thus we find adjectives with both forms (*comic, comical; tragic, tragical*). The historical relationship and semantic differences are explored at length in Kaunisto (2007). Both suffixes occasionally act as independent formatives (*prelatical* 1614, *operatical* 1775) (Nevalainen 1999: 403) but the frequency of this group (Barber 1997 finds *-al/-ic/-ical* to be the most productive non-native adjectival affix in Early Modern English) is certainly complex.

Other adjectival suffixes are semantically narrower and consequently appear on a subset of bases. For instance, *-ese* (It. *Milanese*; Fr. *Chinois*) is added to national proper names only (*Japanese*); it is extended to other proper names much later (*Johnsonese* 1843). Similarly, *-ian* which comes from loans Fr. *Barbarien* > *barbarian* and Latin *Christianus* > *Christian* is associated with proper names such as *Cameronian* 1690, despite some Latinate coinings like *equestrian* 1656 on *equestri-s*. Whilst *-an* is added to Lt. adjectives in *-arius* (*agrarius* > *agrarian*) or

English adjectives in -*ary* (*disciplinarian*), the complex form -*ian* is mostly associated with ideologies (*sublapsarian* 1656). There are some jocular formations on native bases in the 18th century (*nothingarian* 1776). Finally, -*ite*, which appears in Greek/Latin loans like *Israelite*, forms person nouns such as *Jacobite* 1400, *Wyclifite* 1580.

3.2.3 Verb suffixes

Before 1500 the only overt morphological processes available to form verbs were the native prefix *be-* (*bejewel*) and suffix -*en* (*deafen*), and the prefix *en-* (*embody*) which emerges from Fr. loans in Middle English (*endanger*). Deadjectival conversions "often compete" with -*en* suffixations, as in *slack* and *slacken* (Nevalainen 1999: 388; 406; 429). Conversion to verb was a much more common process, and so whilst the above verb-forming prefixes were not really in use after 1600, conversion continued and survived into Modern English.

Nevalainen (1999: 407) describes -*ize* as the most productive of the new verb-forming morphological processes of Early Modern English, a situation which continues into Modern English (Plag 1999). This may be partly to do with the fact that -*ize* appears in relatively fewer Lt. loan words than other borrowed suffixes. Its origins are Greek, from Gk. loans into Latin such as *baptize*. Because -*ize* does not appear in so many Lt. loans, most of the -*ize* words in English such as *popularize* (1593) are coined, although almost always on non-native bases with some exceptions (*womanize* 1593). The fashion for -*ize* verbs attracted controversy in the 16th century, yet they continued to fill up the hard-word dictionaries of the 17th century before their demise in the 18th century (Görlach 1991: 176–177).

The story of -*ify* is closer to other Latinate morphology in that most items are renderings of original Lt. verbs in -*ficare* as in *pacify* < *pacificare*; *horrify* < *horrificare*). The suffix is also absorbed through Fr. loans (*liquefy* < *liquefier*). Coined words such as *beautify* (1526) are quite rare in Early Modern English. Their addition to native bases is marked as "jocular" or "trivial" (OED, Simpson [ed.] 2000–) in words such as *truthify* 1647 and *speechify* 1723.

As we saw above, Lt. past participles in -*atus*, -*ata*, -*atum* were a source of English adjectives. Some of these adjectives were treated as verbs (*separate* 1432). Subsequently English verbs in -*ate* were formed directly on the Lt. participial stems as in *venerate* from *venerari*. In the 16th and 17th centuries some -*ate* verbs were even coined on Romance nouns (*capacitate* 1657 from *capacity*; *fertilitate* 1634 from *fertility*), and Latin nominal stems (*camphorate* 1691 on *camphoratus*) (Nevalainen 1999: 407). These -*ate* verbs were stigmatized as "ynkpot termes" in the 16th century. The author of Thomas Wilson's famous ynkehorne letter from the *Arte of Rhetorique* (1553) pleads "I obtestate your clemencie, to inuigilate thus muche for me". Similar items were fabricated by Cockeram in his dictionary of 1623 (Görlach 1991: 176). The exact number of *-ate* verbs formed through back-formation of *-ation* nouns, as in *locate* (1652) from *location* (1592), is not known, but it is likely to be high throughout the period (Nevalainen 1999: 407; Görlach 1991: 176; Plag 1999). Given the limited productivity of the verb suffixes, it is unsurprising that they are considered to be in complementary distribution (Bauer 2001: 177). Rare "doublets" cited by Plag (1999: 228) (*dandify/dandyise*; *plastify/plasticize*) are 19th century.

The popular native adverb-forming suffix *-ly* had already emerged in Middle English. Highly generalized, in Early Modern English it is applied to adjectives (*bawdily*), including adjectives in *-ly* (*livelily*), a practice subsequently discouraged; participles (*shortsightedly*), numerals (*thirdly*), and even nouns (*agely*). However the suffix is less common in adverbs appearing as intensifiers than it is in Modern English (*exceeding well*) (Nevalainen 1997: 405).

4 References

Allen, Cynthia. 2008. *Genitive Case in Early English: Typology and Evidence*. Oxford: Oxford University Press.

Altenberg, B. 1982. *The Genitive v. the of-Construction. A Study of Syntactic Variation in 17th Century English*. Lund: Gleerup.

Aronoff, Mark and Frank Anshen. 1998. Morphology and the lexicon: Lexicalization and productivity. In: Andrew Spencer and Arnold M. Zwicky (eds.), *The Handbook of Morphology*, 237–248. Oxford: Blackwell.

Barber, Charles. 1997 [1976]. *Early Modern English*. 2nd edn. Edinburgh: Edinburgh University Press.

Bauer, Laurie. 2001. *Morphological Productivity*. Cambridge: Cambridge University Press.

Brewer, Charlotte. 2006. Eighteenth-century quotation searches in the Oxford English Dictionary. In: R. W. McConchie, Olga Timofeeva, Heli Tissari, and Tanja Säily (eds.), *Selected Proceedings of the 2005 Symposium on New Approaches in English Historical Lexis (HEL-LEX)*, 41–50. Somerville, MA: Cascadilla Proceedings Project.

Brown, Roger and Albert Gilman. 1960. The pronouns of power and solidarity. In: Thomas A. Sebeok (ed.), *Style in Language*, 253–276. Cambridge, MA: MIT Press.

Brown, Roger and Albert Gilman. 1989. Politeness theory and Shakespeare's four major tragedies. *Language in Society* 18(2): 159–212

Burnley, David. 1992. Lexis and semantics. In: Norman Blake (ed.), *The Cambridge History of the English Language*. Vol. II. *1066–1476*, 409–499. Cambridge: Cambridge University Press.

Dalton-Puffer, Christiane. 1996. *The French Influence on Middle English Morphology: A Corpus-based Study of Derivation*. Berlin/New York: Mouton de Gruyter.

Durkin, Philip. 2002. Changing documentation in the third edition of the Oxford English Dictionary: Sixteenth-century vocabulary as a test case. In: Teresa Fanego, Belén Méndez-Naya,

and Elena Seoane (eds.), *Sounds, Words, Texts and Change: Selected Papers from 11 ICEHL*, 65–81. Amsterdam/Philadelphia: John Benjamins.
Finkenstaedt, Thomas, Ernst Leisi, and Dieter Wolff. 1970. *A Chronological English Dictionary*. Heidelberg: Carl Winter.
Finkenstaedt, Thomas, Ernst Leisi, and Dieter Wolff. 1973. *Ordered Profusion: Studies in Dictionaries*. Heidelberg: Carl Winter.
Gadde, Fredrik. 1910. *On the History and Use of the Suffixes* -ery, -age *and* -ment *in English*. Ph.D. Dissertation. Lund: Gleerupska University.
Garner, Bryan A. 1987. Shakespeare's Latinate neologisms. In: Vivian Salmon and Edwina Burness (eds.), *Reader in the Language of Shakespearean Drama*, 207–228. Amsterdam/Philadelphia: John Benjamins.
Gordon, George. 1928. *Shakespeare's English*. Society for Pure English Tract no. XXIX. Oxford: Clarendon.
Görlach, Manfred. 1991. *Introduction to Early Modern English*. Cambridge: Cambridge University Press.
Hughes, Geoffrey. 2000. *A History of English Words*. Oxford: Blackwell
Kastovsky, Dieter. 1986. The problem of productivity in word-formation. *Linguistics* 24: 585–600.
Kastovsky, Dieter. 1992. The formats change – the problems remain: Word-formation theory between 1960 and 1990. In: Martin Pütz (ed.), *Thirty Years of Linguistic Evolution: Studies in Honour of René Driven on the Occasion of His Sixtieth Birthday*, 285–310. Amsterdam/Philadelphia: John Benjamins.
Kaunisto, Mark. 2007. *Variation and Change in the Lexicon: A Corpus-based Analysis of Adjectives in English Ending in* -ic *and* -ical. Amsterdam: Rodopi
Kytö, Merja. 1996. The best and most excellentest way: The rivalling forms of adjective comparison in late Middle and Early Modern English. In: Jan Svartvik (ed.), *Words: Proceedings of an International Symposium, Lund, 25–26 August 1995*, 123–144. Stockholm: Kungliga Vitterhets Historie och Antikvitets Akademien.
Kytö, Merja and Suzanne Romaine. 1997. Competing forms of adjective comparison in modern English: What could be more quicker and easier and more effective? In: Terttu Nevalainen and Leena Kahlas-Tarkka (eds.), *To Explain the Present. Studies in the Changing English Language in Honour of Matti Rissanen*, 329–352. Helsinki: Société Néophilologique.
Lass, Roger. 1999. Phonology and morphology. In: Lass (ed.), 23–155.
Lass, Roger (ed.). 1999. *The Cambridge History of the English Language*. Vol. III. *1476–1776*. Cambridge: Cambridge University Press.
Marchand, Hans. 1969. *The Categories and Types of Modern English Word Formation*. 2nd edn. Wiesbaden: Otto Harrassowitz.
Matthews, Peter H. 1991 [1974]. *Morphology*. 2nd edn. Cambridge: Cambridge University Press.
Mühleisen, Susanne. 2010. *Heterogeneity in Word-Formation Patterns: A Corpus-based Analysis of Suffixation with* -ee *and its Productivity in English*. Amsterdam/Philadelphia: John Benjamins.
Nevalainen, Terttu. 1999. Early Modern English lexis and semantics. In: Lass (ed.), 332–458.
Nevalainen, Terttu. 2006. *An Introduction to Early Modern English*. Edinburgh: Edinburgh University Press.
Nevalainen, Terttu and Helena Raumolin-Brunberg. 2003. *Historical Sociolinguistics: Language Change in Tudor and Stuart England*. London: Longman.
Osselton, Noel E. 1958. *Branded Words in English Dictionaries before Johnson*. Groningen: Wolters.

Plag, Ingo. 1999. *Morphological Productivity: Structural Constraints in English Derivation*. Berlin/New York: Mouton de Gruyter.
Riddle, Elizabeth. 1985. A historical perspective on the productivity of the suffixes *-ness* and *-ity*. In: Jacek Fisiak (ed.), *Historical Semantics: Historical Word-formation*, 435–461. Berlin/New York: Mouton de Gruyter.
Rissanen, Matti. 1999. Syntax. In: Lass (ed.), 187–331.
Romaine, Suzanne. 1985. Variability in word formation patterns and productivity in the history of English. In: Jacek Fisiak (ed.), *Papers From the 6th International Conference on Historical Linguistics*, 451–65. Amsterdam/Philadelphia: John Benjamins.
Schäfer, Jurgen. 1973. *Shakespeares Stil: Germanisches und ronianisches Vokabular*. Frankfurt: Athenaum.
Schäfer, Jurgen. 1980. *Documentation in the OED: Shakespeare and Nash as Test Cases*. Oxford: Oxford University Press.
Simpson, John (ed.). 2000–. *The Oxford English Dictionary*. 3rd edn. online. Oxford University Press. www.oed.com/
Starnes, Dewitt T. and G. E. Noyes. 1946. *The English Dictionary from Cawdrey to Johnson, 1604–1755*. Chapel Hill: University of North Carolina Press.
Stein, Dieter. 1988. On the mechanisms of morphological change. In: Michael Hammond and Michael Noonan (eds.), *Theoretical Morphology: Approaches in Modern Linguistics*, 235–249. London: Academic Press.
Taylor, E. W. 1976. Shakespeare's use of *-eth* and *-es* endings of verbs in the First Folio. *CLA Journal* 19(4), 437–457. [Reprinted in Vivian Salmon and Edwina Burness (eds.), *Reader in the Language of Shakespearean Drama*. Amsterdam/Philadephia: John Benjamins, 1987.]
Thomason, Sarah G. and Terrence Kaufman. 1988. *Language Contact, Creolization and Genetic Linguistics*. Berkeley: University of California Press.
Wales, Katie. 1983. *Thou* and *you* in Early Modern English: Brown and Gilman re-appraised. *Studia Linguistica* 37(2): 107–25.
Wermser, Richard. 1976. *Statistiche Studien zur Entwicklung des englischen Wortschatzes*. Bern: Francke.

Elena Seoane
Chapter 5:
Syntax

1   Introduction —— 68
2   Genitive —— 70
3   The loss of impersonal constructions —— 71
4   Changes in verbal periphrases —— 73
5   Changes in the complementation system —— 77
6   Negation —— 80
7   The regulation of word order —— 83
8   Conclusions —— 85
9   References —— 85

Abstract: Early Modern English is an important period of transition between a still largely synthetic language heavy with variants and a fairly analytic, standardized one. The study of EModE syntax benefits greatly from the abundant and heterogeneous linguistic data available in this period, which allows for the inclusion of sociolinguistic and stylistic factors in the analysis of the changes. In this chapter I concentrate on the description of those which are considered quintessential to the period. These are changes in relation to the long-term transformation of English from a synthetic to an analytic language, such as major developments in the verbal system, as well as changes indicative of the emergence of the written standard, with a reduction of variation and the establishment of rules of usage in areas such as negation and word order. Finally, I also focus on those changes which first emerged in this period and which are still developing today, such as the restructuring of the complement system.

1 Introduction

The works of William Shakespeare, Ben Jonson, John Dryden, and many other writers provide evidence of considerable syntactic changes during the EModE period. For example, in *Hamlet*, Shakespeare has Bernardo ask Horatio "What think you on't?" (I.i), while Lord Polonius asks King Claudius "What do you think

---

Elena Seoane: Vigo (Spain)

DOI 10.1515/9783110525069-005

of me?" (II.ii). A wealth of such variants, most of them inherited from Middle English, characterize the beginning of the period, whereas by the turn of the 18th century variation has been greatly reduced, and the language that then emerges is quite similar to the standard we have today.

The 16th and 17th centuries witness the establishment of the written standard, and therefore it comes as no surprise that during this period rules of usage and functional differentiations become established and settled in many areas of English syntax. Changes conforming to this general process of regularization include the differentiation between the preterit and the perfect (Section 4.1) and the fixation of new word order rules (Section 7). Other changes, however, are merely incipient in our period, and would only develop fully in the 19th or 20th century; these include the encroachment of the gerund on the territory of the *to*-infinitive within the complement system (Section 5). Most of the changes observed in Early Modern English are in direct relation to the transformation of English from a synthetic to an analytic language which started in Old English: the loss of case and verb inflection implied a greater development of the verbal system, for example in the functional and formal expansion of the progressive periphrasis (Section 4.2), the introduction of an obligatory subject, with the consequent loss of impersonal constructions (Section 3), and the fixation of svo word order (Section 7).

The sources of data for the study of syntactic change in Early Modern English are abundant and offer a wide range of styles and registers, especially in comparison with Old and Middle English. Though access to truly oral data, the initial locus of change, is not possible, corpora such as the *Helsinki Corpus* (henceforth HC) (Rissanen et al. 1991), the *Corpus of English Dialogues* (1560–1760), the *Corpus of Early English Correspondence Sampler*, the *Parsed Corpus of Early English Correspondence*, the *Lampeter Corpus of Early Modern English Tracts*, the *Penn-Helsinki Parsed Corpus of Early Modern English*, *The Corpus of Scottish Correspondence* (1500–1715), and the first part of *ICAMET*, that is, the *Innsbruck Letter Corpus* (1386 to 1688), allow the researcher to form hypotheses about the sociolinguistic factors conditioning the development of particular changes.

This chapter presents a selection of the major syntactic changes in the EModE period, excluding two which have been dealt with in their own chapters, the development of periphrastic *do* (see Warner, Chapter 13) and changes in relative clauses (see Johansson, Chapter 15). Examples provided are taken from studies of the particular phenomena under discussion as well as from the HC (Rissanen et al. 1991). For the many other interesting syntactic changes that have necessarily been left out of this chapter, such as the restrictions in the use of adjectives as head of NPs, the decline of the subjunctive, the development of modal auxiliaries, the loss of reflexive verbs, the loss of the use of "pleonastic" *that* after adverbial conjunctions, the variation and changes in the realm of causative and conditional links, the reader is referred to the exhaustive *Cambridge History of the English Language* chapter by Rissanen (1999: 187–331).

2 Genitive

One of the most surprising changes in the syntax of NPs in English takes place in our period, namely the revival of the *s*-genitive. In Old English the productive synthetic genitive or *s*-genitive (as in PDE *Mary's car*) was used to express many different types of relations between the head and modifier, while the analytic *of*-construction (*the wheels of the car*) was only marginal at best. In Middle English, in compliance with the long-term shift of English from a synthetic to an analytic language, the *of*-construction gains ground and takes over most of the functions of *s*-genitives. Contrary to what might be expected, however, after a long period of replacement by the *of*-genitive, the *s*-genitive in Early Modern English increases its frequency again. This recent finding by Rosenbach and Vezzosi (2000) and Rosenbach et al. (2000), further discussed in Rosenbach (2002: Chapter 7), comes to contradict the widely established view that the replacement of the *s*-genitive by the *of*-genitive which started in Middle English continued in Early Modern English forming a typical S-curve process (Altenberg 1982: 302; Rissanen 1999: 201).

In this period there is also evidence of a change of status for the '*s*, from an inflection to a clitic-like element. Similarly, the *s*-genitive in this period develops a new function, that of a definite determiner. Both developments, which are discussed and justified in Rosenbach (2002: 201–230), paved the way towards a more frequent use of the *s*-genitive.

The variation between the two constructions in our period is determined by the following (hierarchically-ordered) factors: animacy, topicality, and type of relations. This way, the *s*-genitive is restricted to human and animate possessors exclusively, and is likewise favored for highly topical possessors (i.e. referentially given and definite) and for the expression of typically possessive relations between the NPs concerned.

Other interesting developments in the realm of the genitive is the emergence of the group genitive, as in (1), and the spread of the so-called double genitive and absolute genitive, as in (2) and (3), both of which had emerged in Middle English (cf. Rissanen 1999: 202–204):

(1) They met two of **the king of Spaines armadas or Gallions** (1600 Chamberlain 94; Rissanen 1999: 202)

(2) *He keeps her the prettiest pacing Nag with **the finest Side-saddle of any Womans** in the Ward* (1672 Shadwell 128; Rissanen 1999: 204)

(3) *Where did he lodge then? [...] At **Mr. Jyfford's,** or **Mr. Harwell's*** (1680 *The Trial of Titus Oates*, P IV, 82.C1; HC, Rissanen 1999: 203)

3 The loss of impersonal constructions

Much has been written about impersonal verbs and impersonal constructions in the history of English (cf. especially Elmer 1981; Fischer and van der Leek 1983, 1987; Denison 1990, 1993; Ogura 1990; Allen 1995; Fischer et al. 2000; Möhlig-Falke 2012; Miura 2015). For obvious reasons of space, I will not discuss the different classifications and theories put forward in the literature (let alone the terminological entanglement) regarding impersonal verbs, but will concentrate on the state of affairs in Early Modern English, which sees the decline and disappearance of the last impersonal verb constructions. While in Old and Middle English constructions without a syntactic (nominative) subject were common, their use decays rapidly in late Middle English, and is replaced by the use of constructions with dummy subject *it* or with a non-experiencer subject. In Early Modern English both types of structures can be found: impersonal verbs without an overt subject, as in (4) below, or with dummy *it* or a non-experiencer NP as subject, as in (5) and (6).

(4) *And therfore me **semeth** beste to holde my peace, least I shoulde do as the knyght of the toure dyd* (1534 Anthony Fitzherbert, *The Book of Husbandry* 97; HC)

(5) *whiche your worshipfull benignitee, could sone impetrate for me, if it would **like** you to extend your scedules, and collaude me in them,* (1553 Sir Thomas Wilson, *The Arte of Rhetorique*; Görlach 1991: 221)

(6) *this lodging **likes** me better* (1599 Shakespeare, *King Henry V* IV.i; Brinton and Arnovick 2011: 369)

Subjectless structures such as (4) decline and eventually disappear in the 16th century, and, as already mentioned, are replaced either by constructions of the type illustrated in (5) and (6) (*me likes this* > *it/this likes me*) or by a personal construction (*I like*). Around the 17th century, impersonal constructions with *it* as subject also disappear, though Present-day English retains a few, such as *it seems to me that* or *it happened that* (Brinton and Arnovick 2011: 369).

A number of subjectless phrases, among them *methinks, methought*, and *meseems*, deserve special mention. These survive longer than other impersonal verb constructions probably because they acquire adverbial status in Early Modern English and have already become stereotyped by the 16th century. With regard to *methinks*, the most frequent of all, it loses its original compositional meaning denoting a process of cognition, and develops interpersonal meaning, marking evidentiality; in fact, no pronouns other than *me* are attested in this combination in Early Modern English (**him thinks*; cf. Rissanen 1999: 250–251). The occurrence of formations such as *my thought(s)* or *methoughts* (cf. (7) below) show that *methinks* is no longer perceived as the combination objective pronoun *me* and impersonal verb *thinks*.

(7) **Methoughts** *that I had broken from the Tower And was embark'd to cross to Burgundy;* (1597 Shakespeare, *Richard III* IV.i)

For some scholars *methinks* undergoes a process of grammaticalization in our period (cf. Brinton 1996; Palander-Collin 1999), while for others it is a combination of grammaticalization and lexicalization (Wischer 2000; cf. also López-Couso 1996).

The traditional explanation for the loss of impersonal verbs, as found, for example, in Jespersen (1909–49: III, 11.2), involves the reanalysis of the (normally) preverbal oblique pronoun as subject (*Me likes it* > *I like it*), triggered by the loss of inflections, which would render many structures ambiguous, and the fixation of SVO order. However, this traditional account has faced sound criticism by those who argue that reanalysis would entail variation between speakers, whereas what evidence shows is variation across lexical verbs (Allen 1995: 450–451). Their criticism is also based on the fact that empirical data reveal that the proportion of alleged ambiguous constructions resulting from loss of inflections is notably low (cf. Allen's 1986 paper on *like*; see also von Seefranz-Montag 1984). Moreover, the reanalysis theory would not account for the emergence of new impersonal verbs in Middle English (such as *remember*) and the development of impersonal uses of already existing verbs (such as *behove*, see Allen 1997; for a full discussion of the criticism to the traditional view, cf. Loureiro-Porto 2010). In 2008, Trousdale offers an analysis of the loss of impersonal verbs from the point of view of Construction Grammar; this is undoubtedly a fascinating area of research in need of further insights.

4 Changes in verbal periphrases

4.1 The perfect *be/have* + past participle

The perfect periphrasis in Early Modern English differs from Present-day English in two broad respects: firstly, with regard to the function for which it is used, and secondly, regarding the auxiliary it takes, which can be either *have* or *be*. Illustrative of the first difference are the following examples:

(8) *I **have delivered** it an hour since* (c.1601 Shakespeare, *All's Well that Ends Well* IV.ii; Elsness 1997: 250)
*You **spoke** not with her since?* (c.1608 Shakespeare, *King Lear* IV.iii; Barber 1997: 190)

In (8) the perfect is used where today we would find a preterit (*I delivered it an hour ago*), while the reverse situation is found in (9) (*You have not spoken with her since?*). These two examples show how the perfect, which originated in Old English and became part of the tense and aspect system in Middle English, competed with the preterit for the expression of past time in Early Modern English. In other words, the clear-cut functional differentiation between the two had not yet been reached; in fact, the PDE rules for their use became established only in the early 18th century (Fridén 1948: 27–37; Görlach 1991: 111; Rissanen 1999: 224–227; Fischer and van der Wurff 2006: 140–141).

Regarding the auxiliaries that could mark the perfect in Early Modern English, we find variation between *have* and *be*, the two auxiliaries which, since OE times, could be used for that purpose (cf. Brinton 1988: 99–102). The variation between them at this point can be described as follows. *Have* is normally selected with transitive verbs, and is also predominant with intransitive verbs if these are non-mutative. Mutative intransitives (denoting change of state or place) alternate *have* and *be* (cf. 10 and 11), but *be* is much more frequent. According to Kytö (1997), *have* occurs in 95% of the perfect periphrases with non-mutative intransitives, while it occurs in only 30% of the periphrases with mutative intransitives.

(10) *and then if she find us on the Bed, she will verily conceive that we **have gone** astray, and Erred from the Light.* (1633–1703 Pepys, *Penny Merriments* 148; HC)

(11) *Wough, she **is gone** for euer, I shall hir no more see.* (1533 Udall, *Roister Doister* l. 1077; HC)

The factors influencing the choice between the two auxiliaries in intransitives include the author's idiolect as well as a number of linguistic factors. The most important of these is the intended meaning: if the focus is on the action expressed by the verb, *have* is preferred, whereas *be* tends to be used to highlight the state resulting from the action (cf. 10 and 11). Due to the association between *have* and action contexts, *have* also tends to be singled out in (i) irrealis or hypothetical contexts (e.g. conditional clauses, counterfactuals), where a resultative state is not normally reached and the emphasis is therefore on the (hypothetical) action; and (ii) in iterative and durative contexts (e.g. with an adverbial expressing duration) (cf. Fridén 1948: 44–57; Denison 1993: 355–356; Rissanen 1999: 213–214; Fischer and van der Wurff 2006: 141–142).

Through the period, *have* progressively gains ground at the expense of *be*. Some scholars, such as McWhorter (2002), attribute this process to Scandinavian influence. However, the reason most commonly adduced for the disappearance of *be* as a perfect auxiliary in English is the ambiguity derived from the fact that *be*-perfects are identical to passive periphrases, which in Early Modern English were also expressed with the combination *be* + past participle. That both *is* and *has* could appear as 's added to the confusion between both periphrases (Rissanen 1999: 215; Fischer and van der Wurff 2006: 142).

Despite the steady retreat of *be*, it is still predominant in mutative intransitives at the end of our period and will only be superseded by *have* in the early 19th century (Kytö 1997: 19), except for some relics where *be* is still found today (as in *Dinner is served*, cf. Brinton and Arnovick 2011: 373).

4.2 The progressive *be* + *-ing*

The progressive (*She **is reading** a book*) was established in late Middle English (cf. Fischer 1992: 250–256), but it is in Early Modern English when its frequency increases and its use is expanded to cover nearly all the functions it has in Present-day English, as has been shown conclusively in a number of studies (Nehls 1988; Denison 1993: Chapter 13; Elsness 1994; Núñez-Pertejo 2004). The origin of the progressive is highly disputed. There is no agreement as to whether it derives from one of the following OE constructions or from a combination of both: (i) *be* and the present participle ending in *-ende*, and (ii) the construction made up of *be*, the preposition *on*, and a gerund in *-ing/-ung*, which conveys a meaning similar to that of the progressive (cf. Fischer 1992: 250–256; Traugott 1992: 187–190; Denison 1993: 400–408). Our period witnesses the last remnants of the gerundial construction and a crucial development of the progressive *be* + *-ing*. The grammaticalization of the progressive, however, is not complete in Early

Modern English but takes place later, during the Late Modern English period (cf. Nehls 1988: 183; Denison 1993; Smitterberg 2005; Fischer and van der Wurff 2006: 136).

In this section I will first illustrate the use of the gerundial construction in Early Modern English, and then concentrate on the development of the progressive in Early Modern English and the differences it exhibits with Present-day English, as regards both its meaning and its paradigm.

As already mentioned, the OE construction with *be* + *on* + verbal noun in *-ing* still lingers on in Early Modern English, specially in colloquial styles. Nehls (1988: 184) reports, for instance, that while it does not occur in the elevated style of John Evelyn's *Diary*, it is relatively frequent in the diary of Samuel Pepys, this latter being more colloquial in nature. Similarly, in the EModE section of the *Helsinki Corpus* (HC) (Rissanen et al. 1991) this construction features exclusively in fiction, private letters and comedies (Rissanen 1999: 217; Núñez-Pertejo 2004: 153–154). Another characteristic of the gerundial construction is that it generally contains either an intransitive verb (very commonly one of motion, cf. 12) or a verb with passive meaning (as in 13). In both cases the verb is not followed by an object, and this tendency to appear without an overt object is interpreted by Elsness (1994: 22) as caused by the nominal origin of the *-ing* form involved. As illustrated by Nehls (1988: 184, cf. example 14), however, these gerundial constructions have been attested with objects as well.

(12) *Whither* **were** *you* ***a-going***? *To the Cardinal's;* (c.1613 Shakespeare, *King Henry VIII* I.iii.50; Nehls 1988: 184)

(13) *Yr gowne and things* ***are a making***, *but will not be done against whittsunday* (1620–44 Thomas Knyvett, *The Knyvett Letters* 57; HC, Elsness 1994: 16)

(14) *I kill'd the slave that* ***was a-hanging*** *thee* (c.1608 Shakespeare, *King Lear* V. iii.274; Nehls 1988: 184)

It is not only *a*, the weakened form of *on*, that is possible in our period; other prepositions, such as *in* or *upon*, are also recorded, though at lower frequencies (cf. Elsness 1994: 13; Rissanen 1999: 217; Núñez-Pertejo 2004: 152–156).

The development of the progressive in this period is remarkable on several counts. For one thing, its frequency more than tripled (from 16.8 occurrences per 100,000 words in 1500–1570, to 55.5 in 1640–1710), being considerably more frequent in informal than in formal registers: 53.8 tokens per 100,000 words as against 25.0 (data from the *Helsinki Corpus* in Núñez-Pertejo 2004: 161, 173; see also Elsness 1994: 11). As we know, this trend toward a frequent use and a preference for colloquial registers would continue to characterize progressives in Late Modern and Present-day English (Denison 1998). Closely related to this sharp rise in frequency is the fact that in Early Modern English the progressive begins to function as an aspectual marker, mainly indicating limited duration, as illustrated in (15).

(15) *That done, I **will be walking** on the works;* (1603 Shakespeare, *Othello* III.ii.3; Nehls 1988: 182)

Together with the unequivocal expression of aspect, most of the functions that characterize the modern progressive were present in Early Modern English, such as the expression of futurity (*I am leaving tomorrow*), the use of the progressive with *always* (*He is always doing that*) and the so-called interpretative progressives (Smitterberg 2005: Chapter 7; for a detailed discussion of the semantics of the progressive cf. Brinton 1988: 7–10, 38–45; for Early Modern English in particular cf. Núñez-Pertejo 2004: 177–191).

Despite its highly significant development, the progressive in Early Modern English still differed from Present-day English in a few important respects. Firstly, in contrast to Present-day English, the use of the progressive for the expression of limited duration was only optional, which shows that the grammaticalization of the periphrasis was not yet complete (Nehls 1988: 181–182; Fischer and van der Wurff 2006: 136). Sentence (16), for example, illustrates the use of a simple present to express limited duration, which would not be possible today. Another example of the unsettled use of the progressive in Early Modern English is (17), where a progressive is employed instead of a simple present form to express unlimited duration, possibly for stylistic purposes (cf. Rydén 1997: 422). Finally, (18) instantiates the use of the progressive with a stative verb, which would be highly unexpected in Present-day English.

(16) *No! what does she here then? Say, if it be not a woman's lodging, what **makes** she here?* (1675 Wycherley, *The Country Wife* 135; Nehls 1988: 182)

(17) *And first we cam to Torrens Cedron, which in somer tyme ys Drye, And in winter, and specially in lente, it **ys** mervelows **flowing** with rage of water that comyth with Grett violence thorow the vale of Josophat.* (1517 Torkington, *Ye Oldest Diarie of Englysshe Travel* 27; HC, Núñez-Pertejo 2004: 165)

(18) *I know you expect I should tel you what is become of the money I brought along with me: and I will gladly satisfy you in any thing. Some of it **is** yet **remaining** in my hands, for uses:* (1643–1737 Strype, *Letters* 181; HC, Elsness 1994: 20)

Another relevant difference between Early Modern English and Present-day English is the fact that the paradigm of the progressive was still incomplete, since the progressive passive (*She was being arrested*) is not recorded until the end of the 18th century. Instead, the EModE speaker would employ an active progressive with passive meaning, as in (19).

(19) *Also, they told us for certain that the King's statue **is making** by the Mercers Company (who are bound to do it) to set up in the Exchange.* (1660 Pepys, *Diary* I 113.26; Denison 1993: 390–391)

These constructions, commonly called "passival" (cf. Visser 1963–73: Sections 1872–1881), have an inanimate subject which would correspond to the subject in a true passive and to the object in a true active. Passival constructions survived well into the 19th century (Denison 1998: 151), and there are some remnants in Present-day English (as in *This movie is shooting in Vancouver*, cf. Brinton and Arnovick 2011: 374). Progressive passive import could also be conveyed by gerundial constructions, as illustrated in (13) above (*your things are a making* 'are being made'). The availability of these alternative forms of expressing progressive passive meaning delayed the development of the progressive passive periphrasis, a development which was probably resisted also because it involved the progressive of the verb *be*, not available until Late Modern English (cf. Denison 1998: 146–147), and the occurrence of two consecutive auxiliaries *be*, which did not take place in any other context (Brinton and Arnovick 2011: 374).

The next period would see the continuation of the trend that started in Early Modern English towards a multifunctional and more frequent use of the progressive, especially in informal registers. Also, Late Modern English would host other changes in the progressive leading to its final grammaticalization, such as a more frequent use of the progressive with inanimate subjects, its expansion to non-dependent clauses, the obligatorification of its use as an aspectual marker, and the emergence of the progressive passive.

5 Changes in the complementation system

Early Modern English marks the beginning of a series of changes that would lead to the "massive restructuring of the complement system" (Fanego 2007: 162) which takes place in modern times. Such restructuring involved radical changes in the inventory, frequency and distribution of the different types of sentential complements available in the language. For reasons of space, I will concentrate on the most relevant of these changes: (i) first and foremost, the emergence and spread of gerundive clauses, which would eventually encroach upon the territory of *to*-infinitives in both subject and object positions; and (ii) the spread of the recently established *for* ... *to* construction to new environments.

While all major types of sentential complements date back to Old English, gerundive clauses with and without a subject (cf. 20 and 21 below) emerge in medieval times.

(20) *John resents* **my / me working in a bar**

(21) **Accepting the job** *was a good idea*

The gerunds in these clauses have a nominal origin; the *-ing* suffix comes from the OE derivational suffix *-ing / -ung*, which was used to create deverbal nouns of action, such as OE *sceawung* 'observation' < *sceawian* 'observe' (Kastovsky 1992: 388). In Middle English *-ing* nouns often occurred in phrases which were ambiguous between a nominal and a verbal reading, since they lacked determiners and involved constituents that could occur in NP or VP structure, such as (22) below. As Fanego (2004: 18–26) demonstrates, this is the locus for the reanalysis of the ME noun in *-ing* as a verb, which took place in late Middle English.

(22) *Vnder þe Monument ʒeo stod wiþoute wepyng sore* (c.1280 *Southern Passion* 1874; Tajima 1985: 101)
'she stood close by the sepulcher without weeping bitterly / without bitter weeping'

Though the first signs of the verbalization of the gerund can be traced back to Middle English, its use with fully verbal characteristics was not systematic until the end of the EModE period (cf. Tajima 1985; Donner 1986; Fanego 1996b). Consequently, in Early Modern English gerunds can be fully nominal, as in (23) below, fully verbal, as in (24), or appear in a number of hybrid constructions, which combine nominal and verbal characteristics, as in (25), where the gerund has nominal premodification and a direct object.

(23) *the maine point belonging therunto is the Hus-wiues cleanlinesse* **in the sweet and neate keeping of the Diary House**. (1615 Markham, *Countrey Contentments* 109; HC, Fanego 1996b: 97)

(24) *the whole nation now exceedingly alarm'd by the French fleete* **braving our Coast even to the very Thames mouth:** (1689–90 Evelyn, *Diary* 927; HC, Fanego 1996b: 97)

(25) *to adore that great mystery of Divine Love (which the Angels, better and nobler Creatures than we are, desire to pry into)* **God's sending his onely Son into the world to save sinners** (1671 Tillotson, *Scoffing at Religion* 429; HC, Fanego 1996b: 97)

Closely related to the emergence and spread of verbal gerunds is the fact that gerunds experience a considerable rise in their frequency of use, especially those occurring in constructions which mirror vp structure, that is, gerunds containing post-head dependents. On the contrary, gerunds with only pre-head modifiers decrease in frequency, which is clearly linked to the increasing verbalization of gerunds in our period (Fanego 1996b: 115; 2004: 11–18).

The verbalization of gerunds took place first in prepositional environments, illustrated in (26) below. Other environments, such as subjects or objects, were often blocked by the productive *to*-infinitive, which nevertheless could not occur after prepositions other than *to*. From this prepositional environment, however, verbal gerunds soon spread to other syntactic positions, so that by the end of the EModE period the verbalization of gerunds had nearly reached completion in all syntactic contexts (cf. Fanego 1996b: 125; 2007: 169–170).

(26) *This Vlixes [...]   callis   hym   the   cavse   **of**   **cacchyng**   this   town*
    This Ulysses   calls   him   the   cause   of   capturing   this   town
    (?a1400 'Gest Hystoriale' of the *Destruction of Troy* 12204; Tajima 1985: 76)

Thus, the 16th century sees the first clear cases of verbal gerunds as sentential complements, in particular as objects of subject-control verbs, as in (27). So-called subject-control verbs (such as *refrain* below) govern a complement clause which has an unexpressed subject (pro) whose antecedent or controller is the matrix subject (*he*).

(27) *They come so to purpose, that hee can not refraine **telling them**.* (1561 T. Hoby tr. Castiglione's *Courtyer* (1577) D iv; OED, s.v. *refrain* v., def. 5b [Fanego 1996a: 38])

After our period, verbal gerunds extended their use to new environments, where only *to*-infinitives had been possible before. In other words, Early Modern English hosts the beginning of the process whereby gerundives progressively gain ground at the expense of *to*-infinitives, a process which seems to have reached its highest peak in the 19th century but still goes on today (Denison 1998: 256). Fanego (2007) shows that this process can be characterized as a drift (in Sapir's 1921 terms), that is, as "a long-term succession of changes [...] towards a greater specialization of the infinitive, which has largely come to be used in complementary distribution with the gerundive" (Fanego 2007: 162–163).

Early Modern English also witnesses significant changes in another type of complement, namely the *for* NP *to*-infinitive type, as in (28).

(28) *Water of mynte [...] were good* **for my cosyn to drynke** *for to make hym to browke* (1473 *Marg Paston Lett.* III; Cuyckens and De Smet 2007: 90)

The origin of this construction lies in the reanalysis of the ME sequence [*for* NP] [*to*-infinitive], where *for* is a preposition introducing a benefactive NP followed by a *to*-infinitive. This sequence is reanalyzed into a complementizer *for* introducing the non-finite complement [NP *to*-infinitive], in which the NP functions as subject of the following *to*-infinitive (cf. Fischer 1992: 330–333; Cuyckens and De Smet 2007: 92–94). The first unambiguous examples date back to late Middle English, cf. (28) above. However, it is in Early Modern English when this construction becomes frequent (around 20 occurrences per 100,000 words) and acquires considerable functional development. Originally, the most frequent function is that of extraposed subject (28), which reached its most marked increase in Early Modern English, but in this period the construction also extended to function as subject (29), adjunct (30) and a myriad of other functions (for a discussion of the motivations behind the functional spread, cf. Cuyckens and De Smet 2007).

(29) *and for the quantity of milke,* **for a Cow to giue two gallons at a meale***, is rare, and extraordinarie;* (1615 Markham, *Countrey Contentments*, 613; HC, Cuyckens and De Smet 2007: 99)

(30) *Item that the Wever whiche shall have the wevyng of eny wollen yerne to be webbed into cloth shall weve werk and put into the webbe* **for Cloth to be made therof** (1511–12 *The Statutes of the Realm III*; HC, Cuyckens and De Smet 2007: 101)

6 Negation

This section concentrates on the development of negation in Early Modern English, which is closely related to the development of the dummy auxiliary *do*. The term that best captures the essence of negation in Early Modern English is variation, since several negation patterns, old and new, converge and coexist in this period. Starting with the oldest patterns, the OE and ME negative form *ne* is still recorded in some examples, sometimes on its own but normally together with *not* (from OE *nawiht*).

(31) **Ne** they be **not** in commune [...] **nor** one man hath **nat** al vertues (1531 Elyot, *The Boke named The Governour*; Barber 1997: 198)

Not starts to be used in Middle English in combination with *ne* in order to reinforce the negation and becomes very frequent in Early Modern English. The result is multiple negation, as shown in (31), which can often accumulate three or four negative words in a clause. Multiple negation is very much reduced in frequency in 17th century written English, but survives to face the prescriptive fury of early grammarians in the 18th century and, as we know, it is still amply recorded in Present-day non-standard English (Denison 1998: 243; Rissanen 1999: 272; Mazzon 2004: Chapter 5).

Along with multiple negation, cases of negation using only *not* can also be found in Early Modern English. The original placement of *not* is postverbal (cf. 32), given its reinforcing function, but after the disappearance of *ne* the postverbal position was probably felt to be "unnatural" for *not*, since (i) negatives were traditionally associated with preverbal position (where *ne* used to appear), (ii) *not* in postverbal position separated the transitive verb from its object in a period when fixation of svo word order was taking place, and (iii) there was a general tendency in our period to move light adverbs to preverbal position (Ellegård 1953: 194; Rissanen 1999: 267–268). For this reason, variation between the old postverbal and a new preverbal position for *not*, as in (33), is common:

(32) Wednesday, the vj Day of Januarii, the wynde Rose a yens vs, with grett tempest, thonnderyng and lyghtnyng all Day and all nyght, So owtrageowsly, that we know **not** wher wee war. (1517 Torkington, *Ye Oldest Diarie of Englysshe Travell* 60; HC)

(33) I **not** doubt He came aliue to Land (c.1610 Shakespeare, *The Tempest* I.i; Rissanen 1999: 271)

The most commonly occurring pattern, however, was auxiliary -not -v, as in (34) below, probably because it preserved the natural preverbal position for the negative particle and, in addition, did not separate the subject from the verbal element carrying tense and number. This is the pattern where the relationship between the development of *do* in negatives and the preference of *not* for preverbal position seems to be one of mutual dependency and reinforcement (Denison 1993: 467; Rissanen 1999: 271; Fischer and van der Wurff 2006: 157–158).

(34) Mr Edmondes. Vntill this very day wee haue **not** heard one worde of yo^w since your departure, wch kept vs in douptfulnes of your safetie (1570–1640 Robert Cecil, *Letters*; HC)

Other negative elements expressing negation alone or in combination with each other (and with *not*) are *nothing, none,* or *never*, cf. (35).

(35) *But if ye will sel it, send word to your son what ye will doe, for I know **nothing** els wherwith to help you with* (1500–70 Isabel Plumpton, *Letters to Husband*; HC)

The occurrence of examples like this, where *never* or *nothing* occur as sole negators, have led scholars to believe that these forms were on their way to becoming bleached and grammaticalized, just as *not* resulted from the grammaticalization of the OE emphatic negative particle *nawiht* 'nothing'. While these forms did undergo bleaching in other varieties (e.g. *never / ne'er* in some contemporary non-standard British dialects, cf. Cheshire 1998: 129–130), their grammaticalization would have been blocked in Early Modern English by the fixing of the standard (Blake 1983: 110; Mazzon 2004: 61).

Another difference between Early Modern and Present-day English is the rate of occurrence of negative raising, whereby the negative element in a subordinate clause, as in (36), moves to the main one, as in (37).

(36) *I **think** M. Wyat would **no** Englishman hurt, and this Enterprise cannot be done without the hurt and slaughter of both Parties;* (1554 *The Trial of Sir Nicholas Throckmorton* I.55 c1; HC)

(37) *It does **not** seem to have any eye-lids, and therefore perhaps its eyes were so placed, that it might the better cleanse them with its fore-legs;* (1665 Hooke, *Micrographia* 13.5, 211; HC)

In both constructions the scope of the negation is the complement rather than the matrix verb itself, so that in (37) the meaning is 'it seems not to have any eye-lids.' Though negative raising has been on record since the OE period, its frequency increased steadily over time so that in Early Modern English it was fairly common, though not as much as in Present-day English, where it is said to be characteristic of colloquial styles (Denison 1998: 244).

7 The regulation of word order

One of the major syntactic changes in the history of English is the word order shift that it underwent at some time between Old, Middle, and Early Modern English, whereby English ceased to have a general SOV word order with a verb-second (V2) constraint in declarative sentences and became the SVO language it is today. This change has been the subject of extensive research, and has been ascribed to a complex interplay of factors (cf. Seoane 2006).

By late Middle English, the shift from verb-final to verb-medial word order was visible in the majority of subordinate clauses, and V2 was no longer predominant in declarative sentences. Early Modern English inherits from Middle English this strong tendency towards SVO word order; however, it also exhibits word order patterns which survive from Old English and which would cease to be possible in the 17th century. The following EModE examples have a word order which is disallowed today:

(38) **Then** *doo they vaunt themselues ouer the common multitude* (1592 Nash, *Pierce Penniless*; Barber 1997: 191)

(39) *and* **only by theyr holle consent** *theyr citie and dominions were gouerned:* (1531 Elyot, *The Boke named The Governour*; Barber 1997: 192)

(40) **Thys** *did I here hym saye* (1500–70 Mowntayne, *Autobiography* 210; HC, Rissanen 1999: 266)

(41) *As we his subjects have in wonder* **found** (1599 Shakespeare, *King Henry V*; Brinton and Arnovick 2011: 377)

(42) *I can thee thanke that thou canst* **such answeres** *deuise. But I perceyue thou doste me thoroughly knowe* (1533 Udall, *Roister Doister* I.ii; HC, Rissanen 1999: 268)

(43) **Would I** *haue my flesh Torne by the publique hooke, these quulified hangmen Should be my company* (1603 Jonson, *Sejanus: His Fall* II.iii; Rissanen 1999: 309)

Example (38) exhibits VS or inverted word order after the initial adverbial *then*, a trace of the old V2 constraint. Such a word order pattern was also common, though not categorical, after *also, here, now, so, there, therefore, thus,* and *yet*. Jacobsson (1951) provides statistics for sentences beginning with some of these adverbs in our period, and his figures go from 34% of inverted patterns in the 16th century to only 7% in the 17th century. The verbs *have, say, come* and *stand* favor inversion much longer (Rissanen 1999: 265), but the regularization is nearly complete by the end of the EModE period.

Example (39), on the contrary, has no inversion after the (semantically) restrictive adverbial *only by theyr holle consent*, a type of adverbial that, together with negative ones (such as *never, nor*), triggers mandatory inversion in Present-day English. The PDE rules for inversion after adverbials of this type were established over the course of the 17th century, first for negative adverbials (*never, nor*) and soon after for restrictive ones (*seldom, rarely, little*, etc.).

Example (40) illustrates inversion of verb and subject (auxiliary – s – v) after a fronted direct object, another vestige of the old V2 constraint which would become progressively rarer in our period. The same fate would await examples (41) and (42). In (41) the subordinate clause retains the Old and Early Middle English verb-final (sov) word order, and in (42) the verb phrase is split around the direct object, with verb-final order as well. Finally, example (43) is a conditional clause with inversion (auxiliary – s – v) and no conditional conjunction. Inverted conditional clauses are still possible today but are less frequent and are limited to the verbs *be, have,* and *do* (*Were he to arrive earlier, please let him in*; Rissanen 1999: 308). In the last three examples word order choices may have been influenced by metrical demands, since they are verse texts.

The word order patterns illustrated in examples (38) to (43) are all optional, that is, in Early Modern English, like in Old and Middle English, there were no word order categorical rules but just strong tendencies of use. Word order variation in Early Modern English is controlled by an array of factors, such as metric and rhythmic considerations; the relative weight of the elements involved, that is, of the subject and object, also plays a role, in such a way that nominal subjects tend to occur postverbally more frequently than pronominal subjects, by virtue of their being longer. Stylistic factors have also been held responsible for word order variation, such as the connection between inversion and stylistic flourish (Rissanen 1999: 265). Finally, the author's idiolect also determines the frequency of inversion in Early Modern English: thus, while William Roper, More, and Sydney prefer inversions after non-negative adverbials, Caxton's use of inversion in this context amounts to only 8% of the cases (cf. Jacobsson 1951: 96–97). As already mentioned, the establishment of word order rules as we know them today took place in the 17th century, with the consequent fixation of word order and a parallel increase in the use of alternative means of topicalization and order rearranging devices, such as the passive voice (cf. Seoane 2006).

8 Conclusions

I hope to have shown, through the analysis of a selection of topics, that Early Modern English is a crucial period of transition between the still largely synthetic language found in Middle English and the new analytic and standardized English language we know today. This is a period when rules start to be fixed and when new changes, which are still ongoing today, begin to emerge. Though Early Modern English is no longer the neglected period of study it used to be and many powerful insights have shed light on its numerous developments, research is still needed in many areas, specially regarding the factors – linguistic, social – conditioning the changes it witnesses.

Acknowledgments: I am grateful for generous financial support to the following institutions: the Spanish Ministry of Science and Innovation and the European Regional Development Fund (grant no. HUM2007-60706/FILO, FFI2011-26693-CO2-01, and FFI2011-26693-CO2-02); the Autonomous Government of Galicia (Directorate General of Scientific and Technological Promotion, grant no. 2008-047 the Directorate General for Research, Development and Innovation, INCITE grant no. 08PXIB204016PR).

9 References

Allen, Cynthia L. 1986. Reconsidering the history of like. *Journal of Linguistics* 22: 375–409.
Allen, Cynthia L. 1995. *Case Marking and Reanalysis. Grammatical Relations from Old to Early Modern English*. Oxford: Clarendon Press.
Allen, Cynthia L. 1997. The development of an "impersonal" verb in Middle English: The case of behoove. In: Jacek Fisiak (ed.), *Studies in Middle English Linguistics*, 1–21. Berlin/New York: Mouton de Gruyter.
Altenberg, Bengt. 1982. *The Genitive v. the of-Construction. A Study of Syntactic Variation in 17th Century English*. Malmö: CWK Gleerup.
Barber, Charles. 1997. *Early Modern English*. Edinburgh: Edinburgh University Press.
Blake, Norman F. 1983. *Shakespeare's Language: An Introduction*. London: Macmillan.
Brinton, Laurel J. 1988. *The Development of English Aspectual Systems: Aspectualizers and Post-verbal Particles*. Cambridge: Cambridge University Press.
Brinton, Laurel J. 1996. *Pragmatic Markers in English. Grammaticalization and Discourse Function*. Berlin/New York: Mouton de Gruyter.
Brinton, Laurel J. and Leslie K. Arnovick. 2011. *The English Language. A Linguistic History*. 2nd edn. Oxford: Oxford University Press.
Brunner, Karl. 1955. Expanded verbal forms in Early Modern English. *English Studies* 26: 218–221.
Cheshire, Jenny. 1998. English negation from an interactional perspective. In: Peter Trudgill and Jenny Cheshire (eds.), *The Sociolinguistic Reader*. Vol. I. 127–144. London: Arnold.

Cuyckens, Hubert and Hendrik De Smet. 2007. *For… to* infinitives from Early to Late Modern English. In: Pérez-Guerra (eds.), 77–103. Bern: Peter Lang.
Denison, David. 1990. The Old English impersonals revived. In: Sylvia Adamson, Vivien A. Law, Nigel Vincent, and Susan Wright (eds.), *Papers from the 5th International Conference on English Historical Linguistics. Cambridge 6–9 April 1987*, 111–140. Amsterdam/Philadelphia: John Benjamins.
Denison, David. 1993. *English Historical Syntax*. Harlow: Longman.
Denison, David. 1998. Syntax. In: Suzanne Romaine (ed.), *The Cambridge History of the English Language*. Vol. IV. *1776–1997*, 92–329. Cambridge: Cambridge University Press.
Donner, Morton. 1986. The gerund in Middle English. *English Studies* 67: 394–400.
Ellegård, Alvar. 1953. *The Auxiliary do: The Establishment and Regulation of its Use in English*. Stockholm: Almqvist and Wiksell.
Elmer, Willy. 1981. *Diachronic Grammar. The History of Old and Middle English Subjectless Constructions*. Tübingen: Max Niemeyer.
Elsness, Johan. 1994. On the progression of the progressive in Early Modern English. *ICAME* 18: 5–25.
Elsness, Johan. 1997. *Diachronic Grammar. The History of Old and Middle English Subjectless Constructions*. Berlin/New York: Mouton de Gruyter.
Fanego, Teresa. 1996a. The development of gerunds as objects of subject-control verbs in English (1400-1760). *Diachronica* 13: 29–62.
Fanego, Teresa. 1996b. The gerund in Early Modern English: Evidence from the Helsinki Corpus. *Folia Linguistica Historica* 17: 97–152.
Fanego, Teresa. 2004. On reanalysis and actualization in syntactic change: the rise and development of English verbal gerunds. *Diachronica* 21(1): 5–55.
Fanego, Teresa. 2007. Drift and the development of sentential complements in British and American English from 1700 to the present day. In: Pérez-Guerra (eds.), 161–235.
Fischer, Olga. 1992. Syntax. In: Norman Blake (ed.), *The Cambridge History of the English Language*. Vol. II. *1066–1476*, 207–408. Cambridge: Cambridge University Press.
Fischer, Olga, Ans van Kemenade, Willem Koopman, and Wim van der Wurff. 2000. *The Syntax of Early English*. Cambridge: Cambridge University Press.
Fischer, Olga and Frederike van der Leek. 1983. The demise of the Old English impersonal construction. *Journal of Linguistics* 19: 337–368.
Fischer, Olga and Frederike van der Leek. 1987. A "case" for the Old English impersonal. In: Willem Koopman, Frederike van der Leek, Olga Fischer, and Roger Eaton (eds.), *Explanation and Linguistic Change*, 79–120. Amsterdam/Philadelphia: John Benjamins.
Fischer, Olga and Wim van der Wurff. 2006. Syntax. In: Richard M. Hogg and David Denison (eds.), *A History of the English Language*, 109–198. Cambridge: Cambridge University Press.
Fridén, Georg. 1948. *Studies on the Tenses of the English Verb from Chaucer to Shakespeare*. Uppsala: Almqvist and Wiksell.
Görlach, Manfred. 1991. *Introduction to Early Modern English*. Cambridge: Cambridge University Press.
Hogg, Richard M. (ed.). 1992. *The Cambridge History of the English Language*. Vol. I. *The Beginnings to 1066*. Cambridge: Cambridge University Press.
Jacobsson, Bengt. 1951. *Inversion in English with Special Reference to the Early Modern English Period*. Uppsala: Almqvist and Wiksell.
Jespersen, Otto. 1909-49. *A Modern English Grammar on Historical Principles*. 7 vols. Copenhagen: Ejnar Munksgaard.

Kastovsky, Dieter. 1992. Semantics and Vocabulary. In: Hogg (ed.), 290–408.
Kytö, Merja. 1997. Be/have + *past participle: The choice of the auxiliary with intransitives from Late Middle to Modern English*. In: Matti Rissanen, Merja Kytö, and Kirsi Heikkonen (eds.), *English in Transition: Corpus-Based Studies in Linguistic Variation and Genre Styles*, 17–85. Berlin/New York: Mouton de Gruyter.
López-Couso, María José. 1996. On the history of methinks: *From impersonal construction to fossilised expression. Folia Linguistica Historica* XVII: 153–169.
Loureiro-Porto, Lucía. 2010. A review of Early English impersonals: Evidence from necessity verbs. *English Studies* 91(6): 674–699.
Mazzon, Gabriella. 2004. *A History of English Negation*. London: Longman.
McWhorter, John. 2002. What happened to English? *Diachronica* 19(2): 217–272.
Miura, Ayumi. 2015. *Middle English Verbs of Emotion and Impersonal Constructions: Verb Meaning and Syntax in Diachrony*. Oxford: Oxford Universtiy Press.
Nehls, Dietrich. 1988. On the development of the grammatical category of verbal aspect in English. In: Josef Klegraf and Dietrich Nehls (eds.), *Essays on the English Language and Applied Linguistics on the Occasion of Gerhard Nickel's 60th Birthday*, 173–198. Heidelberg: Julius Groos.
Núñez-Pertejo, Paloma. 2004. *The Progressive in the History of English with Special Reference to the Early Modern English Period: A Corpus-based Study*. München: Lincom Europa.
Ogura, Michiko. 1990. What has happened to "impersonal" constructions? *Neuphilologische Mitteilungen* 91: 31–55.
Palander-Collin, Minna. 1999. *Grammaticalization and Social Embedding: I THINK and METHINKS in Middle and Early Modern English*. Helsinki: Société Néophilologique.
Pérez-Guerra, Javier, Dolores González-Álvarez, Jorge Luis Bueno-Alonso, and Esperanza Rama-Martínez (eds.), 2007. *"Of Varying Language and Opposing Creed": New Insights into Late Modern English*. Bern: Peter Lang.
Rissanen, Matti, Merja Kytö, Leena Kahlas-Tarkka, Matti Kilpiö, Saara Nevanlinna, Irma Taavitsainen, Terttu Nevalainen, and Helena Raumolin-Brunberg. 1991. *The Helsinki Corpus of English Texts*. In: *ICAME Collection of English Language Corpora (CD-ROM)*, 2nd edn., Knut Hofland, Anne Lindebjerg, and Jørn Thunestvedt (eds.), The HIT Centre, University of Bergen, Norway. For manual, see http://clu.uni.no/icame/manuals/; last accessed 14 April 2017.
Rissanen, Matti. 1999. Syntax. In: Roger Lass (ed.), *The Cambridge History of the English Language*. Vol. III. *1476–1776*, 187–331. Cambridge: Cambridge University Press.
Rosenbach, Anette. 2002. *Genitive Variation in English. Conceptual Factors in Synchronic and Diachronic Studies*. Berlin/New York: Mouton de Gruyter.
Rosenbach, Anette, Dieter Stein, and Letizia Vezzosi. 2000. On the history of the s-*genitive*. In: Ricardo Bermúdez-Otero, David Denison, Richard M. Hogg, and Chris B. McCully (eds.), *Generative Theory and Corpus Studies: A Dialogue from 10 ICEHL*, 183–210. Berlin/New York: Mouton de Gruyter.
Rosenbach, Anette and Letizia Vezzosi. 2000. Genitive constructions in Early Modern English: New evidence from a corpus analysis. In: Rosanna Sornicola, Erich Poppe, and Ariel Shisha-Halevy (eds.), *Stability, Variation and Change of Word-Order Patterns over Time*, 285–307. Amsterdam/Philadelphia: John Benjamins.
Rydén, Mats. 1997. On the panchronic core meaning of the English progressive. In: Terttu Nevalainen and Leena Kahlas-Tarkka (eds.), *To Explain the Present. Studies in the Changing English Language in Honour of Matti Rissanen*, 419–429. Helsinki: Société Néophilologique.

Sapir, Edward. 1921. *Language. An Introduction to the Study of Speech*. New York: Harcourt, Brace and Co.
Seoane, Elena. 2006. Information structure and word order: The passive as an information rearranging strategy. In: Ans van Kemenade and Bettelou Los (eds.), *Handbook of the History of English*, 360–391. Oxford: Blackwell.
Smitterberg, Erik. 2005. *The Progressive in 19th Century English: A Process of Integration*. Amsterdam: Rodopi.
Tajima, Matsuji. 1985. *The Syntactic Development of the Gerund in Middle English*. Tokyo: Nan'un-do.
Traugott, Elizabeth Closs. 1992. Syntax. In: Hogg (ed.), 168–289.
Trousdale, Graeme. 2008. Words and constructions in grammaticalization: The end of the English impersonal construction. In: Susan M. Fitzmaurice, and Donka Minkova (eds.), *Studies in the History of the English Language IV: Empirical and Analytical Advances in the Study of English Language Change*, 301–326. Berlin/New York: Mouton De Gruyter.
Visser, Frederikus Theodorus. 1963–73. *A Historical Syntax of the English Language*. 3 vols. Leiden: E. J. Brill.
von Seefranz-Montag, Ariane. 1984. "Subjectless" constructions and syntactic change. In: Jacek Fisiak (ed.), *Historical Syntax*, 521–553. Paris/The Hague: Mouton de Gruyter.
Wischer, Ilse. 2000. Grammaticalization versus lexicalization: "Methinks" *there is some confusion*. In: Olga Fischer, Anette Rosenbach, and Dieter Stein (eds.), *Pathways of Change. Grammaticalization in English*, 355–370. Amsterdam/Philadelphia: John Benjamins.

Ian Lancashire
Chapter 6:
Lexicon and semantics

1 Introduction —— 89
2 Resources for the study of Early Modern English lexis —— 91
3 Lexicon —— 93
4 Semantics
5 Research issues —— 100
6 References —— 103

Abstract: As printing technology itself once did, cyberinfrastructure is changing research into the Early Modern English lexicon and semantics. The Online OED, *Early English Books Online, Lexicons of Early Modern English, The Textbase of Early Tudor English*, and other resources now enable us to chart the growth of English in great detail. The mother tongue remained small, well under 10,000 words, until the 17th century. Printed books, however, by saving and disseminating learned and technical words, expanded available vocabulary by 75% from 1500 to 1600. Hundreds of glossaries and dictionaries printed word-entries that mapped English terms to each other and to other tongues and stimulated interest in semantics. Nouns and verbs were no longer assumed to be names for things and actions, as the famous Lily-Colet grammar taught, but (especially influenced by John Locke in 1690) became pointers to ideas in individual minds. Under the early Tudors, English was widely maligned as a minor tongue lacking the vocabulary and the sophistication of ancient and modern languages. Researchers can now chart a full account of how the English made their own tongue competitive.

1 Introduction

Speakers of Early Modern English (EModE) lived through a language-technology revolution comparable to what we have experienced since 1964, when IBM introduced its Magnetic Tape/Selectric Typewriter, an early industrial forerunner of the word processor (see http://www-03.ibm.com/ibm/history/exhibits/modelb/modelb_office.html; last accessed 14 April 2017). Printing enabled early Tudor

---
Ian Lancashire: Toronto (Canada)

writers to archive and disseminate their new words and senses, leading to the making of widely-available bilingual and monolingual dictionaries and grammars. This in turn contributed to lexico-semantic enrichment, strengthened the case for standardization, and spawned revisionist spelling systems and universal-language schemes (Cohen 1977; Slaughter 1982). The EModE period, for these reasons, was a time of more than just routine semantic change. It witnessed a sizable increase in vocabulary and a new interest in semantics itself. Speakers, readers, and writers had to pay attention to word meaning, thanks to the growth of word-loans in works translated from other languages, of so-called "terms of art" created by professional, technical, and social groups with a special expertise, and of simple zero-derivation, an innovative technique favored by Shakespeare, whereby a new word could be made almost transparently from an existing term by altering its part of speech. Anyone could create new words and senses, and few reading or listening to them were alert enough to detect, or object to, these lexical sports. By 1656, when Thomas Blount published *Glossographia*, a hard-word lexicon, readers faced a schizophrenic, split lexicon: a mother tongue or "common core" (Nevalainen 2006: 47) anchored in the ordinary talk of illiterate and literate alike, and by the rites and scriptures of the Church of England; and a blizzard of invented, borrowed, and transformed words to which no guide existed. For the first time, also, the English lexicon suffered few enduring, unredeemable losses. Given the archival value of printed books, words that passed out of usage at that time are still available.

Our knowledge of the state of the EModE lexicon far surpasses that of most people alive in that period. Educated men and women in Tudor England knew more about and respected Latin better than their own tongue. Sir Thomas Elyot's *Dictionary* (1538) was extended by Thomas Cooper in many re-editions up to 1584 before it was eclipsed by Latin lexicons from the likes of Thomas Thomas (1587) and John Rider (1589), which competed more effectively than had earlier dictionaries by Richard Huloet (1552) and John Baret (1574). The average English nobleman in 1617 could have purchased remarkably full lexicons of Latin, French, Italian, and Spanish, as well as John Minsheu's (1617) astonishing *Ductor in Linguas*, an etymological lexicon of English that cited eleven languages. If not always despised, English was regarded as a severely understocked old tongue, dependent on absorbing words from many other languages if it was to remain viable. Even defenders of English, like Sir Philip Sidney (1598), insisted that it ought not be taught, despite Merchant Taylors' schoolmaster Richard Mulcaster's urgings to the contrary. Those who praised English to the skies, like Richard Carew in "The Excellency of the English Tongue" (1614), proposed as an advantage that "the most parte of our wordes [...] are Monasillables, and soe the fewer in tale, and the sooner reduced to memorye" (Görlach 1991: 241). It is little wonder that Shakespeare confessed himself, as a vernacular playwright, to be one who "sold cheap what is most dear" (Sonnet 110) in comparison to an envied rival poet, likely George Chapman, the translator of Homer's *Odyssey*.

The Renaissance produced some astounding feats of lexico-semantic analysis, but they had little to do with the English language. Robert Estienne's great dictionary of classical Latin, and his son's comparable achievement for Greek, belonged to France; the Accademia della Crusca produced the first great dictionary of a vernacular language, Italian, in its *Vocabolario* of 1612; and the *Dictionnaire de l'Académie Française*, first published in 1694, gave dignity to French. Considine (2014) has recently discussed such major works. The great English literature of the mid-Renaissance in England, works such as Spenser's *The Faerie Queene*, Shakespeare's tragedies, and the King James Bible, however, used a national language that was lexicographically unrecorded except in bilingual lexicons. Most grammar schools taught from the partly translated Lily-Colet Latin grammar (1549). The first monolingual textbook of spelling, dates, and hard words, intended for pre-grammar-school students and uneducated adults, was Edmund Coote's *The English School-maister* (1997 [1596]): it eventually became a standard work. Using his own non-standard spelling system, William Bullokar published books on English grammar in the 1580s; Alexander Gill's English grammar, *Logonomia Anglica* (1619–21), was entirely in Latin, aside from English-language examples in his own non-standard spelling. However sophisticated may have been the linguistic ideas of a very few, most EModE authors in the first half of our period gave little credit to the vernacular. Jones (1953: 3–167) describes how contemporaries viewed English as uneloquent, inadequate, and misspelled.

2 Resources for the study of Early Modern English lexis

Analysis of this period's vocabulary and word-meaning began seriously with the publishing of the complete *Oxford English Dictionary* (OED) (and first supplement) in 1933, and the start of the ongoing University Microfilms Microfilm Project in 1938, which aimed to make available images of all printed books in the *Short-Title Catalogue* (STC) (Pollard and Redgrave 1976–91; Wing 1972–88 and their supplements).

When the planned Early Modern English Dictionary (EMED) project lapsed in the late 1930s, the OED became the default source for the period's lexico-semantic data. Richard Bailey published a large card-file of EMED additions to and antedatings of OED word-forms and senses in 1978. Jürgen Schäfer (1980) then made two significant contributions to the study of the period language by demonstrating the bias inherent in OED citation selection for the Early Modern period and by supplementing OED with data on 5,000 words found in English printed glossaries from 1526 to 1640 (Schäfer 1989). Two other great national dictionaries for old Scots (Aitken and Craigie 1931–2002) and Welsh (Thomas et al. 1967–2002) have since appeared. In 2006, the University of Toronto Press and Libraries also brought out my online database, *Lexicons of Early Modern English* (LEME) (Lancashire [ed.] 2006–), which now includes 858,896 word-entries from 223 dictionaries and glossaries of the period. LEME replaces a prototype Web textbase, *Early Modern English Dictionaries Database* (EMEDD) (Lancashire [ed.] 1999), which I developed online from 1996 to 1999.

In 2003, ProQuest introduced *Early English Books Online* (EEBO; Chadwyck-Healey 2003–2011), which in its first five years has made available image reproductions of about 122,000 works from STC, Wing, and their supplements. STC and its collections have been supplemented by two magnificent research projects by the late Robin Alston (1965): *Bibliography of the English Language [...] to 1800*, a *magnum opus* that identifies, classifies, and extends the body of language texts that EEBO now covers; and 365 facsimile reprints of such books for Scolar Press's series *English Linguistics, 1500–1800*. In 1999 the University of Michigan and ProQuest entered, with member institutions worldwide, into the Text Creation Partnership (TCP) to digitize 25,000 works from these collections. As of February 2017, EEBO-TCP (Welzenbach 1999–) has released 60,300 searchable full-texts. It is possible to search the spelling-list from these data now, but the number of English word-forms or lemmas that these spellings represent is not known. The EEBO-TCP index treats uppercase and lowercase forms separately and does not distinguish between English and other languages. For example, querying the index for spellings of "definition" retrieves twenty spellings, including "definition" (14,944 occurrences), "definitions" (3,686), "definitione" (536), "diifinicion" (355), and "diffinitions" (33). The work of the CIC CLI Virtual Modernization Project in bringing variant EEBO/TCP spellings under their lemma, led by Martin Mueller, should enable the OED to assimilate many new words, senses, and antedatings. However, manual lemmatizing is an immense task, and the error-rate of semi-automatic lemmatization probably still remains too high at the present time.

The Online Oxford English Dictionary, which has over 600,000 word-entries and 3.5 million quotations, is unquestionably the greatest scholarly resource for the English language. Completely searchable, linked to period dictionaries and the Historical Thesaurus, and constantly in revision and expansion (Gilliver 2016), OED is authoritative and inexhaustibly rich. Turning a dictionary into a database has greatly multiplied the queries that can be posed of the data. OED now both answers existing research questions and generates new ones.

Modern editions of period dictionaries, diachronic corpora, and analytic dictionaries of the period by present-day lexicographers add substantially to a researcher's lexico-semantic data. The Early English Text Society has turned out editions of *Catholicon Anglicum* (1483; Herttage [ed.] 1881), *Promptorium Parvulorum* (1440–99; Mayhew [ed.] 1908), and Peter Levins's *Manipulus Vocabulorum* (1570; Wheatley [ed.] 1867). Other stand-alone editions include *Vocabularium Saxonicum* by Laurence Nowell (c.1565; Marckwardt [ed.] 1952), *Dictionarie of the Vulgar Russe Tongue* by Mark Ridley (c.1594–99; Stone [ed.] 1996), *L'éclaircissement de la langue française* by John Palsgrave (1530; Baddeley [ed.] 2003), *Libellus de re herbaria novus* by William Turner (1538; Rydén et al. [eds.] 1999), and *Table Alphabetical* by Robert Cawdrey (1604). Contemporary essays on English, and prefaces and introductions to dictionaries, grammars, and language textbooks, which Manfred Görlach (1991) surveys, are a valuable barometer of language consciousness in the period. The *Helsinki Corpus* (Rissanen et al. 1991; see also Kytö 1996; Rissanen et al. 1993) and the *Corpus of Early English Correspondence* (Nevalainen et al. 1998; see also Nurmi 1998) focus on grammatical and syntactic features but also encode texts (and thus their vocabulary) for various features that bear on semantics. Waite's *The Textbase of Early Tudor English* (2008) is a TEI-encoded Web collection of some 260,000 lines of verse, 1485–1550, that plans to develop a rhyme index and an index of early Tudor spellings.

3 Lexicon

The Early Modern period begins with the introduction of printing to England. This technology created an archive for English. Tudor lexicographers and translators froze new words in print, where they could survive long after anyone stopped uttering them or writing them down. Stein (1985) showed why Robert Cawdrey's (1604) little hard-word lexicon was far from being the first English dictionary – as so many claimed it was for much too long – when she traced a line of English lexicographical works well back into the Old English period. The growth of the hard-word glossary – which Schäfer (1989) documents from 1526 on – testifies to such word-loans, mostly from Latin, technical "terms of art" from trade and craft guilds and from professions like law, pharmacology, and medicine. The 16th and 17th centuries so expanded this mass of new, unfamiliar words that it became a second English, rivalling the mother tongue that people used unselfconsciously and thought little about.

In *Ordered Profusion*, Finkenstaedt et al. (1973) used the first-occurrence dates of OED headwords in their *Chronological English Dictionary* (CED) (Finkenstaedt et al. 1970) to identify 1560–1660 as the peak period of vocabulary growth.

McDermott (2002) linked the CED rate of lexical expansion with the number of books printed year-by-year according to the STC (the latter calculated by Bell and Barnard 1992). Printed books are a persistent quantitative measure in the period, and books created the language's lexical archive. The most lexically rich works are dictionaries. Totals of new CED words increase over a century from 1490–1509 to 1590–1609 by 75%. That astonishing rate of growth resembles the increase of lexicon production more than the increase of all STC books. By 1500, English had just over 36,100 different word-forms, and 64,300 by 1600. This is an increase of 78%, or 3% more than CED numbers from 1973.

The OED Online (Simpson [ed.] 2000–), appearing forty years after the publication of the CED, now allows us to recalculate these data. John Simpson, the editor of the OED, described a simple strategy to select, for instance, the "available vocabulary" between 1650 and 1660: "go to the Advanced search page (leaving 'entries' selected, rather than 'quotations'), search for 500–1660 in the first search field (by 'quotation date'), AND 1650–2008 in the second search field (again by 'quotation date')" (p.c. of March 13, 2008). His result includes affixes and combining forms, which are not awarded "first dates" by the database, and so yields a slightly higher count. My preliminary count of lemmas in LEME uses over 95% non-OED texts but indicates an increase of 75%, like the CED.

Ongoing large-scale antedatings of OED headwords first dated in the Early Modern period indicate that the actual rate of increase of Early Modern English vocabulary may be lower. More and more, we are finding that words occurred earlier than the OED record shows. Bailey's (1978) collection of additions and antedatings to English vocabulary, 1475–1700, has 4,400 entries, of which about 2,900 included antedatings (based on a hand-count of antedatings on twelve pages of the 330-page "Additions and Antedatings.") Schäfer's (1980) study of OED sources revealed that the early Oxford lexicographers had relied overly on citations from major authors, especially Shakespeare, and under-represented the more lexically inventive, such as Thomas Nashe. In 1989 Schäfer also demonstrated that OED overlooked information in hard-word glossaries from 1526 up to the mid-17th century. The 5,000 word-entries in his *Early Modern English Lexicography* (Schäfer 1989) make about 2,600 antedatings to the OED (based on a hand-count of antedatings on twelve pages of the 177-page "Additions and Corrections"). Thus, by 1989 just two scholars had antedated 5,500 OED Early Modern headwords, out of a total of 64,000. We can also infer that the growth of printing, as previously mentioned, archives new words in a way not possible in the Middle English period. The wordlist from the STC books recently digitized by EEBO-TCP (Welzenbach 1999–) will also have an impact. This process of antedating – up to 50% of OED headwords – is spreading vocabulary growth out more evenly through the Tudor period and may diminish the "acceleration" effect. The total archival and mother lexicons of

English will still increase, but their growth-rate in the Tudor period may flatten somewhat unless the OED's new sources produce a balancing number of neologisms. The evidence for these may already exist because, as John Considine (who has worked at the OED) tells me, its office "has large files of 'pre-1800 notins', i.e. words known from sources of before 1800 which are *not* registered *in* the dictionary because their sense is obscure, or they appear to have been imperfectly naturalized, or they're just very rare" (p.c. December 10, 2008).

Was it just hard-word English that expanded, or did the common core also? The schoolmaster of the Merchant Taylors' School in London, Richard Mulcaster (1582) lists 8,143 different English words as the basis for a monolingual English dictionary of "our ordinarie speche" that, he hopes, someone else will compile. He allows for having missed some vocabulary items, but he also conflates the mother tongue, which he describes as the native vocabulary that everyone uses naturally, with newly enfranchised words (that is, word-loans) that people must learn before they can use. The English words employed in bilingual lexicons beginning with John Palsgrave's English–French *L'éclaircissement* (1530) may be expected to come from the mother tongue, words that required no explanation. For example, John Withals, whose pocket lexicon (1553) was popular throughout the 16th century, wrote as if he expected his grammar-school students to have a basic English vocabulary of fewer than 4,000 words. Even the written subset of Shakespeare's vocabulary over twenty years, from 1590 to 1613, was only twice the size of Mulcaster's list. Alfred Hart (1943) estimated it to be 17,677 word-forms. (The nearly 40,000 entries in the Riverside concordance of Shakespeare [Spevack 1973] can be used to exaggerate Shakespeare's personal working lexicon. The concordance includes variant spellings, and plural forms of words, among its headwords.)

There are thus acceptable grounds for a small EModE mother tongue that had many fewer words than the 64,300 lemmas recorded by the OED Online (Simpson [ed.] 2000–). By 1600, the population of England was divided among the country (90%), greater London (5%) (Sheppard 1998: 363), and the other provincial cities (5%; Guy 1988: 34–35). That is, nine of every ten persons lived in places that had no book-sellers. Existing data tell us that some 80% of all Elizabethan men were illiterate, and 95% of women. Even by the 1640s, 70% of men in rural England could not sign their name, in contrast with 22% of Londoners (Guy 1988: 417), although Keith Thomas (1986: 103) expresses doubt that the number of people who could sign their name is a reliable marker of literacy. He believes the literacy rate was much higher than existing data indicate. Country folk as a rule, however, may have had only one book, the English Bible. For example, William Tyndale had used the common mother tongue so that scripture could be understood when it was read aloud at home and church. The plowboy-reader that he had in mind did not need any help to understand what the Bible meant; the vocabulary of the New Testament was modest.

If the mother tongue, the English language used by 90% of the English people, had grown markedly, ordinary people would have needed general-purpose monolingual English dictionaries, but none was published until the early 18th century. John Kersey first brought out what he described as a general dictionary of English in 1702. Few before that time documented the mother tongue that parents passed on to children in daily usage, although teachers of English spelling did so. John Evans (1621), in his *The Palace of Profitable Pleasure*, listed "all English words" alphabetically, each one divided into syllables: the number of words needed to read the Bible and other books, he says, adds up to 6,665. David Crystal (2004: 317) finds 8,000 lexemes in the King James Bible, a number that generally confirms Mulcaster's estimate forty years before.

What grew were occupational sociolects, the specialized vocabularies of city folk, especially the 10% of the population that lived in London (which had tripled in size by the late 16th century) and the provincial cities. A mass of loan-words from the Latin of the educated, and the French, Italian, and Spanish of the merchants, combined with "terms of art" in burgeoning fields of knowledge such as medicine (McConchie 1997), law, and pharmacopoeia (mainly herbs) to form a second tongue, rival to the mother tongue. By the Stuart period, hard words had grown to such an extent that hard-word lexicons by Robert Cawdrey (2007 [1604]), John Bullokar (1611), and Henry Cockeram (1623) had to be printed. By the late 17th century, lexicographers like Thomas Blount (1656) and Elisha Coles (1676) were producing full-length dictionaries that served *only* hard words. The internationalist diplomacy of James I, the religious and political turmoil of the civil war, and the rising sciences that would join into the Royal Society in 1660, among other things, explosively accelerated the growth of this second tongue in the post-Tudor world.

The English did not learn hard words and terms of art from the publication of lexicons but rather because of professional and social communities in London that created conditions for specialized sociolects. Vocabulary expertise gave people a path to wealth in a land where population had doubled and resources had not. The growth of population, the failure of commodities to keep up to need, the declining purchasing power of the wages of most English laborers, the centralization of the crown and its income in London, and the huge development of new media – the printing press and the playhouse – led ingenious people to expand their professional vocabularies. Most OED sources for the Early Modern period are books published in London for an emerging knowledge-based elite, which was at most 10% of the population. Rural and poor speakers could neither use nor make money from specialized vocabularies, but urban professionals could, and their need for money was the root of the growth of a second tongue.

4 Semantics

In the first half of the Early Modern period, most literate English speakers had only the most rudimentary understanding of word meaning and semantics. Caxton's observations on English nearly exhaust what the literate English then knew about the semantics of their own speech: change dominated it, whether for dialectal reasons or personal taste.

> Loo what sholde a man in thyse dayes now wryte. egges or eyren/ certaynly it is harde to playse euery man / by cause of dyuersite & chaunge of langage. For in these dayes euery man that is in ony reputacyon in his countre. wyll vtter his commynycacyon and maters in suche maners & termes / that fewe men shall vnderstonde theym (1490 Caxton's Preface to Virgil's *Eneydos* A1v).

Renaissance scholars writing and conversing in Latin, especially on the Continent, knew much more about semantics than Caxton did (Salmon 1990), of course, but they did not favor English as a subject of study. Early in the reign of Henry VIII, Erasmus (who never learned English during his half a dozen years in England) described English as a tongue of monosyllables – a trait that the Cornishman Richard Carew, a century later, boasted about – and said that the vernacular he had heard used in taverns by men who were hawking merchandise sounded like barking (Giese 1937: 11).

Once the lexicon markedly grew, thanks to printing and other factors (such as the translation of works from other languages, and the growth of bilingual dictionaries), even the educated English speaker only very gradually woke up to the problematic meaning of words. English words in the Tudor period were generally understood to have just two semantic traits: they were easy or hard, and they denoted something in the external world.

Early Modern English glossographers, accordingly, had one main function: to offer, for any hard English word, easier synonyms and corresponding expressions. Monolingual glossaries explained those English words or terms of art which native speakers had to learn by easy terms they knew naturally (as Mulcaster 1582: 166–168 says). Bilingual lexicons gave easy English words for foreign-language words. The dozens of these dictionaries and glossaries that reached print did not document meaning in the common understanding we have of it today. The modern concept of a lexical definition was not to be found in them until 1755, outside occasional texts about mathematics, geometry, and the like. Early lexicographers often used synonyms, ornamented by anecdotes, for the post-lemmatic explanation field (cf. Stein 1986; Lancashire 2006). Samuel Johnson (1979 [1755]) did not recognize the lexical use of the word "definition".

Native speakers who recognized that words had different senses did not seek to explain these differences carefully. The Lily-Colet grammar book [1549] that the English Crown assigned for use in schools in the reign of Edward VI, and that lasted for more than a century, asserted that nouns were names of things in the world (cf. Anderson 1996; Lancashire 2002). When Shakespeare's Juliet asked "What's in a name?" and said that "a rose / By any other word would smell as sweet" (II.ii.43–44), she assented to a theory of semantics that was concept-vacant. Francis Bacon alludes to the prevalence of this belief when he said that "the first distemper of learning, [is] when men studie words, and not matter" (Görlach 1991: 247). This lexical model did not link words with concepts or ideas, a theory put forward in the late 15th century by the Italian humanist Lorenzo Valla, who believed that words, themselves changing over time like material things, could signify themselves (Wasno 1987: 109–10). John Locke in his *Essay Concerning Human Understanding* (1690) persuasively established this semantic notion in England much later. He wrote that "*Words* then are made to be signs of our Ideas", which were originally (and still are, often enough) "sensible *Ideas*" (Görlach 1991: 401–402; cf. Cohen 1977).

We owe this shift in metasemantic thought to Locke and philosophy, and it was to have enormous influence in centuries to come. Once the human mind could be said to have, within it, everything in the world merely by reason of naming those things, people could shake off the constraints that tied their words directly to the world. It became possible to build inner mental worlds as models for how to shape history and nature. Ironically, the founding of the Royal Society in 1660 did not entirely support a scientific method. When John Wilkins in 1668 published an analysis of English semantics that charted connotation and thesaural relationships among words, he was remaking language as an intellectual system, independent of empirical observation. This followed from the myth of the Tower of Babel, when God punished overreaching man by making him speak different tongues. Before Babel, everyone was thought to share the same Adamic tongue. Acting as God's regent on earth, the first man gave names to all the animals. Those names could hardly be arbitrary unless God acted without reason. After Wilkins and Locke, words and the ideas they signified were synonymous and inherently subjective. A key to exercising power over human beings and their world lay in forging a semantically self-consistent inner vision that subjected words to working concepts, and in then getting others to accept that semantic map.

The easy name-to-thing denotation that the Lily and Colet (1549) grammar book assumes became problematic when English speakers grew more interested in analyzing English words rather than, in a straightforward way, just assigning to them synonymous terms. Elyot (1542) expanded his scope from words to phrases, and he added "true definitions of all syckenesses and kyndes of maladyes" (sig. a2v). Elyot merged some definitions *of things* into a dictionary of words. Richard Huloet (1552: sig. [x]2v) observed in the preface to his English-Latin lexicon that, in Britain, English words appeared in Latin text, and Latin words in English text. Both languages, then, deserved equitable treatment. Thomas Wilson (1553), an early defender of English, wrote that "Some seke so farre for outlandishe Englishe, that thei forget altogether their mothers language" (p2r). Richard Mulcaster (1582) plainly observed that "verie manie men, being excellentlie well learned in foren speche, can hardlie discern what theie haue at home" (x4r). "Our naturall tung," he said, "cummeth on vs by hudle [in confusion]" (x4v), and yet "the word being knowen, which implyeth the propertie the thing is half known, whose propertie is emplyed" (y1r). Thomas Thomas (1587: 4) five years later cited approvingly Plato's dictum that whoever knows the names of things will know the things also. Robert Cawdrey (2007 [1604]: a3r) copied Wilson's above remark (Crystal 2004: 291). Francis Bacon (1605) in his *Aduancement of Learning* argued that "wordes, are the tokens currant and accepted for conceits" (II, 60), in this way associating semantics with thought. When John Bullokar (1616), in his hard-word dictionary, claims to "open the signification of such [strange] words" (a3v), some readers understood "signification" as more than acting as signs for things. For example, individuals were confident of their personal interpretations of scripture, a practice that seeded puritan sects on both sides of the Atlantic, sects that promoted widespread religious dissent, a civil war, and the Interregnum.

The growth of the core and hard-word lexicons highlighted semantic issues. When synonyms for a single mother-tongue term multiplied in word-loans from different sources, copiousness resulted, and so did doubts about usage. John Florio (1598) enjoyed multiplying terms and senses and praised English, given the "manie-folde Englishes of manie wordes" in his explanations, for out-vying Italian itself (b1v). Under what circumstance was one synonym used rather than another? Another issue was ambiguity, when a single word acquired two or more senses, commonly because it developed a narrower sense in a professional or trade register. How could a speaker resolve puzzlement when a common term was used in an unexpected way because of its professional or technical context? Edmund Coote (1997 [1596]), for one, solved this problem by glossing only hard, less familiar words (l1r). The monosyllabic mother tongue of small size that Coote taught did not create many such problems, but when English almost doubled in a century because of word-loans and terms of art, readers and speakers could indeed become "gravelled" (Blount 1656: A2r) in understanding their own tongue.

The prefaces of Early Modern dictionaries thus supply milestones in the English speaker's gradually growing awareness of semantic issues. First was Sir

Thomas Elyot's shocked recognition that natural understanding of mother-tongue words was sometimes wrong. In 1538, he expressed dismay at one class of such errors, the misidentification of herbs by ignorant medical practitioners (Elyot 1538). Elyot had to rely on England's first great herbalist, William Turner, to untangle the relationship between names and herbs. Until John Rider (1589) enumerated senses in his English-Latin dictionary, most English lexicographers had separated synonyms and senses indiscriminately by commas. By 1658, Edward Phillips proposed "to distinguish the terms, several derivations, differences, definitions, interpretations, proper significations of the words of our Tongue" (Phillips 1658: a3v), even if he did not, in practice, know what all of these were, having plagiarized most of his dictionary from Blount.

After the foundation of the Royal Society, lexicographers such as John Worlidge, John Ray, and Stephen Skinner made substantial contributions to neglected fields of English vocabulary. Worlidge (1669) analyzed dialectal variation in husbandry – that is, farming terminology. Ray (1674) surveyed British dialectal variation, north and south, and compiled word-lists for birds and fishes. The first glossary of Chaucer's medieval words had come out in 1602: this showed that historical time as well as profession or trade could give rise to semantic ambiguity. This recognition led to the making of etymological lexicons (Liberman 1998). Stephen Skinner (1671) corrected etymologies in John Minsheu's 1617 derivative, often erroneous *Ductor in Linguas*, drawing on William Somner's 1659 dictionary of Anglo-Saxon, the product of almost a century of scholarship by half a dozen people.

5 Research issues

Analyzing Early Modern English semantic change satisfactorily, a principal interest of present-day researchers, is, as Manfred Görlach (1991: 200) says, "a difficult and largely unsolved problem". Researchers have successfully classified specific instances of semantic change as "expansions, reductions and transfers" (Görlach 1991: 207), or as generalization, specialization, pejoration, and amelioration (Nevalainen 1999: 433–434). However, until we can interrogate the OED database to search for word-entries that document the addition and the loss of senses, year by year, research will be partial and somewhat impressionistic. At present, the OED Online (Simpson [ed.] 2000–) advanced search function does not permit queries on senses. We could benefit from a count of lemmata that have undergone semantic change within successive, short periods of time. Then we could analyze each change for its possible causes and effects. Did one or more synonyms appear in the preceding decades and replace the headword, which was then available for semantic reassignment? Were some translations especially productive of sense-shifts? Did social, technological, religious, or intellectual developments highlight gaps in the lexicon that had to be filled? The OED does not intend to answer some of these questions, but other publications, such as Kay et al.'s (2009) *Historical Thesaurus of English* (now part of the OED), may help us do so.

To understand semantic change is in part to comprehend to whom the native speakers of the language at the time ceded the right to influence how they used words. Crown patronage – in publishing dictionaries and reference works such as herbals, in supporting antiquarian studies in archaic forms of English, in enabling or censoring debate over controversial subjects – had an impact on new-word formation and storage. Sir Thomas Elyot went so far as to credit his 1538 Latin-English dictionary to Henry VIII because of the king's enthusiasm for the project and willingness to open up the royal library to his research. The English Crown normally expressed its patronage by allowing lexicographers to dedicate works directly to them or to their chief ministers (Williams 1962). The state and the church, whenever revising educational standards, liturgies, or the translation of the Bible, nudged forward new intellectual models or paradigms of language itself into the public eye. We should consider asking who has political power and money before assigning a cause for given semantic changes. Did the avowed preferences of William Cecil, Lord Burghley, for Latin over English, or of herbals and lexicons over poems and plays, influence Tudor English? After all, he brought Elizabeth to the throne, and he guarded her for fifty years. How did the assumption of James I in 1603, the arrival of thousands of Scots in London, his choice of Francis Bacon as Chancellor, and his humiliation of John Cowell and his legal lexicon, *The Interpreter* (1607), affect English, which had been taken for granted for more than a century? James saw himself as a European monarch: he sought alliances for his children across the English Channel. It was possible to buy two huge bilingual dictionaries of French (Randle Cotgrave 1530) and Italian (John Florio 1598), both dedicated to royals, in 1611, when English itself had to make do with the non-headword position in these massive language works. John Minsheu (1617) had English headwords in his *Ductor in Linguas*, but they were remarkably limited to 12,550 headwords and overwhelmed by the ten other languages whose etymological relations to English the lexicon's word-entries highlighted.

The OED Online (Simpson [ed.] 2000–) has unrivalled scholarship on Early Modern English semantics, but neither the technology to extract it (yet), nor sufficiently representative illustrative contemporary quotations. If we link authors of quotations in the OED with biographical entries about potential authors in the *Oxford Dictionary of National Biography* (Matthew et al. [eds.] 2004–08), we find a discontinuity. About 25 quotations by William Cecil, 50 by Elizabeth I, and 55 by James I appear in the OED, but over 5,600 by Shakespeare.

In the tradition of Samuel Johnson, the OED originally founded its base of quotations on excellent speakers and writers of *literary* English, not on men and women who exerted a powerful influence on all aspects of the nation, and in particular its language. Yet we have a substantial manuscript literature written by Cecil and (especially) James, and no mean remains from Elizabeth. The same is true of dictionary writers. Their neglect, as a group, is so marked that less than 5% of the word-entries in *Lexicons of Early Modern English* (LEME) (Lancashire [ed.] 2006–) are (independently) cited by the Online OED.

Is it possible that the semantics of Early Modern English appears so intractable a problem to language historians because present-day researchers analyze its language separately from the people who spoke it, and the world they describe? A hard English headword in a glossary of the time gave glossographers an opportunity to write a definition, but they seldom did so. They often preferred anecdotes, personal reflections, and information about the thing that the word denoted. The perception of lexical senses, unstandardized at this time, was individuated and contextualized in ways important to the writer and speaker. John Rastell's early law lexicon gives earlier instances of a glossographer whose explanations closely mirror the living context in which they were used. His *Exposiciones Terminorum Legum Anglorum* (1523–24) "glosses 'derke termys' in ways that serve royal power" (Lancashire 2006: 13). Much later, Thomas Blount's (1656) entry on "Landskip" ('landscape') sharply contrasts with the current definition for this sense of the word in the OED (s.v. *landscape*, def. 1b 'The background of scenery in a portrait or figure-painting', 1656–76):

> Landskip (Belg.) Parergon, Paisage or By-work, which is an expressing of the Land, by Hills, Woods, Castles, Valleys, Rivers, Cities, &c. as far as may be shewed in our Horizon. All that which in a Picture is not of the body or argument thereof is Landskip, Parergon, or by-work. As in the Table of our Saviors passion, the picture of Christ upon the Rood (which is the proper English word for Cross) the two theeves, the blessed Virgin Mary, and St. John, are the Argument: But the City Jerusalem, the Country about, the clouds, and the like, are Landskip. El. Ar.

OED Online gives Blount's entry as its earliest citation in this sense, but Blount copies the glossary entry for "LANDSKEP" (Dd4v) almost verbatim from Edmund Bolton's earlier *Elements of Armories* (1610). LEME finds a brief explanation of this sense of the word in both Cotgrave (1611) and Florio (1598). However, Bolton and Blount were Roman Catholics and associated landscape with religious images, the background for Christ's crucifixion. The sense of this term was, as it were, marked by individual religious belief. When John Milton's nephew Edward Phillips (1658), in his *New World*, plagiarized Blount's dictionary, he copied the entry on "Landskip" but, like the OED, excised the reference to the religious image that, for Bolton and Blount, whose faith worshipped images, was relevant to the word's signification. Milton and Phillips despised the Roman Catholic hegemony.

What does this small instance of semantic change tell us, if not that classifying early senses by type – for example, as reductions – is bound to be unsatisfying? The intentions and context of the contemporary English speaker and writer, elusive though they may be, may be better explicators of historical semantic change.

Acknowledgments: The research for this chapter was done at my Lexical Analysis Laboratory, Room 7061, Robarts Library, a facility that I owe to the support of Geoffrey Rockwell's TAPoR network, IBM Canada, the Canada Foundation for Innovation, and the University of Toronto Libraries.

6 References

Aitken, A. J. and William A. Craigie (eds.). 1931–2002. *A Dictionary of the Older Scottish Tongue, from the Twelfth Century to the End of the Seventeenth*. 12 vols. London/Chicago: Oxford University Press and University of Chicago Press.

Alston, R. C. 1965. *A Bibliography of the English Language from the Invention of Printing to the Year 1800*. Leeds: E. J. Arnold.

Anderson, Judith. 1996. *Words that Matter: Linguistic Perception in Renaissance English*. Stanford: Stanford University Press.

Bacon, Francis. 1605. *The Twoo Bookes of Francis Bacon. Of the Proficience and Aduancement of Learning, Diuine and Humane*. London: Henry Tomes.

Bailey, Richard W. (ed.). 1978. *Early Modern English: Additions and Antedatings to the Record of English Vocabulary 1475–1700*. New York: Georg Olms Verlag.

Baret, John. 1574. *An Aluearie or Triple Dictionarie, in Englishe, Latin, and French*. London: Henry Denham.

Bell, Maureen and John Barnard. 1992. Provisional count of STC titles, 1475–1640. *Publishing History* 31: 48–64.

Blount, Thomas. 1656. *Glossographia*. London: Thomas Newcomb for Humphrey Moseley and George Sawbridge.

Bolton, Edmund. 1610. *The Elements of Armories*. London: George Eld.

Bullokar, John. 1616. *An English Expositor: Teaching the Interpretation of the Hardest Words in our Language*. London: John Legatt.

Carew, Richard. 1614. The excellencie of the English tongue. In: William Camden (ed.), *Remaines, concerning Britaine*, 36–44. London: John Legatt for Simon Waterson.

Cawdrey, Robert. 1604. *A Table Alphabeticall, Conteyning and Teaching the Understanding of Hard Usuall English Wordes, Borrowed from the Hebrew, Greeke, Latine, or French, & c.* London: E. Weaver.

Cawdrey, Robert. 2007 [1604]. *The First English Dictionary, 1604. Robert Cawdrey's A Table Alphabeticall*. Intro. by J. A. Simpson. Oxford: Bodleian Library.

Caxton, William (trans.). 1490. *Virgil's* Eneydos. Westminster: William Caxton.

Chadwyck-Healey. 2003–2011. *Early English Books Online, 1475–1700* (EEBO). Ann Arbor: ProQuest. http://eebo.chadwyck.com/home; last accessed 14 April 2017.
Cockeram, Henry. 1623. *English Dictionarie: or, an Interpreter of Hard English Words*. London: Eliot's Court Press for N. Butter.
Cohen, Murray. 1977. *Sensible Words: Linguistic Practice in England 1640–1785*. Baltimore: Johns Hopkins University Press.
Coles, Elisha. 1676. *An English Dictionary: Explaining The difficult Terms that are used in Divinity, Husbandry, Physick, Phylosophy, Law, Navigation, Mathematicks, and other Arts and Sciences*. London: Samuel Crouch. Wing C 5070.
Considine, John. 2014. *Academy Dictionaries 1600-1800*. Cambridge: Cambridge University Press.
Considine, John (ed.) 2012. *Ashgate Critical Essays on Early English Lexicographers. Volume 4: The Seventeenth Century*. Ian Lancashire (gen. ed.) Farnham: Ashgate.
Coote, Edmund. 1997 [1596]. *The English Schoole-maister*. Ian Lancashire, Linda Hutjens, Brent Nelson, Robert Whalen, and Tanya Wood (eds.). Toronto: University of Toronto Library. http://www.library.utoronto.ca/utel/ret/coote/ret2.html; last accessed 14 April 2017. (Originally published: London: Widow Orwin for R. Jackson and R. Dexter.)
Cotgrave, Randle. 1611. *A Dictionarie of the French and English Tongues*. London: Adam Islip.
Cowell, John. 1607. *The Interpreter: or Booke Containing the Signification of Words*. Cambridge: John Legate.
Crystal, David. 2004. *The Stories of English*. London: Allen Lane.
Elyot, Sir Thomas. 1538. *The Dictionary of Syr Thomas Eliot*. London: T. Berthelet.
Elyot, Sir Thomas. 1542. *Bibliotheca Eliotae Eliotis Librarie*. London: Thomas Berthelet.
Evans, John. 1621. *The Palace of Profitable Pleasure*. London: W. Stansby.
Finkenstaedt, Thomas, Ernst Leisi, and Dieter Wolff (eds.). 1970. *A Chronological English Dictionary: Listing 80 000 Words in Order of their Earliest Known Occurrence*. Heidelberg: Winter.
Finkenstaedt, Thomas, Dieter Wolff, Joachim Neuhaus, and Winfried Herget. 1973. *Ordered Profusion: Studies in Dictionaries and the English Lexicon*. Heidelberg: Winter.
Florio, John. 1598. *A Worlde of Wordes, or, Most Copious, and Exact Dictionarie in Italian and English*. London: Arnold Hatfield for Edward Blount.
Giese, Rachel. 1937. Erasmus' knowledge and estimate of the vernacular languages. *The Romanic Review* 28: 3–18.
Gill, Alexander. 1619. *Logonomia Anglica*. London: Iohannes Beale.
Gilliver, Peter. 2016. *The Making of the Oxford English Dictionary*. Oxford: Oxford University Press.
Görlach, Manfred. 1991. *Introduction to Early Modern English*. Cambridge: Cambridge University Press.
Guy, John. 1988. *Tudor England*. Oxford: Oxford University Press.
Hart, Alfred. 1943. The growth of Shakespeare's vocabulary. *Review of English Studies* 19: 242–254.
Herttage, S. J. H. (ed.). 1881. *Catholicon Anglicum, an English Latin Wordbook, Dated 1483*. (Early English Text Society, O. S., 75.) London: Trübner.
Huloet, Richard. 1552. *Abcedarium Anglico Latinum*. Londini: Gulielmi Riddel.
Johnson, Samuel. 1979 [1755]. *A Dictionary of the English Language*. Intro. by Robert W. Burchfield. London: Times Books.
Jones, Richard Foster. 1953. *The Triumph of the English Language*. London: Oxford University Press.

Kay, Christian, Jane Roberts, Michael Samuels, and Irené Wotherspoon (eds.). 2009. *Historical Thesaurus of the Oxford English Dictionary*. 2 vols. Oxford: Oxford University Press.

Kersey, John. 1702. *English Dictionary: Or, a Compleat: Collection Of the Most Proper and Significant Words, Commonly used in the Language*. London: Henry Bonwicke and Robert Knaplock.

Kytö, Merja (ed.). 1996. *Manual to the Diachronic Part of the Helsinki Corpus of English Texts: Coding Conventions and Source Texts*. 3rd edn. Helsinki: Department of English, University of Helsinki. http://clu.uni.no/icame/manuals/; last accessed 14 April 2017.

Lancashire, Ian (ed.). 1999. *The Early Modern English Dictionaries Database (EMEDD)*. http://homes.chass.utoronto.ca/~ian/emedd.html; last accessed 14 April 2017.

Lancashire, Ian. 2002. "Dumb Significants" and Early Modern English definition. In: Jens Brockmeier, Min Wang, and David R. Olson, *Literacy, Narrative and Culture*, 131–154. Richmond, Surrey: Curzon.

Lancashire, Ian. 2006. Law and Early Modern English lexicons. In: R. W. McConchie, Olga Timofeeva, Heli Tissari, and Tanja Säily (eds.), *HEL-LEX: New Approaches in English Historical Lexis*, 8–23. Somerville, MA: Cascadilla Press. http://www.lingref.com/cpp/hel-lex/2005/paper1342.pdf; last accessed 14 April 2017.

Lancashire, Ian (ed.). 2006–. *Lexicons of Early Modern English (LEME)*. Toronto: University of Toronto Library and University of Toronto Press. http://leme.library.utoronto.ca/; last accessed 14 April 2017. LEME no longer charges a licensing fee for full access, and it includes Samuel Johnson's dictionary (1755).

Levins, Peter. 1867. *Manipulus Vocabulorum: A Rhyming Dictionary of the English Language, by Peter Levins. (1570)*. H. B. Wheatley (ed.). (Early English Text Society, O. S., 27.) London: Trübner.

Liberman, Anatoly. 1998. An annotated survey of English etymological dictionaries and glossaries. *Dictionaries* 20: 21–96.

Lily, William and John Colet. 1549. *A Short Introduction of Grammar, 1549*. (English Linguistics 1500–1800, ed. by R. C. Alston, 262.) Menston: Scolar Press, 1970.

Locke, John. 1690. *An Essay Concerning Humane Understanding*. London: for Thomas Basset by Edward Mory.

Matthew, Colin, Brian Harrison, and Lawrence Goldman (eds.). 2004–08. *Oxford Dictionary of National Biography Online*. Oxford: Oxford University Press. http://www.oxforddnb.com/index.jsp

Mayhew, Anthony Lawson (ed.). 1908. *The Promptorium Parvulorum. The First English Dictionary. c. 1440 A. D.* (Early English Text Society, E.S., 102.) London: Kegan Paul, Trench, Trübner, and Henry Frowde, Oxford University Press.

McConchie, R. W. 1997. *Lexicography and Physicke: The Record of Sixteenth-century English Medical Terminology*. Oxford: Clarendon Press.

McConchie, Roderick (ed.) 2012. *Ashgate Critical Essays on Early English Lexicographers. Volume 3: The Sixteenth Century*. Ian Lancashire (gen. ed.) Farnham: Ashgate.

McDermott, Anne. 2002. Early dictionaries of English and historical corpora: In search of hard words. In: Javier A. Díaz Vera (ed.), *A Changing World of Words: Studies in English Historical Lexicography, Lexicology and Semantics*, 197–226. Amsterdam/Atlanta, GA: Rodopi.

Minsheu, John. 1617. *Ductor in Linguas*. London: John Browne.

Mulcaster, Richard. 1582. *The First Part of the Elementarie*. London: Thomas Vautroullier.

Nevalainen, Terttu. 1999. Early Modern English lexis and semantics. In: Roger Lass (ed.), *The Cambridge History of the English Language*. Vol. III. *1476–1776*, 332–458. Cambridge: Cambridge University Press.

Nevalainen, Terttu. 2006. *An Introduction to Early Modern English*. Edinburgh: Edinburgh University Press.

Nevalainen, Terttu, Helena Raumolin-Brunberg, Jukka Keränen, Minna Nevala, Arja Nurmi, and Minna Palander-Collin. 1998. *Corpus of Early English Correspondence* (CEEC). Department of English, University of Helsinki. http://www.helsinki.fi/varieng/CoRD/corpora/CEEC/index.html; last accessed 14 April 2017.

Nowell, Laurence. 1952. *Laurence Nowell's Vocabularium Saxonicum*. Albert H. Marckwardt (ed.). Ann Arbor: University of Michigan Press.

Nurmi, Arja. 1998. *Manual for the Corpus of Early English Correspondence Sampler*. Helsinki: Department of English, University of Helsinki. http://clu.uni.no/icame/manuals/; last accessed 14 April 2017.

Palsgrave, John. 2003 [1530]. *L'éclaircissement de la langue française, 1530: texte anglais original / John Palsgrave*. Susan Baddeley (ed. and trans.). Paris: Champion.

Phillips, Edward. 1658. The New World of English Words, 1658. *(English Linguistics 1500–1800*, ed. by R. C. Alston, 321.) Menston: Scolar Press, 1969.

Pollard, A. W. and G. R. Redgrave. 1976–91. *A Short Title Catalogue of Books Printed in England, Scotland, & Ireland, and of English Books Printed Abroad, 1475–1640*. 2nd edn. 3 vols. William A. Jackson, F. S. Ferguson, and Katherine F. Pantzer (eds.) London: The Bibliographical Society.

Ray, John. 1674. *A Collection of English Words. Not Generally used, with their Significations and Original*. London: H. Bruges.

Rider, John. 1589. *Bibliotheca Scholastica*. Oxford: Joseph Barnes.

Ridley, Mark (attributed). 1996. *A Dictionarie of the Vulgar Russe Tongue Attributed to Mark Ridley*, Gerald Stone (ed.). Köln/Weimar/Wien: Böhlau Verlag.

Rissanen, Matti, Merja Kytö, Leena Kahlas-Tarkka, Matti Kilpiö, Saara Nevanlinna, Irma Taavitsainen, Terttu Nevalainen, and Helena Raumolin-Brunberg. 1991. *The Helsinki Corpus of English Texts*. In: *ICAME Collection of English Language Corpora (CD-ROM)*, 2nd edn., Knut Hofland, Anne Lindebjerg, and Jørn Thunestvedt (eds.), The HIT Centre, University of Bergen, Norway. For manual, see http://clu.uni.no/icame/manuals/; last accessed 14 April 2017.

Rissanen, Matti, Merja Kytö, and Minna Palander-Collin (eds.). 1993. *Early English in the Computer Age: Explorations through the Helsinki Corpus*. Berlin/New York: Mouton de Gruyter.

Salmon, Vivian. 1990. Some views on meaning in sixteenth-century England. In: Peter Schmitter (ed.), *Essays towards a History of Semantics*, 33–53. Münster: Nodus.

Schäfer, Jürgen. 1980. *Documentation in the OED: Shakespeare and Nashe as Test Cases*. Oxford: Clarendon Press.

Schäfer, Jürgen. 1989. *Early Modern English Lexicography*. 2 vols. Oxford: Clarendon Press.

Shakespeare, William. 1997. *The Riverside Shakespeare*. 2nd edn. Boston: Houghton Mifflin.

Sheppard, Francis. 1998. *London: A History*. Oxford: Oxford University Press.

Sidney, Sir Philip. 1595. *The Defence of Poesie*. London: William Ponsonby.

Simpson, John (ed.). 2000–. *The Oxford English Dictionary*. 3rd edn. online. Oxford University Press. www.oed.com/

Skinner, Thomas. 1671. *Etymologicon Linguæ Anglicanæ*. London: T. Roycroft.

Slaughter, Mary M. 1982. *Universal Languages and Scientific Taxonomy in the Seventeenth Century*. Cambridge: Cambridge University Press.

Somner, William. 1659. *Dictionarium Saxonico-Latino-Anglicum*. Oxford: William Hall for Daniel White.

Spevack, Marvin. 1973. *The Harvard Concordance to Shakespeare*. Cambridge, MA: Belknap Press of Harvard University Press.
Stein, Gabriele. 1985. *The English Dictionary before Cawdrey*. Tübingen: Niemeyer.
Stein, Gabriele. 1986. Definitions and first-person pronoun involvement in Thomas Elyot's dictionary. In: Dieter Kastovsky and Aleksander Szwedek (eds.), *Linguistics across Historical and Geographical Boundaries, 1465–1474*. Berlin/New York: Mouton de Gruyter.
Thomas, Keith. 1986. The meaning of literacy in Early Modern England. In: Gerd Baumann (ed.), *The Written Word: Literacy in Transition*, 97–131. Oxford: Clarendon Press.
Thomas, R. J., Gareth A. Beven, and P. J. Donovan. 1967–2002. *Geiriadur Prifysgol Cymru. A Dictionary of the Welsh Language*. 4 vols. Cardiff: University of Wales Press.
Thomas, Thomas. 1587. *Dictionarium Linguae Latinae et Anglicanae*. Cambridge: Richard Boyle.
Turner, William. 1999. *Libellus de Re Herbaria Novus*. Mats Rydén, Hans Helander, and Kerstin Olsson (eds. and trans.). Uppsala: Almqvist & Wiksells.
Waite, Greg (ed.). 2008–. *The Textbase of Early Tudor English*. Dunedin, NZ: University of Otago. http://www.otago.ac.nz/english-linguistics/tudor/; last accessed 14 April 2017.
Waswo, Richard. 1987. *Language and Meaning in the Renaissance*. Princeton: Princeton University Press.
Williams, Franklin B., Jr. 1962. *Index of Dedications and Commendatory Verses in English Books before 1641*. London: Bibliographical Society.
Wilson, Thomas. 1553. *The Arte of Rhetorique*. London: Richardus Grafton.
Wing, Donald. 1972–88. *Short-Title Catalogue of Books Printed in England, Scotland, Ireland, Wales, and British America, and of English Books Printed in Other Countries, 1641–1700*. 2nd edn. 3 vols. New York: The Index Committee of the Modern Language Association of America.
Withals, John. 1553. *A Shorte Dictionarie for Yonge Begynners*. London: T. Berthelet.
Worlidge, John. 1669. *Dictionarium Rusticum*. London: T. Johnson.

Dawn Archer
Chapter 7:
Pragmatics and discourse

1   Introduction —— 108
2   Speech acts in the EModE period —— 109
3   Im/politeness studies relating to the EModE period —— 113
4   Discourses and discourse strategies —— 117
5   Summary —— 121
6   References —— 122

Abstract: This chapter provides an overview of the most widely studied discoursal/pragmatic phenomena of Early Modern English discourse: speech acts, address terms, politeness, discourse markers, and (other) discourse strategies. The Early Modern English period is assumed here to cover approximately three hundred years, starting shortly after the introduction of the printing press to England in 1476; thus, some scholars may want to place several of the studies included here within the late Early Modern English period or at the beginning of the Modern English period (see, e.g., Jucker 2000: 7; Görlach 1991: 9). This chapter also highlights (researchers' awareness of) the importance of considering the "interplay between the individual, language and society" (Palander-Collin 2010) when seeking to explain discoursal/pragmatic phenomena of times past.

1 Introduction

There is a lack of consensus in respect to what constitutes Historical Pragmatics, Historical Discourse Analysis, and Historical Dialogue Analysis as disciplines, and the extent to which they overlap (for useful discussions of their similarities and differences see Brinton 2001; Jacobs and Jucker 1995; Jucker et al. [eds.] 1999; Traugott 2004). One point of similarity relevant to this chapter, however, is the attention given (by advocates of the three disciplines) to the phenomena of speech acts, address terms, politeness, discourse markers, and discourse strategies in the Early Modern English (henceforth EModE) period. Indeed, the afore-

---

Dawn Archer: Manchester (UK)

mentioned constitute the most widely studied discoursal/pragmatic phenomena (within the EModE period) and, as such, are to be the focus of this chapter, beginning with an investigation of speech acts (see Section 2). Where relevant, I will also discuss the (prevalent) use of corpus-linguistic techniques within the various fields.

2 Speech acts in the EModE period

The study of speech acts in their historical context is older than one might imagine if we include non-English studies. For example, Schlieben-Lange and Weydt began investigating the historicity of Romance speech acts in the 1970s (see, e.g., Schlieben-Lange 1976, 1983; Schlieben-Lange and Weydt 1979). The bulk of speech act studies relating to the EModE period date from the 1990s onwards, however, and focus on:
– directives such as requests and orders – that is, verbal acts whereby S (= Speaker) attempts to get H (= Hearer) to do something (e.g. Rudanko 1993; Busse 2002, 2008; Culpeper and Archer 2008);
– expressives such as insults, curses, compliments, and thanks – that is, verbal acts whereby S expresses a psychological state towards H or in respect to a proposition (e.g. Jacobsson 2002; Culpeper and Semino 2000; Jucker and Taavitsainen 2000; Taavitsainen and Jucker 2008b);
– commissives such as promises – that is, verbal acts whereby S commits to do some future act(s) for H (e.g. Arnovick 1994, 1999; Valkonen 2008);
– "rogatives" (i.e. questions) – that is, verbal acts whereby S seeks information from H (e.g. Claridge 2005; Archer 2005).

The above studies draw on literary sources as well as sources that are taken to be representative of "real-life" speech events, as the former are considered to be a valuable means by which to investigate past speech events (for further discussion, see Jucker et al. [eds.] 1999: 16; Jucker and Taavitsainen 2003: 8–9). For example, Busse (2008) provides an inventory of directives in Shakespeare's *King Lear*; Rudanko (1993) investigates questions and requests in Shakespeare's *Othello* and *Coriolanus*; Culpeper and Archer (2008) explore requests in comedy plays and courtroom proceeding transcripts taken from the *Sociopragmatic Corpus* (1640–1760); Archer (2005) draws from the courtroom proceedings of the *Sociopragmatic Corpus* to study questions; Claridge (2005) explores questions, using the *Lampeter Corpus of Early Modern English Tracts* (1640–1740); and Jacobsson (2002) identifies expressions associated with thanking from the six text-types which make up the *Corpus of English Dialogues 1560–1760* (plays, fiction, didactic works, language teaching texts, witness depositions, and courtroom proceedings).

2.1 Methodologies and approaches utilized

Schlieben-Lange's (1976, 1983) work on Romance speech acts enabled her to pioneer an approach that has been hugely influential for English speech act studies (see, e.g., Arnovick's [1999] culturally-rich descriptions of insults, promises, curses and partings). Schlieben-Lange's (form-based) approach involves attending to both "diachronic process" and "historical contrast": that is, gleaning evidence of verbal activity from texts through the identification of performative speech-act verbs, and then confirming the historical appropriacy of the (speech act) labels utilized via historical dictionaries and additional contextual information/evidence ("histories of institutions", law treatises, etc.). More recently, Kohnen (2002: 238, 241) has made a distinction between form-based approaches that engage in "structured eclecticism" and form-based approaches that engage in "illustrative eclecticism". The latter involves researchers picking out relevant examples of a given speech act in the respective periods covered by their particular study on the basis of their (intuitive) reading of the data and of the relevant literature (see, e.g., Jucker and Taavitsainen 2000). In contrast, structured eclecticism involves "a [more] deliberate [and systematic] selection of typical patterns which [researchers] trace by way of a representative analysis throughout the history of English" (Kohnen 2002: 238). As one might expect, given the emphasis on "typical patterns", structured eclecticism (i) tends to be adopted when studying speech acts that occur in routinized forms, and (ii) is the suggested/favored approach when engaging in computerized searches for specific speech acts (Kohnen 2002). Indeed, Jucker and Taavitsainen (2008) have shown how, because Present-day English realizations of apologies are highly routinized and depend on a small range of conventionalized lexical forms, these patterns can offer an excellent point of departure from which to (seek to) identify apologies in Renaissance data. Similarly, Valkonen (2008) has sought to identify promises in the ARCHER corpus and the *Chadwyck-Healey Eighteenth Century Fiction* database, using a small set of lexical-morphosyntactic search patterns (such as PROMIS*, PLEDG*, VOW*, SWEAR*, SWORN, VOUCH*, GUARANTE*), which were originally derived from Wierzbicka's (1987) list of (verbs for) promises.

As an approach based on structured eclecticism will only allow for the automatic detection of performative instances of speech acts, and Culpeper and Archer (2008) wanted to capture all instances of directives (direct and indirect) in their *Sociopragmatic Corpus*, they have developed a (manually applied) annotation scheme as a means of identifying directives in their drama and trial data. Although directives are regarded as being less sensitive to cultural/historical variation than speech acts such as apologies, complaints and compliments (Kohnen 2002), Culpeper and Archer (2008: 58, 47–48) nevertheless advocate a "multi-feature view of speech acts", which makes use of:

- formal features (such as particular conventionalized pragmalinguistic strategies or Illocutionary Force Indicating Devices [IFIDs]: see, e.g., Searle 1975; Aijmer 1996);
- contextual beliefs (such as Searle's [1969] observation that it is not obvious that [the desired] future action will be performed by the target in the normal course of events);
- co-textual features (such as pre-requests: see, e.g., Edmonson and House 1981; Levinson 1983: 356–364; Tsui 1994: 110–111);
- outcomes (such as the target performing the action specified in the earlier speech act: see, e.g., Austin 1962).

This effectively equates to capturing speech-act function and context-of-utterance as well as form and, as such, seeks to avoid "pragmatic false friends", i.e., constructions such as Ford's question to Falstaff (*Would you speak with me?*), "which, against a contemporary background, [can] suggest a wrong pragmatic interpretation"; for example, a request for Falstaff's attention as opposed to a clarification question along the lines of *Did you want to talk to me?* (see Kohnen 2002: 239–240).

2.2 Directives in the EModE period: assessing in/directness

Culpeper and Archer (2008) have also sought to determine the diachronic applicability of the in/directness approach first advocated by Blum-Kulka et al. (eds.) (1989), as Blum-Kulka and House (1989) have suggested that conventional indirectness may be "universal" in our modern world (in/directness, as utilized here, does not relate to Searle's [1975] non-mapping of form and function, but to the transparency with which the illocutionary point of a particular utterance is signalled). Culpeper and Archer's (2008) findings appear to invalidate Blum-Kulka and House's (1989) claim, however, for more than two-thirds of the directives in their late EModE data were achieved directly, via impositive strategies, the majority of which utilized an imperative form (such as *Take away her sword*). Moreover, when conventionally indirect strategies were in evidence, they were used by relatively powerful people/intimates of high-status, rather than by people with less power, as we might expect today. These "powerful" interactants also exhibited a perceived preference for directives marked by contextual beliefs – specifically, volition (cf. *I would speak with you*) or obligation (cf. *We must go to the city*) – a factor that contrasts starkly with a key feature of present-day conventionally-indirect directives: modern-day (British) users are said to orient their requests to the preparatory condition of ability (i.e. a contextual belief, relating to the ability of the target to perform a future action: cf. the widely-discussed request, *Can you pass the salt?*). Culpeper and Archer (2008) point to the "democratisation of discourse" (see Fairclough 1993: 98) and the subsequent reduction in overt markers of power asymmetry between people of unequal institutional power as a possible explanation for the change(s). A perceived need in the EModE period to signal (a level of) volition and/or obligation in one's directives may also help to explain the prevalence of *let*-requests in the *Sociopragmatic Corpus*, in particular, and the EModE period more generally (see Kohnen 2004), as *let* requests exhibited both volition and obligation, depending on whether they requested that something be "allowed" or suggested that something be "desired".

2.3 The "fuzziness" of speech acts/speech act categories

Jucker and Taavitsainen (2000) have suggested a "fuzziness" approach to speech act research, which allows for both synchronic and diachronic variation. What this means, in practice, is a rejection of the application of speech act theory (in its most conservative Searlean sense) in favor of a view of speech acts as prototypes linked by a shared "pragmatic space". For example, they argue that insults (synchronic and diachronic) share the same starting point: they contain[ed] "a predication about the target" that is/was "disparaging" in some way (Taavitsainen and Jucker 2008a: 6). However, (the actual realizations of) insults are/were located across several clines, for example, form ("ritual/rule governed-creative"), context-dependence ("conventional-particular"), and speaker attitude ("ludic-aggressive", "intentional-unintentional"), etc. They go on to suggest that the framework they initially drafted for insults can also be applied to other speech acts/speech act categories as long as we allow the latter to dictate which of the components of the multidimensional framework are foregrounded and which are backgrounded: for example, Taavitsainen and Jucker predict that, with apologies, the form category is likely to be most prominent, as apologies tend to be "expressed in routinised, perhaps even ritual and rule-governed forms"; the dimension of "irony versus sincerity" (a third aspect of speaker attitude) will become "prominent with compliments"; and speaker attitude is also likely to be "of special concern" when constructing directives (Taavitsainen and Jucker 2008a: 7; cf. Culpeper and Archer 2008).

The benefit of a "fuzziness" approach is that it allows for the fact that individual instances of a particular speech act may vary in their degree of conformity to the prototypical manifestation of that act – to the extent that their group identity can be vague. Archer (2005: 127–128, 339–340) therefore opts to identify macro speech act categories when documenting the speech acts that were utilized in the historical English courtroom (1640–1760). By way of illustration, commissive/directive speech acts are captured by the "Counsel" macro speech act category, and include caution, warn, threaten, coerce, advise and recommend; directive (and, more specifically, requirement) speech acts are captured by the "Require" macro speech act category, and include command, order, direct and demand; and directive (and, more specifically, requestive) speech acts are captured by the "Request" macro speech act category, and include desire, plead, beseech, implore and appeal.

3 Im/politeness studies relating to the EModE period

The speech acts that have received most attention to date (in both a synchronic and diachronic context) are those that constitute face-threatening acts (henceforth FTAs); requests, apologies, complaints, and thanks. For example, Busse (2008), Jacobsson (2002) and Taavitsainen and Jucker (2008b) are amongst a number of speech act researchers to make use of Brown and Levinson's (1987 [1978]) politeness theory to explain EModE requests, thanks, and compliments. As Brown and Levinson's theory promotes Goffman's (1967: 5) idea that every rational human being understands s/he and his/her conversational interactant(s) have face wants that are maintained/enhanced using a variety of (super-)strategies, it has also proved useful to Fitzmaurice (2000), when demonstrating how the modal verbs *can*, *may* and *will* were manipulated during the EModE period so as to express both tentativeness and insistence (see Section 3.2.). The majority of researchers, however, (e.g. Brown and Gilman 1989; Calvo 1992; Hope 1994; Kopytko 1993, 1995; Nevalainen and Raumolin-Brunberg 1995; Raumolin-Brunberg 1996; Nevala 2004; Walker 2007) have utilized Brown and Levinson's approach to investigate EModE address terms (including pronominal usage). Brown and Gilman's (1989) exploration of Shakespeare's use of address terms in *Hamlet, King Lear, Macbeth*, and *Othello* is probably the most well-known politeness study of the EModE period. Studies involving *you* and *thou* include Hope's

(1994) investigation of (conversations recounted in) depositions made to the Durham ecclesiastical court in the 1560s, and Walker's (2007) investigation of trial, drama, and witness deposition data (taken from the *Corpus of English Dialogues*). Walker's work, in particular, documents the relationship between the demise of *thou* during the EModE period and factors such as the context-of-utterance and the age, sex and rank of the interlocutors (cf. Brown and Gilman 1960: 225–227).

3.1 Address forms and politeness: a case study of the Bacons

One of the main findings in respect to EModE address formulae is that – like their modern counterparts – they exhibit positive and negative politeness (see, e.g., Nevalainen and Raumolin-Brunberg 1995; Raumolin-Brunberg 1996; Nevala 2004). For example, Nevala (2004) investigated the (early) 17th-century correspondence of a prestigious Norfolk family (the Bacons) as a means of determining the way(s) in which relative power and social distance affected the forms of address/reference utilized in respect to Sir Nicholas (Lord Keeper for Elizabeth I and head of the Bacon family) and his eldest son, Nathaniel (cf. Brown and Levinson's [1987 (1978)] argument that power, distance and the FTA's "ranking of imposition" determine politeness levels). Nevala (2004: 2138) found that, when directly addressing Sir Nicholas, writers utilized strategies denoting "extreme negative politeness, regardless of the distance" between them, and concluded that this was due to Sir Nicholas's superior social status, as well as his role as head of the family (in what was a highly stratified society). In contrast, the direct address that Nathaniel Bacon received from his correspondents was very much dependent on (his relationship with) them: nuclear family members tended to use positive politeness strategies (i.e. first name, last name, kinship term or a combination of the three); family servants utilized negative politeness (i.e. *right worshipful, your worship,* or *your honour*); (more) distant writers alternated between neutral and negatively polite formula (i.e. *cousin Bacon, Sir, Right Worshipful*). Nevala (2004: 2147) contends that Brown and Levinson's model therefore accounts well for the usage of EModE address terms. But she is less convinced of its value in respect to reference terms: nuclear family members would occasionally use both kinship term and title to identify Sir Nicholas, for example. Nevala also found evidence of non-kin writers (both equal in power and subservient to the referent) using kinship terms, which leads her to suggest that the choice of referential term(s) might have been more conscious than the choice of address term(s). Nevala (2004: 2149) further suggests that the possibility of letters being read by others (and thus the need to accommodate to the terms likely to be used by not only the addressee but also those persons who are not overtly referred to in the letters) may account for this. She goes on to propose a further axis for describing EModE referents (addressee-referent), to complement the axes previously identified by Brown and Levinson (1987 [1978]) and Comrie (1976) in respect to modern data (the speaker-addressee axis, the speaker-referent axis, the speaker-bystander axis and the speaker-setting axis).

3.2 Is "deference" the same as "politeness" in an EModE context?

Brown and Levinson (1987 [1978]) believe that, in a modern context, giving deference links to power and, as such, provides a further example of negative politeness (see also Leech's 1983 approbation and modesty maxims). Watts (2003: 80, 176) disagrees, contending that deference is not politeness if it constitutes the norm for a particular activity type: rather, it equates to "politic" behavior. Nevala (2004) is not convinced of the merit of the "politic" approach to deference in a diachronic context, however, as she believes that address formulae could (and did) "work within, and for, politeness" in the EModE period (see also Raumolin-Brunberg [1996: 168], who argues that the choice of address form was "never [...] predictable" in the *Corpus of Early English Correspondence*).

Klein's (1994a, 1994b) studies of the development of linguistic thinking as it related to politeness in the late 17th and early 18th centuries may offer support to Nevala and Raumolin-Brunberg's stance – especially given the affinity of some of Klein's findings with Brown and Levinson's (1987 [1987]) idea of the "model person": Klein emphasizes the link between a growing politeness awareness and an ideology of standardization, which (rather than merely promoting lexical or grammatical correctness) sought to address "the question of effective language use [...] founded on the conditions of gentlemanly and urban conversation" (Klein 1994a: 43). The Third Earl of Shaftesbury's promotion of a "model of gentlemanly conversation" (Klein 1994a: 43) is thought to have been particularly influential. Klein (1994b) also highlights the importance of the socio historical conditions, in particular:
a. the new discursive/socializing conditions afforded by the declining influence of Church and Court,
b. the newly-emerging patterns of urban development (which would house not only the aristocrats and greater/lesser gentry, but also the "pseudo-gentry, professionals and commercial elements" [Klein 1994b: 11]), and
c. the growth of print media/the deregulation of the press (after 1695).

The cumulative effect, according to Klein (1994b: 12), was that politeness became "a model of cultural action" that not only shaped "talk" in its literal sense, but also helped to "shape a wide range of cultural institutions and practices in the eighteenth century", from letter writing (see, e.g., Fitzmaurice 2000) to educational and scientific treatises (see, e.g., Atkinson 1999). For example, Fitzmaurice (2000) draws on Boyer's (1702: 106, 108) idea of politeness as "a dextrous management of our Words and Actions, whereby we make other People have better Opinions of us and themselves" (cited in Klein 1994b: 4), as a means of justifying Margaret Cavendish's apparent manipulation of the (multiple) semantic-pragmatic meanings of the modals *can*, *may* and *will* in her *CCXI Social Letters*. Cavendish's purpose, it seemed, was to construct a voice (for herself and/or her writing persona) that was not "completely authoritative [n]or wholly tentative" and, as such, was attentive to the face issues of herself/her persona(e) and her audience (Fitzmaurice 2000: 8). Put simply, the "art" of letter writing, at this time, appeared to involve balancing the notions of "appropriate discourse and proper stance" in a way that allowed for "the spirit of philosophical enquiry" (Fitzmaurice 2000: 17–18).

As Watts (2003: 40) highlights, the main focus of Klein's (1994a, 1994b) work is politeness$_1$ as opposed to politeness$_2$: that is, it captures the way(s) in which polite behavior was evaluated and commented on by lay members of the EModE language community – and, more particularly, the "gentrification" that politeness underwent at this time (in order to appropriate a new hegemonic discourse). I would therefore contend that we need more studies that seek (like Fitzmaurice 2000) to explain the linguistic consequence(s) (i.e. the politeness$_1$) of the so-called "gentrification of politeness", if we are to fully appreciate EModE conceptions of facework (i.e. the communicative strategies that interactants used to preserve and/or contravene socially-appropriate behavior).

3.3 EModE impoliteness studies

Researchers have begun to investigate instances of face attack (as opposed to face maintenance), using different Shakespeare plays (see, e.g., Culpeper 1998; Rudanko 2006; Bousfield 2007). For example, Bousfield explores a conversation between two of the main characters of *Henry IV, Part I*, where Hal and Falstaff take on the identities of the characters of Hal's father (King Henry IV) and Hal respectively (II.iv). Using Leech's (1983: 142–144) definition of banter as his starting point (i.e. saying something which is obviously untrue and obviously impolite as a means of achieving solidarity/social bonding with one's interlocutor), Bousfield shows how Shakespeare intersperses the dialogue of Hal-as-King with not only banter – that is, comments about Falstaff that are obviously untrue – but also comments that are actually true and, moreover, extremely offensive. Thus, Falstaff (who is known to be diseased) is described by Hal-as-King as being "a trunk of humours" and a "swollen parcel of dropsies". What we are describing here is a stylistic device utilized by Shakespeare to aid characterization. Nevertheless, Bousfield (2007: 216) is careful to remind readers of Mills's (2003: 14) observation that we can manipulate banter in a modern (and, it would seem, a historical) context so that, although what we say is superficially non-serious, it is actually closer to our "true feelings than perceived to be by H". As such, it becomes "surreptitiously face damaging".

Kryk-Kastovsky (2006) and Archer (2008) draw from EModE courtroom transcripts for their discussions of face attack. Archer does so with an important caveat: that some of the existing impoliteness models (e.g., Culpeper 1996, 2005; Culpeper et al. 2003; Bousfield 2008) need to be extended if they are to capture verbal aggression more generally, and not just intentional impoliteness. Archer has done so in ways that draw upon Goffman's (1967: 14) "intentional", "incidental", and "unintended" categories relating to face threat, as opposed to the first only, as Culpeper et al. (2003: 1550) do (as a means of identifying impoliteness, for example). This has enabled her to differentiate between malicious face attacks (where the primary intent was to cause damage), and instances when, for example, defendants and lawyers undertook verbal acts which they knew might have "offensive consequences" (cf. Goffman 1967: 14).

4 Discourses and discourse strategies

Modals, address formulae, and implicature were not the only means by which face was managed in the EModE period, according to Culpeper and Kytö (1999): hedges such as *about* and discourse markers (henceforth DMs) such as *well* and *why* were also used to strategically manage face (as well as information, discourse, and style). For Culpeper and Kytö (1999: 299), style is "involved whenever a hedge is used", regardless of the activity/text-type: it relates to the interactants' understanding of the in/formality of their particular (discoursal) situation, putting an interactant at ease and/or creating a sense of involvement/solidarity, etc. (all of which also appear to relate to Brown and Levinson's [1987 (1978)] concept of "positive politeness"). In addition, Culpeper and Kytö (1999: 304–305) identify an interesting relationship between activity (or text) types and specific EModE hedges: for example, *about* "occurred with striking frequency" in the EModE witness depositions within the *Corpus of English Dialogues*; this is presumably because it offered the user a strategic means of adding "fuzziness to a claim" without appearing to be deliberately withholding information (cf. "[...] *about* a month agoe, as this Examinate was coming towards his Mothers house [...] *about* ten Roodes distant from the same house: and *about* two or three nights after [...]": taken from a deposition relating to the 1612 examinations of the *Pendle Witches*). Similarly, the DMs *why* and *well* occurred very frequently in their drama data, and appeared to "play a role in managing that discourse" (Culpeper and Kytö 1999: 305): *why*, for example, was used to signal (i) S's surprise and/or "challenge something the previous speaker had said" and, (ii) a change of speaker (see Section 4.1).

4.1 Discourse Markers

Culpeper and Kytö's identification of primarily pragmatic/discoursal strategies is not surprising, given that hedges "help signal speakers' feelings and attitudes to their messages, their co-participants and the situation as a whole" (Nikula 1996: 11–12; cited in Culpeper and Kytö 1999: 294). Brinton confirms that some types of DMs share the pragmatic (textual/expressive), procedural (inferential), metalinguistic, and/or sociolinguistic functions of hedges (e.g. relate to turn-taking and politeness), and also lists their phonological, syntactic and semantic features (Brinton 1996):

- DMs are phonologically short items that normally occur sentence-initially (but can occur in medial or final position; see, e.g., Fraser 1999: 938);
- DMs are syntactically independent elements (often constituting separate intonation units) which occur with high frequency (in oral discourse in particular);
- DMs lack semantic content (i.e. they are non-referential/non-propositional in meaning);
- DMs are non-truth-conditional elements, and thus optional (i.e. they may be deleted).

Fraser (1999: 946, 950) further suggests that (modern-day) DMs tend to be "drawn from the syntactic classes of conjunctions, adverbials, or prepositional phrases". As such, although DMs constitute a pragmatic class (in the sense that their more specific interpretation is "negotiated" by the context), they nevertheless maintain "the syntactic properties associated with their class membership": *but*, for example, will denote its core meaning of "simple contrast" plus whatever additional interpretation is warranted, given the context-of-use.

4.2 Identifying DMs of times past

Historically-focused research relating to DMs can be synchronic (i.e. researchers explore a particular time-period that is fixed (be it years, decades, centuries, etc.) or diachronic (i.e. they explore successive synchronic stages of time). Whether synchronic or diachronic, most studies focus not only on "what they [DMs] are, what they mean, and what function(s) they manifest" (Fraser 1999: 933) but also on how individual DMs "pattern" and how those patterns have been derived over time. For example, Brinton (2006) has identified the following syntactic pathways as ones which might lead to DM development:
- adverb/preposition > conjunction > DM;
- predicate adverb > sentential adverb structure > parenthetical DM (cf. Traugott 1995);
- imperative matrix clause > indeterminate structure > parenthetical DM;
- relative/adverbial clause > parenthetical DM.

In contrast, Traugott and Dasher (2002) have identified pathways that are more semantic in orientation, namely:
- truth-conditional > non-truth conditional > non-truth conditional,
- content > procedural, and nonsubjective > subjective > intersubjective meaning,
- scope within the proposition > scope over the proposition > scope over discourse.

Diachronic studies of DMs capturing the EModE period include Jucker's (1997) study of *well*, Fischer's (1998) study of *marry*, and Schwenter and Traugott's (2000) study of *in fact*. For example, Jucker (1997: 93) traces the development of *well* from the Old English to the Modern English period and concludes that it exhibits both a textual and an intertextual function historically, but that "one function typically predominates over the other" (cf. Traugott [1982], who shows how *well* (*right* and *why*) move from a propositional through a textual to an interpersonal meaning). *Marry* also exhibited textual and intertextual functions, according to Fischer (1998); the former, at the beginning of a turn, and the latter, as a means of expressing a range of speaker attitudes. Drawing on the OED, Fischer (1998) initially shows how *marry* is first attested in the second half of the 14th century, as an "oath or an ejaculatory invocation" (to the Virgin Mary). He goes on to identify a growth in the use of *marry* during the period 1570–1640, but it had come to function as an interjection as opposed to a religious invocation. Fischer suggests that these tendencies (i.e. developing into a pragmatically weaker interjection/losing any religious association) may also account for the (historical development of) other religious oaths. Schwenter and Traugott (2000) adopt a similar form-to-meaning approach to show how the DM *in fact* came to take on epistemic modal meanings in contrastive (or "dialogic") contexts (that is, contexts where the speakers/writers (SPs/Ws) presented opposing arguments to real or imaginary interlocutors). The development of *in fact* is shown to be as follows by Schwenter and Traugott (2000: 12): manner adverb > adversative adverb (expressing contrast to someone else's or to the locutor's own prior proposition) > elaborating DM (signalling that what follows is a stronger argument than what precedes, with respect to SP/W's purpose at the point in the discourse). We have also come to associate the *all I said/did was X* pattern with adversitivity and refutation: the specificational *all*-cleft construction (with an ALL-NP-V-BE-X string) arose around 1600 (in dialogic contexts), and then quickly moved from an 'everything' meaning to an 'only' meaning with a clausal focus, becoming conventionalized in the later part of the 17th century (i.e. the 'only' meaning became semanticized into the construction). As such, the construction exhibited a similar switch-referencing characteristic to modern *all*-clefts (cf. Bonnelli's 1992 "change of posture"). That is to say, "in most cases the most important function appears not to be to fill an open proposition, but rather to highlight an upcoming statement as salient, and impose an exhaustive reading on it" (Traugott 2008: 162). Traugott (2008: 159) provides us with the following example (1), dating from 1658, taken from the Chadwyck Healey website (lion.chadwyck.com; last accessed 14 April 2017):

(1) [...] he doth me notorious wrong, I did not mention any Principles of Vnity in this place [...] *All I said was this, That we doe not separate from other Churches, but from their Accidentall Errours* (1658 Bramhall, *Schisme Garded*)

EModE synchronic studies of DMs include Taavitsainen (1995), Blake (1992, 1996), Brown and Gilman (1989), Kryk-Kastovsky (1998), and Busse (1999). Using representations of direct speech taken from literature texts, Taavitsainen (1995: 439, 465) shows how some interjections (such as *ah, alas, benedicte, eh, fie,* and *tush*) exhibited DM-like characteristics: that is, "they encode[d] speaker attitudes and communicative intentions", they sought to deliberately manipulate "reader involvement", and they also served textual functions (but see Fraser [1999: 943], who argues that interjections are best regarded as pragmatic idioms). Blake (1992: 1996) investigates the discourse markers *why* and *what* in Shakespeare's *Henry VI Part 3, Two Gentlemen of Verona,* and *Othello*, showing how the former was used to draw a logical conclusion from what has gone before (and often gave a tone of superiority and potential disparagement), and the latter was used to express surprise or incredulity (and, on occasion, to express contempt or scorn). Kryk-

Kastovsky (1998), Brown and Gilman (1989) and Busse (1999) have all analysed the DMs *pray* and *prithee*; Kryk-Kastovsky, in transcripts of the EModE trials of Titus Oates and Lady Alice Lisle, and Brown and Gilman and Busse, in Shakespearean plays. Kryk-Kastovsky found that *pray* and *prithee* were amongst the most frequent of the DMs in her trial data (although they were not overly frequent). *Pray and prithee* constituted shortened forms of their fuller (propositionally-intact) forms *I pray you* and *I pray thee* in the EModE period; their purpose was to add deference to, for example, questions and requests. This makes them ideally suited to the (historical) courtroom context. That said, Brown and Gilman and Busse have also found that they were used quite extensively by Shakespeare. They disagree, however, on whether they should be seen as ingroup identity markers or deference markers (for further detail of these and other EModE DMs, see Jucker 2002; for diachronic studies, see Akimoto 2000; Traugott and Dasher 2002: 252–255; Brinton 2010).

5 Summary

This chapter has documented studies that have utilized dramatic dialogue, courtroom data, pamphlets, and letters (etc.) to explore particular pragmatic/discoursal features within the EModE period. Some of these studies have adopted a "usage-based approach to language change", which prioritizes the grammaticalization of linguistic elements over time (see, e.g., Traugott 2004: 538). Others have taken an approach that is more overtly sociolinguistic in orientation (see, e.g., the investigations relating to im/politeness). What I have not discussed in detail is the number of researchers who focus on multiple pragmatic/discoursal features within a given text-type/genre in order to say something meaningful about (the structure of) EModE discourse/genre(s) more generally – or, indeed, the work of a particular playwright. Length constraints prevent a detailed overview of all of the genres that have been studied to date. Readers are therefore encouraged to utilize the studies in Jucker et al. (eds.) (1999), as a starting point for further investigation. Suffice it to say, there is a wealth of data exploring Shakespeare's works: Rudanko (1993), for example, has utilized Grice's (1975) cooperative principle, Brown and Levinson's (1987 [1978]) politeness theory, and speech act theory in his studies of *Othello*, *Coriolanus*, and *Timon of Athens*. Magnusson (1999) has also drawn on Brown and Levinson (1987 [1978]), in conjunction with Bourdieu's (1991) idea of the linguistic market, to explore the rhetoric of verbal interaction in Shakespeare. In addition, she compares Shakespeare's works with those of his contemporaries (e.g., Erasmus). Taavitsainen is among a number of researchers who have investigated the dialogic elements of EModE medical/scientific writing;

drawing on a corpus of medical treatises originally published between 1375–1750 (see, e.g., Taavitsainen and Pahta 1997). Taavitsainen (1999) shows how instruction in scientific handbooks was often given in the form of fictional conversations between a master and a pupil. Her approach involves combining close reading with computerized searches for elements with dialogic potential (see Jucker et al. 1999: 20). Correspondence is probably the most-researched genre in the EModE period, however. The bulk of the studies have benefited from the development of the *Corpus of Early English Correspondence*. Indeed, the latter has been used to study address terms, directives and salutations, personal pronouns, discourse markers, reporting, subjectivity and stance (see, e.g., Nevalainen and Raumolin-Brunberg 1995; Raumolin-Brunberg 1996; Fitzmaurice 2000).

Many of the historical studies highlighted above are socio-pragmatic in orientation. For example, researchers who study correspondence regularly take account of issues relating not only to the production and distribution of letters, but also to the levels of literacy, relevant social distinctions (in particular, social status and gender), the conventional form of the letter and the possible impact of letter-writing manuals on the latter (see, e.g., Palander-Collin 2010). Some researchers have also developed socio-pragmatic annotation schemes, which provide historically appropriate information respecting the status, role, age and gender of the interactants *at the utterance level* (see, e.g., Archer and Culpeper 2003), and have used these schemes to explain the discursive strategies of, for example, courtroom participants in the later EModE period (see, e.g., Archer 2005). This would suggest that an emerging trend, when looking at historical language use, is one which pays attention to the "interplay between the individual, language and society" (Palander-Collin 2010; see, also, Culpeper 2010); that is to say, to what is happening, linguistically, within a given text or speech event (i.e. the micro-interactional aspects), to what was happening around it (which necessitates our making use of both the insights of historians and also contemporary opinion/ideas), and, finally, to "how" and "why" (i.e., the purpose[s] for which) it was produced.

6 References

Aijmer, Karin. 1996. *Conversational Routines in English*. London: Longman.
Akimoto, Minoji. 2000. The grammaticalisation of the verb "pray". In: Olga Fischer, Annette Rosenbach, and Dieter Stein (eds.), *Pathways of Change: Grammaticalisation in English*, 67–84. Amsterdam/Philadelphia: John Benjamins.
Archer, Dawn. 2005. *Questions and Answers in the English Courtroom (1640–1760)*. Amsterdam/Philadelphia: John Benjamins.

Archer, Dawn. 2008. Verbal aggression and impoliteness: Related or synonymous? In: Derek Bousfield and Miriam Locher (eds.), *Impoliteness in Language: Studies on its Interplay with Power in Theory and Practice*, 181–207. Berlin/New York: Mouton de Gruyter.
Archer, Dawn and Jonathan Culpeper. 2003. Sociopragmatic annotation: New directions and possibilities in historical corpus linguistics. In: Andrew Wilson, Paul Rayson, and Tony McEnery (eds.), *Corpus Linguistics by the Lune: A Festschrift for Geoffrey Leech*, 37–58. Frankfurt: Peter Lang.
Arnovick, Leslie K. 1994. The expanding discourse of promises in Present-Day English: A case study in historical pragmatics. *Folia Linguistica Historica* 15(1–2): 175–191.
Arnovick, Leslie K. 1999. *Diachronic Pragmatics. Seven Case Studies in English Illocutionary Development*. Amsterdam/Philadelphia: John Benjamins.
Atkinson, Dwight. 1999. *Scientific Discourse in Sociohistorical Context: The Philosophical Transactions of the Royal Society of London, 1675–1975*. Mahwah, NJ: Laurence Erlbaum.
Austin, John L. 1962. *How to Do Things with Words*. Oxford: Oxford University Press.
Blake, Norman F. 1992. Why and what in Shakespeare. In: Toshiyuki Takamiya and Richard Beale (eds.), *Chaucer to Shakespeare: Essays in Honour of Shinsuke Ando*, 179–193. Cambridge: D. S. Brewer.
Blake, Norman F. 1996. *Essays on Shakespeare's Language*. Misterton: The Language Press.
Blum-Kulka, Shoshana and Juliane House. 1989. Cross-cultural and situational variation in requesting behavior. In: Blum-Kulka (eds.), 123–154.
Blum-Kulka, Shoshana, Juliane House, and Gabriele Kasper (eds.). 1989. *Cross-cultural Pragmatics: Requests and Apologies*. Norwood, NJ: Ablex
Bonnelli, Elena T. 1992. "All I'm saying is …" : The correlation of form and function in pseudo-cleft sentences. *Literary and Linguistic Computing* 7(1): 30–42.
Borgmeier, Raymond, Herbert Grabes, and Andreas H. Jucker (eds.). 1998. *Anglistentag 1997 Giessen Proceedings*. Trier: Wissenschaftlicher Verlag.
Bourdieu, Pierre. 1991. *Language and Symbolic Power*. Cambridge: Polity Press.
Bousfield, Derek. 2007. "Never a truer word said in jest": A pragmastylistic analysis of impoliteness as banter in Henry IV, Part I". In: Marina Lambrou and Peter Stockwell (eds.), *Contemporary Stylistics*, 210–220. London: Continuum.
Bousfield, Derek. 2008. *Impoliteness in Interaction*. Amsterdam/Philadelphia: John Benjamins.
Boyer, Abel. 1702. *The English Theophrastus*. London: W. Turner.
Brinton, Laurel J. 1996. *Pragmatic Markers in English*. Berlin/New York: Mouton de Gruyter.
Brinton, Laurel J. 2001. Historical discourse analysis. In: Deborah Schiffrin, Deborah Tannen, and Heidi E. Hamilton (eds.), *The Handbook of Discourse Analysis*, 138–160. Oxford: Blackwell.
Brinton, Laurel. 2006. Pathways in the development of pragmatic markers in English. In: Ans van Kemenade and Bettelou Los (eds.), *The Handbook of the History of English*, 307–334. London: Blackwell.
Brinton, Laurel J. 2010. Discourse markers. In: Jucker and Taavitsainen (eds.), 285–314.
Brown, Penelope and Stephen C. Levinson. 1987 [1978]. *Politeness. Some Universals in Language Usage*. Cambridge: Cambridge University Press.
Brown, Roger and Albert Gilman. 1960. The pronouns of power and solidarity. In: Thomas A. Sebeok (ed.), *Style in Language*, 253–276. Cambridge, MA: MIT Press.
Brown, Roger and Albert Gilman. 1989. Politeness theory and Shakespeare's four major tragedies. *Language in Society* 18(2): 159–212.

Busse, Ulrich. 1999. "Prithee now, say you will, and go about it". Prithee *vs.* pray you *as discourse markers in the Shakespeare corpus*. In: Fritz-Wilhelm Neumann and Sabine Schülting (eds.), *Anglistentag 1998 Erfurt Proceedings*, 485–500. Trier: Wissenschaftlicher Verlag.

Busse, Ulrich. 2002. Changing politeness strategies in English requests: A diachronic investigation. In: Jacek Fisiak (ed.), *Studies in English Historical Linguistics and Philology: A Festschrift for Akio Oizumi*, 17–35. Frankfurt/Main: Peter Lang.

Busse, Ulrich. 2008. An inventory of directives in Shakespeare's King Lear. *In:* Jucker and Taavitsainen (eds.), 85–114.

Calvo, Carla. 1992. Pronouns of address and social negotiation in As You Like It. *Language and Literature* 1(1): 5–27.

Claridge, Claudia. 2005. Questions in Early Modern English pamphlets. *Journal of Historical Pragmatics* 6(1): 133–168.

Cole, Peter and Jerry Morgan (eds.). 1975. *Syntax and Semantics 3: Speech Acts*. New York: Academic Press.

Comrie, Bernard. 1976. *Linguistic Politeness Axes: Speaker-addressee, Speaker-referent, Speaker-bystander*. Pragmatics Microfiche 1.7: A3. Cambridge: Department of Linguistics, University of Cambridge.

Culpeper, Jonathan. 1996. Towards an anatomy of impoliteness. *Journal of Pragmatics* 25: 349–367.

Culpeper, Jonathan. 1998. (Im)politeness in drama. In: Peter Verdonk, Mick Short, and Jonathan Culpeper (eds.), *Exploring the Language of Drama: From Text to Context*, 83–95. London: Routledge.

Culpeper, Jonathan. 2005. Impoliteness and The Weakest Link. *Journal of Politeness Research* 1 (1): 35–72.

Culpeper, Jonathan. 2010. Historical sociopragmatics. In: Jucker and Taavitsainen (eds.), 69–94.

Culpeper, Jonathan and Dawn Archer. 2008. Requests and directness in Early Modern English trial proceedings and play texts, 1640–1760. In: Jucker and Taavitsainen, (eds.), 45–84.

Culpeper, Jonathan and Merja Kytö. 1999. Modifying pragmatic force: Hedges in a corpus of Early Modern English dialogues. In: Jucker (eds.), 293–312.

Culpeper, Jonathan and Elena Semino. 2000. Constructing witches and spells: Speech acts and activity types in Early Modern England. *Journal of Historical Pragmatics* 1(1): 97–116.

Culpeper, Jonathan, Derek Bousfield, and Anne Wichmann. 2003. Impoliteness revisited: With special reference to dynamic and prosodic aspects. *Journal of Pragmatics* 35(10–11): 1545–1579.

Edmonson, Willis J. and Juliane House. 1981. *Let's Talk and Talk about it: A Pedagogic Interactional Grammar of English*. Munich: Urban & Schwarzenberg.

Fairclough, Norman F. 1993. *Discourse and Social Change*. Cambridge: Polity Press.

Fischer, Andreas. 1998. Marry*: From religious invocation to discourse marker*. In: Borgmeier (eds.), 35–46.

Fitzmaurice, Susan. 2000. Tentativeness and insistence in the expression of politeness in Margaret Cavendish's Sociable Letters. *Language and Literature* 9(1): 7–24.

Fraser, Bruce. 1999. What are discourse markers? *Journal of Pragmatics* 31: 931–952.

Goffman, Erving. 1967. *Interaction Ritual*. Chicago: Aldine.

Görlach, Manfred. 1991. *Introduction to Early Modern English*. Cambridge: Cambridge University Press.

Grice, H. Paul. 1975. Logic and conversation. In: Cole and Morgan (eds.), 41–58.

Hope, Jonathan. 1994. The use of thou *and* you *in Early Modern spoken English: Evidence from depositions in the Durham Ecclesiastical Court Records.* In: Dieter Kastovsky (ed.), *Studies in Early Modern English*, 141–152. Berlin/New York: Mouton de Gruyter.
Jacobs, Andreas and Andreas H. Jucker. 1995. The historical perspective in pragmatics. In: Jucker (ed.), 3–33.
Jacobsson, Mattias. 2002. Thank you *and* thanks *in Early Modern English. ICAME Journal* 26: 63–80.
Jucker, Andreas H. 1997. The discourse marker *well* in the history of English. *English Language and Linguistics* 1(1): 91–110.
Jucker, Andreas H., Gerd Fritz, and Franz Lebsanft. 1999. Historical dialogue analysis: Roots and traditions in the study of the Romance languages, German and English. In: Jucker (eds.), 1–34.
Jucker, Andreas H. 2000. *History of English and English Historical Linguistics.* Stuttgart: Klett.
Jucker, Andreas H. 2002. Discourse markers in Early Modern English. In: Richard J. Watts and Peter Trudgill (eds.), *Alternative Histories of English*, 210–230. London: Routledge.
Jucker, Andreas H. (ed.). 1995. *Historical Pragmatics. Pragmatic Developments in the History of English.* Amsterdam/Philadelphia: John Benjamins.
Jucker, Andreas H. and Irma Taavitsainen. 2000. Diachronic speech act analysis: Insults from flyting to flaming. *Journal of Historical Pragmatics* 1(1): 67–95.
Jucker, Andreas H. and Irma Taavitsainen. 2003. Diachronic perspectives on address term systems: introduction. In: Irma Taavitsainen and Andreas H. Jucker. (eds.), *Diachronic Perspectives on Address Term Systems*, 1–26. Amsterdam/Philadelphia: John Benjamins.
Jucker, Andreas H. and Irma Taavitsainen. 2008. Apologies in the history of English: Routinized and lexicalized expressions of responsibility and regret. In: Jucker and Taavitsainen (eds.), 229–244.
Jucker, Andreas H., Gerd Fritz, and Franz Lebsanft (eds.). 1999. *Historical Dialogue Analysis.* Amsterdam/Philadelphia: John Benjamins.
Jucker, Andreas H. and Irma Taavitsainen (eds.). 2008. *Speech Acts in the History of English.* Amsterdam/Philadelphia: John Benjamins.
Jucker, Andreas H. and Irma Taavitsainen (eds.). 2010. *Handbook of Historical Pragmatics.* Berlin/New York: De Gruyter Moutor.
Klein, Lawrence E. 1994a. "Politeness" as linguistic ideology in late seventeenth- and eighteenth- century England. In: Dieter Stein and Ingrid Tieken-Boon van Ostade (eds.), *Towards a Standard English 1600–1800*, 31–50. Berlin/New York: Mouton de Gruyter.
Klein, Lawrence E. 1994b. *Shaftesbury and the Culture of Politeness: Moral Discourse and Cultural Politics in Early Eighteenth-century England.* Cambridge: Cambridge University Press.
Kohnen, Thomas. 2002. Methodological problems in corpus based historical pragmatics: The case of English directives. In: Karin Ajimer and Bengt Altenberg (eds.), *Language and Computers. Advances in Corpus Linguistics. Papers from the 23rd International Conference on English Language Research on Computerized Corpora (ICAME 23). Göteborg, 22–26 May,* 237–247. Amsterdam: Rodopi.
Kohnen, Thomas. 2004. "Let mee bee so bold to request you to tell mee": Constructions with "let me" and the history of English directives. *Journal of Historical Pragmatics* 5(1): 159–173.
Kopytko, Roman. 1993. *Polite Discourse in Shakespeare's English.* Poznań: Wydawnictwo Naukowe Uniwersytetu im. Adam Mickiewcza w Poznaniu.
Kopytko, Roman. 1995. Linguistic politeness strategies in Shakespeare's plays. In: Jucker (ed.), 515–540.

Kryk-Kastovsky, Barbara. 1998. Pragmatic particles in Early Modern English court trials. In: Borgmeier (eds.), 45–56.
Kryk-Kastovsky, Barbara. 2006. Impoliteness in Early Modern English courtroom discourse. *Journal of Historical Pragmatics* 7(2): 213–244.
Leech, Geoffrey N. 1983. *Principles of Pragmatics*. London: Longman.
Levinson, Stephen C. 1983. *Pragmatics*. Cambridge: Cambridge University Press.
Magnusson, Lynne. 1999. *Shakespeare and Social Dialogue: Dramatic Language and Elizabethan Letters*. Cambridge: Cambridge University Press.
Mills, Sarah. 2003. *Gender and Politeness*. Cambridge: Cambridge University Press.
Nevala, Minna. 2004. Accessing politeness axes: Forms of address and terms of reference in early English correspondence. *Journal of Pragmatics* 36: 2125–2160.
Nevalainen, Terttu and Helena Raumolin-Brunberg. 1995. Constraints on politeness: The pragmatics of address formulae in Early English correspondence. In: Jucker (ed.), 541–601.
Nikula, Tarja. 1996. *Pragmatic Force Markers: A Study in Interlanguage Pragmatics*. Studia Philologica Jyväskyläensia: University of Jyväskylä.
Palander-Collin, M. 2010. Correspondence. In: Jucker and Taavitsainen (eds.), 651–677.
Raumolin-Brunberg, Helena. 1996. Forms of address in Early English correspondence. In: Terttu Nevalainen and Helena Raumolin-Brunberg (eds.), *Sociolinguistics and Language History: Studies based on the Corpus of Early English Correspondence,* 167–181. Amsterdam: Rodopi.
Rudanko, Juhani. 1993. *Pragmatic Approaches to Shakespeare. Essays on* Othello, Coriolanus *and* Timon of Athens. Lanham: University Press of America.
Rudanko, Juhani. 2006. Aggravated impoliteness and two types of speaker intention in an episode in Shakespeare's Timon of Athens. *Journal of Pragmatics* 38(6): 829–841.
Schlieben-Lange, Brigitte. 1976. Für einer historische Analyse von Sprechakten. In: Heinrich Weber and Harald Weydt (eds.), *Sprachtheorie und Pragmatik, Akten des 10. Linguistischen Kolloquiums Tübingen 1975*, 113–119. Tübingen: Niemeyer.
Schlieben-Lange, Brigitte. 1983. *Traditionen des Sprechens*. Stuttgart: Kohlhammer.
Schlieben-Lange, Brigitte and Heinrich Weydt. 1979. Streitgespräch zur historität von Sprechakten. *Linguistiche Berichte* 60: 65–78.
Schwenter, Scott A. and Elizabeth C. Traugott. 2000. Invoking scalarity: The development of in fact. *Journal of Historical Pragmatics* 1: 7–25.
Searle, John R. 1969. *Speech Acts: An Essay in the Philosophy of Language*. Cambridge: Cambridge University Press.
Searle, John R. 1975. Indirect speech acts. In: Cole and Morgan (eds.), 59–82.
Taavitsainen, Irma. 1995. Interjections in Early Modern English: From initiation of spoken to conventions of written language. In: Jucker (ed.), 439–465.
Taavitsainen, Irma. 1999. Dialogues in Late Medieval and Early Modern English medical writing. In: Jucker, Fritz, and Lebsanft (eds.), 243–268.
Taavitsainen, Irma and Andreas H. Jucker. 2008a. Speech acts now and then: Towards a pragmatic history of English. In: Jucker and Taavitsainen (eds.), 1–23.
Taavitsainen, Irma and Andreas H. Jucker. 2008b. "Methinks you seem more beautiful than ever": Compliments and gender in the history of English. In: Jucker and Taavitsainen (eds.), 195–228.
Taavitsainen, Irma and Päivi Pahta. 1997. The Corpus of Early English Medical Writing. *ICAME Journal* 21: 71–78.

Traugott, Elizabeth Closs. 1982. From propositional to textual and expressive meanings: Some semantic-pragmatic aspects of grammaticalization. In: Winfred P. Lehmann and Yakov Malkiel (eds.), *Perspectives on Historical Linguistics*, 245–271. Amsterdam/Philadelphia: John Benjamins.

Traugott, Elizabeth Closs. 1995. The role of the development of discourse markers in a theory of grammaticalization. Paper presented at the Twelfth International Conference on Historical Linguistics, Manchester, August 1995. http://www.stanford.edu/~traugott/ect-papersonline.html; last accessed 14 April 2017.

Traugott, Elizabeth Closs. 2004. Historical pragmatics. In: Laurence Horn and Gregory Ward (eds.), *The Handbook of Pragmatics*. Oxford: Blackwell, 538–561.

Traugott, Elizabeth Closs. 2008. "All that he endeavoured to prove was …": On the emergence of grammatical constructions in dialogual and dialogic contexts. In: Robin Cooper and Ruth Kempson (eds.), *Language in Flux: Dialogue Coordination, Language Variation, Change and Evolution*, 143–177. London: Kings College Publication.

Traugott, Elizabeth Closs and Richard Dasher. 2002. *Regularity in Semantic Change*. Cambridge: Cambridge University Press.

Tsui, Amy B. M. 1994. *English Conversation*. Oxford: Oxford University Press.

Valkonen, Petteri. 2008. Showing a little promise: Identifying and retrieving explicit illocutionary acts from a corpus of written prose. In: Jucker and Taavitsainen (eds.), 247–272.

Walker, Terry. 2007. Thou *and* you *in Early Modern English Dialogues: Trials, Depositions and Drama Comedy*. Amsterdam/Philadelphia: John Benjamins.

Watts, Richard J. 2003. *Politeness*. Cambridge: Cambridge University Press.

Wierzbicka, Anna. 1987. *English Speech Act Verbs: A Semantic Dictionary*. Sydney: Academic Press.

Anneli Meurman-Solin
Chapter 8:
Dialects

1 The concept of dialect —— **128**
2 Sources for the study of regional variation in Early Modern English —— **132**
3 Linguistic systems and subsystems illustrating dialectal variation —— **136**
4 Further research —— **145**
5 References —— **147**

Abstract: In comparison with both Middle English and Late Modern, and Present-day English, regional variation in the Early Modern English period has been a less intensively researched area owing to the lack of quantitatively and qualitatively valid data in digital form. Instead of the data-driven and data-oriented approach, historical dialectology focusing on this period has often yielded to language attitudes and the prescriptivist tradition, defining dialect use as non-standard and describing it with reference to marked features exclusively. In the 21st century, several new corpora have been compiled to increase the diatopic representativeness of EModE databases, those drawing on manuscripts being particularly relevant. In modern corpus-based dialect research, the description of linguistic systems at the local and regional levels is based on comprehensive inventories of all features in a particular area, not a pre-selected set of features, probably biased or prejudiced, alleged to permit a diagnosis of a particular variety as dialectal.

1 The concept of dialect

In English historical linguistics, dialects have been examined from a wide range of perspectives. These seem to reflect the prevailing theoretical and methodological approaches adopted in research on particular periods in the history of English, for example, the focus on standardization distinguishing dialectology in the Early Modern English period from that which draws on data from the earlier time-periods. The main claim in this chapter is that dialectology is rarely about diatopic variation exclusively. Research on dialects, in Modern and Present-day English in particular, tends instead to discuss attested variation in a particular

---

Anneli Meurman-Solin: Helsinki (Finland)

region or locality referring to a wide range of variables, chiefly sociolinguistically defined.

The diverse approaches to the discipline can be illustrated for example by the following four themes dialectologists have been concerned about. Firstly, dialects have been considered as reified entities (Milroy 1999; Benson 2001). As pointed out in Meurman-Solin (2004):

> There is a tendency to objectify or reify regional varieties by assuming they form relatively homogeneous – perhaps even relatively self-contained – entities or systems, a tendency to historicise by stressing socio-political rather than linguistic factors as legitimising the naming and describing of regional varieties in a particular way, and a tendency to hierarchicise, leading to the analysis of a regional variety with exclusive reference to a standardised variety (Meurman-Solin 2004: 27).

In this approach, the debate is often about whether a particular variety is a dialect or in fact a language, the case in point being the debated status of Scottish English in the Early Modern English period. This is a period in which a systematic preference for chiefly or uniquely Scottish features has been recorded, patterns of variation and change also, reflecting a sufficiently high degree of variety-internal uniformity to permit the use of the term "Scottish Standard" (Devitt 1989; Meurman-Solin 1993; see also Görlach 1996: 468–470; Dossena 2005: 37–55).

Secondly, regional variation has been studied from an explicitly sociolinguistic perspective, highlighting the pace and direction of change, the diffusion of innovative variants, in particular as conditioned by variables such as the informant's age, social rank, geographical and social mobility, and education. Among recent research, considerable advances in historical sociolinguistics have been made possible by the team involved in creating the family of the Early English Correspondence corpora (CEEC) (Nevalainen et al. 1998) (e.g. Nevalainen and Raumolin-Brunberg 1996, 2003; see Raumolin-Brunberg, Chapter 11). In these studies, "region" is just one of the many variables affecting how the CEEC family of corpora have been compiled and how long-term diachronic developments recorded in the data have been interpreted.

Thirdly, the approach adopted in the creation of linguistic atlases at the Institute for Historical Dialectology (IHD), University of Edinburgh, is to investigate diachronic, diatopic and diastratic variation. However, because the main goal is to map variation and change (i.e. to present the areal diffusion as maps of various kinds as illustrated in Williamson 2004: 126–128), theoretical thinking and the creation of sophisticated tools for data retrieval and analysis have focused on how to conceptualize the variables of time and space in synchrony and diachrony and to localize texts by the so-called "fitting technique" (on this pioneering work in historical dialectology at the IHD, see, for example, Laing

2004; Williamson 2004; and Laing and Lass 2006; for information on current projects of the IHD, see http://www.lel.ed.ac.uk/ihd/laos1/laos1.html (for LAOS) and http://www.lel.ed.ac.uk/ihd/laeme2/front_page/about_laeme.html (for LAEME); accessed 14 April 2017). It is noteworthy, however, that methods as well as principles and practices of corpus compilation tailored for periods such as Middle English and Older Scots are not directly transferable to the study of Early Modern English dialects but will have to be developed further for periods in which distinguishing the conditioning of time and space in isolation from that of other variables may not be possible. With the introduction of printing, the preferred practices of printing houses as well as the perceived wider appeal of standardized varieties meant that writing in a particular dialect was restricted to a limited range of genres. Consequently, explicitly defined criteria will have to be formulated to identify texts that can be claimed to represent a particular dialectal variety.

Fourthly, in the perhaps most widespread approach to dialects and dialectology, research in the field has invited the introduction of language attitudes. This suggests that dialectal features are – implicitly or explicitly – conceptualized as marked, or even stigmatized. The term type which reflects the comparative angle is also widespread: in contrast with standard varieties, dialects are non-standard or sub-standard, even though features cited as representing a particular dialect may be basic to a particular local or regional standard. Thus Görlach (1999) distinguishes between regional and local varieties by comparison with supraregional standards, focusing in his chapter on illustrating contemporary attitudes to the former, and commenting on how prescriptivist trends are reflected in grammars and word-lists recommending good usage and the avoidance of "non-standard" features (cf. Dossena 2005 on Scotticisms). Instead of drawing on texts that can be claimed to represent a particular dialectal variety by language-external criteria, Görlach quotes comments on distinctively dialectal language use in contemporary, or sometimes later literature, or varieties constructed for literary purposes, such as Stage Irish.

Research on dialects tends to focus on orthography, phonology and lexis. Görlach points out that

> Of all the linguistic levels, it is probably most difficult to distinguish between regional and social non-standard features in syntax, since both would have been levelled away by the prescriptive influence of the schools in the surviving written texts. Moreover, syntactic variation is more often a consequence of stylistic choice, depending on formality, text type and topic: where one writer may deliberately flout the rules of 'correct' syntax by using conversational style (in a private letter or in a personal diary not intended for anyone else to read), another may use simple syntax because he cannot do any better (Görlach 1999: 491).

The present chapter claims that the concept of dialectal variation should not be viewed as related to "non-standard features", nor is it appropriate to relate dialectal language use to stylistic choice. The passage quoted above does however illustrate the confusing ways of using the concept of dialect, the reference to register variation ("conversational style") being quite inappropriate in this context (cf. the discussion of stylistic competence in Johnston 1997: 51). In contrast with what seems to be implied by these remarks on style, private documents such as letters scarcely reflect conversational style, since, in early correspondence, writers tended to borrow polite formulae and use the quite formal negative politeness strategies considered appropriate in this particular communicative function in contemporary society.

As regards spelling variation, data extracted from corpora do not justify Görlach's view that "the occasional mis-spellings that are found in later Early Modern English private documents are generally diagnostic of social status rather than of dialect" (Görlach 1999: 506). In fact, spelling variation in letters has been shown to reflect local and regional practices (Meurman-Solin 2000a, 2001).

In the present approach, the term "dialect" is used to refer to language use attested in a particular geographical area, the data comprising both supraregional and regional or local features. In other words, instead of concentrating on distinctive or marked features exclusively, language use in a particular region is described by using a comprehensive inventory. The general assumption is that at least some degree of systematicity as regards distinctive preferences at the local or regional level can be identified as well as some degree of influence by contacts with other local or regional varieties and supraregional standardized varieties. Thus my concern here is not to identify what is chiefly or exclusively local or regional but to provide a full account of linguistic systems drawing on a representative corpus of texts originating from a particular locality or region in a particular time-period.

Recently developed methods of historical dialectology will be illustrated here by drawing on digital corpora representing some southern and northern English varieties in the 16th and 17th centuries. The approach to Scottish English here is to view language use in particular regions in Scotland as reflecting variation and change in English, leaving aside the debate about whether Scots is an independent language or not (cf. Görlach 1996, 1999: 468–469). It will also become clear that I prefer to make a distinction between the theoretical and methodological approach of historical sociolinguistics (as in Nevalainen and Raumolin-Brunberg 2003) and that of historical dialectology. These approaches are often merged in various ways (e.g. Görlach 1999: 470–474), making it difficult to understand mechanisms of language variation and change conditioned by geographical space. Since I find it necessary to define the domain of historical dialectology in stricter terms, its main task is to "describe" in detail language use over time and space. Only in the attempt to "interpret" variation and change attested in the data is it legitimate to start enquiring whether there are sociolinguistically relevant variables which correlate with the frequencies and distributions of linguistic features.

2 Sources for the study of regional variation in Early Modern English

2.1 New corpora

Starting from the 15th century, written English represents local or regional language use quite unevenly due to the diffusion of a new standard norm constituting a supraregional variety of English. The range of writing using local or regional varieties became more restricted in the sense that texts representing some genres were viewed as appealing to wider audiences, their printing in particular strengthening the need to use the supraregional standard. Scottish English became anglicized during the 17th century (see Devitt 1989; Meurman-Solin 1993, 1997); according to Görlach (1999: 468), "Wales was still predominantly Welsh-speaking in the nineteenth century, and Cornish survived until the eighteenth."

At present, there is an increased awareness of a scarcity of research on regional variation in the Early Modern English period due to lack of quantitatively and qualitatively valid data. The most neglected area is probably the investigation of manuscript sources in the various record offices and archives. These relevant data sources should be transcribed and digitized to make them internationally available. In selecting texts for a corpus, language-external criteria should be applied. Since most existing corpora supply a wide variety of both literary and non-literary texts representing the range of genres traditionally included in general-purpose corpora, the focus in complementing these corpora should be on genres which have a local or regional communicative function. The new corpora or new supplements to existing ones would include legal texts of various kinds produced by the local administrative and legal institutions as well as private transactions such as land transfers arranged by advocates, official correspondence, and a wide range of private writing, diaries, autobiographies, accounts, commonplace books, and letters in particular. The linguistic examination of these will inevitably show that there are quite complex texts among these; some texts, such as trial proceedings consist of a number of different texts, witness depositions often reflecting local linguistic practices, while some other texts represent legalese, for example, formulaic language use adapting Latin or French models.

It is generally agreed that historical dialectology in the Early Modern English period is not as advanced as that focusing on Middle English. While the *Linguistic Atlas of Late Middle English* (LALME) (McIntosh et al. 1986) and especially the recently launched *Linguistic Atlas of Early Middle English* (LAEME) (Laing and Lass 2007) have completely changed our ability to reconstruct dialectal variation in Middle English, the situation is quite different in Early Modern English, as Kytö, Grund, and Walker (2007) point out:

> We still know comparatively little about regional Early Modern Englishes: they have been difficult to study since edited material that can be clearly anchored in a specific region of England is scarce. The ongoing standardisation of English during the period also means that regional features were being increasingly suppressed in favour of the norm in most formal written records (Kytö, Grund, and Walker 2007: Section 4).

As regards the availability of relevant data, innovative work by Kytö et al. (Kytö, Walker, and Grund 2007; see also Kytö, Grund, and Walker 2007) has improved the situation by producing a digital edition of manuscripts of English witness depositions dating from 1560–1760, representing four regions of England (the North, South, East, and West) and the London area. As they rightly claim, "[w]ritten records of the oral testimony of a witness in a criminal or ecclesiastical trial give a glimpse into the lives and language of ordinary people in the past". However, they also stress that, even though in principle witness depositions could be considered an ideal source for investigating regional variation, there are caveats. Kytö, Grund, and Walker (2007) list the following:

> since legal writing is a very formal genre, standardisation is only to be expected, and so is perhaps even the removal of "inappropriate" regional language. Although the presence of dialectal vocabulary does show that all regionalisms were not sifted out by the scribe, it is frequently difficult to determine whether the language reported by the scribe is indeed that of the witness: the language may in fact be partly or wholly that of the scribe (see Kytö and Walker 2003; Grund, Kytö, and Rissanen 2004; Grund 2007). The level of training of the scribe probably contributed to the picture: the more highly educated would perhaps have been more discriminating, while less trained scribes may have followed the actual language of the deponents more closely. Unfortunately, there is little information on the scribes, and more studies on the Early Modern legal scribes that worked for justices of the peace and different courts remain a desideratum (Kytö, Grund, and Walker 2007: Section 4).

However, Huber (2007) considerably increases our understanding of the practices of scribes by discussing those involved in the production of the *Old Bailey Proceedings*.

At present, regional variation has been described in studies drawing on different data sources, but, most usefully, this fragmentary evidence is complementary, as Kytö, Grund, and Walker (2007) illustrates. While the CEEC (Nevalainen et al. 1998) corpora contain data on the North, East Anglia and the London area, the witness depositions originate from the counties of Northumberland, Cumberland, Westmorland, Yorkshire, Lancashire, Norfolk, Suffolk, Essex, Oxfordshire and Somerset in addition to the London area.

The compilation and annotation principles of the manuscript-based *Corpus of Scottish Correspondence* (CSC) (Meurman-Solin 2007a), 1500–1715, have been affected by those applied to the *Linguistic Atlas of Early Middle English* and the *Linguistic Atlas of Older Scots* (see the online introductions to LAEME [Laing and Lass 2007] and LAOS [Williamson 2007], and Meurman-Solin 2007a, 2007b, 2017). One of the goals of the CSC corpus is to be diatopically representative. In the 2007 version that the illustrations in Section 3 are based on, the dialect areas represented are as follows: Ross and Cromarty, Sutherland, Aberdeenshire, Angus, Perthshire, Fife, Lothian, the Border counties, Lanarkshire, Ayrshire, Argyllshire and Dumfries and Galloway. Following the principles applied to the *Scottish National Dictionary* (Grant and Murison 1931–76) and the *Concise Scots Dictionary* (Robinson 1985–96), these areas have been grouped into six regions: Northern Scots, North-East Scots, East Mid Scots, West Mid Scots, South Mid Scots, and Southern Scots. South Mid Scots and Southern Scots have mostly been ignored in presenting some illustrative data in Section 3, since samples representing them are not yet of a statistically valid size.

2.2 Assessment of data sources for historical dialectology

The validity of findings in research on regional variation in Early Modern English is drastically reduced by the frequently stated fact that the data only represents the literate, i.e. mostly members of the higher social ranks (see Nevalainen and Raumolin-Brunberg 2003; on Scottish women's literacy, see Meurman-Solin 2001: 21–22).

Two factors in particular diminish our ability to provide a balanced reconstruction of historical varieties of English used in different localities. Firstly, there is as yet no purpose-built database enabling a thorough investigation of how rural and urban varieties relate to one another in the various regions and localities in the Early Modern English period. Beside the cline from local to regional and supraregional, there are other clines; for example, from peripherally located rural areas to rural areas within easy access in the network of transport and communication, and from economically self-supporting and culturally self-contained towns to lively royal boroughs favoring trade, with further enriching dimensions such as a university and important administrative and legal institutions.

Secondly, social, cultural, and economic distance may play a more important role in linguistic variation and change than mere geographical distance. My earlier corpus-based research suggests that "distance" as a social, economic, and cultural construct, rather than as a concept defined purely geographically, is a significant conditioning factor in patterns of variation and change attested in the history of Scots (Meurman-Solin 2000a, b). In fact, in studying local and regional variation, it is necessary to define quite complex variables as factors conditioning linguistic choice. While the scalar concept of distance permits us to define relations in terms of core and periphery, for example, with respect to economic significance, the concept of network allows the assessment of type, direction and frequency of ties.

In principle, all texts originating from a particular area can be claimed to represent it. However, their representativeness varies, there being a set of variables by which the texts can be positioned on a cline. As discussed in Meurman-Solin (2004, 2007a), texts written by members of a speech community are diatopically more representative than those by members of discourse and text communities. To comment on the latter two, members of discourse communities share a wide range of conventionalized discourse properties with geographically distant communities. Since there are important differences between what texts, genres and text types were available and circulated in a particular locality or region in a particular time-period, information about text community type also permits us to create criteria for assessing the validity and relevance of data for the study of dialectal variation. Since all the sources represent written language, fully authentic data that could be claimed to reflect spoken practices is rare. Letters by privately trained and inexperienced writers are often mentioned as the best source of local language use but the potential influence of models must be taken into account even in these. Moreover, the relatively low level of linguistic and stylistic competence of these writers may increase the number of hapax variants, the attested variants being idiosyncratic rather than diagnostic of a particular geographical area (see Meurman-Solin 1999, 2001, 2004, 2005).

As with Old English and Middle English material, information about text histories will permit the quality assessment of data sources used for historical dialectology in the Early Modern English period. Texts may exist in different versions, their relation requiring detailed study. Printing may have had a major effect, standardizing being part of most printers' policies. Texts spoken in a particular variety may have been written down by a scribe using a different variety. In principle, only diplomatic digital editions of manuscripts can be considered reliable, there being ample evidence of editorial practices applied in later centuries (including the present one) having permitted major processes of modernisation or normalisation (for standards in philological editing, see Lass 2004).

Depending on how much language-external information is available and how reliable it is, texts can be positioned on a cline from primary witnesses, or "anchor texts", to texts the status of which is unclear (cf. Nevalainen and Raumolin-Brunberg 1996: 43). A database must also be assessed from the perspective of whether it is valid for answering a particular research question, lexical studies not necessarily requiring the same standards of philological editing as phonological and morpho-syntactic questions. In general, the relevance and validity of a corpus depends on which particular feature is investigated. Language-external variables may condition the general frequency of a feature, so that a quantitative analysis aiming to identify diatopically relevant patterns of variation may provide misleading results. For example, 45% of the instances of the personal pronoun SHE have been recorded in women's letters in the CSC (Meurman-Solin 2007a), even though the proportion of these letters in the corpus is only circa 20%. Assessing the relative weight of region or locality and other variables defined by the sociolinguistic framework is a necessary but often difficult exercise.

3 Linguistic systems and subsystems illustrating dialectal variation

Limitations of space prevent me from giving a full account of how the methodological approaches in recent historical dialectology succeed in depicting a particular linguistic system. This section will thus only provide some illustrations of patterns of diffusion across space using material from the CSC (Meurman-Solin 2007a) and CEEC (Nevalainen et al. 1998) corpora. The goal is merely to illustrate corpus-based analyses of diachronic developments in a number of regional varieties, and the findings based exclusively on letters have of course no validity across genres. In the letter genre, however, there are numerous representatives of local language use that cannot be recovered from among representatives of other genres. The linguistic features in the illustrations have been selected to permit comparison with data extracted from the CEEC (Nevalainen et al. 1998), discussed extensively in the publications of the compilers.

3.1 The relative system

The relative system is an obvious choice for illustrating the theoretical and methodological approach of present-day historical dialectology, seeing that there is a long history of research in this area in Scottish studies (e.g. Caldwell 1974; Romaine 1982; Devitt 1989; Meurman-Solin 2000b, 2007c; see also Busse, Chapter 12; Johansson, Chapter 15).

3.1.1 Variant forms of *which*

Formal variation in the relative *which* in the CSC (Meurman-Solin 2007a) can be traced by examining the variants as classified into three main types: the *quhilk* type, the transitional types *quhich* and *whilk*, here grouped together, and the *which* type. In this analysis, no distinction is made between occurrences in restrictive and non-restrictive relative clauses, the restrictive relative clauses introduced by *which* being quite infrequent in the CSC corpus (9% of the total of occurrences of *which*). Since the approach here is purely comparative, Figure 8.1 gives the findings in percentages. In the statistics, the *quhilk* type includes variants of *quhilkis* and *the quhilk*, and the *which* and *quhich/whilk* types include variants of *the which* and *the quhich/whilk* respectively.

In the 16th century, all occurrences of this relative represent the *quhilk* type (there is no 16th-century data representing Northern Scots in the CSC). We can therefore focus on developments in four regions in the 17th century.

As illustrated by Figure 8.1, all occurrences in the period 1650–1715 represent the *which* type in East Mid and Northern Scots, whereas the proportion of the *quhilk* type is still 10% and 2%, and that of *quhich/whilk* 20% and 3% in North East and West Mid Scots respectively. The quite large proportion of transitional variants in North East Scots as late as post-1650 letters is a particularly interesting finding.

As regards the period 1600–1649, in which variation and change is generally most intense in the history of Scottish English, the proportion of the *quhilk* type is lowest in West Mid Scots (18%) and highest in the North (83%) and the North East (55%). However, the percentage is also quite high in East Mid Scots (48%). The high degree of variation attested does not exclusively result from *quhilk* variants being replaced by *which* variants. This can be illustrated by the variational pattern recorded in West Mid Scots, the percentage of the *quhich/whilk* type, i.e. the transitional variants, being as high as 28%, with the *quhilk* type representing 18% and the *which* type 54%. The proportion of the transitional variants is lowest in the North (1%) but considerably higher in East Mid and North East Scots (9% and 20% respectively).

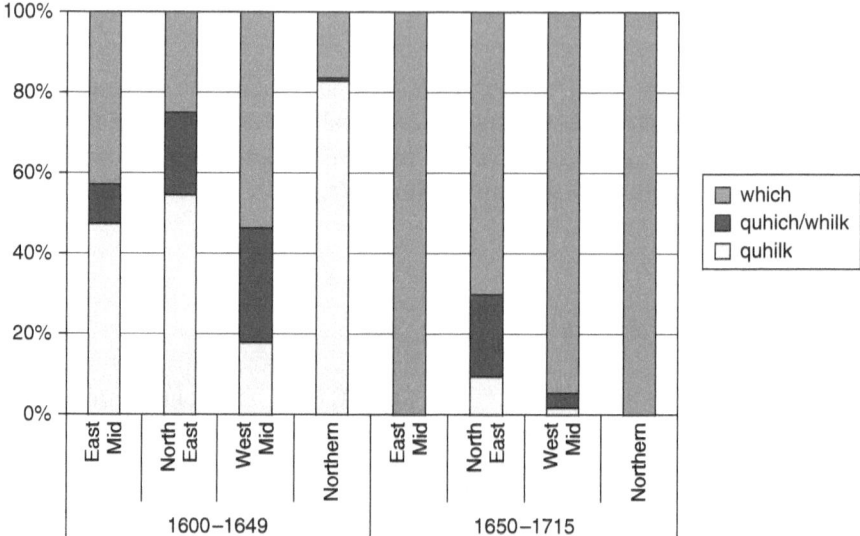

Figure 8.1: Percentages of *the quhilk*, *quhich/whilk* and *which* types in four regions in the CSC

Overall, the variational patterns of the forms of the relative *which* resemble one another in East Mid and North East Scots in comparison with the quite different profiles of West Mid and Northern Scots. The main difference between the two groups is the greater number of transitional variants in the West and a clear time-lag in the spread of the *which* type recorded in Northern Scots. Moreover, only very few transitional variants have been attested in Northern Scots.

This investigation has identified clear differences in the pace at which incoming variants spread across regions rather than demonstrating the existence of distinctive variants which are diagnostic of particular regional varieties. In comparing processes of diffusion, regions also differ from one another in the number and range of transitional variants. Figure 8.2 illustrates the proportion of transitional variants in the four regions (the type has not been attested in the 16th century).

While the relative proportion of *quhich/whilk* decreases to 3% in West Mid Scots and maintains the same level in North East Scots (20%), the type disappears from post-1650 letters representing East Mid and Northern Scots.

As regards the minority variants of *quhilk* and *which*, the plural variant *quhilkis* is considerably more frequent in East and West Mid Scots than North East Scots. Nevalainen and Raumolin-Brunberg (2000) have studied variation between *which* and *the which*, drawing on data extracted from the *Corpus of Early English Correspondence*. Figure 8.3 is based on information in Table 10 in Nevalainen and Raumolin-Brunberg (2000: 320).

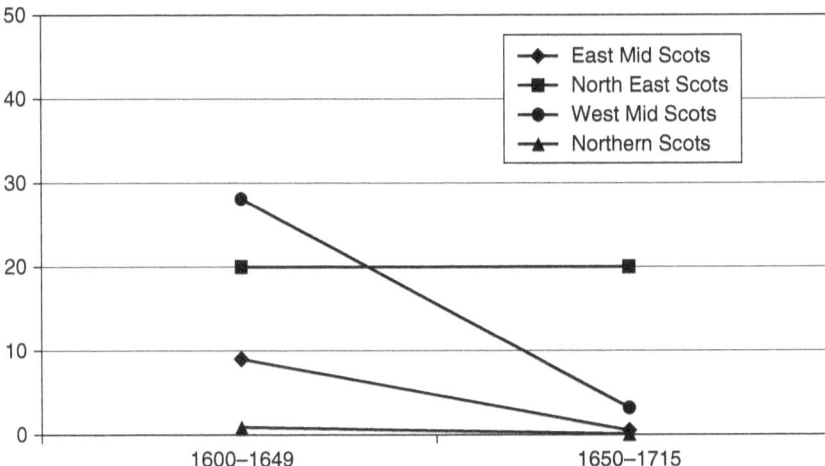

Figure 8.2: Percentages of the *quhich/whilk* type in four regions in the 17th century in the CSC

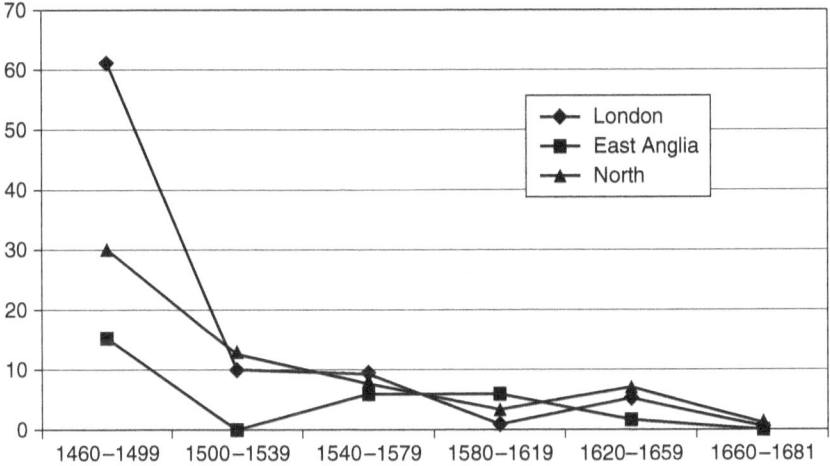

Figure 8.3: Percentages of *the which* type in the three dialect areas in the CEEC

We notice that there is a rather abrupt change in the proportion of the *the which* type in the CEEC (Nevalainen et al. 1998) data, developments in the English and Scottish regions resembling one another from 1500 onwards (Figure 8.4).

In the Scots data, a clearly larger proportion of *the quhilk/which* has been recorded in West Mid Scots in the first half of the 16th century and a regained 10% frequency in East Mid Scots in the first half of the 17th; otherwise there is a constant decrease in the use of this variant.

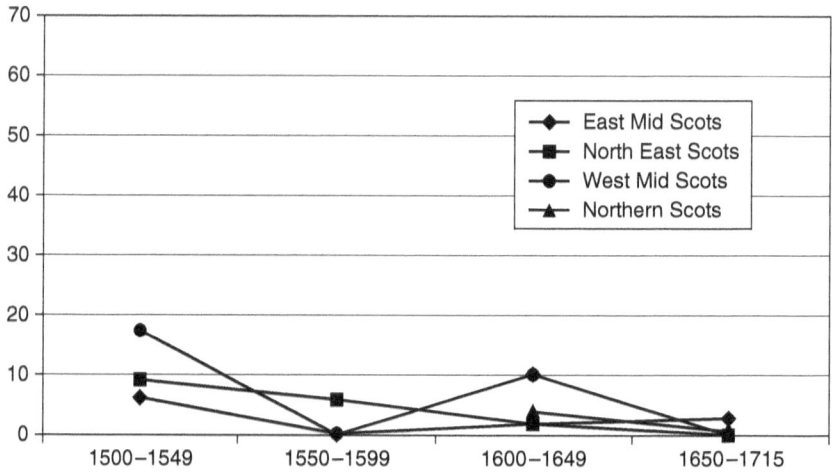

Figure 8.4: Percentages of *the quhilk/which* in four regions in the CSC

3.1.2 Relative *that*, *which*, *who* and a zero link in four regions of Scotland

Due to limitations of space, only some patterns in the relative system can be illustrated here. It is possible to examine their diatopic distribution in greater detail since zero realizations of relative links have been signalled in the annotation applied to the CSC (see Meurman-Solin 2007a). Figure 8.5 illustrates zero relatives in the function of object with an inanimate antecedent, the most frequent function in which zero realizations occur:

Figure 8.5 displays a highly interesting similarity between developments in all the regions except West Mid Scots, where the general direction of change finally becomes convergent with the other regions at the beginning of the 17th century. A zero realization is attested in the range of 60–86% in 16th-century West Mid Scots.

Figure 8.6 illustrates variation in the choice of a relative link in East Mid Scots.

The analysis identifies a considerable increase in the proportion of zero realizations and a decrease in the proportion of the relative *that* in East Mid Scots. Of course, a quantitative result of this kind only provides one perspective on the description of the relative system in East Mid Scots.

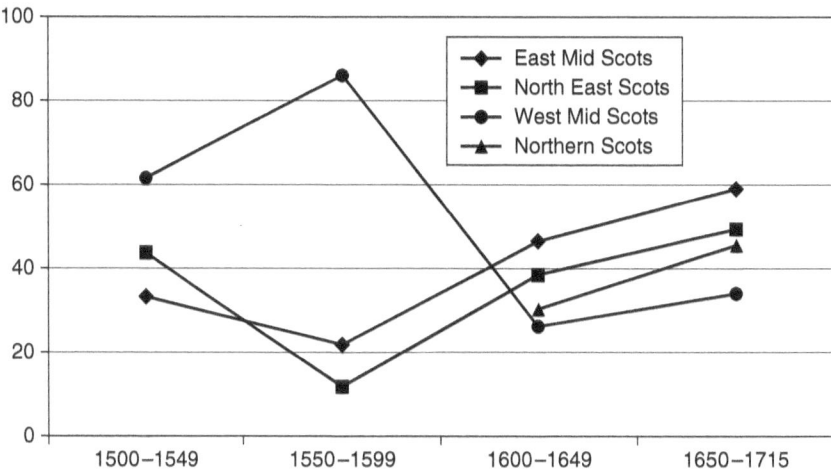

Figure 8.5: Percentages of zero relatives in the function of object with an inanimate antecedent in four regions of Scotland in the CSC

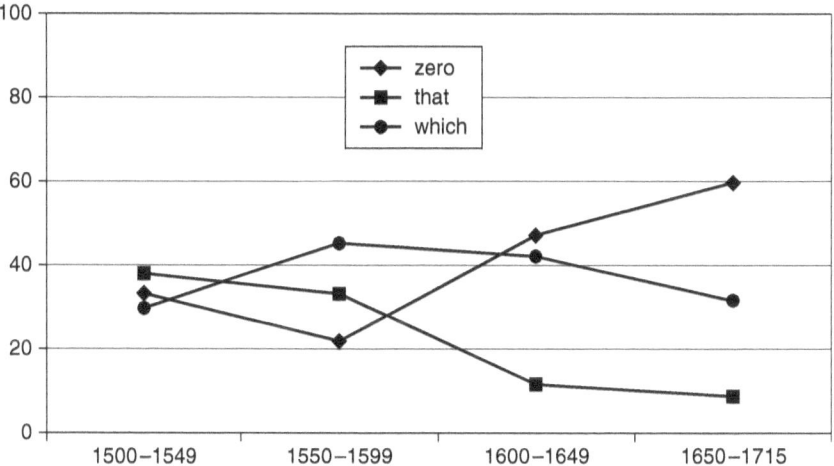

Figure 8.6: Percentages of the realizations of a relative link in the function of object with an inanimate antecedent in East Mid Scots in the CSC

3.2 Subject–verb agreement

The second case study considers subject–verb concord in the present indicative and also presents some quantitative analyses on variation between *s*-variants, *th*-variants and zero-variants in the CSC (Meurman-Solin 2007a). This feature was selected since Nevalainen and Raumolin-Brunberg, the leaders of the CEEC project, have discussed it in great detail in their publications (see also Meurman-Solin 1992).

3.2.1 -s versus zero in the first person singular present indicative

The main perspective is that of tracing the degree of homogeneity in the application of the Northern Subject–Verb rule. Figure 8.7 illustrates the diffusion of s-variants in the first person present indicative with a non-adjacent pronoun subject:

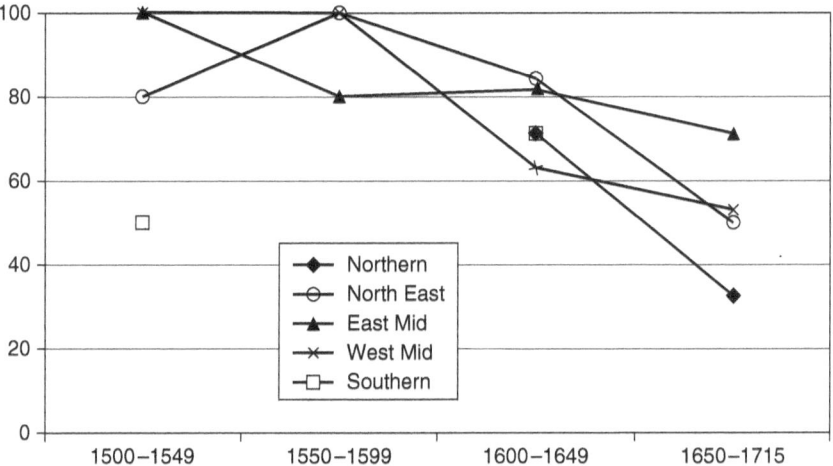

Figure 8.7: Percentages of s-variants in the first person singular present indicative with a non-adjacent pronoun subject in the CSC

Figure 8.7 shows that the Northern Subject–Verb rule is most consistently used in East Mid Scots, the heartland of the so-called "Scottish Standard" in the 16th century and the first half of the 17th, the proportion of the s-variant remaining as large as 71% as late as the last sub-period. In at least 50% of the occurrences, the s-variant is also preferred throughout in West Mid and North East Scots, this variant being chosen in 80–100% of the cases in these areas in the 16th century. It is noteworthy that the rule loses its strength first in Northern Scots, the most peripheral area.

3.2.2 -s and -th versus zero in the third person plural present indicative with NP subject

As regards the present indicative with adjacent third person plural NP subject, the suffixed verb, either with -s or -th, is the rule in the 16th-century texts except for a single occurrence of the unsuffixed variant in Stirlingshire in 1550. No instances of zero inflection have been recorded in North East, South Mid and Southern Scots in the 17th century. As regards other regions, the earliest examples of zero inflection in Northern letters date from 1660, in West Mid Scots from 1641, and in East Mid Scots from 1600. The suffixed verb represents the majority variant except in the early 18th-century letters representing Northern Scots. It is noteworthy that letters written by women contain no unsuffixed variants in the corpus in this context. With adjacent subjects containing singular NPS in co-ordination, the following present tense verb is also suffixed except in the early 18th-century letters.

Another context to which the Northern Subject–Verb Rule applies is the present indicative in relative clauses with antecedents in the plural. In this context, the suffixed verb is the only variant in pre-1600 letters, and the unsuffixed verbs remain in the minority in the 17th century, and absent in Northern, North East, and South Mid Scots. The rare occurrences of zero inflection have been attested in East Mid Scots (Stirlingshire 1630, 1643, and Fife 1682), West Mid Scots (Lanarkshire 1659 [a female writer], 1692, and Ayrshire 1641) and in Southern Scots (Border counties 1600). The variant -th is rare in both of these contexts (only six occurrences).

The th-variant is in a minority in the third person singular present indicative in 16th- and 17th-century Scots. To stress its minority status, its spread across six regions is illustrated in Table 8.1 by mean frequencies:

Table 8.1: Mean frequencies (/10,000) of the th-variant in the third person singular present indicative in six regions of Scotland in the CSC

	Northern	North East	East Mid	West Mid	South Mid	Southern
1600–1649	0.4	1.2	5.4	4.2	7.5	4.3
1650–1715	3.0	8.2	3.5	6.7	0	0

The mean frequencies show that the th-variant was considerably less frequent in North East and Northern Scots in the first half of the 17th century, the highest having been attested in South Mid Scots. While the spread of the th-variant reached approximately the same level in post-1650 letters in North East, East Mid and West Mid Scots, it remains quite rare in Northern Scots and is absent in South Mid and Southern Scots.

3.3 Demonstrative pronouns

In the Older Scots system of demonstrative pronouns, the plural of the proximal *this* is *thir* and the plural of the distal *that* is *thai* (see King 1997: 168–169; see also Beal 1997: 350–351). *These* and *those* occur almost exclusively in the 17th-century letters in the CSC (Meurman-Solin 2007a) data. In the 16th century, there is only one example in 1550 and another in 1596, both of them nominal uses. In a more detailed study of the Scottish English system of demonstratives, close attention should be paid to the fact that "the tendency to use *these* where Standard English would have *those* persists into the 20th century, at least in the phrase *in these days*, referring to the distant past" (Beal 1997: 350). Since *thir* is only used attributively, the following comparative account of the mean frequencies of *thir*, *these*, *thai* and *those* in four regions excludes nominal uses (for example, of the total of occurrences of *these*, approximately 60% are nominal uses). In examining the introduction of *these* and *those* and the decrease in *thir* and *thai* in East Mid Scots, we find developments of the following kind:

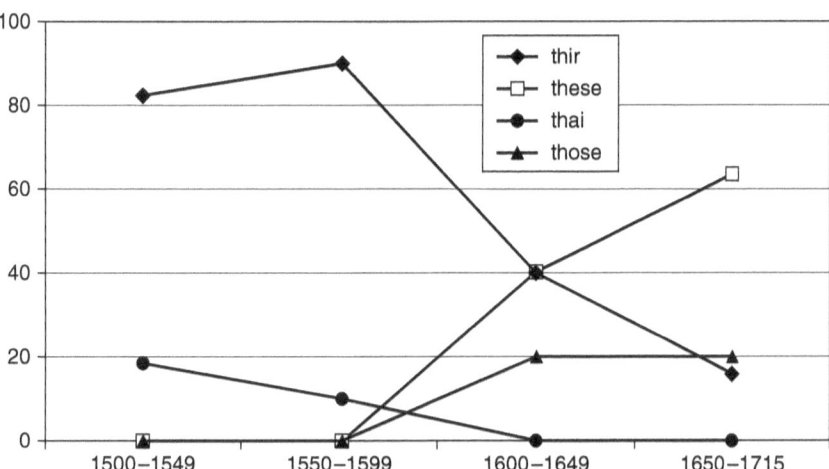

Figure 8.8: Percentages of plural demonstratives in East Mid Scots in the CSC

Figure 8.8 illustrates a remarkable change over time, with the diverging developments of *thir* and *thai* moving towards a lower frequency and *these* towards a higher.

Figure 8.9 shows that *thir*, which is considerably more frequent in East Mid Scots, the basis of the so-called "Scottish Standard", decreases in frequency most dramatically in this region during the first half of the 17th century. A time-lag can be seen in West Mid Scots in the same period:

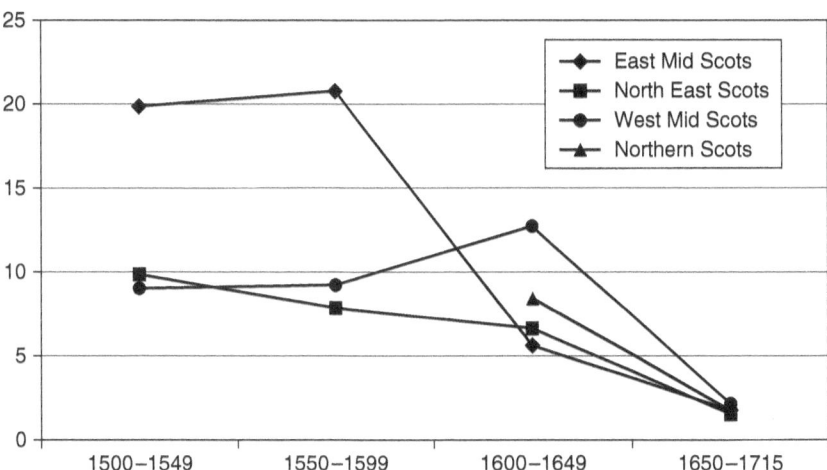

Figure 8.9: Mean frequencies (/10,000) of *thir* in four regions in the CSC (Meurman-Solin 2007a)

These brief illustrations in Section 3 show that space – here regions in Britain – and time – here the 16th and 17th centuries – can be conceptualized as autonomous variables in research based on sufficiently large corpora in which both variables belong to the core of rigorously defined compilation principles. In this purely quantitative approach, it has been possible to identify favored practices in a particular region at a particular time, as well as patterns in the chronology of spread across regions. However, as has been well documented in recent research, a thorough syntactic and semantic-pragmatic analysis of these quantitative findings is required to understand fully the conditioning factors of variation and change. A further central dimension is the influence of contact between varieties.

4 Further research

Space and spatiality have been claimed to be largely untheorized variables in research on local and regional variation (Britain 2002: 603):

> Given the historical origins of variationism in traditional dialectology, and given the advances the discipline has made over the past decades in unpacking the initially rather crude attempts at understanding the social embedding of variation and change [...], it is

paradoxical that one of the social categories that has received least attention of all is space. Almost without exception, space has been treated as a blank stage on which sociolinguistic processes are enacted. It has been unexamined, untheorized, and its role in shaping and being shaped by variation and change untested.

Britain's critical survey is highly relevant in assessing where the major advances and future challenges are in historical dialectology. The three dimensions of spatiality – Euclidean, social and perceived space (Britain 2002: 604) as well as models concerning knowledge about human geography in a particular region such as the description of the history of the Fens (Britain 2002: 604–606) – provide new insights into cross-disciplinary methodologies in the field.

The approach to historical dialectology presented above (in Section 3) could be defined as data-driven and data-oriented. Methodologically, the claim here is that the study of language use in Euclidean space is complementary to that in social and perceived space in a highly relevant way, and, as shown by work at the Institute for Historical Dialectology in Edinburgh, also feasible with the assistance of sophisticated software applied to large quantities of data. In my view, combining the three conceptions of space into a complex merger of perspectives does not provide a methodologically useful tool. Instead, the three space types should be conceptualized as suggesting a sequence of perspectives, the first stage of data analysis taking place with reference to geographical coordinates, with time and space as primary variables, the data being then investigated from the perspective of social space, and, finally, from the perspective of perceived space.

Even in this multi-perspective methodology, a dialectologist tends to marginalize the influence of discourse properties. However, since historical dialectology in the early periods of the English language exclusively draws on written data representing a wide range of different genres, space defined by discourse and text community type (see Section 2.2) is also a highly relevant conditioning factor.

The present chapter claims that the most important advances in historical dialectology drawing on Early Modern English data can be found in research directly related to the creation of new digital databases. The creators of these new databases (Kytö, Grund, and Walker 2007; Kytö, Walter, and Grund 2007 in particular) base their compilation principles and practices on precisely defined and transparent criteria applicable to the assessment of diatopic representativeness. For example, to increase the relevance and validity of comparative descriptions over time and space, they restrict their work to one particular genre, trials, thus avoiding generalisation across genres. An equally relevant database can be extracted from corpora representing correspondence; however, it is usually necessary to shape a subcorpus, only including informants who are relatively homogeneous as regards variables such as education and geographical and social mobility.

Overall, work towards a thorough description of regional variation in the Early Modern English period has only just started. Since the majority of texts now available in editions tend to represent the canon of literary and non-literary texts comparable to that used as source material for dictionaries, continued work towards making locally and regionally functional material on Early Modern English dialects available is required to improve the quality and quantity of research.

5 References

Beal, Joan. 1997. Syntax and morphology. In: Jones (ed.), 335–377.
Benson, Phil. 2001. *Ethnocentrism and the English Dictionary*. London/New York: Routledge.
Britain, David. 2002. Space and spacial diffusion. In: Jack K. Chambers, Peter Trudgill, and Natalie Schilling-Estes (eds.), *The Handbook of Language Variation and Change*, 603–637. Malden, MA/Oxford: Blackwell.
Caldwell, Sarah J. G. 1974. *The Relative Pronoun in Early Scots*. Helsinki: Société Néophilologique.
Devitt, Amy J. 1989. *Standardizing Written English. Diffusion in the Case of Scotland 1520–1659*. Cambridge: Cambridge University Press.
Dossena, Marina and Roger Lass (eds.). 2004. *Methods and Data in English Historical Dialectology*. Bern: Peter Lang.
Dossena, Marina. 2005. *Scotticisms in Grammar and Vocabulary*. Edinburgh: John Donald Publishers.
Görlach, Manfred. 1996. And is it English? *English World-Wide* 17(2): 1–22.
Görlach, Manfred. 1999. Regional and social variation. In: Roger Lass (ed.), *The Cambridge History of the English Language*. Vol. III. *1476–1776*, 459–538. Cambridge: Cambridge University Press.
Grant, William and David Murison (eds.). 1931–76. *The Scottish National Dictionary*. Edinburgh: Scottish National Dictionary Association.
Grund, Peter. 2007. From tongue to text: the transmission of the Salem witchcraft examination records. *American Speech* 82(2): 119–150.
Grund, Peter, Merja Kytö and Matti Rissanen. 2004. Editing the Salem Witchcraft Records: an exploration of a linguistic treasury. *American Speech* 79(2): 146–167.
Huber, Magnus. 2007. The Old Bailey Proceedings, 1674–1834: Evaluating and annotating a corpus of 18th- and 19th-century spoken English. In: Anneli Meurman-Solin and Arja Nurmi (eds.), *Annotating Variation and Change* Vol. 1. http://www.helsinki.fi/varieng/journal/volumes/01/huber/; last accessed 14 April 2017.
Johnston, Paul. 1997. Older Scots phonology and its regional variation. In: Jones (ed.), 47–111.
Jones, Charles (ed.). 1997. *The Edinburgh History of the Scots Language*. Edinburgh: Edinburgh University Press.
Kastovsky, Dieter and Arthur Mettinger (eds.). 2000. *The History of English in a Social Context. A Contribution to Historical Sociolinguistics*. Berlin/New York: Mouton de Gruyter.
King, Anne. 1997. The inflectional morphology of Older Scots. In: Jones (ed.), 156–181.

Kytö, Merja and Terry Walker. 2003. The linguistic study of Early Modern English speech-related texts: How "bad" can "bad" data be? *Journal of English Linguistics* 31(3): 221–248.

Kytö, Merja, Terry Walker, and Peter Grund. 2007. English witness depositions 1560–1760: An electronic text edition. *ICAME Journal* 31: 65–85.

Kytö, Merja, Peter Grund, and Terry Walker. 2007. Regional variation and the language of English witness depositions 1560–1760: Constructing a "linguistic" edition in electronic form. In: Päivi Pahta, Irma Taavitsainen, Terttu Nevalainen, and Jukka Tyrkkö (eds.), *Towards Multimedia in Corpus Studies* Vol. 2. http://www.helsinki.fi/varieng/journal/volumes/02/kyto_et_al/; last accessed 14 April 2017.

Laing, Margaret. 2004. Multidimensionality: time, space and stratigraphy in historical dialectology. In: Dossena and Lass (eds.), 49–96.

Laing, Margaret and Roger Lass. 2006. Early Middle English dialectology: Problems and prospects. In: Ans van Kemenade and Bettelou Los (eds.), *Handbook of the History of English*, 417–451. Oxford: Blackwell.

Laing, Margaret and Roger Lass. 2007. LAEME: *A Linguistic Atlas of Early Middle English, 1150–1325*. University of Edinburgh. http://www.lel.ed.ac.uk/ihd/laeme1/laeme1.html; last accessed 14 April 2017.

Lass, Roger. 2004. Ut custodiant litteras: Editions, corpora and witnesshood. In: Dossena and Lass (eds.), 21–48.

McIntosh, Angus, Michael L. Samuels, and Michael Benskin. 1986. *A Linguistic Atlas of Late Mediaeval English*. 4 vols. Aberdeen: Aberdeen University Press.

Meurman-Solin, Anneli. 1992. On the morphology of verbs in Middle Scots: Present and present perfect indicative. In Matti Rissanen, Ossi Ihalainen, Terttu Nevalainen, and Irma Taavitsainen (eds.), *History of Englishes. New Methods and Interpretations in Historical Linguistics*, 611–623. Berlin/New York: Mouton de Gruyter.

Meurman-Solin, Anneli. 1993. *Variation and Change in early Scottish Prose. Studies based on the Helsinki Corpus of Older Scots*. Helsinki: Suomalainen Tiedeakatemia.

Meurman-Solin, Anneli. 1997. Differentiation and standardization in early Scots. In: Jones (ed.), 3–23.

Meurman-Solin, Anneli. 1999. Letters as a source of data for reconstructing early spoken Scots. In: Irma Taavitsainen, Gunnel Melchers, and Päivi Pahta (eds.), *Writing in Nonstandard English*, 305–322. Amsterdam/Philadelphia: John Benjamins.

Meurman-Solin, Anneli. 2000a. On the conditioning of geographical and social distance in language variation and change in Renaissance Scots. In: Kastovsky and Mettinger (eds.), 227–255.

Meurman-Solin, Anneli. 2000b. Geographical, socio-spatial and systemic distance in the spread of the relative *who* in Scots. In: Ricardo Bermúdez-Otero, David Denison, Richard M. Hogg, and C. B. McCully (eds.), *Generative Theory and Corpus Studies: A Dialogue from 10 ICEHL*, 417–438. Berlin/New York: Mouton de Gruyter.

Meurman-Solin, Anneli. 2001. Women as informants in the reconstruction of geographically and socioculturally conditioned language variation and change in 16th and 17th century Scots. *Scottish Language* 20: 20–46.

Meurman-Solin, Anneli. 2004. Data and methods in Scottish historical linguistics. In: Ermanno Barisone, Maria Luisa Maggioni, and Paola Tornaghi (eds.), *The History of English and the Dynamics of Power*, 25–42. Alessandria: Edizioni dell'Orso.

Meurman-Solin, Anneli. 2005. Women's Scots: Gender-based variation in Renaissance letters. In: Sally Mapstone (ed.), *Older Scots Literature*, 424–440. Edinburgh: John Donald Publishers.

Meurman-Solin, Anneli. 2007a. *Corpus of Scottish Correspondence* (CSC). University of Helsinki. http://www.helsinki.fi/varieng/CoRD/corpora/CSC/; last accessed 14 April 2017; For manual, see https://www.kielipankki.fi/wp-content/uploads/ScotsCorr_Manual_2016.pdf; last accessed 23 July 2017.

Meurman-Solin, Anneli. 2007b. Annotating variational space over time. In: Anneli Meurman-Solin and Arja Nurmi (eds.), *Annotating Variation and Change* Vol. 1. http://www.helsinki.fi/varieng/series/volumes/01/; last accessed 14 April 2017.

Meurman-Solin, Anneli. 2007c. Relatives as sentence-level connectives. In: Ursula Lenker and Anneli Meurman-Solin (eds.), *Connectives in the History of English*, 255–287. Amsterdam/Philadelphia: John Benjamins.

Meurman-Solin, Anneli. 2017. ScotsCorr: The Helsinki Corpus of Scottish Correspondence 1540–1750. Kielipankki. http://urn.fi/urn:nbn:fi:lb-201411071; last accessed 23 July 2017.

Milroy, James. 1999. The consequences of standardisation in descriptive linguistics. In: Tony Bex and Richard J. Watts (eds.), *Standard English: The Widening Debate*, 16–39. London/New York: Routledge.

Nevalainen, Terttu and Helena Raumolin-Brunberg. 1996. The Corpus of Early English Correspondence. In: Terttu Nevalainen and Helena Raumolin-Brunberg (eds.), *Sociolinguistics and Language History. Studies based on the Corpus of Early English Correspondence*, 39–54. Amsterdam/Atlanta, GA: Rodopi.

Nevalainen, Terttu, Helena Raumolin-Brunberg, Jukka Keränen, Minna Nevala, Arja Nurmi, and Minna Palander-Collin. 1998. *Corpus of Early English Correspondence* (CEEC). Department of English, University of Helsinki. http://www.helsinki.fi/varieng/CoRD/corpora/CEEC/index.html; last accessed 14 April 2017.

Nevalainen, Terttu and Helena Raumolin-Brunberg. 2000. The changing role of London on the linguistic map of Tudor and Stuart England. In: Kastovsky and Mettinger (eds.), 279–337.

Nevalainen, Terttu and Helena Raumolin-Brunberg. 2003. *Historical Sociolinguistics: Language Change in Tudor and Stuart England*. London: Longman.

Robinson, Mairi (ed.). 1985–96. *Concise Scots Dictionary*. Edinburgh: Chambers.

Romaine, Suzanne. 1982. *Socio-Historical Linguistics, Its Status and Methodology*. Cambridge: Cambridge University Press.

Williamson, Keith. 2004. On chronicity and space(s) in historical dialectology. In: Dossena and Lass (eds.), 97–136.

Williamson, Keith. 2007. *A Linguistic Atlas of Older Scots, Phase 1: 1380–1500* (LAOS). http://www.lel.ed.ac.uk/ihd/laos1/laos1.html; last accessed 14 April 2017.

Laura Wright
Chapter 9:
Language contact

1   Introduction —— 150
2   Contact with Romance languages (the mixed-language business variety) —— 151
3   Contact with Celtic languages —— 152
4   Other foreign language contact within Britain —— 154
5   Dialect contact within Britain —— 157
6   English transported abroad —— 159
7   Summary —— 163
8   References —— 163

Abstract: This chapter discusses contact between English and other languages, and also contact between different dialects within Britain. Such contact is likely to have led to grammatical changes, lexical borrowings and the rise of Standard English. Non-standard, predominantly Southern, English carried abroad by colonizers is also treated, as this is the period when English first became established in the New World and southern hemisphere. The main languages referred to in this chapter are Anglo-Norman, Medieval Latin, the Celtic languages spoken in Britain, Dutch, and French.

1 Introduction

By 1475, English had already been greatly influenced by contact with other Indo-European languages, predominantly Old Norse and Anglo-Norman French. Spoken Anglo-Norman and Latin had influenced English well before the Early Modern period, but immediately prior to 1475 it seems to have been the written varieties of Anglo-Norman (AN) and Medieval Latin (MLt.), the languages of written record, which exerted an influence on business practice. Over the course of our period they were to be replaced by English, but their semantic and orthographic legacy continued. The first section considers the way in which

---

Laura Wright: Cambridge (UK)

Anglo-Norman and Medieval Latin were routinely mixed when keeping accounts.

2 Contact with Romance languages (the mixed-language business variety)

Until around 1475 (earlier in the case of some archives, later in others), accounts and inventories were written in a mixed-language variety which combined Medieval Latin, Anglo-Norman, and Middle English. This might sound like a limited text-type, but keeping track of money in and money out is and was one of the fundamentals of business, and then as now was a major motivation for putting pen to paper. For example, here is a short extract from an account of money spent by the London Bridge House Estate in the financial year 1477–78 on repair. This is what business writing in the early part of the Early Modern period looked like, combining the three languages in an orderly fashion, (1):

(1) Item *Cuidam harnden per CCxvj dies Johanni Boyle per CCxvj dies Thome Cowherd per CCviij dies henrico Milhale per CCxij dies & Johanni Reyne per lxvij dies fremasons operantes in hewyng & apparellyng lapides vocatis brigge assheler ac in factura & posicione illius nouo Groyne ad finem occidentalem Capelle sub tenemento in tenura Johannis Robgent* / (London Metropolitan Archives, MS CLA/007/FN/02/003, London Bridge Wardens' Annual Accounts volume 3, 1460–1484, folio 288, financial year 1477-8. Roman indicates expanded forms)
'And to a certain Harnden for 216 days, John Boyle for 216 days, Thomas Cowherd for 208 days, Henry Milhale for 212 days and John Reyne for 67 days, freemasons, working in hewing and apparelling stone called bridge ashlar, and in making and positioning that new groin at the Western end of the chapel under the tenement in the tenure of John Robgent'

In this text-type the grammatical matrix is that of Medieval Latin, but nouns, adjectives, deverbal *-ing* forms, and proper names could optionally be realized in English, with both languages informed semantically by Anglo-Norman. In this Medieval Latin extract, there are the following non-Latin nouns and deverbal *-ing* forms: *hewyng* (OE+OE), *apparellyng* (AN+OE), *brigge* (OE), *assheler* (AN), *groyne* (?AN). This is not because the scribes did not know Latin; rather, a set of language-mixing rules had developed in this text-type, and plenty of documents written in this kind of mixed language still exist in archives around Britain. It was the supra-regional professional norm during the centuries preceding our period, and its effect on the development of written English (particularly with regard to spelling and lexis) is currently under investigation (see e.g. Wright 2000, 2001a, 2002a, 2002b, 2005, 2012, forthc.; Trotter 2010; Ingham forthc.). Several other text-types routinely used language mixing, including medical, astronomical, mathematical, and other scientific texts, sermons and other religious writings, legal texts, administrative texts, literary prose, drama and verse (see Schendl 2000, 2002). So the first point is that Early Modern written English followed on directly from five hundred years' worth of mixed-language usage, and carried over many of its Romance-influenced ways, including much technical vocabulary. At the beginning of the Early Modern period, writing was a still a predominantly trilingual affair, and monolingual writing in English was only just becoming the norm.

3 Contact with Celtic languages

Within the British Isles, at the beginning of the Early Modern period, not everyone would have spoken English. The Celtic group of languages spoken in Britain – Welsh, Cornish, Irish Gaelic, Scottish Gaelic, Manx, perhaps Cumbrian – were mainly restricted to their various regions, but within those regions held sway. There has long been an acceptance that the Celtic languages did not exert much influence on English because there seem to be very few Celtic loan-words in English, or Celtic place-names in England (see Coates 2002: 72–75). This view has been countered by, amongst others, White (2003: 42), who points out that it is to be expected that a high-status peoples would be unlikely to borrow lexemes from a low-status substrate language, and that the relevant place-names refer to places that were only settled in late Anglo-Saxon times. Whether these Celtic languages caused any other kind of contact phenomena has been the subject of several recent papers, such as those in Tristram (ed.) (2000, 2003); and Filppula et al. (eds.) (2002). To consider those which fall within the remit of our period: Klemola (2000) suggests that the verb constraint known as the "Northern Subject Rule" might stem from substratum influence from the Brythonic group of Celtic languages, as it has parallels in Welsh, Cornish, and Breton. (The Northern Subject Rule operates in those Northern dialects where third-person plural present-tense markers are constrained by the adjacency of the pronoun *they*. An utterance from the *Survey of English Dialects* for Lancashire illustrates: *they* **peel** *them and* **boils** *them* – where the presence of *they* next to the verb *peel* blocks the suffix *-s*, which is otherwise realized on *boils*.) The Northern Subject Rule is first attested in Northern Middle English and Middle Scots texts, and is still current in some

Scottish dialects. It can be found in Early Modern London English writing; Schendl (1996) analyzed third person plural present-tense indicative morphology in selected works of fifteen London authors and found it to be variably present. He analyzed selected Shakespearean texts, and found that "none of the c.160 instances of plural – (e)s in Shakespeare occurs in the pattern 'they + adjacent plural present indicative verb', though this construction is attested more than 300 times in Shakespeare's works" (Schendl 1996: 150).

With respect to the progressive, Mittendorf and Poppe (2000), Poppe (2003), and Filppula (2003) considered evidence for the possibility that the English progressive construction (*to be* + v-*ing*, as in *Mary* **is** *sing***ing**) might stem from a Celtic substratum. Filppula (2003: 154–158) provides a summary of earlier scholars' work, and opines that it is indeed likely to be the result of contact with Celtic languages. The progressive gained ground in the Early Modern period and is still widening its scope today. The spread and subsequent retrenchment of periphrastic *do* is one of the most well-known changes of our period. Klemola (2002) considers the rise of periphrastic *do* and its possible substratum in Brythonic Celtic (the Welsh, Cornish, Breton group). The earliest attestations of periphrastic *do* are found in affirmative declaratives in 13th-century South-western texts, and in negative declaratives and questions from the late 14th century (Denison 1993: 264–265). Periphrastic *do* in affirmative declaratives then began to decline during the latter half of the 16th century, standardizing to emphatic contexts only by about 1700 (see Warner, Chapter 13). Klemola (2002) suggests that the 19th-century geographical distribution of periphrastic *do* in South-western dialects, centering on Dorset, Wiltshire, Somerset, and Gloucestershire, indicates the probable Middle English heartland of this construction, and opines that Celtic influence is a likely contributory factor in the rise of periphrastic *do*. It should be highlighted that there is a distinction to be made between Celtic contact at point of settlement, resulting in the subjection of the Celts and their languages (murder, enslavement, exodus, and other types of cultural withdrawal, resulting in not much language contact phenomena – although with rather more place-name continuity than has hitherto been appreciated [Coates 2002: 73–75]), and prolonged Celtic contact with living speakers in the relevant parts of Britain culminating in our period, possibly resulting in such convergence features as the Northern Subject Rule, the progressive, and periphrastic *do*.

4 Other foreign language contact within Britain

Turning now to speakers of languages from outside British territory: there is much evidence that other foreign languages were heard within Britain during the Early Modern period, but overall, and possibly with exceptions, it seems likely that their speakers accommodated to English rather than the other way around. Let us consider the evidence for their presence: two volumes by Goose and Luu (eds.) (2005) and Luu (2005) detail "alien" and "stranger" presence in Early Modern Britain. As a simplification, we can say that foreigners came to Britain either to trade, for economic betterment, or to escape persecution in their homelands. Of the latter, three groups stand out – Dutch, Flemish and Walloon refugees avoiding Spanish persecution in the southern Netherlands from the middle of the 16th century; the Moriscos, expelled from Spain in 1609; and the Huguenots who fled from France in the 1680s (Goose 2005: 1). Leaving aside London for the moment,

> All of the more significant provincial immigrant settlements are to be found in the south and east of England, in the towns of Norwich, Canterbury, Colchester, Sandwich, Maidstone, Southampton, Great Yarmouth, Dover, Thetford, King's Lynn, Stamford, Halstead, Rye, Winchelsea, and later also on Canvey Island in Essex and in the fens of Lincolnshire and Cambridgeshire, at Sandtoft and Thorney respectively. Their foundations, with the exceptions of the fenland and Canvey Island communities, date from between 1561 and 1576 (Goose 2005: 17–18).

There were at least 16,000 aliens living in Canterbury, Colchester, London, Norwich, Sandwich, and Southampton by the 1570s (Luu 2005: 90), and "it is very likely that collectively the provincial immigrant communities outnumbered those in London in the late sixteenth century, and in total there may have been as many as 23,000–24,000 aliens in England by the 1590s" (Goose 2005: 17–18).

The largest immigrant community outside London during our period was in Norwich. This began with the official importation of Flemish wool workers to boost the local economy in 1565. Next in size was Canterbury, with French-speaking Walloons manufacturing draperies and silks in 1575, reinforced by migrants from Calais in the 1640s, and the Huguenot immigration of the later 1600s. The Sandwich settlement of Flemings, also cloth-workers, dates from 1561. Numbers fluctuated over the decades, but suggested peak alien figures are Sandwich: 53% in the 1570s, Norwich: 40% in the 1580s, and Canterbury: 33% in the 1590s (Goose 2005: 18–21).

These were the largest and longest-lasting immigrant communities outside London, where Dutch and French would have been routinely used. Trudgill (2001) has suggested that it is this process of language contact with Dutch and French that resulted in East Anglian leveling of the present-tense verb paradigm to zero, so that instead of third-person singular *she walks*, the traditional form in this area is ***she** walk*. Language contact is a plausible explanation for a morphological simplification of a system (as happened here), as it is well-known that speakers of mutually unintelligible languages who interact persistently in adulthood produce new systems that are morphologically simpler than the input systems – which is how pidgin languages are created. In fact, speakers in much of East Anglia had already been placed in a language contact situation by the advent of Viking Old Norse speakers in earlier centuries (see Poussa 1999; Nevalainen et al. 2001), so that the advent of the Dutch may be regarded as having exacerbated a language-contact process already set in motion. It is quite a challenge to disentangle processes of language contact and change initiated at the end of the first millennium from those introduced five hundred years later. By the mid-20th century the traditional English dialects had either leveled to -*s* or to zero (these being the only two options available by then, all other suffixes having been lost, with the exception of some vestigial usages of ***thou** walkest*), so all the dialects simplified with regard to present-tense verb morphology, with or without language contact.

Turning now to London, Luu (2005: 87–140) provides data on immigrants in Elizabethan London, including whereabouts in the City they lived and where they originally came from. That it was cosmopolitan is not in doubt:

> Throughout all of the conflicts and controversies of the period London remained notably cosmopolitan, accommodating not only Dutch and French, but also small communities of Spanish, Italians, Germans and other nationalities, while there is little to indicate that – except for brief periods of national crisis or in relatively isolated incidents – foreign conflict ever translated into concerted action against the immigrants in our midst (Goose 2005: 9).

By 1483–84, the alien population in London had increased to 3,400, forming at least 6% of the population (Luu 2005: 89). The medieval Hansard and Italian communities were somewhat in decline in our period as trade shifted to Antwerp, with probably as few as seventy Italian and eighty Hanse merchants resident in London in the early 1500s (Luu 2005: 87). At this date there were possibly a further 1,800 artisan aliens living in London with their families, out of a total population of about 50,000 in 1500 (Goose 2005: 13). In 1550 a change to this pattern was introduced: a charter was granted to religious refugees to set up their own churches in London, resulting in waves of religious and political refugees, with perhaps 30,000 people entering England between 1567 and 1573. At its peak in 1553, London accommodated around 10,000 strangers out of an estimated total population of about 80,000 (Luu 2005: 88–91; Goose 2005: 13), forming roughly 12% of the population. Thereafter, numbers of immigrants declined in the capital, despite continued immigration, as more English people migrated to the city, and immigrants moved elsewhere in England or returned home. Estimates are down to about 10% by the 1570s (Luu 2005: 97). Even the late 17th-century Huguenot immigration probably did not significantly increase the proportion.

With regard to languages spoken in the capital, in 1593 Luu estimates that Dutch-speakers constituted 55% of aliens in the capital, with French speakers constituting 34% and Italian speakers 3% (Luu 2005: 99). They settled overwhelmingly north of the river, concentrated largely on the edges of the city. There is little doubt that peoples of the same culture interacted together, but, of necessity, acquired English to a greater or lesser extent. To take one example, Wessell Webling, a brewer from Cleves, arrived in London around 1565 at the age of sixteen. He began work as a servant to his brother, a brewer in Southwark, and when his brother died in 1568 he continued in partnership with his brother's widow. Webling not being as experienced in brewing as his brother, the business failed to make a profit and the partnership was dissolved. Webling then went to work with an English brewer who had married the widow of one of his brother's alien colleagues, but this partnership, too, failed. By 1586, Webling had crossed the river and was living in the Steelyard. By 1593 he was running a large brewery employing more than thirty-four servants, and he eventually died a wealthy man in 1610, leaving a small bequest to the poor of his home town, Groten Recken in Westphalia, as well as larger sums to London friends and relatives (Luu 2005: 270, 276, 282). To return to 1576, when his fortunes were finally on the up but not yet established, we find him, along with a group of his countrymen, consorting with local women, (2):

(2) *Wessell Weblinge beinge here called & chardged to haue offended wth mary Poyntell & to haue had thuse of her body He doth confesse yt that he is in falte ^therin^ and is content to geve of his benevolens to the poore xl^s Desyringe to be spared of his ponyshement And therefore the Courte is content to Dischardge hym for all offencs vntill this Daye/* (Bridewell Court Minute Book fo. 161v, 23 January 1576, London, Guildhall Library, MS Minutes of the Court of Governors of Bridewell and Bethlem: Microfilm Reels MS33011/1–2, 22 April 1559–6 May 1576)

Prostitution between foreign men and local women gave rise to language-contact opportunities in a weak-tie network context. Weak-tie networks are thought to be a conduit of language change, and the concept belongs to social network theory. Social network theory, initially developed in the field of sociology but adopted by biologists, geographers, and anthropologists as well as linguists, is a technique for accounting for the interactions between humans as they go about their lives in different social groupings – family, workplace, clique of friends, and so on. It was notably applied by Lesley Milroy (1987) when studying speech communities in

Belfast, and has become a predominant paradigm in the field of historical sociolinguistics. Once a network of speakers has been identified the network is analyzed for density and multiplexity, that is, the frequency and kind of interaction that occurs between individuals. Ties between individuals are said to be strong if the individuals in a network interact frequently, repeatedly and in several social contexts, and to be strong ties if the individual members interact in this way with many other members of the same network. Ties are said to be weak if individuals interact infrequently in a single social context, and a loose-knit network with weak links is one where individuals interact with few others from that group on infrequent or single occasions. There are currently two predominant interpretations with regard to linguistic change and network ties. The first interpretation is that innovators of linguistic change are thought to have usually weak links to a network, but that strong ties facilitate actual adoption of innovations at a later stage. The second is that linguistic change is led by strong-tie innovators who sit at the hub of a web of high-frequency, multiplex strong and weak links. The first view has been developed by Milroy and Milroy (1985), the second by Labov (2001), but Raumolin-Brunberg (2006) has suggested that these linguists have been looking at different stages of the dissemination of linguistic change, with the Milroys concentrating on the initial stages, and Labov on the later developments.

To conclude this section; there was systemic influence on English from Old Norse and Anglo-Norman (before the period considered here, but with continuing effect), written Anglo-Norman and Medieval Latin (in the early part of our period), and possibly the Celtic languages (with continuing effect in the Early Modern period); and day-to-day influence from speakers with other first languages (notably Dutch and French) in, particularly, London, Canterbury, Colchester, and the port towns of Norwich, Southampton, and Sandwich. Once immigrants had settled in Britain they embarked upon a lifelong process of English language acquisition and development.

5 Dialect contact within Britain

Let us return to our immigrant, Wessell Webling. He maintained network ties with his countrymen for forty-five years, but also interacted with such English speakers as his employers (when he was younger) his workforce (when he was older), the younger members of his family, his local English friends, and community members. How can such lifelong influences on his English be reconstructed and analyzed, supposing him to have left sufficient data in the form of letters or other personal papers? Longitudinal studies over the lifespan are a recent development in the field of historical linguistics, the study of changes over an individual's life having been made possible by the amassing of computer-searchable data. One such is Raumolin-Brunberg (2009), who looked at how Sir Walter Ralegh (from Devon), Philip Gawdy (from Norfolk) and John Chamberlain (Londoner) changed their grammar in adulthood with regard to the morphological variables *my/thy* vs *mine/thine*, *-s* vs *-th*, affirmative and negative *do*, and subject relativizer *who*, in a study of their personal letters. These changes seem to have occurred as a result of their shifting social networks as they moved around geographically and rose socially in Elizabethan society. In particular, Ralegh and Gawdy changed their grammar when they were middle-aged. Raumolin-Brunberg hypothesizes that either they just carried on increasing proportions of incoming variants acquired in childhood, or, as migrants to London, they accommodated to forms heard in their new environment, leading even to hypercorrection. She also notes that they, unlike Chamberlain, were socially ambitious, and that this ambition might be reflected in their adult language acquisition. Work detailed in Nevalainen and Raumolin-Brunberg (2003) charts the grammar of some more of these socially shifting migrants to London from other parts of Britain by analyzing personal letters held in the *Corpus of Early English Correspondence* for morphological variables.

One of the great differences between the end of the Middle English period and the start of the Early Modern is the increase of visitors to the capital from both outside the capital and outside the country for reasons of trade (see Keene 2000; Wright 2001a) and social betterment. These included both migrants to the capital from other parts of Britain and the Continent, and people coming repeatedly on short-term visits and then returning home. I suggest that here we have a case of cause and effect: the cause being the increasing amount of visits to the capital from speakers outside it, and the effect being the rise of Standard English. Standard English bears the traces of a dialect-contact variety, from its simplified morphology to its mixed-dialect lexis. Whereas London English of the early Middle English period used predominantly regionally marked, Southern morphology, proto-Standard English (that is, English written for formal purposes from 1475 into the 1500s) came to adopt more and more linguistic features from the regional dialects, which features subsequently lost their regional marking. These include:

- Southern present-tense indicative verb plural *-th* came to be replaced by Midland *-en* and *-s*. Subsequently, *-th* and *-n* were lost and zero became the Standard English marker, with *-s* still in use as a verb plural form in London English.
- Southern present-tense indicative verb third person singular *-th* was replaced by Northern *-s*.

- present participle markers changed from regionally marked *-and(e), -end(e), -ind(e)* to non-regional *-ing*.
- Northern *are* took over as the plural third person present form of the verb *to be* and Southern *be(n), beth* were, eventually, lost.
- South-western auxiliary *do* expanded in function.
- adverbial suffixes reduced from Southern *-liche* to Northern *-ly* (or this change can be regarded as simply the loss of the regionally marked final syllable).
- Northern pronouns *they, them, their* ousted *hei, hem, here*.

Some of these developments can be regarded as the effect of dialect leveling, which is the process whereby interaction between speakers of different dialects leads to a kind of 'consensus' output, with features that are regionally marked lost, and features that are held in common retained. Thus, the regional plural indicative present-tense markers *-th*, *-n*, and *-s* were lost and zero adopted; non-regional present participle *-ing* took over from regionally marked *-and(e), -end(e), -ind(e)*; and regional adverbial *-liche* went to non-regional *-ly*. In other cases, one regional form came to predominate in Standard English which, although originating outside the South-East, then lost its local marking. Third person singular *-s, are*, the *th-* pronouns, and *do*, all regional forms in late Middle English, no longer had regional connotations by the end of the Early Modern period (see the essays in Wright [ed.] (2000) for more on the processes of the standardization of English).

6 English transported abroad

As English speakers began to colonize territories in the New World, the English language came into contact with indigenous languages, and also the languages of other colonizers. This situation led to the creation of New Englishes and English-lexicon creoles (Schneider 2007). As the bulk of this speaker contact lies outside our timeframe, in the Late Modern period (Hickey 2004a), I shall mention just the first English-speaking colony in America, the first in what is now Canada, the first Caribbean Englishes, and the first Southern Hemisphere English.

The first English-speaking colony to survive successfully in North America was the Virginia Colony, with its township at Jamestown, founded by 104 Englishmen on 13 May 1607, with the first slaves thought to have arrived from Africa in 1619. The first young man to be sentenced to transportation to Virginia by the London Court of Bridewell was on 2 October 1607 (William Person, a dyer's apprentice, found guilty of cozening ('stealing') his master's goods and running away), and young people continued to be transported officially into the 1640s –

and unofficially thereafter, due to the lucrative illegal practice of "spiriting" or kidnapping. Other London courts continued sentencing people to Virginia into the 1700s and to New England from 1643 (see, for example, Wright 2001b, 2003, 2004 and Wareing 2000, which analyzes data from the Middlesex Sessions Papers [1645–1718], recording the transporting of offenders to the New World from the Middlesex Courts). Not too much is known about early language contact with Algonkian speakers, although there is some record, and it is worth noting that native Americans went to London (Salmon 1992). Unfortunately, one at least seems to have come to grief there, (3):

(3) *Kicko an Indian* par *Lord Maio^r kept. William Campion John Harding Humfrey Young Thom^{as} Rich John Basse Beniamen Carter Thom^{as} Clement Nicholas Moore William Pottes* par *Const*able *Cleworth Langborne* vagrant *boyes to be sent to Virginia* (Bridewell Court Minute Book fo. 238, 26 August 1631, London, Guildhall Library, MS Minutes of the Court of Governors of Bridewell and Bethlem: Microfilm Reels MS33011/7, 1 March 1626–7 May 1634)

The main debates with regard to early American English have been about dialect influence on the development of American English from Ulster Scots (which lies substantially after our period) and about language contact with speakers of West African languages under conditions of slavery, putatively giving rise to present-day African American Vernacular English. This is a much-disputed topic, but as there is scant direct evidence from our period, it will not be pursued here (see Winford 1997, 1998 for a summary).

The first English-speaking colony in what is now Canada was founded on the island of Newfoundland in 1583 (Clarke 2004). However, settlement patterns were seasonal, with residents returning to their homes in the West Country after one or two fishing seasons. The main language variety with which English came into contact in this locality was mostly Irish English (although there were some monolingual Irish Gaelic speakers) from 1675, but the bulk of the Irish immigration came considerably later (see Clarke 2004: 244–245).

In the North Atlantic, Bermuda was colonized by English-speakers in 1609, with the first slaves on the islands by 1617. We hear of the first vagrants and petty criminals sentenced to Bermuda from the London Court of Bridewell in May 1619. The first Caribbean Islands to be colonized by English-speakers were St Kitts in 1623 and Barbados in 1626 (Baker 1998: 337–339; note that this is old-style dating – 1624 and 1627 are given as the founding dates in e.g. Hickey 2004b: 331). African slaves are known of on St Kitts from 1626, and young London vagrants were sentenced to St Kitts from June 1628 and to Barbados from January 1632. Initially, Barbados is thought to have had a hundred or more British settlers, thirty-two Amerindians from the Guianas, and in 1629 an influx of settlers from St Kitts (Baker 1998: 348) and in the 1640s from Ireland (Hickey 2004b: 331; for an overview of English-language contact in the Caribbean, see Hickey 2004b). Parkvall (1998: 64–5) gives information about the early colonization of St Kitts, with English speakers in contact with speakers of French and African languages during the 1600s. Baker (1998: 346–347) suggests that a language-contact "medium for inter-ethnic communication" would have come into being on St Kitts in the first few decades of settlement, although it should be noted that this view is contentious (cf. Hickey 2004b: 332). Baker's argument is that previous commentators have assumed that slaves tried to speak the language of their masters, and that their English was effectively a learner variety with substrate interference, whilst the English-speakers simply addressed slaves in English. He posits another scenario: namely, all Kittitian speakers, freemen and slaves, would have tried to communicate with each other, thereby causing a medium for interethnic communication to come into being and eventually stabilize. This scenario holds good for all multilingual colonies consisting of adult monolingual speakers, and, indeed, explains why Surinam Creoles (for instance) have a predominantly English lexicon despite being only briefly under English rule (from 1651–67) and whence the majority of English settlers and English-owned slaves had departed by 1675. If, as Baker suggests, an English-lexicon medium of interethnic communication had arisen before 1675, then there would have been no need to abandon it simply because the monolingual English-speakers had left and new Dutch administrators had arrived. It would still have functioned successfully as a code between slaves speaking non-mutually intelligible languages, and the Dutch administrators would have then spoken it, to a degree (Baker 1998: 348).

Baker's scenario can be supported by data from the oldest Southern Hemisphere English, that of the South Atlantic island of St Helena. From the late 1500s to 1673 St Helena was contested by the Portuguese, Dutch, French, and English. In 1673 the island was granted to the British East India Company in London to hold in perpetuity. The Company set up the island's infrastructure, including keeping court records in the St Helena Consultations Books (British Library India Office G Factory Record Series MS G/32/2 St Helena Consultations 1676–1696), two copies of which survive. The East India Company and the free planters who settled on St Helena owned slaves from West Africa, Java, India, Madagascar, Sumatra, Borneo, and Malaya, amongst other places; and there is evidence in the St Helena Consultations that in the late 17th century such slaves spoke three or even four separate linguistic codes:
a. first, the St Helena slaves are represented as speaking the same kind of non-Standard Southern English spoken by the free planters and the soldiers. This is the default language which the slaves and everyone else are recorded as

speaking before the Court. It is possible that the Court Recorder standardized the slaves' English and that it is presented as more competently spoken than it really was, but there is no evidence for this.

b. second, some slaves reported that they could not understand others who spoke in Portuguese, a language used deliberately by some (rebelling) slaves so that other (non-rebelling) slaves would not understand. This may have been contemporary Portuguese, or a Portuguese-lexicon creole.

c. third, in December 1695 the St Helena Consultations contain a small amount of a restructured or minimal-pidginized variety of English, mostly in negative constructions: "you noe savy", "I noe tell you", "me noe save spake English", "you haue no good hart", "Jack noe such foole". There is very little, but as it is at such an early date it is important. It is compounded by the fact that some slaves are recorded as using elements of such pidgin to talk to each other as well as the Court, and the speakers who used it are also recorded as using English and hence are codeswitchers, possibly for social reasons.

d. fourth, there is mention that some slaves spoke to others in their "country language"; that is, presumably, the language used in their country of origin (see Wright 2013a, 2013b, 2014; Schreier and Wright 2010).

It is also worth mentioning that a few lines containing similarly restructured English dating from a few years earlier, 1686, are extant in the Bodleian Library from a slave-trading station of the Gold Coast of West Africa (Huber 1999: 87–88). Huber (1999: 93) goes on to make the point that, wherever they were shipped to (and some went to St Helena), these slaves would have used such English (or restructured English) as they had gleaned for purposes of interethnic communication, so their variety cannot have been a fully expanded pidgin as such (expanded pidgins being unintelligible to speakers of the lexifier language). Finally, it should be emphasized that the variety of English inputting to all these New Englishes was, to a large extent, the regional variety of the people sentenced to go there from the London courts, or the poorer kind of planters and soldiers, and not Standard English.

To conclude this section: there is little data on English language contact in the colonies during the Early Modern period, but as it was a significant, formative period for the resultant New Englishes and English-lexicon creoles, it deserves mention.

7 Summary

Other types of Early Modern English language contact not dealt with in this chapter include the vast amount of word creation from Classical Latin and Greek roots that is to be found specifically in scientific writing (see, e.g., Norri 1992) and more generally in words of a formal register, and also borrowings due to specific activities, such as Italian in the field of music. The main thrust of this chapter has been to demonstrate that some Early Modern English speakers would have been, directly or indirectly, in a language-contact situation, whether because they came into contact with non-English speaking Celtic indigenes, because they came into contact with foreigners (with French and Dutch being the predominant languages involved), or because they came into contact with speakers from other dialect areas (with London being the largest city where this occurred). Simplification is one of the outcomes of language contact amongst adult speakers, and the processes of dialect contact are particularly significant in our period because one of the main differences between the Middle and the Early Modern periods is the tremendous amount of regional variation present in all the Middle English dialects as compared to the comparative lack of variation in Standard English. Had there been no contact between English speakers (especially those in London) and speakers of other languages, or contact between speakers of different English dialects, then English would not have standardized when and where it did.

8 References

Baker, Philip. 1998. Investigating the origin and diffusion of shared features among the Atlantic English creoles. In: Baker and Bruyn (eds.), 315–364.
Baker, Philip and Adrienne Bruyn (eds.). 1998. *St Kitts and the Atlantic Creoles: The Texts of Samuel Augustus Mathews in Perspective*. London: University of Westminster Press.
Clarke, Sandra. 2004. The legacy of British and Irish English in Newfoundland. In: Hickey (ed.), 242–261.
Coates, Richard. 2002. The significance of Celtic place-names in England. In: Filppula (eds.), 47–85.
Denison, David. 1993. *English Historical Syntax: Verbal Constructions*. London: Longman.
Filppula, Markku. 2003. More on the English progressive and the Celtic connection. In: Tristram (ed.), 150–168.
Filppula, Markku, Juhani Klemola, and Heli Pitkänen (eds.). 2002. *The Celtic Roots of English*. Joensuu: Joensuu University Press.
Filppula, Markku, Juhani Klemola, and Heli Paulasto (eds.). 2008. *English and Celtic in Contact*. London: Routledge.
Goose, Nigel. 2005. Immigrants in Tudor and Early Stuart England. In: Goose and Luu (eds.), 1–40.

Goose, Nigel and Lien Luu (eds.). 2005. *Immigrants in Tudor and Early Stuart England*. Sussex Academic Press: Brighton.

Hickey, Raymond. 2004a. Timeline for varieties of English. In: Hickey (ed.), 621–626.

Hickey, Raymond. 2004b. English dialect input to the Caribbean. In: Hickey (ed.), 326–359.

Hickey, Raymond (ed.). 2004. *Legacies of Colonial English: Studies in Transported Dialects*. Cambridge: Cambridge University Press.

Huber, Magnus. 1999. Atlantic English creoles and the Lower Guinea Coast: A case against Afrogenesis. In: Magnus Huber and Mikael Parkvall (eds.), *Spreading the Word: The Issue of Diffusion among the Atlantic Creoles*, 81–110. London: University of Westminster Press.

Ingham, Richard. 2013. Language mixing in medieval Latin documents: Vernacular articles and nouns. In: Judith Jefferson and Ad Putter (eds.), *Medieval Multilingualism in Later Medieval Britain: Sources and Analysis*, 105–122. Turnhout: Brepols.

Keene, Derek. 2000. Metropolitan values: Migration, mobility and cultural norms, London 1100–1700. In: Wright (ed.), 93–116.

Klemola, Juhani. 2000. The origins of the Northern Subject Rule: A case of early contact? In: Tristram (ed.), 329–346.

Klemola, Juhani. 2002. Periphrastic DO: Dialectal distribution and origins. In: Filppula (eds.), 199–212.

Labov, William. 2001. *Principles of Linguistic Change*. Vol. II *Social Factors*. Oxford: Blackwell.

Luu, Lien B. 2005. *Immigrants and the Industries of London 1500–1700*. Aldershot: Ashgate.

Milroy, James and Lesley Milroy. 1985. Linguistic change, social network and speaker innovation. *Journal of Linguistics* 21: 339–384.

Milroy, Lesley. 1987. *Language and Social Networks*. Oxford: Blackwell.

Mittendorf, Ingo and Erich Poppe. 2000. Celtic contacts of the English progressive? In: Tristram (ed.), 117–145.

Nevalainen, Terttu and Helena Raumolin-Brunberg. 2003. *Historical Sociolinguistics: Language Change in Tudor and Stuart England*. London: Longman Pearson Education.

Nevalainen, Terttu, Helena Raumolin-Brunberg, and Peter Trudgill. 2001. Chapters in the social history of East Anglian English: The case of the third-person singular. In: Trudgill and Fisiak (eds.), 187–204.

Norri, Juhani. 1992. *Names of Sicknesses in English, 1400–1550: An Exploration of the Lexical Field*. Helsinki: Suomalainen Tiedeakatemia.

Orton, Harold, Eugen Dieth 1962–71. *Survey of English Dialects: The Basic Material*. Leeds: E. J. Arnold.

Parkvall, Mikael. 1998. A short note on the peopling of English St Kitts. In: Baker and Bruyn (eds.), 63–74.

Poppe, Erich. 2003. Progress on the progressive? A report. In: Tristram (ed.), 65–84.

Poussa, Patricia. 1999. Dickens as sociolinguist: Dialect in David Copperfield. In: Irma Taavitsainen, Gunnel Melchers, and Päivi Pahta (eds.), *Writing in Nonstandard English*, 27–44. Amsterdam/Philadelphia: John Benjamins.

Raumolin-Brunberg, Helena. 2006. Leaders of linguistic change in Early Modern England. In: Roberta Facchinetti and Matti Rissanen (eds.), *Corpus-based Studies of Diachronic English*, 115–134. Frankfurt am Main: Peter Lang.

Raumolin-Brunberg, Helena. 2009. Lifespan changes in the language of three early modern gentlemen. In: Arja Nurmi, Minna Nevala, and Minna Palander-Collin (eds.), *The Language of Daily Life in England (1400–1800)*, 165–196. Amsterdam/Philadelphia: John Benjamins.

Salmon, Vivian. 1992. Thomas Harriot (1560–1621) and the origins of Amerindian Linguistics. *Historiographia Linguistica* 191: 25–56.
Schendl, Herbert. 1996. The 3rd plural present indicative in Early Modern English – variation and linguistic contact. In: Derek Britton (ed.), *English Historical Linguistics 1994. Papers from the 8th International Conference on English Historical Linguistics*, 143–160. Amsterdam/Philadelphia: John Benjamins.
Schendl, Herbert. 2000. Linguistic aspects of code-switching in medieval English texts. In: Trotter (ed.), 77–92.
Schendl, Herbert. 2002. Mixed language texts as data and evidence in English historical linguistics. In: Donka Minkova and Robert Stockwell (eds.), *Studies in the History of the English Language. A Millenial Perspective*, 51–78. Berlin/New York: Mouton de Gruyter.
Schneider, Edgar W. 2007. *Postcolonial English: Varieties Around the World*. Cambridge: Cambridge University Press.
Schreier, Daniel and Laura Wright. 2010. Earliest St Helenian English in writing. In: Raymond Hickey (ed.), *Varieties in Writing. The Written Word as Linguistic Evidence*. Amsterdam/Philadelphia: John Benjamins.
Tristram, Hildegard L. C. (ed.). 2000. *Celtic Englishes II*. Heidelberg: Universitätsverlag C. Winter.
Tristram, Hildegard L. C. (ed.). 2003. *The Celtic Englishes III*. Heidelberg: Universitätsverlag C. Winter.
Trotter, David. 2010. Bridging the gap: The (socio)linguistic evidence of some medieval English bridge accounts. In: Richard Ingham (ed.), *The Anglo-Norman Language and its Context*, 51–62. York/Woodbridge: York Medieval Press in association with Boydell and Brewer.
Trotter, David A. (ed.). 2000. *Multilingualism in Later Medieval Britain*. Woodbridge: D. S. Brewer.
Trudgill, Peter. 2001. Third-person singular zero: African-American English, East Anglian dialects and Spanish persecution in the low countries. In: Trudgill and Fisiak (eds.), 179–186.
Trudgill, Peter and Jacek Fisiak (eds.). 2001. *East Anglian English*. Woodbridge: D. S. Brewer.
Wareing, John. 2000. *The Regulation and Organisation of the Trade in Indentured Servants for the American Colonies in London, 1645–1718*. Unpublished Ph.D dissertation, University of London.
White, David L. 2003. Brittonic influence in the reductions of Middle English nominal morphology. In: Tristram (ed.), 29–45.
Winford, Don. 1997. On the origins of African American Vernacular English – A creolist perspective. Part 1: Sociohistorical background. *Diachronica* 14(2): 305–344.
Winford, Don. 1998. On the origins of African American Vernacular English – A creolist perspective. Part 2: Linguistic features. *Diachronica* 15(1): 99–154.
Wright, Laura. 2000. Bills, accounts, inventories: Everyday trilingual activities in the business world of later medieval England. In: Trotter (ed.), 149–156.
Wright, Laura. 2001a. The role of international and national trade in the standardisation of English. In: Isabel Moskowich-Spiegel Fandiño, Begoa Crespo García, Emma Lezcano González, and Begoña Simal González (eds.), *Re-interpretations of English. Essays on Language, Linguistics and Philology* (I), 189–207. A Coruña: Universidade da Coruña.
Wright, Laura. 2001b. Third person singular present-tense -s, -th and zero, 1575–1648. *American Speech* 76(3): 236–258.
Wright, Laura. 2002a. Code-intermediate phenomena in medieval mixed-language business texts. *Language Sciences* 24: 471–489.

Wright, Laura. 2002b. Standard English and the lexicon: Why so many different spellings? In: Mari C. Jones and Edith Esch (eds.), *Language Change: The Interplay of Internal, External and Extra-linguistic Factors*, 181–200. Berlin/New York: Mouton de Gruyter.

Wright, Laura. 2003. Eight grammatical features of Southern United States speech present in Early Modern London prison narratives. In: Stephen J. Nagle and Sara L. Sanders (eds.), *English in the Southern United States*, 36–63. Cambridge: Cambridge University Press.

Wright, Laura. 2004. The language of transported Londoners: Third-person-singular present-tense markers in depositions from Virginia and the Bermudas, 1607–1624. In: Hickey (ed.), 158–171.

Wright, Laura. 2005. Medieval mixed-language business texts and the rise of Standard English. In: Janne Skaffari, Matti Peikola, Ruth Carroll, Risto Hiltunen, and Brita Wårvik (eds.), *Opening Windows on Texts and Discourses of the Past*, 381–399. Amsterdam/Philadelphia: John Benjamins.

Wright, Laura. 2012. On variation and change in London medieval mixed-language business documents. In: Merja Stenroos, Martti Mäkinen and Inge Særheim (eds.), *Language Contact and Development around the North Sea*, 99–115. Amsterdam/Philadelphia: John Benjamins.

Wright, Laura. 2013a. The contact origins of Standard English. In: Daniel Schreier and Marianne Hundt (eds). *English as a Contact Language. Studies in English Language*, 58–74. Cambridge: Cambridge University Press.

Wright, Laura. 2013b. The language of slaves on St Helena, South Atlantic, 1682–1724. In: Marijke J. Van Der Wal and Gijsbert Rutten (eds.). *Touching the Past. Studies in the historical sociolinguistics of ego-documents*, 58–74. Amsterdam: Benjamins.

Wright, Laura. 2014. Some early creole-like data from slave speakers: The Island of St Helena, 1695–1711. In: Michael D. Picone and Catherine Evans Davies (eds.), *New Perspectives on Language Variety in the South: Historical and Contemporary Approaches*, 203–218. Tuscaloosa: University of Alabama Press.

Wright, Laura. forthc. A multilingual approach to the history of Standard English. In: Paivi Pahta, Janne Skaffari and Laura Wright (eds.). *Multilingual Practices in Language History: New Perspectives*. Language Contact and Bilingualism 15. Berlin: Mouton de Gruyter.

Wright, Laura (ed.). 2000. *The Development of Standard English 1300–1800: Theories, Descriptions, Conflicts*. Cambridge: Cambridge University Press.

Lilo Moessner
Chapter 10: Standardization

1   Basic concepts —— 167
2   Reduction of variation —— 170
3   Elaboration of function —— 180
4   Summary —— 183
5   References —— 184

Abstract: The chapter starts with a discussion of the concepts Early Modern English (EModE) and standardization. Early Modern English is established as the period between Middle English (ME) and Late Modern English; it covers the 16th and 17th centuries. Reduction of variation and elaboration of function are viewed as the processes which contributed most to EModE standardization. Reduction of variation is illustrated in Section 2, with examples from the levels of spelling, morphology, and syntax. Section 3 describes the conscious elaboration of the functions of the vernacular after it replaced Latin as the language of learned discourse. It started with the expansion of the vocabulary, which was necessary for the development of new text categories and changes in already existing ones. The last section summarizes the main issues of the chapter and places them in a broader historical perspective.

1 Basic concepts

1.1 Early Modern English

Linguistic periods, like dialects, are abstractions. Their borderlines are fuzzy, and the criteria by which they are established are matters of dispute. There is not even agreement as to the types of criteria to be used; they can be language-internal or language-external or a combination of both.

Originally, historians of the English language worked with a binary model with the two periods Anglo-Saxon and English. At the end of the 19th century, it was replaced by a three-period model with the periods Old English, Middle

---

Lilo Moessner: Aachen (Germany)

English, and Modern English (Sweet 1891: 211). In this model, Early Modern English figures as a sub-period of Modern English, covering the time span 1500–1650. The most recent newcomer to the period model is Late Modern English. Although it already formed part of Sweet's three-period model, where it figured as the sub-period from 1650 onwards, it is now conceived as a full-fledged period covering the 18th and 19th centuries. Its wide acceptance as a separate period is witnessed by a series of conferences, the first of which took place in Edinburgh in 2001.

Late Modern English is perhaps too new a period to have caused discussions about its beginning and end. This is different for Early Modern English. Barber (1997) and Nevalainen (2006) agree on 1500 and 1700 as the beginning and the end of the EModE period without justifying these dates as more appropriate than others. But both scholars also mention other possible dates based on language-internal criteria. After reviewing earlier suggestions about the dating of Early Modern English, Görlach (1991: 9–11), too, proposes 1500 and 1700 as its limits. The dates 1476–1776 in the title of volume III of the *Cambridge History of the English Language* mark a wider time span for Early Modern English with cultural and political events as points of demarcation. In the introduction to the volume, Lass (1999: 6) defends the establishment of Caxton's printing press in England as the starting-point of a linguistic period by the repercussions it had on the text production process. The American Declaration of Independence as the end-point of the period is justified, because it initiated the development of English into a global language. Lass makes it quite clear that changes of the language system are related "in subtle and complex ways" to contemporary political, social, and cultural changes, but that neither can be considered the cause of the other. Therefore the extralinguistically defined end-point is not in conflict with his restriction of the linguistic period of Early Modern English to the years 1500–1700 (Lass 1999: 9).

Finally, there is a pragmatic reason for sticking to this periodization in the present chapter, too. Many of the studies on the development of individual features to be discussed in Section 3 are based on the *Helsinki Corpus of English Texts* (HC) (Rissanen et al. 1991), and in this invaluable research tool Early Modern English is considered to cover the years 1500–1710.

1.2 Standardization

We take it for granted that the general reference works on modern languages describe their standard varieties, i.e. the products of the process of standardization. Even when we consider only the written form of Present-day English (PDE), it is difficult to specify the criteria by which Standard English is defined. The

Cambridge Grammar (Huddleston and Pullum 2002: 4) claims a "widespread agreement" about "what we are calling Standard English"; it relies on the variety used in broadcasting and in edited writing. The authors of the *Comprehensive Grammar of the English Language* (Quirk et al. 1985: 7) stress other properties; for them the standard variety is taught in the schools of the countries with English as a native language, and it is associated with educated users. Descriptions like these reflect the conviction that a standard language is an idea in the mind rather than a reality (Milroy and Milroy 1999: 19). Strictly speaking, this concept of a standard language is a paradox, because the two properties most intimately associated with standard languages are their lack of variation and their stability. Yet it is our experience that languages do change and that even standard languages allow a certain degree of variation.

Milroy and Milroy (1999: 22–23) present a seven-step model for the description of the standardization process. It contains the stages selection, acceptance, diffusion, maintenance, elaboration of function, codification, and prescription. They point out that these stages need neither necessarily follow each other nor proceed with the same speed.

The non-linear character of the standardization process is also stressed by Nevalainen and Tieken-Boon van Ostade (2006: 286) in their chapter "Standardisation" in the *History of the English Language*, and they attribute it "to the fact that it was not a consciously monitored development". On this controversial point they agree with Hope (2000: 51–52), who claims that "[s]tandardisation [...] looks more like a language-internal phenomenon: something motivated and progressed below the conscious awareness of language users".

The overriding principle of EModE standardization was reduction of variation. The reduction process is partly due to the influence of public authorities, as in the case of the standardization of spelling; partly it is the outcome of subconscious choices. This is evident in all stages of the Milroyan model apart from prescription, and it will be illustrated on the levels of spelling, morphology, and syntax. The Milroys' elaboration of function stage was a conscious process in Early Modern English in those fields where the vernacular replaced Latin. This will be illustrated from the field of the English vocabulary, which had to be enlarged before the language could take over new functions.

2 Reduction of variation

Theoretically, variation can be reduced on the levels of spelling, grammar, and lexical semantics. The avoidance of polysemy was one of the goals of the natural philosophers, as the 17th-century representatives of the new experimental sciences were called. But they were realistic enough to see that this goal could not be achieved completely because of the infiniteness of the lexicon. Therefore, this aspect will be left out of consideration here.

Variation was a pervasive feature of EModE spelling, morphology, and syntax, and most of the changes which took place in Early Modern English proceeded in the same direction, towards a reduction of variation. As it is not possible within the limits of this chapter to provide an exhaustive description of all standardization processes going on in Early Modern English, my aim will rather be to give an idea of the different paths reduction of variation can take.

2.1 Spelling

EModE grammar writing followed the tradition of Latin grammar writing. Therefore, the first part of EModE grammars deals with the letters and their "voices", i.e. their relation to sounds or phonemes. Yet before the first English grammars were produced, correct spelling was already an issue in England. Scragg (1974: 58–60) explains this ultimately as a consequence of the borrowing of many Latin words during the 16th century. Due to the prestige of Latin, the spelling of earlier loanwords, which had entered English via French and then been adapted to English phonology and word structure, was changed to make their impressive history more transparent. In some cases, both spellings still exist today, and each adopted a meaning of its own or got restricted to special contexts. Well-known examples are *parson/person* (< Lt. *persona*), *poor/pauper* (< Lt. *pauper*), *frail/fragile* (< Lt. *fragilis*). Very often, however, the more prestigious form replaced the older form completely, e.g. *throne* instead of *trone*, *falcon* instead of *faucon*, *captive* instead of *caitif*. The tendency to associate English words with Latin roots was so pronounced that it also affected words of native origin: the letter <c> is an unetymological addition in *scissors* and *scythe*. They were wrongly associated with Lt. *scindere* 'cut', but the etymon of *scythe* is Old English *siðe*, and *scissors* derives from Late Lt. *cisorium* 'a cutting instrument'. Association with a Latin "etymon" was not even necessary to promote spelling changes. On the analogy of *dumb*, where the final <b> is etymologically motivated, the unetymological spellings *crumb* and *thumb* were introduced. It was only natural that the pronunciation of words such as *throne*, *falcon*, and *captive* was also changed to match the new prestigious spelling (spelling pronunciation). This change of pronunciation took some time so that different pronunciations were current for the same spelling.

The coexistence of different spellings and different pronunciations for the same word gave rise to a heated debate about correct spelling. Whatever the principles were on which correct spelling should be based, it was clear from the outset that spelling must be stabilized. Two currents can be distinguished in the spelling reform debate; Nevalainen (2006: 32) refers to them as phonemic and logographic. The representatives of the former advocated the one phoneme–one letter principle, whereas those of the latter gave more room to tradition and etymology.

John Hart (1569) was one of the fervent defenders of the one phoneme–one letter principle. He blamed the English spelling system because it used more letters in a word than it contained sounds. This is an attack against unetymological spellings of the type *thumb*, but also against the digraph <gh> in words like *eight*. He would not allow either that the same letter was used to represent two different phonemes. As a remedy for these shortcomings he proposed the following rules: Monophthongs are to be represented by a single vowel symbol, vowel length is to be indicated by a subscript dot; <i> and <u> always represent vowels, <j> and <v> consonants; <k> represents the phoneme /k/; the letter <q> is not used at all; for the representation of /tʃ/, /θ/ and /ð/, new symbols are invented.

Although Hart's system did not find much immediate approval, several early grammarians followed his line of argument; among them were William Bullokar (1580, 1586), Alexander Gil (1621), and Charles Butler (1634). In the preface to his grammar, Butler (1634: 7) complains about the lack of "a tru' and constant writing". He addresses two points, namely the variety of spellings for the same word, and the many-to-many relation between phoneme and letter. Both features lead to unnecessary difficulties for the learners of English. Butler (1634: 8) sees the reason for this deplorable situation in the inadequacy of the Latin alphabet, which has not enough letters for the representation of "all the single sounds of the English". He blames contemporary spelling conventions for adopting letters from other alphabets and for using digraphs for the representation of one phoneme. He gives several examples to show that some letters do not evoke an association with the corresponding phonemes, e.g. the letters <i> and <u> representing the phonemes /j/ and /v/. Difficulties also arise from the co-existence of old and new spellings. Butler proposes a spelling reform based on three principles: new characters have to be introduced to compensate for the shortcomings of the Latin alphabet, some have to be given new and appropriate names, and the spelling has to mirror the generally accepted pronunciation of the words. He is sure that the introduction of this new spelling would save learners a lot of trouble and time. Butler's grammar is written along the lines of this new spelling system.

The importance Butler attaches to matters of spelling is evident from the layout of his grammar. It is divided into four chapters, of which the first two take up nearly half the grammar. They deal with letters and their distribution in syllables. All letters are used with three different fonts called Roman, Italic, and English, and they have upper case and lower case variants. Butler's alphabet contains the 26 letters of the Latin alphabet, supplemented by the two digraphs <ee> and <oo> and eight special symbols. A final <e> which is not pronounced is replaced by an apostrophe, e.g. *plac'* for *place*. Butler himself was not too sure that his spelling would find many supporters. At the end of his note to the reader he expresses his fear that the power of custom might get the upper hand against all reason.

Custom is indeed one of the key-words of the opposing party. In his *First Part of the Elementarie*, Richard Mulcaster (1582: 98) argued that a spelling reform was not necessary, because "[t]he vse & *custom* of our cuntrie, hath allredie chosen a kinde of penning, wherein she hath set down her relligion, hir lawes, hir priuat and publik dealings". Since there is so much variation in pronunciation, he considers a phoneme-based spelling system undesirable. In his opinion consistency in spelling is much more important. As a schoolmaster he was primarily concerned with the teaching aspect of spelling. Therefore he included in his book an alphabetical list of about 8,000 words with their recommended spelling. Although this word-list became accepted as an authoritative reference work for spelling, the decisive role in the standardization process of spelling was played by the printers (Scragg 1974: 70; Nevalainen 2006: 36).

One might have expected the regularizing influence of the printers to set in right after the introduction of the printing press by Caxton. But the first effect of the new technology was rather more than less variation, because Caxton had to employ foreign compositors, who were not familiar with English spelling conventions. Some progress was made when native English compositors were recruited. By the middle of the 16th century, quality printing houses followed the practices set up by the scriveners of the manuscript tradition. The variants which remained were not always due to the ignorance or the negligence of the printers, but rather a consequence of the exigencies of type-justification (Scragg 1974: 71–72). When there was too much space at the end of a line, the addition of a final <e> was a handy remedy. Additionally the individual printing-houses did not follow the same spelling conventions. Nevertheless by 1650, the reduction of spelling variants had progressed so far that the system had nearly reached the present-day state. Two factors played an important role in this last stage of standardization: the influence of the spelling-books on the shaping of public taste and the effort of the printing-houses to cater for "the widest cross-section of the book-purchasing public" (Scragg 1974: 74).

2.2 Morphology

Early Modern English as a transitional stage between earlier periods with more and later periods with fewer inflectional endings shows reduction of variation in all open word-classes, but also in its pronominal system. Although the morphology of substantives and adjectives was regularized as well, the most striking instances concern inflectional forms of verbs and especially the system of pronouns.

2.2.1 The third person singular indicative present tense

In the 3P SG PRES IND variation was partly inherited from Middle English, and partly it developed in Early Modern English. The endings *-(e)th* and *-(e)s* were used in Middle English, but they had a different regional distribution. The ending *-(e)s* prevailed in northern texts, *-(e)th* was typical of southern dialects. Stein (1987) distinguishes three stages in the EModE development from *-(e)th* to *-(e)s* in his study of literary texts. In stage A, which he documents with texts between 1525 and 1583, *-(e)th* is "the near-exclusive or 99% predominant ending" (Stein 1987: 407). Then follows stage B with variation between both endings. Their distribution depends on the stem-final phoneme of the verb and on matters of rhythm. The more modern ending is the rule, especially in negations; *-(e)th* is used after stem-final sibilants and when an additional syllable is required. The texts in Stein's corpus which represent this stage date from 1572–1602. The first representative of stage C with a nearly exclusive ending *-(e)s* is Dekker's *The Seven Deadly Sinns of London* (1606).

Whereas Stein studied the *-th/–s* development only in literary texts, Bambas (1998) draws attention to the relevance of the text category for the spread of the *-s* ending. After analyzing 21 literary prose texts from the middle of the 16th to the middle of the 17th century, he comes to the conclusion that although the *-s* ending occurred only rarely in prose works before the last decade of the 16th century, it then held its ground firmly until the middle of the 17th century. He did not find any phonotactic or rhythmic constellations which favored one or the other ending. Variation between the two endings by the middle of the 17th century is also claimed by Nevalainen and Raumolin-Brunberg (2000: 238).

It is interesting to note that Bambas supports his hypothesis of the survival of *-th* endings until well into the 17th century by Ben Jonson's (1640) description of EModE verb morphology in his *English Grammar* and by his use of the *-s* ending in only 20% of all instances.

All scholars who examined the development of the ending of the 3P SG PRES IND agree that at the end of the 17th century, the ending -(e)s was the norm. When -(e)th occurs in later texts, it is used for special stylistic effects.

2.2.2 The second person singular of the personal pronoun and of verbs

One of the important changes towards standardization concerns verbs and pronouns at the same time. The ending -(e)st for the 2P SG PRES/PAST IND disappeared from the inflectional system of verbs, when the variation between the forms *thou* and *you* of the personal pronoun was given up in favor of *you* (cf. Nevalainen 2006: 100).

Already in Middle English, the original plural form *you* had encroached upon the territory of the singular form *thu*, and in Early Modern English both forms were used side by side for some time (cf. Busse, Chapter 12, Section 2.5). Various models have been proposed to account for the distribution of the forms, most prominently the power and solidarity model (Brown and Gilman 1960, 1989). It predicts *y*–forms from +power speakers (i.e. speakers of the upper social ranks) in exchanges with their social equals and with –power speakers (i.e. speakers of the lower social ranks), but *th*-forms from –power speakers in exchanges with their social equals and with +power speakers. Yet this model does not satisfactorily explain many of the occurrences of either form (Hope 1993, 1994; Jucker 2000). In the present context it is important to note that whatever the motives may have been which led to the choice of one or the other form, the frequency of the *th*-forms (*thou* for subject case, *thee* for object case, *thy/thine* as possessive determiner and possessive pronoun) is steadily declining during the EModE period. Evidence from the HC and ARCHER, *A Representative Corpus of Historical English Registers* (Biber and Finegan 1990–93/2002/2007/2010), confirms this statement.

Table 10.1: Tokens of *thou* in the EModE part of the HC (Rissanen et al. 1991) (per 10,000 words)

Helsinki Corpus	Tokens of *thou*
1500–1570	24.45
1570–1640	17.59
1640–1710	12.16

In the HC (see Table 10.1) the figures of the sub-period 1640–1710 reflect the impact of the text category on the preservation of *thou*: 81 of the 208 tokens cluster in one text, namely Queen Elizabeth I's translation of Boethius's *De consolatione philosophiae*. Drama texts and dialogues in fiction texts as well as sermons provide another 61 examples. Plays and sermons are also the text categories which preserve *thou* best in the 18th century. The 18th century texts of ARCHER contain 54 tokens of *thou*, and c.60% of them occur in these two text categories. The parameter text category also proved relevant in Walker's study of the distribution of *thou* and *you* in *A Corpus of English Dialogues 1560–1760*. She found that *thou* was best preserved in depositions (Walker 2007: 288, Figure 9.1). The influence of linguistic factors seems to depend on the choice of data. The hypothesis that *thou* is preferred with auxiliaries, *you* with lexical verbs (Barber 1997: 155, Lass 1999: 149) is supported by my data from the 18th-century ARCHER texts. With two exceptions the examples of *thou* are combined with auxiliaries. By contrast, Walker (2007: 293) found some preference for *you* in this environment in her corpus.

When verbs or auxiliaries occur with *thou*, they preserve their inherited endings, i.e. *-(e)st* for lexical verbs in present and in past tense and *-t* in the forms *art*, *wert*, *shalt*, and *wilt*. When *thou* gets replaced by *you*, the unmarked forms of verbs and auxiliaries for the second person singular are used, and another instance of variation is lost through the spread of one form at the expense of the other.

2.2.3 The neutral possessive determiner

My next example is more complex in that more than two variants are involved and more than one survived after the 17th century. The feature in question is the neuter possessive. The inherited form was *his*, which after the replacement of grammatical by natural gender of substantives was used in combination with animate and non-animate head nouns. Its ME etymon had served as the genitive of the masculine and the neuter gender of the third person singular in the system of personal pronouns. The rise of the new form *its* at the end of the 16th century can be explained as an instance of gap-filling: the three-gender distinction of the personal pronoun was then paralleled by a three-gender distinction of the corresponding possessive determiners (Seppänen 2000: 136). During the 16th century, *his* as a premodifier of non animate head-nouns had an infrequent competitor in the uninflected neuter personal pronoun *it* (Nevalainen and Raumolin-Brunberg 1994: 174). More frequent alternatives were the postnominal modifiers *of it* and *thereof*. The latter has the advantage that it can refer to animate and non-animate, to singular and plural substantives. The variant *of the same* was a minor alternative in official texts.

The first grammarian to include the newcomer *its* into the paradigm of possessive determiners is Charles Butler (1634: 40). This is amazing for two reasons: first, it usually takes much longer before a new item finds its way into grammars; second, in the text of the grammar, Butler refers to non-animate substantives only by *his* (Moessner 2000: 409; Nevalainen and Raumolin-Brunberg 1994: 190). Quite ironically, the first grammarian who mentioned *its* in his grammar and consistently used it in the text of his grammar and in his other works is Guy Miège, whose native tongue was French, and who published his grammar as late as 1688. Dryden's disapproval of Ben Jonson's use of *his* with reference to non-animate nouns indicates that *its* must have been the standard form in the second half of the 17th century (Moessner 2003: 46). This hypothesis is supported by quantitative evidence.

Nevalainen and Raumolin-Brunberg (1994: 189) found a complementary distribution of *his* and *it* in the EModE part of the HC. If only these two variants are compared, *his* has a share of 100% in the first sub-period (1500–1570), and it is completely replaced by *its* in the third sub-period (1640–1710). In the second sub-period, *his* is still the predominant form, but there are already a few occurrences of *its*. The conclusion to be drawn in terms of standardization would be that by the middle of the 17th century, *its* had become the standard form. The situation is complicated by the existence of the additional variants *of it* and *thereof* in post-head position. In the first two sub-periods, when they competed with *his*, they had shares of between 30% and 37% if all variants are taken into account. Nevalainen and Raumolin-Brunberg (1994: 191) explain this high share with "the general tendency of placing items with animate reference before the head, and those with inanimate reference after the head". When the gap was filled by *its*, the frequency of both post-modifiers dropped, and *thereof* became restricted to the genre of legal texts. Despite its frequency drop to 28% in the last sub-period, *of it* is the strongest competitor of *its*.

At the beginning of the EModE period, the paradigm of possessive determiners contained the forms *his*, *of it*, *thereof*, and the minor alternatives *it* and *of the same* as variants of the third person singular neuter. At the end of the 16th century, *its* was added to the paradigm. By the middle of the 17th century, *it* had disappeared and *his* was replaced by *its*. From the second half of the 17th century, *of the same* and *thereof* became restricted to the legal register, *its* and *of it* remained the only competitors.

2.2.4 Comparison of adjectives

Standardization followed a different path in the inflectional paradigm of adjectives. For the formation of the comparative and the superlative two patterns were available for the writers of EModE texts: the native English pattern with the endings *-er* and *-est* and the periphrastic pattern with *more* and *most*, which first appeared in the 13th century under the influence of Latin (Kytö and Romaine 2000: 172). Most EModE grammarians treat these patterns as free variants, and those who give distribution rules do not agree about them (Dons 2004: 55–56). Modern accounts of EModE morphology add a third pattern, namely double comparison (Lass 1999: 158; Baugh and Cable 2002: 242; Barber 1997: 147; Görlach 1991: 84), i.e. a combination of both patterns, as in the following example:

(1) *The Duke of Milan*
*And his **more braver** daughter could control thee* (Shakespeare, *The Tempest* I.ii.439–440)

Dons's (2004: 57–59) quantitative analysis of the HC shows that this strategy played only a minor role. When the form *lesser* is excluded, the percentage share of the double comparative is 2.12 in the sub-period 1500–1570 and drops to 0.68 in the sub-period 1570–1640. In the last sub-period double comparison was not used any longer. This is a clear case of reduction of variation. Changes in the distribution of the other two formation patterns are more complex. The inflectional pattern, which gained in frequency during the EModE period, continued this trend after the 17th century. Kytö and Romaine (1997: 335) provide the following figures for inflectional comparatives: 55% (Late ME), 59% (EModE), 84% (PDE). Changes in the distribution of the two patterns seem to be an ongoing process, because in the period 1900–1950 the share of inflectional comparatives is only 69%. It should be borne in mind, however, that these figures do not tell us anything about the preferred strategy of comparison of individual adjectives. Criteria for the choice of one or the other strategy are similar in Early Modern English and in Present-day English: the number of syllables, the etymology of the adjective, the style level, and the text category.

2.3 Syntax

The standardization processes covered here concern the structure of the verbal syntagm and the syntax of relative pronouns.

2.3.1 Multiple negation

Multiple negation, a construction which was inherited from Middle English, was frequent in the 16th century (Rissanen 1999: 272). It involves the use of a negative particle together with negative determiners, pronouns, adverbs, or conjunctions. It occurred side by side with simple negation. Barber's (1997: 199) claim that multiple negation was used for the purpose of emphasis does not hold for all cases. The examples below from the HC demonstrate that the same author could use both constructions for the same purpose, i.e. non-emphatic negation:

(2)   a. *But **no** Cristen man ys **not** suffered for to come ny it.* (1517 Torkington, Ye Oldest Diarie of Englysshe Travell 30; HC)
      b. *In thys Sepultur ys **no** Cristen man suffred to entre,* (1517 Torkington, Ye Oldest Diarie of Englysshe Travell 36; HC)

This is not to deny that there are instances of multiple negation which are adequately interpreted as emphatic, e.g.

(3)   *I have one heart, one bosom, and one truth,*
      *And that **no** woman has, **nor never none***
      Shall mistress be of it, save I alone. (Shakespeare, Twelfth Night III.i.158–160)

These are the examples which Nevalainen (1998) considered in her study on the loss of multiple negation. Comparing the frequency of multiple and simple negation patterns for emphatic negation in the periods 1520–1550 and 1580–1610, she found that the share of multiple negation dropped from 40% to 12% from the first to the second period, and she concluded from these figures that multiple negation was "definitely on the way out around 1600" (Nevalainen 1998: 275). Since her data were coded for social rank and gender as well, the change can be described in more precise sociolinguistic terms. Men were leading the change, and they belonged to the ranks of the educated and upwardly mobile professionals. They were eager to imitate the new construction, which was quickly adopted by the members of the upper social ranks, and in their overzealousness they used it even more often than those they imitated.

Nevalainen's figures capture only changes in the frequency of the patterns of emphatic negation, and they do not allow quantitative statements about the development of multiple negation in the later part of the 17th century. More corpus research is needed, before we can make more precise statements about multiple negation than Barber's (1997: 199): "It is rarely found in StE [Standard English] after the time of Shakespeare".

2.3.2 The *do*-periphrasis

The development of the *do*-periphrasis is one of the best researched patterns of English syntax (cf. Warner, Chapter 13). For nearly half a century the description provided by Ellegård (1953) went unchallenged. Two reasons are responsible for the long and general acceptance of the results achieved in his study: they are based on a large corpus and obtained by the method of quantitative analysis. Very unusual for his time, Ellegård employed statistical techniques for the interpretation of his figures. These are the stages which he established for the development of the *do*-periphrasis: Periphrastic *do* originated at the end of the 13th century and first occurred in poetic texts as a device for metrical and rhythmical purposes. At the end of the 15th century it became widely used in prose texts. Then it gained in popularity especially among the educated and literate circles. This development reached its peak in the middle of the 16th century. With the exception of affirmative questions, the frequency of periphrastic *do* dropped for several decades. From the last decade of the 16th century, the development of *do* in affirmative declarative sentences continued to drop, whereas in the other sentence types it rose steadily and by 1700 had become almost the rule. More recent investigations, adopting a sociolinguistic and variationist approach, provide evidence for an adjustment of Ellegård's timeline. On the basis of data from the *Corpus of Early English Correspondence*, Nurmi (1999) argues in favor of postponing the date of the decline of *do* in affirmative statements by about 40 years to the first decade of the 17th century. Since her data also document a decline of *do* in negative statements at the same time, she dates the beginning of the regularization process to the years after 1620, when the frequency of *do* in negative statements started to increase again. Very interestingly, she connects the frequency drop before to the accession of James I. His Scottish nobility introduced a new prestige variety with fewer occurrences of *do*. Whereas Nurmi shifted the completion of the standardization process already by about 20 years into the Late Modern English period, Tieken-Boon van Ostade (1987) in her study on the auxiliary *do* in the eighteenth century even suggests that it was an ongoing change in the 18th century. She analyzed informative prose, epistolary prose, and direct speech of 16 authors, and she found average shares of 21.42% of *do*-less negative sentences and of 9.79% of *do*-less questions in these text categories.

2.3.3 The syntax of relative pronouns

The changes in the system of relative pronouns constitute a complex case of reduction of variation (cf. Johansson, Chapter 15). At the opening of the EModE period this system was realized by the forms *who*, *which*, *the which*, and *that*. All of them could refer to animate and to non-animate antecedents, and all of them could occur in restrictive and in non-restrictive attributive relative clauses. Already during the 16th century, the frequency of *the which* decreased, the form got restricted to prepositional syntagms and finally was dropped from the system: "Standardization appears to have worked here to the exclusion of one variant" (Raumolin-Brunberg 1996: 102). The frequency decline is convincingly illustrated by the figures from the HC: 72 occurrences in the first EModE sub-period (= 3.8/10,000 words), 21 occurrences in the second sub-period (1.1/10,000 words), in the third sub-period *the which* no longer occurs (Dons 2004: 77). This evidence is in line with the inclusion of *the which* in the inventory of relative pronouns in the grammars by Butler (1634) and Ben Jonson (1640). The remaining relative pronouns underwent standardization processes of a different kind. In the course of the 17th century the relative pronoun *which* became restricted to non-animate, the relative pronouns *who* and *whom* to animate antecedents, and the relativizer *that* to restrictive relative clauses (Rissanen 1999: 294).

3 Elaboration of function

When at the beginning of the EModE period the vernacular took over in the domains which before were dominated by Latin and French, the inadequacy of English was felt in two fields, namely in matters of style and on the level of lexis. Lack of elegance and lack of copiousness were the shortcomings in the words of the commentators in the 16th century.

3.1 The need for new words

Gaps in the vocabulary were a natural consequence of the quickly changing world-picture: the earth as the center of the universe was replaced by the sun, the invention of the microscope and the telescope made objects visible which were invisible before, and the properties of blood circulation were discovered (Lass 1999: 1–2). The growth of specialized knowledge required new words for new things and concepts. Three strategies were available for the addition of new words to the English vocabulary: borrowing from other languages, the revival of obsolete native English words, and the exploitation of productive word-formation patterns.

The growth of the vocabulary during the EModE period is truly remarkable (cf. Lancashire, Chapter 6). The calculations of new words for the period 1500–1700 range from 12,000 (Baugh and Cable 2002: 233) to 90,000 (Stockwell and Minkova 2001: 40–41). From the figures given in *A Chronological English Dictionary* (Finkenstaedt et al. 1970), it can be inferred that the 17th century contributed even more new words than the 16th century. Wermser (1976), who studied the expansion of the English vocabulary between 1450 and 1900, compared the share of neologisms in the common core of the vocabulary to that in specialized discourse. He found that the share of words belonging to specialized discourse increased throughout the EModE period and that the increase was particularly conspicuous in the natural sciences (Wermser 1976: 127–129).

There is some disagreement on the main source of the new words. Baugh and Cable (2002: 230) state that "[b]y far the greater part of the additions to the English vocabulary in the period of the Renaissance was drawn from sources outside of English". Based on Wermser's figures for the individual sub-periods of his corpus, Nevalainen (1999: 351) concludes that "borrowing is by far the most common method of enriching the lexicon in Early Modern English". These statements cannot be supported when the vocabulary of the natural sciences is analyzed. Robert Boyle, one of the most famous natural scientists and one of the founding members of the Royal Society, contributed as many as 446 neologisms. Only 73 (= 16.4%) are loan-words, but 315 (= 70.6%) belong to the category of affixations (Gotti 1996: 42–43). Henry Power, another scientist and member of the Royal Society, who contributed 109 lexemes to the EModE vocabulary, followed a similar strategy: 70.6% of his neologisms are affixations, and only 12.8% are loan-words. A comparison with the neologisms attested in William Barlow's treatise *Magneticall Aduertisements* (1616) reveals that in the natural sciences, contrary to the common core vocabulary, affixations played a more important role than loan-words already at the beginning of the 17th century. Their share decreases between the first and the second half of the century, whereas the share of affixations increases (Moessner 2007: 250). A similar distribution of coining strategies is observed for the general vocabulary of the period by Barber (1997: 220) and by Stockwell and Minkova (2001: 41).

The desire to enrich the English vocabulary must have led to an overuse of loan-words by some writers in the 16th century. Latin loan-words were an easy choice for those who were familiar with the classical languages, and they served well for filling gaps in the English vocabulary. The supporters of borrowing argued that the Romans used the same strategy and thus produced the copiousness for which Latin was so admired. The opposing party stressed the danger that loan-words were not only used in cases where an English word was not available, but also as a flourish of style to show off the writer's learning. Additionally the meaning of the loan-words was not transparent, and this constituted a hindrance for the less educated part of the reading public. The different evaluation gave rise to the so-called "inkhorn controversy", a public debate about the appropriateness of loan-words. Although the controversy had ebbed down in the 17th century, even a writer like Robert Boyle felt obliged to comment on the right use of loan-words. In his *Proëmial Essay* he writes:

> [A] writer may be allow'd to use Exotick Terms, especially when Custom has not only Denizon'd them, but brought them into request. [...] [I]n Exotick Words, when Custom has once made them familiar and esteem'd, scrupulously to decline the use of them may be as well a fault, as needlessly to employ them (Hunter and Davis 1999: Vol. 2, 17).

Conscientious users of loan-words were aware of their obscurity, and they often added English paraphrases or more lengthy explanations. Barber (1997: 54) quotes Elyot with the paraphrases 'gyue courage to others' for *animate*, and 'bringing vp of noble children' for *education*. Paraphrasing of individual words as they occur in a text is an unsystematic device. Mulcaster (1582: 166) goes one step further and opts for the compilation of a dictionary:

> It were a thing verie praiseworthie in my opinion, and no lesse profitable then praise worthie, if som one well learned and as laborious a man, wold gather all the words which we vse in our English tung, whether naturall or incorporate, out of all professions, as well learned as not, into one dictionarie, and besides the right writing, ..., wold open vnto vs therein, both their naturall force, and their proper vse.

Since he is above all concerned with spelling, the list of about 8,000 items, which he adds at the end of his book, contains only their recommended spelling, but no meanings.

The first monolingual English dictionary with a sizeable number of entries is Edmund Coote's *The English Schoole-Maister* (1596). It contains 1,368 lemmas in alphabetical order (Schäfer 1989: 42). Coote took over those items of Mulcaster's list which would have caused problems for the less well educated readers, "some fewe of the hardest" as he describes them. For most of his entries he added glosses in a different font, e.g. *accident* befall, *amorous* full of loue. Some of his glosses are loan-words as well, e.g. *epilogue* conclusion, *exquisite* perfect. The entries which are not glossed are partly native words (e.g. *almightie*, *bloud*) and partly loan-words (e.g. *circle*, *necessitie*).

All early lexicographers were primarily interested in these "hard words", and their dictionaries specialized in these. The most important representatives of hard word dictionaries are Robert Cawdrey (*A Table Alphabeticall* 1604), John

Bullokar (*An English Expositor* 1616), and Henry Cockeram (*The English Dictionarie* 1623). These were the first steps towards a standardization of the English vocabulary.

The expansion of the vocabulary was a prerequisite for the development of new text categories and for changes in already existing ones. A good example of the former is the rise of the experimental essay (Moessner 2006), and crucial changes affected the category of medical writing (Taavitsainen 2004).

4 Summary

Starting from the concept of EModE standardization as a process which is governed by the principle of reduction of variation and in which functional elaboration became necessary when Latin had yielded the field of learned discourse to the vernacular, several features of the English language between 1500 and 1700 were described which contributed to the development of modern Standard English.

The treatment of standardization processes on the level of pronunciation was deliberately left aside. All through the EModE period there were at least two phoneme systems which existed side by side. Some speakers preferred the realization of the more progressive, others the realization of the more archaic one, and speakers could switch from one to the other. Furthermore, pronunciation is the level on which standardization has never been fully achieved: "When, however, we refer to 'standard' spoken English, we have to admit that a good deal of variety is tolerated in practice" (Milroy and Milroy 1999: 18).

Attempts at reduction of variation were most successful on the plane of spelling, where by 1650 a spelling system was achieved which differs only little from the system still in use today.

It was not my intention to describe all instances of variation reduction which took place on the grammatical level, both morphology and syntax, in Early Modern English. Rather I wanted to show the different ways in which standardization processes affected the grammatical system. Simple loss of one variant in favor of another one was illustrated by the replacement of the ending *-(e)th* by *-(e)s* in the third person singular indicative present of verbs, and by the complete replacement of multiple negation by simple negation. A similarly straightforward, but different type was illustrated by the development of periphrastic *do*, where the originally free variants of verb forms with and without *do* developed into variants in complementary distribution. The case of the replacement of *thou* by *you* showed that standardization processes can also proceed pairwise; with the loss of *thou* the ending *-(e)st* of the second person singular indicative of verbs disappeared, too. More complex processes are involved in the changes affecting the comparison of adjectives and the syntax of relative clauses. In both cases one variant got lost, namely double comparatives and *the which* respectively, and the other variants became restricted to special environments: the inflectional comparatives and superlatives to monosyllabic adjectives and the analytic forms to polysyllabic adjectives, *who* to animate and *which* to non-animate antecedents. The most complex constellation concerned the possessive determiner *its*. Here a completely new form entered the paradigm, where it competed with *his*, *it*, *of it*, and *thereof*. Although *its* is first attested only in 1598, at the end of the EModE period it had ousted *his* and *it* completely and pushed *thereof* into the niche of the legal register. When looking at the individual processes, it became evident that they proceeded at different pace and that some were completed at the end of the EModE period (e.g. the loss of multiple negation, double comparatives), whereas others have to be described as change in progress (e.g. periphrastic *do*, the distribution of synthetic and analytic comparative formation). These are the standardization processes which need to be followed up in the analysis of Late Modern English.

Functional extension required first of all an expansion of the English vocabulary. Lack of copiousness was indeed one of the complaints of the early commentators. Translators and the writers of texts about specialized topics felt the need for new words especially badly. A line of development was traced from statements about the necessity of authoritative word-lists to the compilation of the first monolingual English dictionaries and the rise of the experimental essay as a new genre and the conceptual and linguistic changes in the genre of medical texts. The textual representatives of these genres had reached characteristic profiles at the end of the EModE period, but they were subject to later changes. Standardization processes helped to shape these profiles, but they did not produce stable text categories.

5 References

Bambas, Rudolf. 1998. Verb forms in -s *and* -th *in Early Modern English prose*. In: Mats Rydén, Ingrid Tieken-Boon van Ostade, and Merja Kytö (eds.), *A Reader in Early Modern English*, 65–71. Frankfurt/Main: Peter Lang.

Barber, Charles. 1997. *Early Modern English*. 2nd edn. Edinburgh: Edinburgh University Press.

Barlow, William. 1616. *Magneticall Aduertisements*. Amsterdam/New York: Da Capo Press, 1968. [Facsimile]

Baugh, Albert C. and Thomas Cable. 2002. *A History of the English Language*. 5th edn. London: Routledge.

Biber, Douglas and Edward Finegan. 1990–1993/2002/2007/2010. *A Representative Corpus of Historical English Registers (ARCHER)*. Version 3.1 http://www.llc.manchester.ac.uk/research/projects/archer/; last accessed 14 April 2017.

Brown, Roger and Albert Gilman. 1989. Politeness theory and Shakespeare's four major tragedies. *Language in Society* 18: 159–212.

Brown, Roger, and Albert Gilman. 1960. The pronouns of power and solidarity. In: Thomas A. Sebeok (ed.), *Style in Language*, 253–276. Cambridge, MA: MIT Press.

Bullokar, John. 1616. *An English expositor*. (*English Linguistics 1500–1800*, ed. by R. C. Alston, 11.) Menston: The Scolar Press, 1967.

Bullokar, William. 1580, 1586. *Book at Large (1580) and Bref Grammar for English (1586)*. Facsimile reproductions with an introduction by Diane Bornstein. New York: Scholar's Facsimiles & Reprints, 1977.

Butler, Charles. 1634. *The English Grammar, or The Institution of Letters, Syllables, and Woords in the English Tung*. Oxford: William Turner. [Albert Eichler (ed.), *Charles Butler's English Grammar*. Halle a. S.: Max Niemeyer, 1910.]

Cawdrey, Robert. 1604. *A Table Alphabeticall*. (English Experience, its Record in Early Printed Books Published in Facsimile, 226.) New York: Da Capo Press, 1970.

Cockeram, Henry. 1623. *The English Dictionarie*. (*English Linguistics 1500–1800*, ed. by R. C. Alston, 124.) Menston: The Scolar Press, 1968.

Coote, Edmund. 1596. *The English Schoole-Maister*. (*English Linguistics 1500–1800*, ed. by R. C. Alston, 98.) Menston: The Scolar Press, 1968.

Dalton-Puffer, Christiane and Nikolaus Ritt (eds.). 2000. *Words: Structure, Meaning, Function. A Festschrift for Dieter Kastovsky*. Berlin/New York: Mouton de Gruyter.

Dons, Ute. 2004. *Descriptive Adequacy of Early Modern English Grammars*. Berlin/New York: Mouton de Gruyter.

Ellegård, Alvar. 1953. *The Auxiliary do. The Establishment and Regulation of its Use in English*. Stockholm: Almqvist & Wiksell.

Finkenstaedt, Thomas, Ernst Leisi, and Dieter Wolff. 1970. *A Chronological English Dictionary*. Heidelberg: Winter.

Gil, Alexander. 1621. *Logonomia Anglica*. 2nd edn. (*English Linguistics 1500–1800*, ed. by R. C. Alston, 68.) Menston: The Scolar Press, 1968.

Görlach, Manfred. 1991. *Introduction to Early Modern English*. Cambridge: Cambridge University Press.

Gotti, Maurizio. 1996. *Robert Boyle and the Language of Science*. Milan: Guerini.

Hart, John. 1569. *An Orthographie*. (*English Linguistics 1500–1800*, ed. by R. C. Alston, 209.) Menston: The Scolar Press, 1969.

Hope, Jonathan. 1993. Second person singular pronouns in records of Early Modern "spoken" English. *Neuphilologische Mitteilungen* 94: 83–100.

Hope, Jonathan. 1994. The use of *thou* and *you* in Early Modern spoken English: Evidence from depositions in the Durham ecclesiastical court records. In: Dieter Kastovsky (ed.), *Studies in Early Modern English*, 141–151. Berlin/New York: Mouton de Gruyter.

Hope, Jonathan. 2000. Rats, bats, sparrows and dogs: Biology, linguistics and the nature of Standard English. In: Wright (ed.), 49–56.

Huddleston, Rodney and Geoffrey K. Pullum. 2002. *The Cambridge Grammar of the English Language*. Cambridge: Cambridge University Press.

Hunter, Michael and Edward B. Davis (eds.). 1999–2000. *The Works of Robert Boyle*. 14 vols. London: Pickering and Chatto.
Jonson, Ben. 1640. *The English Grammar (from the works)*. (*English Linguistics 1500–1800*, ed. by R. C. Alston, 349.) Menston: The Scolar Press, 1972.
Jucker, Andreas H. 2000. *Thou* in the history of English: A case for historical semantics or pragmatics? In: Dalton-Puffer and Ritt (eds.), 153–163.
Kytö, Merja and Suzanne Romaine. 1997. Competing forms of adjective comparison in Modern English: What could be *more quicker* and *easier* and *more effective*? In: Terttu Nevalainen and Leena Kahlas-Tarkka (eds.), *To Explain the Present. Studies in the Changing English Language in Honour of Matti Rissanen*, 329–352. Helsinki: Société Néophilologique.
Kytö, Merja and Suzanne Romaine. 2000. Adjective comparison and standardisation processes in American and British English from 1620 to the present. In: Wright (ed.), 171–194.
Lass, Roger. 1999. Introduction. In: Lass (ed.), 1–12.
Lass, Roger. 1999. Phonology and morphology. In: Lass (ed.), 56–186.
Lass, Roger (ed.). 1999. *The Cambridge History of the English Language*. Vol. III. *1476–1776*. Cambridge: Cambridge University Press.
Miège, Guy. 1688. *The English Grammar*. (*English Linguistics 1500–1800*, ed. by R. C. Alston, 152) Menston: The Scolar Press, 1969.
Milroy, James and Lesley Milroy. 1999. *Authority in Language. Investigating Language Prescription and Standardisation*. 2nd edn. London/New York: Routledge.
Moessner, Lilo. 2000. Grammatical description and language use in the seventeenth century. In: Ricardo Bermúdez-Otero, David Denison, Richard M. Hogg, and C. B. McCully (eds.), *Generative Theory and Corpus Studies. A Dialogue from 10 ICEHL*, 395–416. Berlin/New York: Mouton de Gruyter.
Moessner, Lilo. 2003. *Diachronic English Linguistics. An Introduction*. Tübingen: Gunter Narr.
Moessner, Lilo. 2006. The birth of the experimental essay. In: Vijay K. Bhatia and Maurizio Gotti (eds.), *Explorations in Specialized Genres*, 59–77. Bern: Peter Lang.
Moessner, Lilo. 2007. The vocabulary of Early Modern English scientific texts. In: Ute Smit, Stefan Dollinger, Julia Hüttner, Gunther Kaltenböck, and Ursula Lutzky (eds.), *Tracing English through Time. Explorations in Language Variation*, 235–252. Wien: Braunmüller.
Mulcaster, Richard. 1582. *The First Part of the Elementarie which entreateth chefelie of the right writing of our English tung*. London: Thomas Vautroullier.
Nevalainen, Terttu. 1998. Social mobility and the decline of multiple negation in Early Modern English. In: Jacek Fisiak and Marcin Krygier (eds.), *Advances in English Historical Linguistics (1996)*, 263–291. Berlin/New York: Mouton de Gruyter.
Nevalainen, Terttu. 1999. Early Modern English lexis and semantics. In: Lass (ed.), 332–456.
Nevalainen, Terttu. 2006. *An Introduction to Early Modern English*. Edinburgh: Edinburgh University Press.
Nevalainen, Terttu and Helena Raumolin-Brunberg. 1994. *Its* strength and the beauty *of it*: The standardization of the third person neuter possessive in Early Modern English. In: Dieter Stein and Ingrid Tieken-Boon van Ostade (eds.), *Towards a Standard English 1600–1800*, 171–216. Berlin/New York: Mouton de Gruyter.
Nevalainen, Terttu and Helena Raumolin-Brunberg. 2000. The third-person singular *-(e)s* and *-(e)th* revisited: The morphophonemic hypothesis. In: Dalton-Puffer and Ritt (eds.), 235–248.
Nevalainen, Terttu and Ingrid Tieken-Boon van Ostade. 2006. Standardisation. In: Richard Hogg and David Denison (eds.), *A History of the English Language*, 271–311. Cambridge: Cambridge University Press.

Nurmi, Arja. 1999. *A Social History of Periphrastic DO*. Helsinki: Société Néophilologique.
Quirk, Randolph, Sidney Greenbaum, Geoffrey Leech, and Jan Svartvik. 1985. *A Comprehensive Grammar of the English Language*. London/New York: Longman.
Raumolin-Brunberg, Helena. 1996. Apparent time. In: Terttu Nevalainen and Helena Raumolin-Brunberg (eds.), *Sociolinguistics and Language History. Studies based on the Corpus of Early English Correspondence*, 93–109. Amsterdam/Atlanta: Rodopi.
Rissanen, Matti, Merja Kytö, Leena Kahlas-Tarkka, Matti Kilpiö, Saara Nevanlinna, Irma Taavitsainen, Terttu Nevalainen, and Helena Raumolin-Brunberg. 1991. The Helsinki Corpus of English Texts. In: *ICAME Collection of English Language Corpora (CD-ROM)*, 2nd edn., Knut Hofland, Anne Lindebjerg, and Jørn Thunestvedt (eds.), The HIT Centre, University of Bergen, Norway. For manual, see http://clu.uni.no/icame/manuals/; last accessed 14 April 2017.
Rissanen, Matti. 1999. Syntax. In: Lass (ed.), 187–331.
Schäfer, Jürgen. 1989. *Early Modern English Lexicography*. Vol. I. *A Survey of Monolingual Printed Glossaries and Dictionaries 1475–1640*. Oxford: Clarendon Press.
Scragg, Donald George. 1974. *A History of English Spelling*. Manchester: Manchester University Press.
Seppänen, Aimo. 2000. The genitive/possessive pronoun *its*. *Studia Neophilologica* 72: 121–141.
Shakespeare, William. 1997. *The Complete Works*. 2nd edn. G. Blakemore Evans (ed.). Boston/New York: Houghton Mifflin.
Stein, Dieter. 1987. At the crossroads of philology, linguistics and semiotics: Notes on the replacement of *th* by *s* in the third person singular in English. *English Studies* 68(5): 406–432.
Stockwell, Robert and Donka Minkova. 2001. *English Words: History and Structure*. Cambridge: Cambridge University Press.
Sweet, Henry. 1891. *A New English Grammar Logical and Historical*. Part I. Oxford: Clarendon Press.
Taavitsainen, Irma. 2004. Transferring classical discourse convention into the vernacular. In: Irma Taavitsainen and Päivi Pahta (eds.), *Medical and Scientific Writing in Late Medieval English,* 37–72. Cambridge: Cambridge University Press.
Tieken-Boon van Ostade, Ingrid. 1987. *The Auxiliary DO in Eighteenth-century English. A Sociohistorical-linguistic Approach*. Dordrecht: Foris Publications.
Walker, Terry. 2007. Thou *and* You *in Early Modern English Dialogues*. Amsterdam/Philadelphia: John Benjamins.
Wermser, Richard. 1976. *Statistische Studien zur Entwicklung des englischen Wortschatzes*. Bern: Francke Verlag.
Wright, Laura (ed.). 2000. *The Development of Standard English, 1300–1800: Theories, Descriptions, Conflicts*. Cambridge: Cambridge University Press.

Helena Raumolin-Brunberg
Chapter 11: Sociolinguistics

1 Sociolinguistics and language history —— 188
2 Early Modern England 1500–1700 —— 190
3 The sociolinguistic patterns of language change —— 192
4 Summary —— 206
5 References —— 206

Abstract: This chapter shows that there was considerable sociolinguistic variation in Early Modern England. Despite the problems of accessing the lowest social ranks and women due to widespread illiteracy, studies of letter and dialogue data testify to the significance of gender, social rank, region, and register in the diffusion of linguistic change. The chapter focuses on morphosyntactic changes, such as the replacement of the subject pronoun *ye* by *you*, the adoption of the third-person singular suffix *-s* instead of *-th* and the loss of multiple negation.

As today, women seemed to lead changes from below but, unlike today, changes from above were led by men. Social stratification also proved significant, and the capital region, London and the Court, formed the centre from which changes spread elsewhere in the country. The chapter also shows that some individuals changed their language across their lifespans, and weak-tie networks apparently promoted the diffusion of change.

1 Sociolinguistics and language history

Basically, sociolinguistic variation has been approached from two complementary angles, those of the speaker and of the situation of language use. The linguistic choices individual language users make have been observed to correlate with their social backgrounds, i.e. gender, social status, education, ethnic group, etc. Moreover, linguistic choices have also been found to be influenced by the situation of language use and, in particular, the relationship between the interlocutors. Beside these topics, sociolinguistic research has covered other areas of study, such as standardization and prescription, language attitudes,

---

Helena Raumolin-Brunberg: Helsinki (Finland)

social networks, patterns of communication, and multilingualism, to mention just a few.

Most of what we know of sociolinguistic variation stems from studies of present-day languages, but there is no reason to believe that similar phenomena would not have existed in the past. Historical and cultural research has given ample evidence of the existence of social and gender stratification in past societies, for instance, and we can assume that language variation in the past was constrained by social factors, although they were not necessarily the same as in today's societies.

Present-day sociolinguistics and historical linguistics share one important objective: both strive to account for linguistic change. In recent years, historical linguists have begun to apply sociolinguistic methods to their research. The forerunner in this field was Romaine (1982), who used genre variation to trace changes in the relative pronoun system in Middle Scots. A large number of studies using similar methods have followed suit, and research has since also been extended beyond texts to individual language users in the study of one informal genre such as personal correspondence (as in Nevalainen and Raumolin-Brunberg 2003, 2017).

Although sociolinguists, both present-day and historical, take linguistic change as their central topic, there is no reason to claim that all sociolinguistic variation should involve change. However, because stable variation has only received limited attention in historical studies (see, e.g., Raumolin-Brunberg 2002; Laitinen 2007: 212), it seems appropriate here to concentrate on phenomena that have been uncovered in the studies of early modern linguistic changes.

While sociolinguists studying present-day languages can use informal spoken language as their data, historical linguists focusing on developments before the innovation of audio recording have only written language for their use. As regards Early Modern English, there is a great deal of written data available from various genres, some of which are rather informal, representing language that, at least to some extent, resembles the spoken idiom of the time. These genres include personal letters and dialogues, which form the main sources that have been used for research in historical sociolinguistics.

Letters represent the written mode of language, and illiteracy sets its limits to their use as research data. On the other hand, they are good data for sociolinguistic research, as present-day studies (e.g. Biber 1988) show that personal letters in many ways resemble such spoken genres as spontaneous speech and interviews. It is also important to notice that they comprise genuine interaction (for further information on letters as a genre, see Nurmi and Palander-Collin 2008). In addition, the writers and recipients of letters can be traced and this information used for sociolinguistic analysis.

The historical study of dialogue texts such as trial proceedings, witness depositions, and drama is not unproblematic either because of the inaccurate ways spoken language has been recorded in writing or the poor ability of many playwrights to imitate speech. However, as Kytö and Walker (2003: 241) argue, there are speech-related texts which may be fairly reliable records of spoken interaction of the past and hence relevant material for historical sociolinguistics.

The development of electronic text corpora and retrieval programs has been instrumental for historical sociolinguistic research. Most of the material discussed in this article goes back to the electronic *Corpus of Early English Correspondence* (CEEC) (Nevalainen et al. 1998), which was compiled at the University of Helsinki for research in historical sociolinguistics in 1993–97. The CEEC, covering the period c.1410–1681, contains over 6,000 letters, c.2.7 million words, from 778 informants (for further information, see Raumolin-Brunberg and Nevalainen 2007). Material from the *Corpus of Early English Correspondence Supplement* (CEECSU) (Kaislaniemi et al. 2000) covering the period 1402–1663 (c.900 letters and 0.44 million words) was also used.

A multi-genre corpus, the *Helsinki Corpus of English Texts* (HC) (Rissanen et al. 1991) has also provided data for studies drawn on in this article. The HC, consisting of c.1.6 million words of English from c.700–1710, was compiled at the University of Helsinki under the supervision of Matti Rissanen in the 1980s (for further information, see Rissanen et al. 1993). Expanded versions have been provided by the University of Pennsylvania.

Further materials used in historical sociolinguistics include *A Corpus of English Dialogues* (CED) (Kytö and Culpeper 2006), covering the period 1560–1760, compiled at Uppsala University and Lancaster University under the supervision of Merja Kytö and Jonathan Culpeper (for further information, see Kytö and Walker 2003) and, for early American English, the *Salem Witchcraft Records* from 1692, re-edited by an international team (Rosenthal et al. 2009).

2 Early Modern England 1500–1700

It cannot be stressed too much that the pursuit of historical sociolinguistics requires a thorough knowledge of the conditions that prevailed in the society whose language is under examination. In order to provide some background information, this section gives a very brief description of Early Modern England, but a more detailed reconstruction of the society can found in Nurmi (Chapter 2), and in the relevant sociohistorical literature such as Laslett (1983), Wrightson (1991), Barry and Brooks (1994), Heal and Holmes (1994), Fletcher (1995), and

Wrightson (2003). (For further references, see Nevalainen and Raumolin-Brunberg 2003).

Ruled by the popular Tudor and Stuart monarchs, England underwent a change between 1500 and 1700 from the medieval three-estate society, involving clergy, nobility and laborers, into a country with a more complex social structure. Social historians have often described the divisions in hierarchical terms, as in Table 11.1. In line with what seems to be the usage among most social historians, this table and this article as a whole employs the early modern concept "rank" instead of the more controversial modern term "class".

Table 11.1: Rank and status in Early Modern England (after Laslett 1983: 38)

Estate			Grade
			Royalty
GENTRY	Nobility		Duke, Archbishop, Marquess, Earl, Viscount, Baron, Bishop
	Gentry proper		Baronet, Knight, Esquire, Gentleman
	Professions		Army Officer, Government Official, Lawyer, Medical Doctor, (wealthy) Merchant, Clergyman, Teacher, etc.
NON-GENTRY			Yeoman, Merchant, Husbandman, Craftsman, Tradesman, Artificer, Laborers, Cottager, Pauper

The nobility and the upper sections of the gentry proper formed the elite, comprising only a couple of per cent of the population. The upper clergy, the archbishops and bishops, found a place among the nobility because of their influential position. At the other end, laborers, cottagers and paupers occupied the lowest rungs of the social ladder.

Although the main dividing line was usually drawn between the gentry and non-gentry, this was not a rigid division. Beside a specific lifestyle, gentility involved land ownership and no need to work for a living, but the borderline could be crossed by people from the middle ranks. These consisted of people in administrative, legal and medical professions, wealthy merchants, and craftsmen.

The social position of women was mainly derivative, unmarried women being categorized according to their fathers' social position while the married ones followed their husbands.

Education, too, was socially stratified. The way children were trained for adult life varied according to their social background and gender. Home was the most important place for teaching children the skills they needed in the future. The role of school attendance increased with time, but home tuition persisted. Children of the lower social strata rarely went to school and, if they did, their families could hardly afford it for more than a year or two.

The curriculum of the educational institutions for boys, the grammar schools and beyond, was essentially classical, which means that it was predominantly boys from the upper and middling strata of society who acquired a command of Latin, the most prestigious language of the time. The educational system placed the language of law and administration beyond the reach of the lower ranks and women.

The level of literacy was also socially stratified. Most of the estimates of literacy have been counted on the basis of the proportion of the population who signed their names instead of inscribing a mark on various public documents. This method may not have the best accuracy, but does apparently provide a confident estimate of those who were able to read, as reading was taught as a separate skill before writing. In the 17th century, most members of the gentry and professionals were able to read, whereas about only half of yeomen and craftsmen could do so. Women's ability to read was at the same low level as that of male laborers.

Despite the growth of migration within the country, dialectal variation in language was extensive. While it is possible to trace dialectal texts from the early part of the 16th century, it becomes more difficult to do so from later periods because of the increasing standardization of spelling, although this did not affect all private writing. On the whole, although considerable standardization of the written language took place during early modern times, no codified standard language existed before the 18th century.

3 The sociolinguistic patterns of language change

3.1 External constraints: gender, status, region and register

One of the main aims of historical sociolinguistics is to find out how linguistic innovations spread among past populations. Researchers look for answers to questions such as who were the innovators and early adopters of a new form, was it men or women who first used this form, which part of the country did the innovation spread from, and so on. Although early modern society, described briefly above, changed over time, at a relatively abstract level we can consider it the independent variable against which linguistic variation is correlated (Chambers 2003: 18–19).

3.1.1 Gender

Gender has proved to be one of the most robust external constraints in present-day sociolinguistics. In a seminal article, Labov (1990: 213–215) presents two basic principles of women's participation in linguistic change: 1) women adopt prestige forms at a higher rate than men in linguistic change from above; 2) women use higher frequencies of innovative forms than men do in linguistic change from below. These two concepts, change from above and below, are used to account for social awareness in connection with the diffusion of innovative forms. Change from above refers to the importation of elements from outside the language system, e.g., from a foreign language, with full public awareness, while change from below refers to changes from within the language system without social awareness. The two general principles expressed by Labov, paradoxically involving opposing tendencies, suggest that women are more active in promoting linguistic change.

As regards Early Modern England, it has become evident that Labov's first principle of women adopting prestige forms before men does not hold because of women's limited access to learning and classical education. On the other hand, many studies of Early Modern English show females leading changes in the same way as Labov indicates in his second principle, in change from below.

Let us look at women's participation in two early modern changes representing different areas of grammar. The personal-pronoun system underwent significant changes in Tudor and Stuart England, one of which was the replacement of the second-person singular pronoun *thou/thee* by *ye/you*. Furthermore, the old object form *you* rapidly replaced the subject form *ye*. This change took place circa 1480–1580, *you* spreading from the informal genres to the formal ones, thus representing a change from below (for details, see Raumolin-Brunberg 2005b).

Examples (1) and (2) illustrate the use of the second person subject pronoun in the letters of the merchant couple John and Sabine Johnson. While the husband relies on the traditional *ye* subject, his wife has adopted the new form *you*.

(1) *trie owt this matter by examynyng of them eche alone by themselves that **ye** may knowe the trewthe, and then **ye** maie kepe and put from you whome **ye** thincke good, and that **ye** perseave to be fawlte* (1546 John Johnson; CEEC)

(2) *Our Lord knowth, for I stand in doutt, wherefore I moest hartely desyre you to make all the sped hom that* **you** *can. And do* **you** *th[inc]ke, good husbond, what a great comfart it shal be to me to have [\you\] here at that tyme* (1546 Sabine Johnson; CEEC)

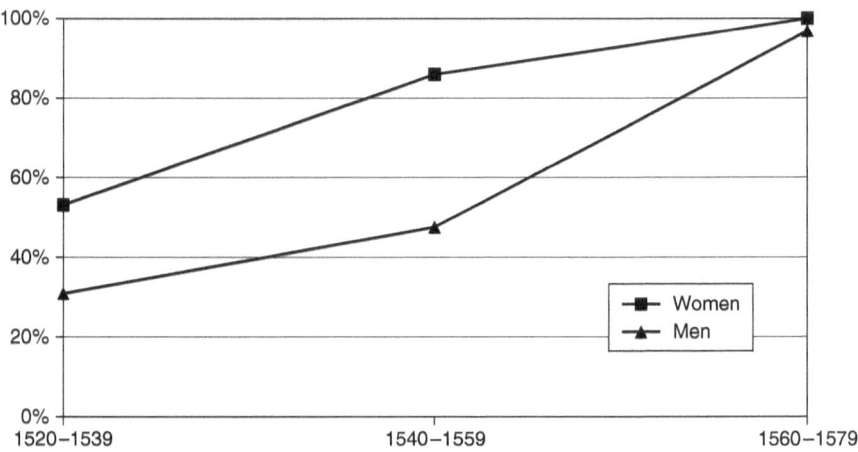

Figure 11.1: The gender distribution of the replacement of subject *ye* by *you*, 1520–1579. Percentages of *you* (CEEC, Nevalainen et al. 1998 and CEECSU, Kaislaniemi et al. 2000).

Figure 11.1, depicting the gender difference in the *Corpus of Early English Correspondence* from 1520–1579, shows that women were at least one generation ahead of men during the rapid change in the first half of the 16th century.

Examples (3) and (4) illustrate another early modern change, the decline of multiple negation, also called double negation and negative concord. Sentential negation in early Middle English usually consisted of two parts, *ne* and *not*. In negative clauses, indefinites were expressed by their negative forms, e.g. *nothing*, and a sentential negator also occurred with *no*, *never*, etc. The first element of the sentential negator disappeared from most genres by 1600, and the negative indefinites were replaced by the assertive ones, e.g. forms beginning with *any*. Coordinate structures, typically including *nor* or *neither*, kept two negators for much longer (for details on multiple negation, see Nevalainen 2006). Example (3) illustrates the old usage with multiple negation, whereas (4) exemplifies the modern single negation with an assertive pronoun.

(3) *and I shall* **not** *put you in* **no** *more troubul but I be sysch you hartly my Lorde that I may have it to morow at nyght at the farest* (1516 Margaret Tudor; CEEC)

(4) *I doe **not** hear of **any man** that dealeth so lustyly with the enemye as he doth*
(1586 Robert Dudley; CEEC)

Figure 11.2 shows the gender distribution of the percentages of single negation of all sentential negations under examination. It indicates that men led the decline of multiple negation throughout the 16th century. In men's letters over half of the cases represent single negation as early as 1500–1539, while women still mostly resorted to multiple negation at this period.

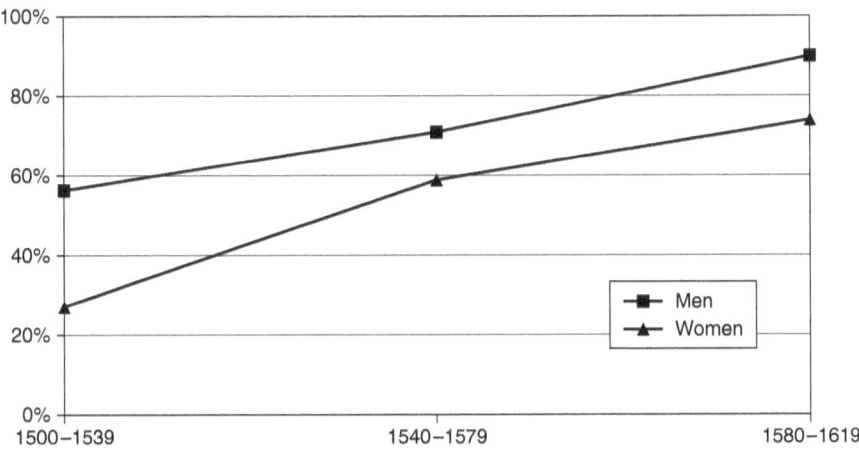

Figure 11.2: The gender distribution of the decline of multiple negation, 1500–1619. Percentages of single negation (CEEC, Nevalainen et al. 1998 and CEECSU, Kaislaniemi et al. 2000).

The lack of a codified standard language in Early Modern England did not mean that prestige was not attached to some varieties, such as the language of the Royal Court and London with its surroundings (Puttenham 1589). However, this type of prestige was different from that of today's standard and, on the whole, it seems that access to learned written language, very rarely open to women, made men leaders in early-modern changes from above, such as the above loss of multiple negation. It was not led by men in general but the leaders were well-educated upper-ranking and professional men who had access to learned types of writing (Nevalainen and Raumolin-Brunberg 2003).

In fact, recent research has discovered more cases of female-led change than male-led change. In addition to the shift from *ye* to *you*, they include such well-known changes as the loss of the nasal from the possessives *mine* and *thine*, the introduction of the prop-word *one*, the replacement of the third-person singular suffix *-th* by *-s* (Nevalainen and Raumolin-Brunberg 2003: 118–125; for details see Section 3.1.2) and the rise of the auxiliary *will* at the expense of *shall* (Nurmi 2003b).

As regards the male-led changes from above, apart from multiple negation we can mention inversion after initial negators (Nevalainen and Raumolin-Brunberg 2003: 129) and the rise of the meaning of 'logical necessity' of the auxiliary *must* (Nurmi 2003a).

Recent studies have also identified changes that switch from male to female advantage. An interesting case is the use of periphrastic *do* in affirmative statements, a change in which men were ahead of women until c.1600, after which there was an increase in this regard led by women in the first decades of the 17th century. During the second half of the century, the difference between the sexes vanished and the use of *do* diminished in general. Nurmi (1999) suggests that the dropping of *do* in men's language could be connected with changing prestige patterns, as the ascent of James I meant increasing Scottish influence on many matters of life, including language. Scottish English at the time used affirmative periphrastic *do* less than the southern varieties.

In sum, there was considerable gender variation in the participation in ongoing changes in Early Modern England. Women led many changes from below as they do today, whereas changes from above, usually materializing as shifts following Latinate models, were led by men who had acquired a classical education.

3.1.2 Social stratification

Social class is a constraint that is more or less taken for granted in the sociolinguistic research into present-day speech communities. There is every reason to believe that social stratification also played a role in the highly hierarchical early modern society.

The creation of an appropriate stratification model for linguistic studies on the basis of the social hierarchies reconstructed by social historians (as in Table 11.1) is not without its problems. After several tests, a four-level model proved to be suitable for research into the material represented by the CEEC. The ranks are as follows:
a. upper ranks: royalty, nobility, gentry and clergy;
b. social aspirers: men of lower or middle ranks who entered the upper ranks by climbing at least two rungs on the social ladder;
c. middle ranks: professionals and wealthy merchants;
d. lower ranks: other non-gentry.

The names of the categories speak for themselves, except that "social aspirers", also called "upwardly mobile", may need an explanation. Present-day studies have shown that upwardly mobile people are often very sensitive to linguistic attitudes so that they both tend to follow prestige patterns and to avoid stigmatized forms.

Several trials on the CEEC have shown that the corpus is not large enough for a more fine-grained division. This is true for the lower ranks in particular, from which the data are inevitably limited because of their missing writing skills. The same is true of women, which is why the following case studies based on the CEEC only discuss the language of the male informants.

Figure 11.3 shows the social rank distribution of the introduction of -s as the indicative third-person singular suffix during the early modern era, as its proportion grows from 8% to 93% in letters written by men. This change had been going on about five hundred years by the beginning of the early modern era, as the use of -s has been documented in the North of England as early as the 10th century. From there it spread to the South, where the corresponding suffix was -th. By the 15th century, -s had reached the late medieval London mercantile community, but -th was still the form the majority chose.

As Figure 11.3 indicates, -s was favored by the lower ranks in the second half of the 16th century. A remarkable change took place around 1600. It is as if a stigma was lifted from -s, when its use increased from 19% to 58% between the twenty-year periods on each side of this dividing line. Even after 1600, the lower ranks had the highest score, but the other ranks also chose -s in over half the cases. Examples (5)–(8) show the variation among the gentry in the 1620s.

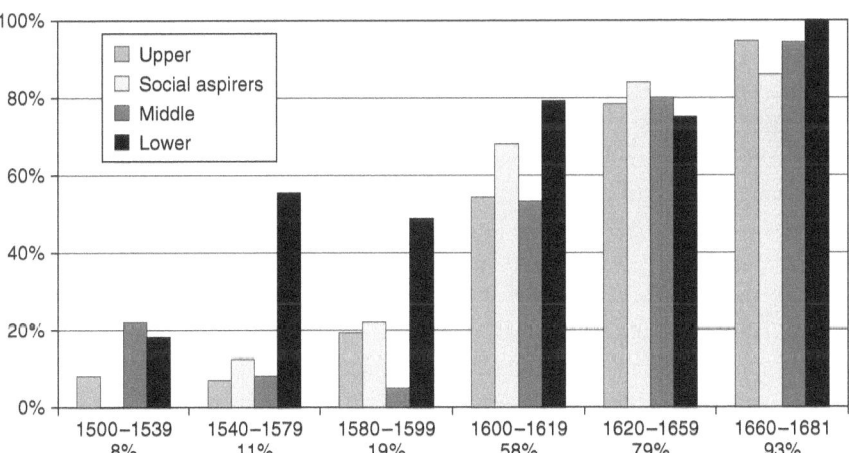

Figure 11.3: Third-person singular suffix -s versus -th. Percentage of -s. *Have* and *do* excluded, male informants (CEEC, Nevalainen et al. 1998; after Nevalainen and Raumolin-Brunberg 2003: 144–145)

(5) *The French King **geueth** no sattisfaction to oe embassadors* (1626 Nathaniel Bacon II; CEEC)

(6) *My sister **giues** you thankes for seending him to her* (1625 Brilliana Harley; CEEC)

(7) *My brother's monument **goeth** well forwarde* (1628 Edward Bacon; CEEC)

(8) *the Counte Mansfeldes bysnis **goes** not forward as it aught* (1625 Thomas Meautys I; CEEC)

It is interesting to see how quickly the usage of the social aspirers changed. It seems that these people sensed the changing attitudes towards the use of -s very early on.

The above case study clearly shows that social stratification was an important factor in the diffusion of early modern linguistic changes. As far as other changes are concerned, the two shifts previously discussed in detail, the replacement of subject *ye* by *you* and the decline of multiple negation, also exhibit social stratification. Unlike the third-person -s, after its introduction in the middle ranks in Late Middle English, *you* spread very quickly into all ranks, including the upper ones. No stigma can have been attached to this change, and it is likely that the early adoption of *you* by the prestigious upper ranks guaranteed its rapid progress in general.

Figure 11.4 shows the early modern distribution of the decline of multiple negation by four social ranks. This graph further illustrates the significance of male education referred to in the previous section. The leadership of this change falls on the social aspirers and middle ranks; in other words, people who were professionals in producing written documents, such as lawyers, administrators, and clergymen. Nevalainen and Raumolin-Brunberg (2003: 151) in fact show that even among the gentry those who held administrative offices or worked as lawyers used single negation more than other gentlemen. The lower ranks are clearly behind the others in the diffusion of this change, and this may well have been a reason for the later stigmatization of double negation.

The *Corpus of English Dialogues* (CED) (Kytö and Culpeper 2006), mostly used for socio-pragmatic research, also provides information about the role of the social rank in the diffusion of linguistic changes. This corpus, like in the *Salem Witchcraft Records*, contains material even from illiterate lower ranks, which is beyond the reach of the letter corpus. For example, in her study of the use of *thou* and *you* in Early Modern English dialogues, Walker (2007) shows that those in superior social position often addressed their social inferiors with *thou* but

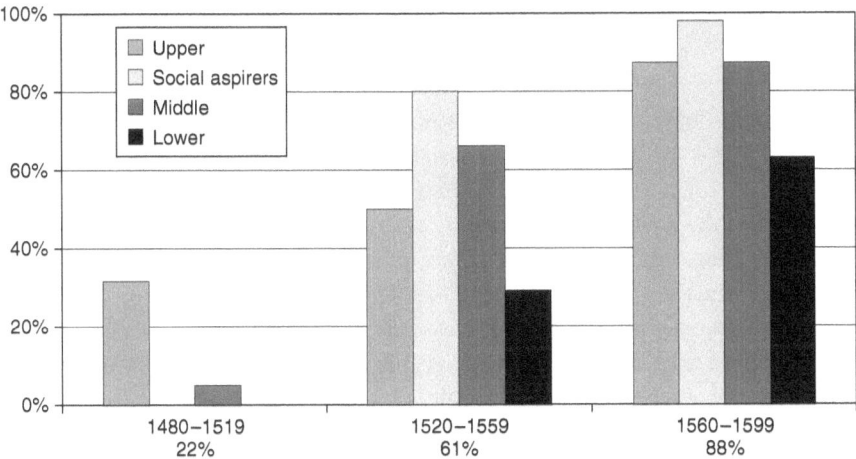

Figure 11.4: Use of single negation versus multiple negation 1480–1599. Percentage of single negation, male informants (CEEC, Nevalainen et al. 1998)

received *you* from them. This usage gradually diminished towards the 18th century, when *you* strengthened its position as the general pronoun of address.

These descriptions of early modern changes testify that social stratification played a part in the diffusion of linguistic changes like that documented for present-day languages.

3.1.3 Region

This section deals with the role regional variation played in the diffusion of changes, in other words, their supralocalization. As a matter of fact, in a VARBRUL analysis of several early modern changes, region proved more significant than gender and register in several cases (Nevalainen and Raumolin-Brunberg 2003: 199).

Research has pinpointed two significant source areas of changes: the North and the London region. The importance of the North has a long history, as it is generally held that a large number of changes, such as the simplification of the inflectional system, originated in the North during the Old English period. The early modern developments can be considered a continuation of this protracted process.

The significance of London, on the other hand, was a newer phenomenon, which was based on the enormous growth of this city during Tudor and Stuart times. Immigration to London created a community with considerable dialect mixing, the development of central administration made London and Westminster the place where the most important people lived, and the growth of the merchant community improved the city's economy. All this raised London's status in the eyes of ordinary Englishmen, and London English had all the prerequisites to become a prestige variety. We know, for instance, that in 1589 George Puttenham recommended the language of the "better-brought-up sort" of London and the Royal Court for aspiring poets.

How, then, did the new forms spread in the country? The traditional hypothesis has been that diffusion takes place according to a wave model; in other words, changes gradually spread outwards from a centre. This is possible if populations are distributed relatively evenly and contacts are maintained in all directions. Geography and potential for communication can change the picture, however, so that mountains or rivers may hinder or promote contacts and linguistic changes with them.

Another attested way of spreading linguistic innovations is dialect hopping. Trudgill (1986) showed that new forms can hop from one urban centre to another bypassing the countryside in between. It seems evident that in past societies it was migration that mostly accounted for this hopping phenomenon, and it is also clear that the capital was the centre that received a large number of immigrants from the countryside. However, people not only moved to London but many moved away from London after a stay of a few years and, of course, took the linguistic forms they had adopted with them.

The regional diffusion of the innovative forms in the CEEC has been studied in four areas, namely London, East Anglia, the North (i.e. the counties north of Lincolnshire) and the Court. These areas should be self-explanatory except for the Court, which refers to the royal family and its courtiers, as well as diplomats and high administrative officers, many of whom lived in Westminster.

Figure 11.5 describes a change that had its origin in the North. During the first decades of the 16th century, we only find -s in the letters written by northerners, although, as mentioned above, it had occurred in late-medieval merchants' letters in London. The abrupt shift around 1600, already referred to in the previous section, is led by Londoners. During this period, East Anglia lags far behind. The following forty-year period testifies to a rapidly growing adoption of -s among courtiers and East Anglians alike. On the whole, here we see how a change with northern origin first spread to London and then from London to the countryside.

The diffusion of subject *you* looks much simpler, as Figure 11.6 testifies. This is a typical change led by the London region, i.e., London and the Court. The curves for East Anglia and the North are almost identical. The spread of single negation as opposed to multiple negation was not very different from that of *you*, but the leading role of the Court was even more conspicuous. Its regional diffu-

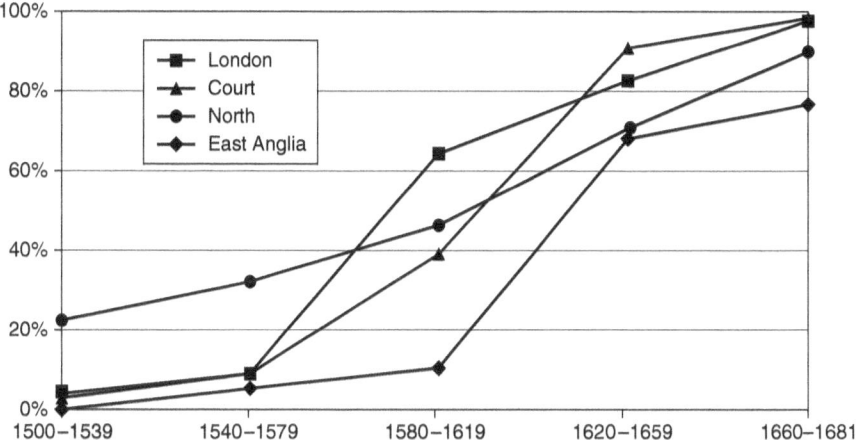

Figure 11.5: The replacement of -*th* by -*s* in verbs other than *have* and *do*, 1500–1681; regional distribution (CEEC, Nevalainen et al. 1998 and CEECSU, Kaislaniemi et al. 2000; excluding Sir Thomas Browne, whose language radically diverged from that of the other informants)

Figure 11.6: The replacement of subject *ye* by *you*, 1480–1599; regional distribution. Percentages of *you* (CEEC, Nevalainen et al. 1998 and CEECSU, Kaislaniemi et al. 2000)

sion actually corroborates the results of the previous section, as courtiers represented the well-educated upper-rank gentlemen who were seen to lead this change.

The significance of regional variation has also been attested in the dialogue corpus. Walker (2007: 102) shows that in witness depositions, *thou* was more frequent in the North – in other words, in areas where it may still occur in the dialect today.

3.1.4 Register and genre

The situational variation of language use is reflected in register and genre variation, which both play an important part in the diffusion of linguistic changes. Studies of multi-genre corpora such as the *Helsinki Corpus* (Rissanen et al. 1991) have shown that changes from below are usually first attested in informal and speech-like genres.

The *Helsinki Corpus* evidence indicates that subject *you* first appeared in oral genres (Raumolin-Brunberg 2005b: 64). As regards the introduction of the third-person suffix -*s*, Kytö (1993: 124) shows that -*s* occurred in the private letters in the Early Modern section of the *Helsinki Corpus* before any other genre. On the other hand, testifying to a change from above, Rissanen (2000: 125) finds a relatively large number of occurrences of single negation in the Late Middle English legal texts in the *Helsinki Corpus*. This offers reason to assume that legal texts may have served as a model for the use of single negation, a practice that first spread among educated men.

Letter data offers the possibility of using the interpersonal relationship as a basis for register variation and diffusion of new items. The division of letters into two groups, (1) letters exchanged between family members and friends and (2) letters between others, has shown that changes from below tend to be seen in the earlier group first. Raumolin-Brunberg and Nevalainen (1997: 711–713) observe that experienced writers, such as Sir Thomas More and Sir Thomas Wyatt, differentiated between family and non-family letters in the use of *you* and *ye*, among other changes. King Henry VIII's letters form an excellent example of register variation between private and official writing. There are no occurrences of *ye* in his autograph love letters to Anne Boleyn, his second wife, although it occurs in his official letters written by secretaries.

In the VARBRUL analysis of five changes, Nevalainen and Raumolin-Brunberg (2003: 199) show that register, analyzed on the basis of the relationship between the letter writers, tends to be less significant than gender and region. It is only in the earliest stages of the introduction of *you* that the group "family and friends" becomes the major factor promoting the use of *you*.

3.2 Idiolectal change

A different view of the diffusion of linguistic changes is offered by examining the behavior of individual language users. There has been increasing interest in the way individuals participate in ongoing linguistic changes (see, e.g., Sankoff and Blondeau 2007; Nevalainen and Raumolin-Brunberg 2017: 202–214). In a speech community, it is possible to find both people who participate and people who do not participate in changes in progress.

The behavior of individuals under ongoing linguistic change is often discussed in terms of generational and communal change. Generational change refers to a situation in which there is idiolectal stability despite ongoing change in the community. In communal change, in turn, people change their language in adulthood, altering their language in the same direction. Labov (1994: 83–84) suggests that sound change and morphological change typically follow the pattern of generational change, while lexical and syntactic changes represent the converse pattern, communal change. Although this often seems to be the case, there is also evidence of lifespan changes, i.e. changes in adulthood, among sound changes (Sankoff and Blondeau 2007).

It is worth pointing out that the well-known concept of apparent time goes back to the generational model, in other words, on the idea that adult speakers' phonology and grammar are fixed. The apparent-time model is a convenient tool with which present-day sociolinguists can examine the diffusion of ongoing linguistic changes by comparing usage across generations of speakers in order to identify the direction and rate of change. Historical research has the advantage of following changes in real time, in other words, how changes actually spread among populations and individuals.

Figure 11.7 is a graphic presentation of the use of the third-person sibilant suffix in the language of nine individual CEEC informants over ten-year periods between 1570 and 1669. All of them have left letters spanning more than twenty years for posterity. At the same time as the figure testifies to extensive inter-individual variation, it also shows that six people changed the frequencies of the new and old forms over their lifespans, while three did not (for the numerical information on and background of the informants, see Raumolin-Brunberg 2005a; Nevalainen and Raumolin-Brunberg 2017: 205).

It is remarkable that there are two stable idiolects at the opposite ends of the scale: Sir Francis Hastings, who used the old form *-th*, and John Chamberlain, who chose the sibilant. Elizabeth, Queen of Bohemia, also exhibits high idiolectal stability during her long letter-writing career. The rest increase their use of *-s* at different rates, except that one informant, Philip Gawdy, both increases and decreases its use in a zig-zag pattern.

The CEEC, with material from the same individuals over longer periods of time, makes it possible to study idiolects and their stability over time. At the same time as the findings so far show extensive inter-individual variation, they also testify to changes in idiolects in the lifespans of several language users.

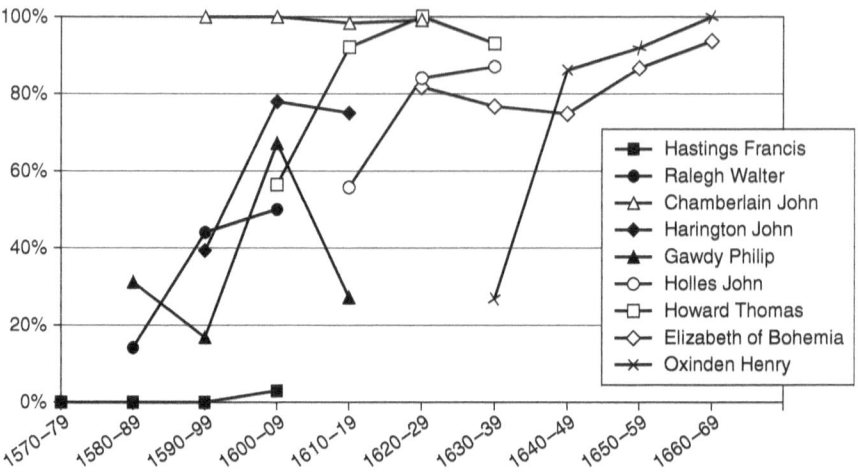

Figure 11.7: The percentage of third-person singular -s in nine idiolects, 1570–1669: a longitudinal study at 10-year intervals (CEEC, Nevalainen et al. 1998 and CEECSU, Kaislaniemi et al. 2000)

3.3 Social networks

The linguistic relationships within social networks form an interesting area of sociolinguistic research in their own right. Here we only raise issues that are connected with the diffusion of linguistic changes. According to James Milroy and Lesley Milroy (e.g. 1985), weak and uniplex ties in loose-knit social networks typically promote change, whereas the norm-enforcing character of networks with multiplex dense ties makes them resistant to change. On this view, linguistic innovators tend to be socially marginal people. On the other hand, on the basis of his Philadelphia data, Labov (2001: 385–411) observes that in the new and vigorous phase of change, the leaders of linguistic change are influential central members of their social networks.

The analysis of social networks should be undertaken cautiously in historical linguistics because of the difficulties in the accurate reconstruction of networks. It seems that the network issue in Early Modern English can be approached in two ways: first, from the macro level, focusing on the general characteristics of the society in question and, second, by looking at particular individuals and their life-stories.

The macro-level approach, based on the general history of Early Modern England, makes use of the fact that internal migration was common and even boosted by two major events, the Reformation in the 16th century and the Revolution with the Civil War in the 17th. As regards the Reformation, one might assume that only religious matters were at issue, but it had a broader effect on society. Among other things, the Church lost its riches and its former lands were sold to laypeople. Both the Reformation and the social turmoil of the Civil War increased weak ties in social networks and possibly accelerated the spread of ongoing linguistic changes (Raumolin-Brunberg 1998).

Furthermore, London's massive growth during the early modern era also led to an increase in weak-tie networks. Thus, it is only natural that the London region grew to be the centre from which linguistic changes spread to other parts of the country.

The second approach, the examination of the social networks of particular individuals, is more difficult, because we seldom know enough of a person's life to reconstruct their networks with sufficient accuracy. Some information has been gained by comparing the leaders of linguistic change at different phases of the diffusion process (Labov 1994:79–82; for the quantification, see Nevalainen and Raumolin-Brunberg 2003: 55). The CEEC data (Raumolin-Brunberg 2006: 130), for instance, suggest that during the incipient phase, when the new form was found at most in 15% of all the occurrences of the variable, the leaders of *you* and *-s* were geographically mobile people, probably with a great many weak links, which, according to Milroy and Milroy (1985), should promote the diffusion of linguistic change. On the other hand, the new and vigorous leaders, i.e. those who led the change when the new form, was found in 15–35% of the occurrences, seem to have been individuals with an influential social position, in other words, the kind of people Labov (2001: 385–411) speaks of as leaders of linguistic change. It is reasonable to suggest, for instance, that the rulers of the country like Henry VIII, leading the use of *you*, and Elizabeth I, an advanced user of third-person *-s*, were central figures in their social networks.

The above suggests that the type of people who lead linguistic changes and their networks vary during the different phases of change. The analysis Milroy and Milroy (1985) seems to concentrate on the incipient phase, while Labov's (2001: 385) arguments explicitly deal with new and vigorous changes. On the whole, despite being a less clear tool of analysis than the speaker variables such as gender, social status, age, etc., the examination of Early Modern social networks may help us understand the diffusion of innovative forms during this period.

4 Summary

Despite the problems of accessing the lowest sections of society and women due to widespread illiteracy, studies of Early Modern English testify to the significance of gender, social rank, region, and register in the diffusion of linguistic change. We have seen that early modern women led a number of changes from below, whereas learned changes were led by men rather than women. Social stratification also proved significant, and it seems that, for rapid diffusion, a new variant needed to be accepted by the topmost ranks, as in the case of the third-person singular -s in the 17th century. The capital region, London and the Court, clearly became the centre from which several changes spread elsewhere in the country. Furthermore, changes from below first occurred in informal genres and registers. Some individuals changed their language across their lifespans, and weak-tie networks apparently promoted the diffusion of change.

By using real-time evidence and linguistic material that represents genuine communication, sociolinguistic research on Early Modern English has enhanced our understanding of the ways grammatical changes diffuse among populations. Further research is needed to diversify and augment the picture that has been acquired so far.

5 References

Barry, Jonathan and Christopher Brooks (eds.). 1994. *The Middling Sort of People: Culture, Society and Politics in England 1550–1800*. London: Macmillan.

Biber, Douglas. 1988. *Variation across Speech and Writing*. Cambridge: Cambridge University Press.

Chambers, J. K. 2003. *Sociolinguistic Theory*. 2nd edn. Oxford: Blackwell.

Fletcher, Anthony. 1995. *Gender, Sex and Subordination in England 1500–1800*. New Haven/London: Yale University Press.

Heal, Felicity and Clive Holmes. 1994. *The Gentry in England and Wales, 1500–1700*. London: Macmillan.

Kaislaniemi, Samuli, Mikko Laitinen, Minna Nevala, Terttu Nevalainen, Arja Nurmi, Minna Palander-Collin, Helena Raumolin-Brunberg, and Anni Sairio. 2000. *Corpus of Early English Correspondence Supplement (CEECSU)*. Department of English, University of Helsinki. http://www.helsinki.fi/varieng/CoRD/corpora/CEEC/ceecsu.html; last accessed 14 April 2017.

Kytö, Merja. 1993. Third-person present singular verb inflection in early British and American English. *Language Variation and Change* 5: 113–139.

Kytö, Merja and Terry Walker. 2003. The linguistic study of Early Modern English speech-related texts: How "bad" can "bad" data be? *Journal of English Linguistics* 31(3): 221–248.

Kytö, Merja and Jonathan Culpeper. 2006. *A Corpus of English Dialogues 1560–1760*. With the assistance of Terry Walker and Dawn Archer. Uppsala University and Lancaster University.

http://www.helsinki.fi/varieng/CoRD/corpora/CED/index.html; last accessed 14 April 2017.

Labov, William. 1990. The intersection of sex and social class in the course of linguistic change. *Language Variation and Change* 2: 205–254.

Labov, William. 1994. *Principles of Linguistic Change. Vol. 1: Internal Factors*. Oxford/Cambridge, MA: Blackwell.

Labov, William. 2001. *Principles of Linguistic Change. Vol. 2: Social Factors*. Oxford/Cambridge, MA: Blackwell.

Laitinen, Mikko. 2007. *Agreement Patterns in English: Diachronic Corpus Studies on Common-Number Pronouns*. Helsinki: Société Néophilologique.

Laslett, Peter. 1983. *The World We Have Lost – Further Explored*. London: Routledge.

Milroy, James and Lesley Milroy. 1985. Linguistic change, social network and speaker innovation. *Journal of Linguistics* 21: 339–384.

Nevalainen, Terttu. 2006. Negative concord as an English "Vernacular Universal": Social history and linguistic typology. *Journal of English Linguistics* 34(3): 257–278.

Nevalainen, Terttu, Helena Raumolin-Brunberg, Jukka Keränen, Minna Nevala, Arja Nurmi, and Minna Palander-Collin. 1998. *Corpus of Early English Correspondence* (CEEC). Department of English, University of Helsinki. http://www.helsinki.fi/varieng/CoRD/corpora/CEEC/index.html; last accessed 14 April 2017.

Nevalainen, Terttu and Helena Raumolin-Brunberg. 2003. *Historical Sociolinguistics: Language Change in Tudor and Stuart England*. London: Pearson.

Nevalainen, Terttu and Helena Raumolin-Brunberg. 2017. *Historical Sociolinguistics: Language Change in Tudor and Stuart England*. Second Edition. London and New York: Routledge.

Nurmi, Arja. 1999. *A Social History of Periphrastic* do. Helsinki: Société Néophilologique.

Nurmi, Arja. 2003a. The role of gender in the use of MUST in Early Modern English. In: Sylviane Granger and Stephanie Petch-Tyson (eds.), *Extending the Scope of Corpus-Based Research: New Applications, New Challenges*, 111–120. Amsterdam and New York: Rodopi.

Nurmi, Arja. 2003b. *Youe shall see I will conclude in it:* Sociolinguistic variation of WILL/WOULD and SHALL/SHOULD in the sixteenth century. In: David Hart (ed.), *English Modality in Context: Diachronic Perspectives*, 89–107. Frankfurt: Peter Lang.

Nurmi, Arja and Minna Palander-Collin. 2008. Letters as a text type: Interaction in writing. In: Marina Dossena and Ingrid Tieken-Boon van Ostade (eds.), *Studies in Late Modern English Correspondence: Methodology and Data*, 21–49. Bern: Peter Lang.

Puttenham, George. 1589. *The Arte of English Poesie*. (*English Linguistics 1500–1800*, ed. by R. C. Alston, 110.) Menston: The Scolar Press, 1968.

Raumolin-Brunberg, Helena. 1998. Social factors and pronominal change in the seventeenth century: The Civil War effect? In: Jacek Fisiak and Marcin Krygier (eds.), *Advances in English Historical Linguistics*, 361–388. Berlin/New York: Mouton de Gruyter.

Raumolin-Brunberg, Helena. 2002. Stable variation and historical linguistics. In: Helena Raumolin-Brunberg, Minna Nevala, Arja Nurmi, and Matti Rissanen (eds.), *Variation Past and Present: VARIENG Studies on English for Terttu Nevalainen*, 101–116. Helsinki: Société Néophilologique.

Raumolin-Brunberg, Helena. 2005a. Language change in adulthood: Historical letters as evidence. *European Journal of English Studies* 9(1): 37–51.

Raumolin-Brunberg, Helena. 2005b. The diffusion of *you*: A case study in historical sociolinguistics. *Language Variation and Change* 17: 55–73.

Raumolin-Brunberg, Helena. 2006. Leaders of linguistic change in Early Modern England. In: Roberta Facchinetti and Matti Rissanen (eds.), *Corpus-based Studies of Diachronic English*, 115–134. Frankfurt: Peter Lang.

Raumolin-Brunberg, Helena and Terttu Nevalainen. 1997. Social embedding of linguistic changes in Tudor English. In: Raymond Hickey and Stanisław Puppel (eds.), *Language History and Linguistic Modelling: A Festschrift for Jacek Fisiak on his 60th Birthday*, 701–717. Berlin/New York: Mouton de Gruyter.

Raumolin-Brunberg, Helena and Terttu Nevalainen. 2007. Historical sociolinguistics: The Corpus of Early English Correspondence. In: Joan C. Beal, Karen P. Corrigan, and Hermann L. Moisl (eds.), *Creating and Digitizing Language Corpora: Diachronic Databases*. Vol. 2, 148–171. Basingstoke/New York: Palgrave Macmillan.

Rissanen, Matti. 2000. Standardization and the language of early statutes. In: Laura Wright (ed.), *The Development of Standard English, 1300–1800: Theories, Descriptions, Conflicts*, 117–130. Cambridge: Cambridge University Press.

Rissanen, Matti, Merja Kytö, Leena Kahlas-Tarkka, Matti Kilpiö, Saara Nevanlinna, Irma Taavitsainen, Terttu Nevalainen, and Helena Raumolin-Brunberg. 1991. *The Helsinki Corpus of English Texts*. In: *ICAME Collection of English Language Corpora (CD-ROM)*, 2nd edn., Knut Hofland, Anne Lindebjerg, and Jørn Thunestvedt (eds.), The HIT Centre, University of Bergen, Norway. For manual, see http://clu.uni.no/icame/manuals/; last accessed 14 April 2017.

Rissanen, Matti, Merja Kytö, and Minna Palander-Collin (eds.). 1993. *Early English in the Computer Age: Explorations through the Helsinki Corpus*. Berlin/New York: Mouton de Gruyter.

Romaine, Suzanne. 1982. *Socio-historical Linguistics: Its Status and Methodology*. Cambridge: Cambridge University Press.

Rosenthal, Bernard, Gretchen Adams, Margo Burns, Peter Grund, Risto Hiltunen, Merja Kytö, Matti Peikola, Benjamin Ray, Matti Rissanen, and Richard Trask (eds.). 2009. *Records of the Salem Witch Hunt*. Cambridge: Cambridge University Press.

Sankoff, Gillian and Hélène Blondeau. 2007. Language change across the lifespan: /r/ in Montreal French. *Language* 83(3): 560–588.

Trudgill, Peter. 1986. *Dialects in Contact*. Oxford: Basil Blackwell.

Walker, Terry. 2007. *Thou and you in Early Modern English Dialogues: Trials, Depositions and Drama Comedy*. Amsterdam/Philadelphia: John Benjamins.

Wrightson, Keith. 1991. Estates, degrees, and sorts: Changing perceptions of society in Tudor and Stuart England. In: Penelope J. Corfield (ed.), *Language, History and Class*, 30–52. Oxford: Blackwell.

Wrightson, Keith. 2003. *English Society 1580–1680*. London: Routledge.

Ulrich Busse
Chapter 12: Pronouns

1 Early Modern English pronouns – an outline —— 209
2 Personal pronouns —— 210
3 Summary —— 221
4 References —— 221

Abstract: The chapter discusses the most important developments and changes of EModE personal and possessive pronouns and the explanations provided in the relevant specialist literature. As many of the pronoun changes were rather long-term developments, often originating in late Old English or Middle English, wherever necessary a short glance backwards or forwards into Modern English will be taken. The rise and the demise of the following variants is treated in detail: the third-person plural pronouns *them* and *hem*, the third-person singular neuter pronouns *his* and *its*, the first and second-person singular possessives *my* and *thy* vs. *mine* and *thine*, the second-person plural pronouns *ye* and *you*, and the second-person singular and plural pronouns *thou* and *you*. Methodologically, the EModE period (1500–1700) is broken down into three isolectal stages showing both the inventory and the use of forms at the beginning, in the middle, and at the end of the period.

1 Early Modern English pronouns – an outline

Pronouns are grammatical (closed-class) words. On the one hand, this suggests that their number cannot be freely increased by processes of word-formation or borrowing. On the other hand, due to their discourse-deictic functions they are less likely than nouns to fall into disuse. Nonetheless, the EModE period saw the introduction of the possessive determiner *its*, the subject relative *who* and the loss of the *thou* (*thee, thy, thine*) paradigm.

For reasons of space, the article deals with personal pronouns in detail, leaving aside all other types of pronoun. (For a concise outline of relative pronouns in Early Modern English, see Johansson, Chapter 15.) The introductions

---

Ulrich Busse: Halle/Saale (Germany)

to Early Modern English by Barber (1997: 148–159), Görlach (1994: 68–71) and Nevalainen (2006: 77–88) provide good overviews of the developments of the relative, interrogative, reflexive, intensive, demonstrative, and indefinite pronouns. Raumolin-Brunberg (1997) deals with reciprocal pronouns. The monograph by Heltveit (1953) deals with demonstrative pronouns, and van Gelderen's (2000) book treats the history of English reflexive pronouns in detail.

2 Personal pronouns

The most decisive change affected the second-person singular pronouns: the *thou* (*thee, thy, thine*) paradigm was replaced by the former plural forms *you/yours/your*. Apart from this major change, leading to the complete demise of the old singular forms in Present-day Standard English, a number of minor changes took place as well (see Table 12.1 below), involving in particular the following pronouns:

- *them* and *hem*, *'em*, with a northern form replacing a southern form,
- *his* and *its*, with the new form *its* supplanting the older form *his*,
- *my* vs. *mine* and *thy* vs. *thine*, resulting in a clear differentiation between determiner (*my, thy*) and independent function (*mine, thine*),
- *ye* and *you*, leading to the generalization of the former objective form *you*.

Table 12.1: Early Modern English personal pronouns (from Nevalainen [2006: 77]; major changes indicated in boldface)

Person/Number	Subjective case	Objective case	Possessive, determiner	Possessive, independent
1P SG	I	me	my/mine → my	mine
1P PL	we	us	our	ours
2P SG	**thou ~ ye → you**	thee ~ you	**thy/thine → thy ~ your**	thine ~ yours
2P PL	**ye → you**	you	your	yours
3P SG personal	he, she	him, her	his, her	his, hers
3P SG non-personal	(h)it → it	him, (h)it → it	**his (thereof) → its (of it)**	(his → its)
3P PL	they	them ('em)	their	theirs

The interesting question is: how was this reduction of variants brought about and which language-internal factors or -external forces were at work? Hence, in the following sections these contrasts will be examined each in turn by describing the social embedding of the respective change and the language-internal factors that led to "streamlining" by sorting out the variants, as it appears from hindsight.

2.1 The third-person plural pronouns *them* and *hem*

The two forms *them* and *hem* for the third-person plural go back to different sources. The form *hem* stems from Anglo-Saxon, while the forms beginning with *th-* were borrowed from Old Norse in the OE period.

> The modern paradigm *they/their/them* is odd: an entire grammatical subsystem borrowed from another language. These come from Scandinavian *þeir* (nom) / *þeirra* (gen) / *þeim* (dat). This system was not, however, borrowed all at once; it took at least 400 years for the new paradigm to be established in the dialect complex that gave rise to the modern standards (Lass 2006: 74–75).

The substitution of the native forms by their Old Norse counterparts happened first in the north of England, where during the late OE period the contact with the Vikings in the area of the Danelaw had been most intense, presumably "because the Old English *h*-forms were ambiguous with singular pronouns" (Hope 2003: 91). During the ME period the Old Norse forms percolated from the north to the south, however, travelling at different speeds, with the nominative spreading faster than the possessive and the objective. "[W]e find the Northern dialect using the Scandinavian *th*-forms in all the three cases (nominative, genitive, and objective), the Midlands dialects using the *th*-forms in the nominative but the *h*-forms in the genitive and objective, and the Southern dialect using the *h*-forms exclusively" (Brinton and Arnovick 2006: 275). Thus, in Late Middle English, for instance in Chaucer, we find nominative *they*, but *hem* and *hir* for the objective and possessive. "This process was completed in the fifteenth century, when the northern third-person plural object form *them* replaced the southern *hem*" (Nevalainen 2006: 78). Barber (1997: 151) is also of the opinion that the Old Norse forms "are the normal ones by 1500", and Hope (2003: 91) remarks that the change was virtually complete in the south when Shakespeare was born in 1564. However, even for Shakespeare's works Spevack (1968–80) lists 222 instances of *'em* as opposed to 2,046 tokens of *them*.

In the course of the period "*hem* becomes less frequent, and is rare in the seventeenth century, though it is still recorded as late as 1660. Its weak form was *em*, with the usual loss of initial /h-/ in unstressed syllables" (Barber 1997: 151). Nevalainen notes that "[t]he change would perhaps have been harder to detect in speech, because the unstressed forms of *hem* and *them* could have identical realisations, often rendered by *'em* in writing imitating speech" (2006: 78).

2.2 The third-person singular neuter pronouns *his* and *its*

In comparison to Modern English with the only forms *it* and *its*, Table 12.1 shows that for the third-person neuter pronouns a number of changes occurred in Early Modern English. In Old English, the neuter pronoun was declined *hit, his, him, hit*. During Middle English, unlike all other pronouns, the accusative and dative case forms were merged under the accusative rather than the dative form, turning the paradigm into *hit, his, hit*, so that at the beginning of the EModE period

> [t]he original form of the nominative and the accusative was *hit*, which was still in use in the sixteenth century. The word *it* is an example of the restressing of a weak form: it arose in ME when initial /h-/ was regularly lost in unstressed syllables. […] The disappearance of *hit* takes place during the sixteenth century, and by 1600 *it* is the normal form (Barber 1997: 150).

Sometimes these forms were even further reduced to *'t*. However, "the *'t* form has not survived in Modern English except in jocular use" (Brinton and Arnovick 2006: 332).

By contrast, *his* remained the proper form of the possessive until the 1600s, making the forms for the possessive and determiner for the third-person masculine and neuter pronouns identical. This "ambiguous" use of *his* did not mirror the distinction between animate and inanimate referents. The clash between grammatical gender in contrast to notional or natural gender was felt by EModE speakers and was resolved in a number of ways. "Various substitutes were tried, clearly indicating a desire, conscious or unconscious, to avoid the use of *his* in the neuter" (Baugh and Cable 2002: 243), namely:

– the use of the simple form *it* as a possessive (beginning in the 14th century), example (1):

(1) *Wherfore I meruaile how our English tongue hath crackt* **it** *credit, that it may not borrow of the Latin as wel as other tongues […]* (1586 Pettie, *The Ciuile Conuersation of M. Stephen Guazzo*; Görlach 1994: 218)

– periphrastic *thereof* and *of it* as alternative constructions, (2):

(2) *The Plantine trees also grow in that countrie, the tree is as big as a mans thigh, and as high as a firre pole, the leaues* **thereof** *be long & broade […]* (1591 Hortrop, *The Trauailes of an English Man*; Görlach 1994: 307)

– the formation of *its*, by adding a possessive ending to *it*, (3):

(3) *And let confession make halfe amends, that euery language hath **it's** Genius and inseparable form [...]* (1603 Florio, *Montaigne's Essays*; Görlach 1994: 219)

The new form spread rapidly. Barber (1997: 150–151) mentions that it was the normal form by the 1620s, and that the use of *his* as a neuter genitive became rare, but "lingered on until about 1670 [...]. But once the form *its* had become firmly established, these other devices [see examples 1–3 above] became unnecessary". However, "[a]t the beginning of the seventeenth century it was clearly felt as a neologism not yet admitted to good use. There is no instance of it in the Bible (1611) or in any of the plays of Shakespeare printed during his lifetime [...]. Toward the close of the seventeenth century its acceptance seems to have gained momentum rapidly" (Baugh and Cable 2002: 244). Yet, this refers only to its function as a determiner. With reference to the grammar of Present-day English, Nevalainen (2006: 81) points out that "the independent possessive pronoun *its* is marginal even today". In following Baugh and Cable (2002), we can thus conclude that

> If grammatical gender had survived in English the continued use of *his* when referring to neuter nouns would probably never have seemed strange. But when, with the substitution of natural gender, meaning came to be the determining factor in the gender of nouns, and all lifeless objects were thought of as neuter, the situation was somewhat different (Baugh and Cable 2002: 243).

For a detailed treatment of the third person neuter possessive see Nevalainen and Raumolin-Brunberg (1994).

2.3 The first and second-person singular possessives *my* and *thy* vs. *mine* and *thine*

By 1500, the pronoun-determiners have alternative forms: *my* or *mine* and *thy* or *thine*. By 1600, *mine* and *thine* have become less frequent, and by 1700 they are no longer used in this function. In short, the rules for the usage of the variant forms can be laid down as follows:

At the beginning of the period in 1500, similarly to *a/an*, *my* and *thy* are used before consonants, and *mine* and *thine* before a vowel, or sometimes <h> + vowel. In case of silent word-initial <h>, as in *honour, host* or *habit*, we find *mine/thine*, and also before a pause. This usage changes in the 16th century. "By 1600, *my* and *thy* are almost without exception the forms used before consonants, while before vowels *my* and *mine* are in free variation, as are *thy* and *thine*: Shakespeare has both *thine eyes* and *thy eye*, both *mine own* and *my own*" (Barber 1997: 152). The following examples (4), (5) and (6) from Shakespeare's plays (see Busse 2002: 224) underline this seemingly random patterning of variants within a single line of text, as they defy the neat distribution usually given in reference works:

(4) In **thine** own person answer **thy** abuse (1590/91 *The Second Part of King Henry the Sixth* II.i.40)

(5) *Throw* **thy** *glove, / or any token of* **thine** *honor else, [...].* (1607/08 *Timon of Athens* V.iv.49–50)

(6) *I'll take* **thy** *word for faith, not ask* **thine** *oath: [...].* (1607/08 *Pericles* I.ii.120)

However, a systematic investigation of the Shakespeare corpus (see Busse 2002: Chapter 9) has revealed that by 1600 *thy* and *thine* were no longer in free variation before vowels, because "minimal pairs" show that meaningful choices were made on grounds of intra-textual constraints, in particular for stylistic reasons, as for euphony, emphasis, parallelism, antithesis, etc. According to Barber (1997: 152) *mine* and *thine* continue to recede during the 17th century, so that in standard literary prose *my* and *thy* can be regarded as the normal forms by 1700.

Concerning the reasons for the ultimate demise of *mine* and *thine*, Görlach (1994: 69) argues that in predicative use, the *n*-forms are characterized by greater intonational emphasis and their ability to occur before a pause or sentence boundary. Owing to this, the *-n* is generally retained. Thus, in the 17th century the Middle English phonetic distinction is understood grammatically. Görlach also points out that the *-n* could be interpreted as a weakened form of *one*, as in *such one*, *this one*, which had become usual in this position after pronouns. Whether this really was the case, cannot be proved.

Strang (1970: 139) argues along the same line: "since the use in final position was pronominal, the distribution could serve as matrix for a new, grammatical, distinction. The now familiar difference of use, +/n/ pronominal, -/n/ attributive, develops from this matrix at the end of the 16c; though in attributive use the old phonological distinction continued in use for a time".

Schendl (1997: 181) has brought forward the hypothesis that both "the synchronic and diachronic variation in the forms of the possessives might correlate with levels of formality and that the *n*-less variants entered the emerging written standard from the spoken language". Schendl concludes that from the first half of the 16th century to the first half of the 17th century the stylistic value of the forms *my/thy* vs. *mine/thine* has resulted in a reversal of markedness. At the first stage, the distribution is basically phonologically determined, then *my/thy* are marked as informal, and finally these forms are unmarked, which leads to the marking of *mine/thine* as poetic. This view is also shared by Nevalainen, but she adds that this change – similar to the one of *them* replacing *hem* – has a regional dimension, too. "The loss of *-n* occurred earlier in the north than in the south. In the course of the sixteenth century the short forms *my* and *thy* spread to most contexts and the long ones were retained only in poetic language and fixed expressions (*mine own, thine eyes*)" (Nevalainen 2006: 78). Nevertheless, Wales (1996: 167–168) still includes *thy* and *thine* in the pronoun paradigm of present standard and non-standard English(es) "because they are still known and used by native standard English speakers as part of a general 'elevated' register". For a concise recent case study of how the nasal in the first and second person possessives was lost, see Raumolin-Brunberg and Nevalainen (2007).

2.4 The second-person plural pronouns *ye* and *you*

First examples for the use of the oblique form *you* functioning as a nominative can be found from the 14th century onwards, but at the beginning of the EModE period, there was still a clear distinction between the nominative and the objective forms of the second-person plural pronoun, with *ye* as the nominative and *you* as the objective form. By 1600, *you* takes over as the nominative form, making *ye* a less common variant. However, until the middle of the 16th century, *ye* still prevails in the nominative. In the second half of the 16th century the use of *you* as a nominative gains momentum, but the archaizing language of the *Authorized Version* of the Bible (1611) maintains *ye* in the nominative as in (7) and (8):

(7) *No doubt but **ye** are the people, and wisdom shall die with **you*** (Job 12, 2)

(8) *The Lord deal kindly with **you**, as **ye** have dealt with the dead, and with me. The Lord grant **you** that **ye** may find rest [...]* (Ruth 1, 8–9; Pyles 1971: 202n.)

Kenyon (1914) has shown that in the *Authorized Version* of the Bible *you* only occurs as a nominative in 7% of all instances. *Ye* is also maintained in Tyndale's translation of the New Testament. Simultaneously, many authors show vacillation in their use of the two variants. For instance, according to Wyld (1937: 330 quoted in Pyles 1971: 202n.), 16th-century authors like Lord Berners and Sir Thomas More clearly differentiated between both forms. Others like Roger Ascham, Bishop Latimer, Cavendish, or Lyly (in *Euphues*) used both forms indiscriminately in the nominative, whereas Queen Elizabeth I used only *you* for both functions.

Beginning in the third quarter of the 16th century, and coming to a close in the 18th, the paradigm is reordered with *you* as the majority form regardless of case. *Ye* is relegated to elevated literary usage such as poetic apostrophes. For example, in Shakespeare's plays there occur a mere 343 tokens of *ye* in comparison to 22,222 tokens of *you*. Within these limits, *ye* frequently occurs in postverbal position in imperatives and in sentences containing the optative subjunctive, in particular greeting formulae such as *fare ye well*. As concerns its discourse functions, *ye* is clearly marked as the affective pronoun in comparison to *you*, because it frequently occurs in exclamatives, which are mostly found as apostrophes in connection with abstract nouns together with either honorific or abusive vocatives (see Busse 2002: Chapter 10).

A number of papers by Terttu Nevalainen and Helena Raumolin-Brunberg based on the *Corpus of Early English Correspondence* (CEEC) (Nevalainen et al. 1998) report on the social diffusion of the change. In these studies, the authors concentrate on extralinguistic variables such as social stratification, gender and apparent time. Apart from the social patterning of usage in the first subperiod (1520–1550) of the CEEC, the most striking result is that there are no instances whatsoever of *ye* in subject position in the second subperiod (1590–1620), "indicating that all the differences between the ranks observed some half a century earlier have been levelled out" (Nevalainen 1996: 66).

In comparison to the other pronouns this development is rather exceptional, because *ye* and *you* are the only pronouns to have given up marking for nominative or oblique case, as this development did not take place for *I-me, we-us, he-him, she-her, they-them* (see Heltveit 1952: 378–379). Most often two explanations are given, a phonological and a syntactic, or rather a combination of the two, i.e. a confusion of weak forms in unstressed contexts and a cross-over analogy to the second person singular pronouns *thou* and *thee*. For example, Barber (1997: 149) says that "it is not entirely clear why it was the accusative form which became thus standardised, but it may have been by analogy with *thou*: the two forms usually had the same vowel in late Middle English, and [...] the form [jəʊ], rhyming with *thou*, still existed in the sixteenth century". Strang also emphasizes this point:

> Phoneticians indicate that in the late 16c the strong form was /jəʊ/ (=PE* [Present-day English] /jaʊ/), weak /jʊ/. While the modern weak form is a continuation of the old one, the strong form is a new analogical creation, by lengthening of the weak one [...]. The marked circumstances of the use of *thou* have, however, enabled the old strong form to survive, though the weak /ðʊ/ has been lost (Strang 1970: 140–141).

Görlach (1994: 69) mentions the following factors: both *ye* and *you* had a common unstressed form [jə], which in addition to the redundancy of case marking led to wrong interpretations. This development received further strengthening through the cross-over analogy of vowels in *thou* and *thee*. He also points out that from the ME period onwards, the function of case marking has been largely supplanted by a fixed svo-word order. With the consolidation of word order, the personal pronouns with their case marking are "over-characterized", which made case shiftings without loss of understanding possible.

According to Fries (1940: 201) the case differentiation of subject and object by means of word order rather than inflection makes progress during the 14th century, and is more or less fixed to svo by 1500, although case marking in the pronouns is retained much longer. For the maintenance of this distinction in the pronominal system, Howe gives the following reasons:

> that morphologically the personal pronouns are [...] on the whole portmanteau forms rather than suffixed inflection, and are thus phonologically less likely to lose inflection through the reduction of endings common in the Germanic languages in adjectives, nouns and verbs. Furthermore, the high degree of suppletion in the personal pronouns means that given phonological reduction, forms which have a suppletive distinction will *tend* to remain formally distinct longer than those with less suppletive distinctions, and this seems to be borne out by examples such as English *ye-you* [...] (Howe 1996: 70).

A further reason that could have contributed to the confusion of forms is their spelling as both *thou* and *you* and *thee* and *ye* could be written with <y>. Lass (1999: 154) offers the following short description and explanation for the replacement of *ye* by *you*, stressing that the process began in the fourteenth century, especially in postverbal position, e.g. as subject of a preposed verb, as in (9):

(9)   *to morwe schal **yow** wedded be* (1492 *Guy of Warick*; Mustanoja 1960: 125, my emphasis)

The spelling <ye> for *you* in unstressed positions and its pronunciation as /jə/ may have added to the confusion of the two forms. "Thus (at least in written language) there is an early precedent for confusing the shapes of the two forms. And the post-verbal use of *you*, even as subject, simply reflects the fact that oblique pronoun forms typically appear in this position as objects – a generalisation of linear position over syntactic function" (Lass 1999: 154).

Lutz (1998: 197) has dealt with this case in detail. She argues that cross-over analogy, which may have had a partial effect on the switch from *ye* to *you*, cannot have been the decisive factor, because the singular nominative and oblique forms *thou* and *thee* do not show signs of confusion throughout the EModE period. For this reason, she instead assumes that the selection of the Middle English plural object form *you* as the only remaining form of direct address in standard English can be attributed to the interplay of various external and internal factors (Lutz 1998: 201).

2.5 The second-person singular and plural pronouns *thou* and *you*

Whereas the previous changes have not received very much attention by scholars, the shift from *thou* to *you* has been studied in detail (see e.g. Finkenstaedt 1963). With the loss of singular *thou* (*thee, thy, thine*) in the standard form of the language and the generalization of *you* (*your, yours*), the number and case distinction got lost (see Table 12.1), thus creating "a notable asymmetry [...] in the personal pronoun system" (Nevalainen 2006: 78).

The gradual replacement of the singular forms began in the 13th century when the plural pronouns *ye/yow* spread as the polite forms in addressing one person. They "owe their new function most probably to French influence, particularly the courtly literature" (Wales 1983: 108). From Chaucer's time well into the EModE period, this contrast played an important role in marking socio-affective distance between interlocutors. The change from *thou* to *you* is most often explained in terms of sociolinguistic and pragmatic models or a combination of both.

Brown and Gilman (1960) trace this use of pronominal address back to the Roman Empire of the 4th century, when the pronoun *vos* appears as a reflex of the *nos pluralis majestatis* of the emperor. From then on, they show the spread of the plural form and the development on two social planes. The vertical dimension of status yields the polite plural pronoun as a deferential address to superiors, and the singular pronoun as an address form for social inferiors. Discourse among social equals, when not intimate or well acquainted, favors a reciprocal exchange of plural pronouns, and the singular pronoun as a sign of intimacy.

The main difficulties within the Brown and Gilman approach to the English language, and to Early Modern English in particular, lie in the fact that the overlay of social and affective usages of *thou* are often difficult or impossible to distinguish. Furthermore, in Shakespearean English there is often momentary fluctuation in pronoun usage among two interlocutors which cannot be explained by a model assuming static social hierarchies (see Wales 1983).

For instance, Eagleson (1971: 13) treats such shifts in pronoun usage in terms of markedness: "*you* had become the unmarked or neutral form, while *thou* was the marked form, being used to register any important shift not simply in rank but especially in emotion, be it love or anger, respect or contempt". He provides us with a striking example (10) taken from *King Lear* (discussed again by Stein 2003: 251).

(10) *Goneril [to Edmund]: Decline **your** head: this kiss, if it durst speak, /Would stretch **thy** spirits up into the air* (1605 *King Lear* IV.ii.22–23)

In trying to win Edmund over for her plans, Goneril tries to deceive him by making him believe that she is in love with him. She subtly achieves this effect by first addressing him with *you*, and after the bestowal of the kiss by passionately thouing him. The socio-pragmatic aspects of Shakespeare's pronominal usage are further explored by Busse (2002), Stein (2003), and U. Busse and B. Busse (2010).

Pronoun choices and in particular pronoun switches have been explained by micro-sociolinguistic or -pragmatic approaches. For example, Hope (1993: 85) argues that "rapidly modulating forms addressed to the same person" have hitherto been explained as being affectively marked deviations from the forms expected on a social basis according to the Brown and Gilman model of power and solidarity. Yet, his work on depositions would suggest that such shifts should, moreover, be interpreted on a micro-pragmatic level.

Hope (1994: 58) finds the situation "with at least three competing systems – a social system, an emotional/politeness-based system, and a system in which 'you' is the only available form – all open to use by speakers" quite confusing. From these systems he only expects the last subsystem to show "socio-historical linguistic patterning consistently", because the social and emotional subsystems "would be expected to disrupt it" (Hope 1994: 58).

With Nevalainen (2006) we can summarize the general development of the change in the following way:

> *Thou* retreated to the private sphere, but could surface in public discourse when emotions ran high. Around 1600, *thou* is found in fiction, drama and poetry and in religious contexts of all kinds, especially with reference to God, as well as in trial records (Nevalainen 2006: 78).

However, the speed of the change, and even more importantly its interpretation, depend on the type of language studied. Taavitsainen (1997) discusses EModE genres and text types under the specific perspective of how personal affect is dealt with linguistically in fiction and adjoining text types. Among the factors she tests for personal affect are also the second person pronouns. From a diachronic statistical analysis, she finds that "the difference between the use of the second person singular in fiction and the adjoining genres is significant" (Taavitsainen 1997: 239), as fiction and to a lesser degree autobiography are the only genres to make use of *thou* throughout all phases of Early Modern English. However, in these text types the function of *thou* is different. "[T]he frequent use of *thou* in fiction is connected with the social classes depicted in these texts: country folk and lower and middle class people among which it was the unmarked pronoun of address [...] In non-literary texts such as autobiography the use of *thou* to express heightened emotionality is evident" (Taavitsainen 1997: 256–257). For history, biography, diary and travelogue the figures for *thou* are almost negligible.

On the basis of the CEEC, Nevala (2004) has studied the varying use of the pronouns of address in "letters written from one family member to another, as well as correspondence between close friends" (Nevala 2004: 159), covering the time span from the early 15th century to the first half of the 18th century. In her own words, the main results of her study are summarized as follows:

> [N]o definite conclusions can be made about the influence of social rank on the use of *thou*. Instead, the writer's social role and thus the power characteristics seem to affect the pronoun usage to a certain degree. [...] Material from the 17th century shows an increase in the users of *thou* [...]. The use of address pronouns also seems to be influenced to a certain degree by the situational level of intimacy and affection between members of a family and close friends (Nevala 2004: 177, 178).

For further studies taking account of the social factors of the change from *thou* to *you* (especially in the 17th century) see Raumolin-Brunberg (1998; 2005).

Walker (2007) has investigated the use of second-person pronouns in the three genres of Trials, Depositions, and Drama Comedy from 1560 to 1760 finding that

> [o]f the three genres, Trials had the lowest percentages of THOU, and there was a marked decline after 1600: THOU was rare in the seventeenth century, and did not occur after 1719 [...]. The Depositions genre, by contrast, had much higher percentages of THOU. There was an unsteady decline across the 200-year period studied, but still as much as 21 per cent THOU in period 5 [1720–1760]. Drama Comedy exhibited a marked decline in THOU after 1640, and a further decline after 1720 (Walker 2007: 288–289).

As regards the factors influencing the use of *thou* and *you*, Walker (2007: 293) found "little evidence in the material that pronoun selection was determined by linguistic factors" such as different sentence and verb types or formulaic phrases. Instead, a wide range of extra-linguistic factors such as social distance, region, characterization, emotion, etc. "have been found to motivate pronoun usage in dialogues in the three speech-related genres" (Walker 2007: 292). In terms of sociolinguistic variables, "age did not seem a prime factor in pronoun selection" and "the influence of the sex parameter was less than clear" (Walker 2007: 292).

These results show that the explanation for the change is not as simple and straightforward as it seems at first sight.

3 Summary

The discussion of changes within the EModE system of personal pronouns shows that a number of minor changes and a fundamental change leading to the replacement of the singular pronoun *thou* (*thee*, *thy*, *thine*) took place. At the beginning of the EModE period in 1500, there is still an overlap in function between second-person singular and plural forms, but at the end of the period, about 1700, the only forms left over in Standard English are *you* and *your*.

Viewed from a typological perspective, this change made the paradigm rather exceptional "not only in comparison with that of the immediately preceding stages of the language and with that of the other Germanic and Indo-European languages [...], but also compared to many entirely unrelated languages" (Lutz 1998: 190), leaving Present-day Standard English with an asymmetrical pronoun system.

All the pronoun changes are long-term developments, often beginning in Late Old English or Middle English. In the case of the replacement of *hem* by *them*, language contact with Old Norse was a decisive factor and the shift from *thou* to *you* has been attributed to the influence of courtly French literature in the ME period. While this shift seems to have been a socio-pragmatic matter, triggered by extra-linguistic factors, the change from *ye* to *you* in subject function shows an interplay of language-internal and -external factors. The introduction of the non-personal third-person singular pronoun *it* resolved the conflict between the older system of grammatical gender and the newer system of notional gender. With *my/mine* and *thy/thine* a formerly phonological contrast is exploited for stylistic purposes before the nasal forms fall into disuse.

4 References

Barber, Charles. 1997. *Early Modern English*. 2nd edn. Edinburgh: Edinburgh University Press.
Baugh, Albert C. and Thomas Cable. 2002. *A History of the English Language*. 5th edn. London: Routledge.
Brinton, Laurel J. and Leslie K. Arnovick. 2006. *The English Language: A Linguistic History*. Oxford: Oxford University Press.
Brown, Roger W. and Albert Gilman. 1960. The pronouns of power and solidarity. In: Thomas A. Sebeok (ed.), *Style in Language*, 253–276. Cambridge, MA: MIT Press.
Busse, Ulrich. 2002. *Linguistic Variation in the Shakespeare Corpus: Morpho-syntactic Variability of Second Person Pronouns*. Amsterdam/Philadelphia: John Benjamins.

Busse, Ulrich and Beatrix Busse. 2010. Shakespeare. In: Andreas H. Jucker and Irma Taavitsainen (eds.), *Historical Pragmatics*, 247–281. (*Handbooks of Pragmatics*, 8.) Berlin/New York: Mouton de Gruyter.

Eagleson, Robert D. 1971. Propertied as all the tuned spheres: Aspects of Shakespeare's language. *The Teaching of English* 20: 4–15.

Finkenstaedt, Thomas. 1963. *You and Thou: Studien zur Anrede im Englischen (mit einem Exkurs über die Anrede im Deutschen)*. Berlin: de Gruyter.

Fisiak, Jacek and Marcin Krygier (eds.). 1998. *Advances in English Historical Linguistics*. Berlin/New York: Mouton de Gruyter.

Fries, Charles Carpenter. 1940. On the development of the structural use of word-order in modern English. *Language* 16: 199–208.

van Gelderen, Elly. 2000. *A History of English Reflexive Pronouns: Person, Self, and Interpretability*. Amsterdam/Philadelphia: John Benjamins.

Görlach, Manfred. 1994. *Einführung ins Frühneuenglische*. 2nd edn. Heidelberg: Winter. [English edition, *Introduction to Early Modern English*, Cambridge: Cambridge University Press, 1991].

Heltveit, Trygve. 1952. Notes on the development of the personal pronouns in English. *Norsk Tidsskrift for Sprogvidenskap* 16: 377–386.

Heltveit, Trygve. 1953. *Studies in English Demonstrative Pronouns: A Contribution to the History of English Morphology*. Oslo: Akademisk Forlag.

Hope, Jonathan. 1993. Second person singular pronouns in records of Early Modern spoken English. *Neuphilologische Mitteilungen* 94: 83–100.

Hope, Jonathan. 1994. *The Authorship of Shakespeare's Plays: A Socio-linguistic Study*. Cambridge: Cambridge University Press.

Hope, Jonathan. 2003. *Shakespeare's Grammar*. London: The Arden Shakespeare.

Howe, Stephen. 1996. *The Personal Pronouns in the Germanic Languages: A Study of Personal Pronoun Morphology and Change in the Germanic Languages from the First Records to the Present Day*. Berlin/New York: Mouton de Gruyter.

Kenyon, John S. 1914. *Ye* and *you* in the King James Version. *PMLA Proceedings of the Modern Language Association of America* 24, New Series 12: 453–471.

Lass, Roger. 1999. Phonology and morphology. In: Lass (ed.), 56–186.

Lass, Roger (ed.). 1999. *The Cambridge History of the English Language*. Vol. III. *1476–1776*. Cambridge: Cambridge University Press.

Lass, Roger. 2006. Phonology and morphology. In: Richard Hogg and David Denison (eds.), *A History of the English Language*, 43–108. Cambridge: Cambridge University Press.

Lutz, Angelika. 1998. The interplay of external and internal factors in morphological restructuring: The case of you. In: Fisiak and Krygier (eds.), 189–210.

Mustanoja, Tauno F. 1960. *A Middle English Syntax*. Vol. 1: *Parts of Speech*. Helsinki: Société Néophilologique.

Nevala, Minna. 2004. *Address in Early English Correspondence*. Helsinki: Société Néophilologique.

Nevalainen, Terttu. 1996. Social stratification. In: Terttu Nevalainen and Helena Raumolin-Brunberg (eds.), *Sociolinguistics and Language History: Studies based on the Corpus of Early English Correspondence*, 57–76. Amsterdam: Rodopi.

Nevalainen, Terttu. 2006. *An Introduction to Early Modern English*. Edinburgh: Edinburgh University Press.

Nevalainen, Terttu and Helena Raumolin-Brunberg. 1994. *Its* strength and the beauty *of it*: The standardization of the third person neuter possessive in Early Modern English. In:

Dieter Stein and Ingrid Tieken-Boon van Ostade (eds.), *Towards a Standard English, 1600–1800*, 171–216. Berlin/New York: Mouton de Gruyter.

Nevalainen, Terttu, Helena Raumolin-Brunberg, Jukka Keränen, Minna Nevala, Arja Nurmi, and Minna Palander-Collin. 1998. *Corpus of Early English Correspondence* (CEEC). Department of English, University of Helsinki. http://www.helsinki.fi/varieng/CoRD/corpora/CEEC/index.html; last accessed 15 April 2017.

Pyles, Thomas. 1971. *The Origins and Development of the English Language*. 2nd edn. New York: Harcourt Brace Jovanovich.

Raumolin-Brunberg, Helena. 1997. Reciprocal pronouns: From discontinuity to unity. *Studia Anglica Posnaniensia* 31: 227–236.

Raumolin-Brunberg, Helena. 1998. Social factors and pronominal change in the seventeenth century: The Civil War effect? In: Fisiak and Krygier (eds.), 361–388.

Raumolin-Brunberg, Helena. 2005. The diffusion of you: A case study in historical sociolinguistics. *Language Variation and Change* 17: 55–73.

Raumolin-Brunberg, Helena and Terttu Nevalainen. 2007. From mine *to* my *and* thine *to* thy: *Loss of the nasal in the first and second person possessives*. In: Ute Smit, Stefan Dollinger, Julia Hüttner, Gunther Kaltenböck, and Ursula Lutzky (eds.), *Tracing English through Time: Explorations in Language Variation*, 303–314. Vienna: Braumüller.

Schendl, Herbert. 1997. Morphological variation and change in Early Modern English: *my/mine, thy/thine*. In: Raymond Hickey and Stanisław Puppel (eds.), *Language History and Linguistic Modelling: A Festschrift for Jacek Fisiak on his 60th Birthday*. Vol. 1: *Language History*, 179–191. Berlin/New York: Mouton de Gruyter.

Spevack, Marvin. 1968–80. *A Complete and Systematic Concordance to the Works of Shakespeare*. 9 vols. Hildesheim: Olms.

Stein, Dieter. 2003. Pronominal usage in Shakespeare: Between sociolinguistics and conversation analysis. In: Irma Taavitsainen and Andreas H. Jucker (eds.), *Diachronic Perspectives on Address Term Systems*, 251–307. Amsterdam/Philadelphia: John Benjamins.

Strang, Barbara M. H. 1970. *A History of English*. London: Methuen.

Taavitsainen, Irma. 1997. Genre conventions: Personal affect in fiction and non-fiction in Early Modern English. In: Matti Rissanen, Merja Kytö, and Kirsi Heikkonen (eds.), *English in Transition: Corpus-based Studies in Linguistic Variation and Genre Styles*, 185–206. Berlin/New York: Mouton de Gruyter.

Wales, Kathleen M. 1983. Thou and you in Early Modern English: Brown and Gilman reappraised. *Studia Linguistica* 37: 107–125.

Wales, Katie. 1996. *Personal Pronouns in Present-day English*. Cambridge: Cambridge University Press.

Walker, Terry. 2007. Thou *and* You *in Early Modern English Dialogues*. Amsterdam/Philadelphia: John Benjamins.

Wyld, Henry Cecil. 1937. *A History of Modern Colloquial English*. 3rd edn. New York: Dutton.

Anthony Warner
Chapter 13:
Periphrastic DO

1 Introduction —— 224
2 Origin —— 228
3 Variation: discourse-based, social, and stylistic factors —— 229
4 Variation: lexical and collocational effects —— 230
5 Variation: phonotactic and syntactic factors —— 231
6 Parametric change and the rise of DO —— 234
7 Regulation of DO —— 236
8 Envoi —— 238
9 References —— 238

Abstract: In Early Modern English the modern use of auxiliary DO *(Did you hear? I did not hear)* largely replaced earlier full verb constructions *(Heard you? I heard not)*. An affirmative without emphasis *(I do hear = I hear)* was also possible, as hardly today. This chapter discusses factors involved in the substantial variation characteristic of the period, possible motivations for the rise of DO, and the emergence of its modern profile. Variation corresponded to a wide range of parameters, including discourse and stylistic properties, the presence of particular lexemes and collocations, and the verb's phonotactics. There were also major differences between clause types. These distributions may reveal motivations for the rise of DO, or simply reflect speakers' choices during a more abstract change (the loss of V-to-I), proceeding at a shared "constant rate" across contexts. Many issues are unsettled, but electronic corpora provide a major opportunity for progress.

1 Introduction

A distinctive property of today's English is its use of DO in clauses negated by *not* and in inverted questions. In Chaucer's period (the late 14th century) the finite lexical verb was used in such constructions, though DO was just beginning to appear. It gains over the finite lexical verb, and Early Modern English (1500–

Anthony Warner: York (UK)

1700) is a period of substantial variation between the two, as finites of DO replace the earlier use of the finite lexical verb. So the playwright Jonson, writing c.1600, has both options available to him in the constructions of Table 13.1, and there is similar variation in negative questions.

Table 13.1: Variation between DO and finite lexical verb in Ben Jonson

	with DO	with finite lexical verb
Affirmative inverted wh-questions	a. *When did you see him?* (1905–8 [1599] Jonson, *Every Man out of his Humour* 1643) b. *O Madam, why do you prouoke your Father, thus?* (1932 [1605] Jonson, *Eastward Ho!* 591, l. 161)	c. *When saw you my neece?* (1905–8 [1599] Jonson, *Every Man out of his Humour* 1284) d. *And how approue you your sisters fashion?* (1932 [1605] Jonson, *Eastward Ho!* 535, l. 132)
Affirmative inverted yes–no questions	a. *Pray you, sir, did you see Master Fastidius Briske?* (1905–8 [1599] Jonson, *Every Man out of his Humour* 2800) b. *Doe you heare, sir?* (1905–8 [1598] Jonson, *Every Man in his Humour* 2432)	c. *O, Carlo! welcome: saw you Monsieur Briske?* (1905–8 [1599] Jonson, *Every Man out of his Humour* 2748) d. *How now Cutberd, succeedes it, or no?* (1937 [1609] Jonson, *Epicoene* 196, l. 10)
Negative declaratives with *not*	a. *I am deafe, I doe not heare you; ...* (1932 [1605] Jonson, *Eastward Ho!* 610, l. 15) b. *I look't in the pot once, indeed, but I did not drinke.* (1905–8 [1599] Jonson, *Every Man out of his Humour* 3933)	c. *No sir, he saw him not.* (1905–8 [1598] Jonson, *Every Man in his Humour* 271) d. *I loue not your disputations, or your court-tumults.* (1937 [1609] Jonson, *Epicoene* 258, l. 46)
Negative imperatives with *not*	a. *Nay, doe not speake in passion so: ...* (1905–8 [1598] Jonson, *Every Man in his Humour* 2707) b. *doe not wrong the gentleman, and thy selfe too.* (1905–8 [1598] Jonson, *Every Man in his Humour* 435)	c. *speake not, though I question you.* (1937 [1609] Jonson, *Epicoene*, 177, l. 7) d. *Come, wrong not the qualitie of your desert, with looking downeward, couz; ...* (1905–8 [1598] Jonson, *Every Man in his Humour* 387)

At the beginning of Early Modern English DO was relatively uncommon, but by the end (1700) it was by far the more frequent variant in inverted questions, and had made substantial progress in negative declaratives and imperatives. In the major types of affirmative question its development followed an s-curve, being fastest in the middle of the 16th century as the curve crossed 50%, but negative questions and declaratives show a more complex development, with a major drop in incidence preceding a later recovery.

In (and before) Early Modern English, DO also occurred rather freely in finite affirmative sentences like (1). This use of DO rose steadily to a peak of rather less than 10%, then declined.

(1) Affirmative declaratives with DO
   a. Sogliardo *You will not serue mee, sir, will you? I'le giue you more then countenance.*
   Shift *Pardon me, sir, I **doe** scorne to serue any man.* (1905–8 [1599] Jonson, *Every Man out of his Humour* 2217)
   b. George *Your meat's ready, sir, and your company were come.*
   Carlo Buffone *Is the loyne of porke enough?*
   George *I, sir, it is enough.*
   Macilente *Porke? heart, what dost thou with such a greasie dish? I thinke thou **dost** varnish thy face with the fat on't, it lookes so like a glew-pot.* (1905–8 [1599] Jonson, *Every Man out of his Humour* 3754)

Here there is no emphasis on the polarity as is normally required today. DO also occurs in sentences where there apparently is such an emphasis, (2), but these are in a minority.

(2) Affirmative declaratives with DO of emphatic polarity
   a. Sogliardo *doe you know me, sir?*
   Macilente *I **doe** know you, sir.* (1905–8 [1599] Jonson, *Every Man out of his Humour* 687)
   b. Clerimont *No, sir, doe not take it so to heart: shee do's not refuse you, but a little neglect you. Good faith, True-wit, you were too blame to put it into his head, that shee do's refuse him.*
   True-wit *Shee **do's** refuse him, sir, palpably, how euer you mince it.* (1937 [1609] Jonson, *Epicoene* 191, l. 131)

Thus at the beginning of the period, speakers and writers had a choice across a range of clause types: instead of using a finite lexical verb, they could use a finite of DO with the lexical verb in the infinitive. Various contextual, social, and stylistic factors apparently weighted this choice, but the two variants were clearly generally acceptable. By the end of the period, the predominant usage was approaching today's, though change continued throughout the 18th century (Tieken-Boon van Ostade 1987). From 1700, most types of inverted questions strongly favored DO, and it was the more common (unmarked) choice with negative declaratives and imperatives. In affirmative declaratives it had become uncommon, but although examples which apparently show emphatic polarity increased in the 17th century, they seem to have remained a minority even towards the end of that century, so the modern situation in which affirmative DO ordinarily carries emphatic polarity or marks an implicit contrast is a later restriction.

The situation can be illustrated from Ellegård's (1953) major investigation of Early Modern English prose works, by giving figures for three romances translated by Caxton from just before the period, five plays by Jonson in the middle, and Swift's *Journal to Stella* just after the end (see Table 13.2).

Table 13.2: Percentages of DO in construction types in specific texts

	Caxton 1483–1489	Jonson, acted 1598–1609, printed 1600–1616	Swift 1710
Affirmative inverted questions	20% (1/5)	67% (231/344)	93% (53/57)
Negative declaratives	3% (4/149)	35% (47/133)	87% (61/70)
Affirmative declaratives	2% (173/7200)	3% (138/4000)	0.2% (5/2800)

Here particular subcategories are omitted in accordance with Ellegård's (1953: 162) practice in his well known graph.

The major general problems raised by this construction are the following:
- origin. How did it originate? What was the original process of grammaticalization? (Section 2)
- distribution. What is the nature of the factors which structure the distribution of DO versus the finite full verb? Here there has been a wide spread of suggestions (phonotactic, syntactic, semantic, pragmatic, and discourse-based characteristics; the impact of processing; and social correlates). (Sections 3, 4, 5)
- motivation. Why did DO make progress, and what is the nature of this change? Did any of the factors controlling its distribution also actually motivate the rise of DO? Or was it a more abstract type of change, in which speakers took choices because of the presence of variation without those choices impacting on the process of change itself? (Sections 5, 6)
- regulation. A further major topic is the development of the modern distribution, in which DO has been characterized in terms of its use as a "last resort" expression of tense, occurring in constructions which require a finite auxiliary (inverted questions, clauses negated by *not*, clauses with emphatic polarity). In contrast, DO has been lost (or all but lost) in affirmative declaratives without emphasis, and substantial progress towards this position had been

made by the end of the Early Modern period, as noted above. Why should the development of DO have been differentiated in this way? (Section 7)

2 Origin

This will be only briefly discussed, since it belongs to the period before Early Modern English. The most persuasive account of the first stages of the grammaticalization of DO derives it from causative uses. These had a common variant which omitted the agent, and was focused on what happened, possibly being perfective. Thus in the Middle English example in (3) the question as to whether Grim made the baskets himself, or had them made is not relevant; the focus is on the fact that they were made (cf. the vagueness of modern "got" in the gloss). There are also contexts in which DO + infinitive is clearly causative, involving an agent who is not specified.

(3) *Gode paniers **dede** he **make**,*
On til him, and oþer þrinne
Til hise sones, to beren fish inne (c.1300 The Lay of Havelok the Dane 760–762; Skeat [ed., revised by Sisam] 1902)
'He [Grim] got good baskets made,
one for himself and another three
for his sons, to carry fish in'

The construction became syntactically isolated, and was subsequently bleached and re-analyzed as containing an empty auxiliary (Denison 1993: 279–281, and see his summaries of the many competing theories of origin).

Other suggestions include reinterpretation of DO + bare action noun, such as *do helpe, do synne, do swynke* – which faces the difficulty that the construction first appears in the south west where distinctive infinitival morphology of some weak verbs survived late – and conjectures that the construction has its source in second language acquisition in contact situations, in child language, or as a sporadic but recurrent form in Germanic dialect. There has also been a recent resurgence of interest in the relevance of contact with Celtic, which shows constructions combining DO with a verbal noun (see Filppula et al. 2008 for discussion and references). This may have involved a mutual development or a substrate influence on English, but it is difficult to draw confident conclusions in this area.

3 Variation: discourse-based, social, and stylistic factors

3.1 Discourse contrasts

Since DO lengthens the verbal group, there is a potential stylistic contrast between *sing* and *do sing* etc., in which *do sing* is the marked choice. One clear effect is that affirmative DO is used for purposes of balance and sentence rhythm when a verb is final, as in (4), or when the verb would otherwise be inappropriately light, as probably in (5).

(4) *in the high-street the Marchants and Tradesmen* **do dwell**, ... (1618 Taylor, *Penniless Pilgrimage*; Rissanen 1991: 331)

(5) *The viij day of januarij* **dyd ryd** *in a care at westmynster the wyff of the grayhond* ... (1557 Machyn, *Diary* 8 Jan., entry 705; Bailey et al. [ed.] 2006).

In verse DO is clearly used to put an infinitive in rhyme. It has also been claimed that it is associated with a variety of effects involving focus or intensity (and these may underlie the later development of the modern use of affirmative DO for emphatic polarity). It is more common with verbs which may show strong emotional content, such as *assure, believe, beseech, confess* (Ellegård 1953: 172), and Stein (1990), among others, claims that DO may mark intensity, and that it has discourse properties, marking prominence, such as that at the climax or peak of a narrative. It may also indicate a change of topic. DO is too general in Early Modern English for it to have had a precise semantic content, but it is the marked alternative in affirmative declaratives, and as such it has a range of marked uses.

3.2 Social and stylistic variation

There is also clear differentiation across texts, some of which reflects social and stylistic variation. In the earlier part of the period, this bears on the question of whether the change is from above or from below. Ellegård claimed that in the 15th century the use of affirmative DO was chiefly a feature of literary language, and this would be consistent with its being a top down change. But Nurmi's results for the first half of the 16th century point to its being a change from below, and this seems more likely. She used data from the *Corpus of Early English Correspondence* (Nevalainen et al. 1998) and found that affirmative DO was more frequent in more informal family letters at this period and that social aspirers tended to avoid it (Nurmi 1999: 106, 189). This is also consistent with Rissanen's (1991) convincing argument that the rise (and decline) of affirmative DO was initially a feature of the spoken language. In the second half of the century, however, it seems that DO had more prestige. It became more frequent in formal letters, and it seems to be particularly characteristic of the stylistically self-conscious Euphuistic writing of the mid-to-late 16th century.

Gender is clearly a relevant (but somewhat puzzling) factor. Nurmi examined the period from 1580 in a sample from the *Corpus of Early English Correspondence*, noting that it shows a change from rise to decline in both affirmative and negative declaratives. She found a clear differentiation of gender between these clause types with a striking switch round. Women used significantly more DO than men in declaratives after 1620, but this reversed the situation found towards the end of the 16th century, when men used more DO than women (Nurmi 1999: 154, 171).

There is also a striking drop in usage of DO *not* in negative declaratives seen in the second half of the 16th century in Ellegård's database, and from 1600 in the *Corpus of Early English Correspondence*. In both corpora there is a recovery later in the 17th century. Nurmi (1999: Chapter 10) suggests that this drop is due to the adoption of a new prestige model with a lower incidence of DO after James VI of Scotland became James I of England in 1603, since DO was diffusing northwards, and had a much lower incidence in northern English and Scottish English. Warner (2005), however, follows the dating of Ellegård's corpus, and proposes an earlier re-evaluation. He claims that Ellegård's database shows a smooth increase of use of DO *not* across time in texts with simpler lexis (many of which are plays), which he interprets as reflecting the vernacular development. But in texts with more complex lexis (including non-fictional prose, such as Milton's *Eikonoklastes*), the level of DO *not* collapses dramatically towards the end of the 16th century, and shows little increase in the 17th. He suggests that this development may have had its roots in an avoidance in more carefully edited prose of the contracted form *don't*, or the reduced forms which preceded it, given that there is evidence of some level of reduction from the 16th century.

4 Variation: lexical and collocational effects

There were clear lexical effects. Some involve individual lexical items, and may be motivated by their properties. *Dyd pryche* 'did preach' is very common in Machyn's *Diary* (1550–63) and it may well be that Machyn was avoiding the final consonant group [tʃt]; note that 40 years later Jonson included *clutcht* among the terrible vocabulary purged from Marston in the *Poetaster* (1601). *Eat* is also common with DO, especially in the preterit: in the Authorized Version (1611) *did eat* is the normal past, and *ate* is entirely absent in the Gospels (Ellegård 1953: 179 note 1), presumably because of ambiguities caused by the fact that its ablaut had developed differently in different dialects and present and past were not always distinct.

The best known lexical effect is that some particular verbs (Ellegård's 1953: 199 '*know* group') are slow to occur with DO in negative declaratives: The group includes *know, care, doubt,* and *fear*, and we may add *come* and *speak* (201). There is a similar group of verbs in questions, including *come, like, make,* and *say*, but *know* is not especially uncommon with DO in questions. Such effects are often restricted to particular constructions, and collocations play an important role here. For example, *I do well understand* is common in the *Cely Letters*, and in Ellegård's database *say* is frequently found in *How say you?, What say you?*, while it is not so much the lexeme *know* itself that lags in its use of DO in negative declaratives in the 17th century, but the collocation *I know not*. Individual items can also be particularly frequent with DO (167). An example is *think* in negative declaratives in Ellegård's 17th century data, which is due mainly to the frequency of collocations with subject *I*: *I do/did not think* versus *I think not, I thought not*. It does not, however, seem to be the case that there is a pattern of lexical diffusion from a group of items which are in the lead (as has been claimed for some physiologically-motivated sound changes). Instead, DO seems to occur more frequently with less common verbs, but noticeably less frequently with a small group of particular lexical items, or particular collocations, as noted above. These are typically (but not invariably) verbs or collocations of high frequency. In this respect the spread of DO seems to be held back by the conservatism of such items, as has been noted for analogically-based morphological or phonological changes which affect the least frequent items first.

5 Variation: phonotactic and syntactic factors

5.1 Phonotactics and the motivation of change

There is some evidence that DO tends to be used with subject *thou* when there would be a consonant group at the end of an inflected verb. This is particularly true of weak past tenses. Stein (1990) interpreted this as a major mechanism which motivated the rise of DO, suggesting that the potential combination of a verb which had a consonant final stem with inflectional *-st, -dst* provided a trigger or motivation, and that DO was used "to circumvent undesired word-final consonant clusters" (171) on inflected main verbs. In his story, the raised use of DO was rapidly generalized to verbs with subject *you*, and subsequently to other categories. A difficulty with the major role assigned to this process as an engine of change is that the striking differences between syntactic categories remarked by Ellegård are not adequately accounted for: Stein claims that questions are in the lead because they have "a greater sensitivity to phonotactic undesiredness" (Stein 1990: 156–157), but he simply takes this point for granted.

5.2 Syntax and the progress of change

Syntactic factors which favor affirmative DO include the separation of subject and verb, notably by an adverb. But the most striking syntactic fact is the differences between major construction types, which can be substantial; see Table 13.2 above for some figures. Here are Ellegård's major categories, ordered in terms of their frequency of DO in the 15th and 16th centuries:

negative inverted questions
affirmative inverted questions (excluding questions with *wh*-object)
negative declaratives
affirmative declaratives
negative imperatives

Ellegård (1953: 201–203) also noted that there was a strong preference for DO in transitive questions where the alternative with the finite full verb would have both subject and object after the verb, as in *When saw you my neece* or *And how approue you your sisters fashion* in Table 13.1 above. He referred to this as "one of the main inconveniences of inversion", pointing out that questions with initial *wh*-object (*What saw you?*) or with intransitive verbs show a considerably lower level of DO.

Kroch (1989a) proposed an account of this in terms of processing complexity. He suggested that by this date English speakers used a parsing strategy which initially interpreted V + NP as V + OBJECT. This would clearly have created a difficulty in inversion contexts where the object had not already been identified, and Kroch advanced an interpretation in which the high level of DO in such transitive questions reflected this parsing difficulty. This raised the possibility that change was driven by such considerations.

He subsequently measured the rate of change for major construction types, supposing that competition between the incoming finite DO and the older finite full verb would result in an s-curve. He used an appropriate function (the logistic) which generated an s-curve, plotted the incidence of DO against time, and measured the rate of change for each context. He found that for the period up to 1575 the rates were not distinct (except for affirmative declaratives). This means that the s-curves for each context are the same shape. He called this identity the "Constant Rate Effect". As a term this is potentially misleading, since clearly a change which proceeds along an s-curve starts slowly, speeds up, achieves a maximum rate of change, and then begins to slow down, and tails off. But the slope of any particular s-curve corresponds to a single coefficient within the equation type Kroch used, and when curves for different contexts have the same slope, this figure is constant. In order to account for this, he suggested that a single change (competition between finite full verb and DO) was taking place at an abstract level, and that surface distinctions between constructions were the result of various processing and discourse factors. Now note that, given the Constant Rate Effect, it is not clear that the construction types with the highest incidence of DO are driving the change. It had previously seemed natural to assume that the highest context would be the fastest (and the first), and this would clearly be the prime candidate for causation. But if all contexts proceed in parallel, none is "fastest". Instead, there might be a single more abstract competition whose progress could be quite separately motivated; for example, as the increasing adoption of the unmarked value of the parameter for V-to-I movement (see below), or of a resulting structurally more economical grammar lacking this movement. Kroch comments that in such a case

> the pattern of favoring and disfavoring contexts does not reflect the forces pushing the change forward. Rather it reflects functional effects, discourse and processing, on the choices speakers make among the alternatives available to them in the language as they know it; and the strength of these effects remains constant as the change proceeds (Kroch 1989b: 238).

We might however suggest that such factors have a potential role in pushing the change forward, depending partly on our interpretation of the more abstract underlying change and its relationship to the rise of DO. This would fit with adaptationist views, in which language alters as strategies which are "fitter" to survive replace other less "fit" strategies. In biological evolution a single adaptation may have more than one advantage from the organism's perspective, and we may imagine that the same will also be true where an abstract construction type is interpreted as the organism. Good candidates as contexts promoting change will be those which have the highest levels of DO, or which have the highest levels in a factor group which has a wide range of levels of occurrence, provided, of course, that there is a coherent set of interpretations of the value of the adaptation (the form with DO). From this perspective, both the parsing difficulty proposed by Kroch and the phonotactic problem noted by Stein may have contributed to the overall advance of DO across all contexts. Social factors (such as covert prestige) might also be implicated.

There is good reason to think that the introduction of DO was a "communal" change in the sense that the community moved forward together, with individuals increasing their use of DO across time. An alternative would be for older individuals to retain an earlier level of usage, perhaps that set at acquisition, showing an "apparent time" effect across ages at any particular date. Ellegård (1953: 166) notes for the 16th century "that there is a marked tendency for writers to use DO more frequently the older they grow", and Stein (1990: 215–217) gives figures for Shakespeare from which it is clear that Shakespeare increased his usage of DO in questions with subject *you* across time. Warner (2004) examines Ellegård's data for questions, and finds that there is no support for an apparent time effect, but that the evidence is throughout consistent with communal change, under which individuals change their level of usage as they grow older. He goes on to suggest that this is consistent with a model of change based in usage, in which adults increase their level of use of DO in response to steady pressure from the kind of parsing difficulty discussed above.

6 Parametric change and the rise of DO

Syntactic factors which have traditionally been thought to promote the rise of periphrastic DO include the general rise of the class of auxiliaries, and the associated higher frequency of periphrastic expression of tense, aspect, modality, and voice. Constructions with DO fit well into this general pattern. The rise of subject–verb–object unmarked order, as the earlier verb second order declined, may have promoted the rise of DO in inverted questions. Note that this sequence is retained when DO is used (DO–subject–verb–object), and it has indeed been suggested that an initial DO may have functioned as an interrogative marker. The position of DO before sentential negation has also been thought to provide a surface ordering (tense–negative–lexical verb) preferable to the alternative (tensed lexical verb–negative).

Generativists have generally adopted a narrower focus, looking at the possibility that the rise of DO should be associated with changes in morphology and in the surface position of adverbs, which they account for more abstractly as the loss of V-to-I movement with full verbs. This process moves V from its position in VP to a higher functional position I, head of the inflectional phrase. This functional position encodes the tense and agreement contrasts which appear on the finite verb. In this higher position it precedes adverbs located at the edge of VP, so that they intervene between verb and object, as in (6).

(6) a. *This most precious bloud that he shed on the Crosse, **cryeth alwayes** mercye for sinners* ... (a1535 Fisher, *English Works* 412; Mayor [ed.] 1876)
b. *These ... **confyrmed alwayes** their lyues to the most holye lawes ... of Chryste.* (1544 Bale, *A Brefe Chronycle concernynge Syr J. Oldcastell* in *Harl. Misc.* [Malh.] I. 257; OED: s.v. *conform*)

But when v-to-i movement is lost, tense and agreement appear on the verb by the minimalist's Agree or by a process of affix lowering, and adverbs located at the edge of vp no longer intervene between verb and object as in (7).

(7) a. *Then I holde it best that we **alwayes condempne** The Byble readers.* (1538 Bale, *A Comedye concernynge Thre Lawes* 1204; OED: s.v. *bible*).
b. *A most loving and carefull housholder, bicause he **alwayes sent** them rayne to prepare them foode.* (1571 Golding, *Calvin on Ps. lxviii.* 10; OED: s.v. *householder*)

This change in verb–adverb ordering is clearly ongoing in late Middle English and Early Modern English (Ellegård 1953: 182–186). If do is taken to supply the position in i which is no longer occupied by a raised v, then the rise of do can be seen as a reflex of the loss of v-to-i movement. The further question, as to what motivated this loss, has been answered by appeal to a parameter of Universal Grammar under which a language has to be sufficiently rich in verbal inflection for v-to-i to be acquired. Since Early Modern English shows a dramatic weakening of the earlier Middle English contrasts of person, number, and tense in the morphology of the verb, this might have led language learners to acquire a grammar which lacked v-to-i movement.

There is a range of issues here, perhaps most pertinently the question as to why developments in Danish, Norwegian, and Swedish are so different. These languages are also held to have lost v-to-i movement but they permit neg + verb outside verb second clauses, and retain verb + subject order in questions. *Not* + verb is found in Early Modern English, but only as a very uncommon option. The details of the loss of "rich inflection" are unclear, and there has been considerable discussion as to how the parameter should be interpreted. One suggestion has been that it was ultimately the loss of inflection for person in the past tense; another, the loss of co-occurring distinct morphemes for tense and person or number. The timing of these losses (and the related loss of infinitival morphology) also needs more detailed investigation. Turning to the decline of verb-adverb order, Kroch makes the interesting claim that Ellegård's figures for the positioning of *never* show that the rate of loss matches that of the increase of do, and that this implies the identity of the processes. But on Ellegård's figures, the loss of verb–

adverb order is comfortably in advance of the rise of DO in the 15th and 16th centuries, and verb–adverb–object order seems to be lost by the late 16th century, though there is a substantial further period in which surface order in negatives could be interpreted as showing V-to-I movement. This might, however, be accounted for under hypotheses which split I into further categories, so that the loss of V-to-I movement is actually a sequence of losses of movement, as has been suggested. For a detailed update on the history of verb–adverb order as related to the rise of DO, and some discussion of other topics in this section, see Haeberli and Ihsane (2016).

7 Regulation of DO

7.1 The decline of affirmative DO

The term "regulation" refers to the development and establishment of the modern distribution of "last resort" DO, the latest stage in grammaticalization, in which DO becomes syntactically predictable. From 1650, DO is clearly moving towards this position. But it is perhaps possible to see the beginning of this development from the point when affirmative DO began to decline. There is an interesting difficulty over timing here, which reflects the nature of the texts being considered. In Ellegård's database affirmative DO seems to level off in the middle of the 16th century, and begin to decline towards the end of the century. But in the *Helsinki Corpus* the overall peak is later (Rissanen 1991), and in the *Corpus of Early English Correspondence* its decline is shown in "the first decades of the 17th century" (Nurmi 1999: 163). The *Helsinki Corpus* (Rissanen et al. 1991) is balanced between genres in a way not attempted by Ellegård, and the *Corpus of Early English Correspondence* (Nevalainen et al. 1998) is based in a single genre. But it is interesting that Rissanen showed that the frequency of DO and timing of change in the *Helsinki Corpus* differed across genres, with trial transcripts and comedies (the text types closest to actual speech) showing a sharp decline from the 16th century, fiction remaining level, while other text types (including letters) continued to show an increase. This suggested to Rissanen that developments in speech and in writing were probably different, with speech losing affirmative DO earlier than writing, in which stylistic considerations supported its use in at least the first part of the 17th century (1991: esp. 328–329). Dating here then seems to depend on genre.

Stylistic considerations were also involved in the decline of DO *not* (as discussed above): in Ellegård's database this is found in the second half of the 16th century, but in the *Corpus of Early English Correspondence* it can be seen at the beginning of the 17th century. Nurmi (1999: Chapter 10) suggested that the decline of DO in declaratives, both affirmative and negative, was a single sociolinguistic fact, due in both cases to the prestige of Scottish English, and she placed the grammatical differentiation of the two constructions well into the 17th century. But Rissanen's findings that the genres closest to speech show an earlier decline of affirmative DO tend to suggest an earlier decline in spoken language. In negative declaratives there is indeed clear evidence (reviewed above) of a differential evaluation in the 17th century. But in the case of affirmative DO, one may wonder whether the decline follows not from a change in evaluation but from a grammatical difference.

7.2 Was there a grammatical change in the late 16th century?

This has been posited by generative grammarians: it is potentially the point at which the modern system becomes discernible. It is also the point at which Kroch claimed that the loss of V-to-I was completed, since Ellegård's figures for the competition between the types of (6) and (7), where adverb position shows V-to-I or its absence, show that for *never*, V-to-I is found in only 3% of instances in 1575–1600 (Ellegård 1953: 184). At this point, Kroch suggested, the different construction types became underlyingly distinct and no longer showed an identical competition between DO and the finite verb, so that the Constant Rate Effect ceased to hold. Kroch (1989b) believed that affirmative declaratives already had a lower coefficient of change than other contexts in the 15th and 16th centuries, and he interpreted this as the result of a competition between a different group of grammatical alternatives than were found in other contexts. A recalculation of the rate of change after some corrections to Ellegård's figures made by Warner (2006), however, shows that the rate is indeed actually the same in affirmative declaratives as in other contexts before the second half of the 16th century. This opens the possibility that a reanalysis at that point is not so much the going to completion of the loss of V-to-I, or of one of the components of the loss of V-to-I in a more articulated model of verbal projections, but instead the (general) adoption of the "last resort" status of DO, whereby DO is available only where other ways of realizing tense and agreement fail.

8 Envoi

Despite the amount of work undertaken on DO, there is clearly much disagreement and major differences resulting from different theoretical positions. From the preceding discussion it is clear that many facts have been established, that much is yet to know, and that the history of DO is plentifully documented, so that it provides a wonderful resource for the investigation of long term linguistic change in a socially structured context. The properties of the variation between DO and finite verb clearly require substantial databases if they are to be studied profitably. Ellegård (1953) collected a major database, and other prominent databases used in work on DO have been the *Helsinki Corpus* (Rissanen et al. 1991) and the *Corpus of Early English Correspondence* (Nevalainen et al. 1998), all mentioned above. The fact that these last two are publicly available in electronic form, the second in a parsed version, makes work on DO hugely easier, and we can expect researchers to take advantage of these and other parsed corpora, including the *Penn-Helsinki Parsed Corpus of Middle English* (Kroch and Taylor 2000), the *Penn-Helsinki Parsed Corpus of Early Modern English* (Kroch et al. 2004) and the *Penn Parsed Corpus of Modern British English* (Kroch et al. 2010). Moreover, Ecay (2015) has taken a major step beyond these. He discusses the methodology of tagging and using a very large database, and the interpretation of results achieved. His database includes over 43,000 texts, some 600,000 negative declaratives, and nearly 7,000,000 affirmative declarative sentences. Look forward to some decades of serious progress!

9 References

Bailey, Richard W., Marilyn Miller, and Colette Moore. 2006. *A London Provisioner's Chronicle, 1550–1563, by Henry Machyn*. University of Michigan Press and the Scholarly Publishing Office of the University of Michigan University Library. http://quod.lib.umich.edu/m/machyn/; last accessed 4 April 2017.

Denison, David. 1993. *English Historical Syntax: Verbal Constructions*. London/New York: Longman.

Ecay, Aaron. 2015. *A Multi-step Analysis of the Evolution of English Do-Support*. University of Pennsylvania PhD dissertation.

Ellegård, Alvar. 1953. *The Auxiliary 'Do': The Establishment and Regulation of its Use in English*. Stockholm: Almqvist & Wiksell.

Filppula, Markku, Juhani Klemola, and Heli Paulasto. 2008. *English and Celtic in Contact*. New York/London: Routledge.

Haeberli, Eric and Tabea Ihsane. 2016. Revisiting the loss of verb movement in the history of English. *Natural Language and Linguistic Theory* 34: 497–542.

Jonson, Ben. 1905–8 [1598]. Every Man in his Humour. In: Willy Bang (ed.), *Ben Jonsons Dramen. Materialien zur Kunde des älteren Englischen Dramas*. Vol 7. Louvain: A. Uystpruyst.

Jonson, Ben. 1905–8 [1599]. Every Man out of his Humour. In: Willy Bang (ed.), *Ben Jonsons Dramen. Materialien zur Kunde des älteren Englischen Dramas*. Vol 7. Louvain: A. Uystpruyst.

Jonson, Ben. 1932 [1605]. Eastward Ho! In: C. H. Hereford and Percy Simpson (eds.), *Ben Jonson*. Vol. 4. Oxford: Clarendon Press.

Jonson, Ben. 1937 [1609]. Epicoene. In: C. H. Hereford and Percy Simpson (eds.), *Ben Jonson*. Vol. 5. Oxford: Clarendon Press.

Kroch, Anthony. 1989a. Function and grammar in the history of English: Periphrastic *do*. In: Ralph W. Fasold and Deborah Schriffin (eds.), *Language Change and Variation*, 132–172. Amsterdam/Philadelphia: John Benjamins.

Kroch, Anthony. 1989b. Reflexes of grammar in patterns of language change. *Language Variation and Change* 1: 199–244.

Kroch, Anthony and Ann Taylor. 2000. *Penn-Helsinki Parsed Corpus of Middle English*. 2nd edn. http://www.ling.upenn.edu/hist-corpora/PPCME2-RELEASE-4/index.html; last accessed 14 April 2017.

Kroch, Anthony, Beatrice Santorini, and Ariel Dietani. 2004. *Penn-Helsinki Parsed Corpus of Early Modern English*. http://www.ling.upenn.edu/hist-corpora/PPCEME-RELEASE-3/index.html; last accessed 14 April 2017.

Kroch, Anthony, Beatrice Santorini, and Ariel Dietani. 2010. *Penn Parsed Corpus of Modern British English*. https://www.ling.upenn.edu/hist-corpora/PPCMBE2-RELEASE-1/index.html; last accessed 14 April 2017.

Mayor, John E. B. 1876. *The English Works of John Fischer, Bishop of Rochester*. (Early English Text Society, E.S., 27.) London: N. Trübner.

Nevalainen, Terttu, Helena Raumolin-Brunberg, Jukka Keränen, Minna Nevala, Arja Nurmi, and Minna Palander-Collin. 1998. *Corpus of Early English Correspondence (CEEC)*. Department of English, University of Helsinki. http://www.helsinki.fi/varieng/CoRD/corpora/CEEC/index.html; last accessed 14 April 2017.

Nurmi, Arja. 1999. *A Social History of Periphrastic DO*. Helsinki: Société Néophilologique.

Rissanen, Matti. 1991. Spoken language and the history of *do*-periphrasis. In: Dieter Kastovsky (ed.), *Historical English Syntax*, 321–342. Berlin/New York: Mouton de Gruyter.

Rissanen, Matti, Merja Kytö, Leena Kahlas-Tarkka, Matti Kilpiö, Saara Nevanlinna, Irma Taavitsainen, Terttu Nevalainen, and Helena Raumolin-Brunberg. 1991. *The Helsinki Corpus of English Texts*. In: *ICAME Collection of English Language Corpora (CD-ROM)*, 2nd edn., eds. Knut Hofland, Anne Lindebjerg, and Jørn Thunestvedt, The HIT Centre, University of Bergen, Norway. For manual, see http://clu.uni.no/icame/manuals/; last accessed 14 April 2017.

Skeat, Walter William. 1902. *The Lay of Havelok the Dane*. 2nd edn. revised and corrected by Kenneth Sisam, 1915, with further corrections 1956. Oxford: Clarendon Press.

Stein, Dieter. 1990. *The Semantics of Syntactic Change: Aspects of the Evolution of 'do' in English*. Berlin/New York: Mouton de Gruyter.

Tieken-Boon van Ostade, Ingrid. 1987. *The Auxiliary Do in Eighteenth-century English: A Sociohistorical-linguistic Approach*. Dordrecht: Foris.

Warner, Anthony. 2004. What drove DO? In: Christian J. Kay, Simon Horobin, and Jeremy Smith (eds.), *New Perspectives on English Historical Linguistics*, Vol 1. *Syntax and Morphology*, 229–242. Amsterdam/Philadelphia: John Benjamins.

Warner, Anthony. 2005. Why *do* dove: Evidence for register variation in Early Modern English negatives. *Language Variation and Change* 17: 257–280.

Warner, Anthony. 2006. Variation and the interpretation of change in periphrastic *do*. In: Ans van Kemenade and Bettelou Los (eds.), *The Handbook of the History of English*, 45–67. Malden: Blackwell.

Manfred Krug
Chapter 14:
The Great Vowel Shift

1   Introduction —— 241
2   Why "Great Vowel Shift"? —— 242
3   On the history of Great Vowel Shift theories —— 255
4   Motivating the Great Vowel Shift and avenues for further research —— 260
5   References —— 263

Abstract: The long-vowel inventories of all modern English accents and dialects differ substantially from the pronunciations that existed around 1400. Most of the relevant changes have been described as being interlinked and part of the so-called "Great Vowel Shift" (GVS), but consensus in the pertinent scholarship is limited. This chapter pursues a discussion of the history of GVS theories, the major issues and arguments. It is seen that some long-standing tenets and theories have a weak foundation and that the GVS is well known only in the sense that it is widely known. Despite a vast literature, many aspects of the changes are still poorly understood and, probably because of the vast literature, most aspects are controversial. Some of the controversies, however, turn out to be definitional rather than factual in nature. In this context, this chapter provides the likely paths of development from Middle to Modern English(es).

1 Introduction

A handbook article on what has occasionally been called the "watershed" of the history of English phonology must aim at broad coverage and focus on what is common ground. The problem for a chapter on what is traditionally labelled the "Great Vowel Shift" is that few things have remained undisputed in the literature, for this is probably the most-written-about development in the history of the English language. A focus on common ground is thus virtually impossible, as is an exhaustive treatment. And although some of the recent literature seems to converge on the position that only the changes which affected the Middle English (hereafter ME) phonemes /iː/, /uː/, /eː/, and /oː/ are interrelated, and thus part of

Manfred Krug: Bamberg (Germany)

a shift (a shift which would then not be so great after all and perhaps not merit capitalization and a definite article), this position may turn out to be ephemeral. For the sake of completeness and to give due attention to older accounts, this chapter will discuss all long vowels and thus include also the developments of the lower half of the vowel space, i.e. the developments that affected ME /ɛː/, /ɔː/, and /aː/. The discussion will start with the uncontroversial, proceed to majority views, and conclude with a treatment of conflicting theories.

The label "Great Vowel Shift" was introduced by Otto Jespersen (1909) almost exactly 100 years ago. But rather than offer yet another review of the literature (see McMahon 2006a or 2006b for a recent synopsis) and rather than present new or more detailed phonetic facts or conjectures based on individual writers' orthoepistic and textual evidence, this chapter will adopt a more global perspective. It will try to shed some new light on the discussion by (a) re-evaluating Dobson's (1968) interpretations of a range of 16th and 17th century sources in a quantitative manner, and by (b) looking at the contemporary intellectual background and the assumptions behind certain theories. In particular, the chapter will focus on the early theories by Jespersen and Luick (1896) from the turn of the 20th century, but also comment in passing on later biology-driven analogies and structuralist theories. Perhaps not surprisingly, it will turn out that the answers to the most fundamental questions – whether the label "shift" and the epithet "great" are appropriate – hinge crucially on a researcher's perspective or definition and that different perspectives entail different merits and problems. In the course of this chapter, some of the classic problems, listed as (i) to (v) below, will therefore lose their poignancy, but new problems will arise. The article will conclude with a discussion of motivations and potential avenues for future research.

2 Why "Great Vowel Shift"?

In the past three decades, research on the series of changes known as the "Great Vowel Shift" has centered on counterexamples and focused on why what happened to the ME long vowels should *not* be considered "great" or a "shift". This chapter will begin with a defense of the traditional label, although it is by no means the first to do so. In another recent handbook article, McMahon (2006a) discusses in a systematic way the classic and partly interrelated five "problems" identified by Lass (1976) and Stockwell and Minkova (1988), around which most of the literature revolves:

(i) Inception: where in the vowel space did the series of changes begin?
(ii) Order: what is the chronology of individual and overlapping changes?

(iii) Structural coherence: are we dealing with interdependent changes forming a unitary overarching change or with local and independent changes?
(iv) Mergers: is the assumption of non-merger, i.e. preservation of phonemic contrasts, viable for language change in general and met in the specific changes of the GVS?
(v) Dialects: how do we deal with dialects which did not undergo the same changes as southern English or in which the changes proceeded in a different order?

After careful consideration of the issues and evaluation of the previous literature, McMahon concludes that while there is no simple answer to any of the above problems, the label "Great Vowel Shift" is justified beyond aesthetic and didactic grounds, certainly for the upper half, but probably also for the lower half, of the vowel space. The analyses offered in the present account will essentially confirm this position.

2.1 Why "great"?

In the late 19th century, linguists like Luick (1896: 306–307) were struck by the fact that all long vowels of the English spoken around Chaucer's time changed qualitatively in subsequent centuries. And the qualitative changes were so significant that for 17th century pronunciations new phonemic labels are necessary in order to avoid crude misrepresentations of the phonetic facts, certainly (but not only) for the predecessors of modern southern British English. For convenience and familiarity among the expected readership, my first reference point will be the accent that is referred to as "Received Pronunciation" or "RP" in its Present-day English (PDE) form, which – although supposedly supraregional – is essentially based on the pronunciation of educated southern British English speakers. Table 14.1 lists all ME long vowels and their PDE RP reflexes. Lexical exceptions as well as dialects and accents other than RP will be dealt with in later sections.

It is true that there exist northern English and Scottish dialects that have not participated in all of the changes sketched in Table 14.1. And yet the vast majority of modern native speakers of English worldwide have pronunciations that diverge in relatively minor ways from modern RP, notably so when their varieties are compared to early Middle English (that is, pre-GVS) pronunciations. In fact, many modern dialects can be shown to be conservative relative to RP and can thus be located somewhere on the paths from ME to RP (whose intermediate stages are specified in Table 14.2 and Figure 14.1 below). Consider, for instance, Edinburgh

Table 14.1: Modern RP pronunciations of the ME long vowels with PDE orthographies ("C" stands for "consonant"; adapted from Barber 1997: 105)

	Middle English		Modern English (RP)	example	typical (and rarer) PDE spellings examples
(I)	iː	>	aɪ	time	iCe, -y, -ie, (i+ld; i+nd) tide, fly, pie (child, kind)
(II)	uː	>	aʊ	house	ou, ow mouse, how
(III)	eː	>	iː	see	ee, ie seed, field
(IV)	oː	>	uː	boot	oo, (oCe, -o) food, (move, who)
(V)	ɛː	>	iː	sea	ea, ei, eCe heath, conceit, complete
(VI)	ɔː	>	əʊ	sole	oCe, oa, (o, oe) hope, boat, (so, foe)
(VII)	aː	>	eɪ	name	aCe make, dame

English dialects which are currently diphthongizing their reflexes of ME /uː/, /ɛː/ and /ɔː/ (Schützler 2009). This, of course, does not mean that RP is more advanced in the sense of "being superior" or even a natural endpoint of diatopic or diastratic variation, as is immediately obvious from the fact that modern RP speakers – similar to Australian and New Zealand English speakers – are diphthongizing /iː/ again in words like *see, me, tea*. Just how complex the situation is can be seen in American English, which varies between [oː], [o] and [oʊ] for ME /ɔː/ in words like *go* and *goat*: depending on the history of a dialect, the monophthongal variants [oː] and [o] can be either progressive (i.e. monophthongizations of [oʊ]) or conservative (i.e. reflect one-step raisings from ME /ɔː/, as in most modern Scottish and Irish English dialects outside Edinburgh and Dublin; see also Section 3 below for discussion).

In any case, such evidence lends further support to the uniformitarian hypothesis (see Christy 1983), which most modern research on phonetic and phonological change is based on and according to which changes that are impossible today were impossible in the past because the same principles hold for changes irrespective of the period during which they occur. Lass (1997: 24–32) offers an illuminating updated account of the uniformitarian hypothesis, including the Uniform Probabilities Principle, which states that "the (global, cross-linguistic) likelihood of any linguistic state of affairs (structure, inventory, process, etc.) has always been roughly the same as it is now" (Lass 1997: 29). From this follows that present-day changes are in principle no different from historical ones and may thus shed light on the past. This chapter therefore considers conservative as well as progressive dialects if they exhibit changes that may enhance our understanding of the GVS.

Let us leave aside for a moment the question of whether or not the changes in Table 14.1 are interlinked and thus merit the label "shift" (for discussion, see Sections 2.2 and 2.4 below). Allowing for some simplification – as all models, theories, and handbook articles must – the changes involved certainly meet the criteria for a number of strong labels in historical phonology. In the dialects that participated in the shift almost the entire English lexicon was affected by the changes in (I) to (VII). In other words, whatever the individual histories and intermediate stages, it is obvious that it was essentially phonemes that changed. We can thus label each individual change without oversimplifying too much an "unconditioned", i.e. "context-free" sound change that deserves to be called a "neogrammarian" sound change – though not in the strongest form of the hypothesis, which claims that sound change affects all words and all speakers of a speech community simultaneously, because some items (like *do, good*) were affected by the changes earlier than others (cf. Ogura 1987; Lass 1999: 78 and the discussion in Labov 1994: Chapter 17 on sound change vs. lexical diffusion). Indeed, precisely the fact that some exceptions to the GVS can be explained by the existence of phonetic variants underpins the neogrammarian label: low-stress items like *and* or *my* [mɪ], as in *me mum*, for instance, simply had no long vowel because high frequency and low stress lead to vowel lenition (cf. Bybee 2003); and differences like *sane* vs. *sanity* or *divine* vs. *divinity* display a regular pattern, too (cf. McMahon 2007).

It is at this early point that a chapter on the Great Vowel Shift must leave the comfortable ground of unanimous scholarly consensus and enter the field of majority views because the phonetic details or developmental paths with intermediate stages that have led to modern English RP are not uncontroversial, although even here the differences in opinion are smaller than they seem at first sight. Different symbols like [iy, ɪi, ɪj] today often do not represent differences in views on the phonetic facts but are explainable in terms of different transcription traditions and conventions. Bloch and Trager (1942) as well as Trager and Smith (1951) systems from the 1940s and 1950s (with the glides /j/ and /w/ as the endpoints of long monophthongs and diphthongs) are common even in recent American publications. The present chapter uses IPA-based systems (with pure long monophthongs and exclusively vocalic elements in the diphthongs), which have been dominant in British publications since Daniel Jones's time, i.e. since the early 20th century (e.g. Jones 1909). A conspectus of the current majority view of each ME long vowel's developmental path is offered in Table 14.2 and Figure 14.1.

Table 14.2: Paths from Middle English long vowels to RP pronunciations

	Middle English							Modern English (RP)
(I)	iː	>	ɪi			>	əɪ	>	aɪ
(II)	uː	>	ʊu			>	əʊ	>	aʊ
(III)	eː					>			iː
(IV)	oː					>			uː
(V)	ɛː	>	eː			>			iː
(VI)	ɔː	>	oː			>	oʊ	>	əʊ
(VII)	aː	>	æː	>	ɛː	>	eː	>	eɪ

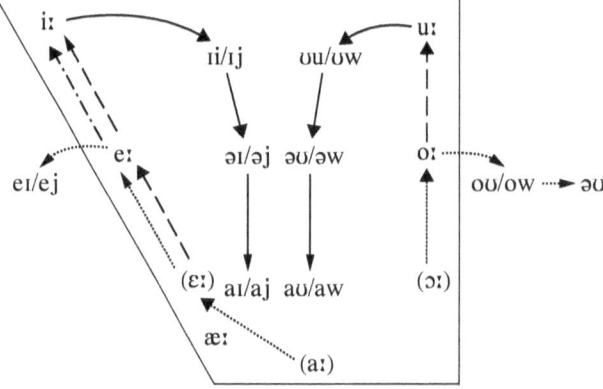

Figure 14.1: Paths from Middle English long vowels to RP pronunciations (Great Vowel Shift and subsequent developments)

Each arrow type (e.g. a sequence of arrows consisting of a dotted line) in Figure 14.1 represents one vowel trajectory, where the arrows with big arrowheads are part of the GVS and those with thin arrowheads are regarded by the majority of researchers as post-GVS developments. As will be shown in some detail in later sections, the changes of the ME vowels in the lower half of the phonetic space (the vowels given in brackets) start considerably later than those in the upper half. As was mentioned above, there is broad consensus in recent studies that at least the changes starting in the upper half, i.e. paths (I) to (IV), belong to the GVS or "GVS proper" (Lass 1992, 1999, 2006; Labov 1994: 234; Stockwell 2002; Krug 2003a; McMahon 2006a; see next section for detail). Furthermore, variants like [ɪi/ɪj] and [ʊu/ʊw] of diphthongization stages are not purely notational in Figure 14.1. If Present-day English can serve as a guide, the phonetically most realistic assumption is that both pairs were essentially in complementary distribution: ME [ɪi] and [ʊu] would then be prototypical realizations in prepausal and preconsonantal contexts, while [ɪj] and [ʊw] are prevocalic prototypes serving to avoid hiatus (on the loss of hiatus during Middle English see Section 4 below). Finally, for the paths of ME /iː/ and /uː/ – (I) and (II) in Table 14.2 – some authors have used a more back first element for the modern RP vowels [aʊ] and [aɪ], namely [ɑʊ] and [ɑɪ], respectively, while others again have used intermediate stages [ʌɪ] and [ʌʊ]. Early accounts including Jespersen (1909), Chomsky and Halle (1968), and Wolfe (1972) assume peripheral diphthongization paths for the ME long high vowels, i.e. ME /iː/ via [ei/ɛi] and /uː/ via [ou/ɔu]. Most recent research converges on the central path, one of the reasons being the non-merger of the ME phonemes /iː/ and /ai/ (see Labov 1994: 234 for details). The two alternative paths are, however, to a certain extent compatible if we assume competing standard variants (cf. Lass 1999: 102).

In summary, for a number of reasons at least the epithet "great" seems justified for the series of changes under discussion here. Not a single long vowel of the major standard PDE varieties has remained in the position it occupied during the 14th century; the ModE reflexes differ greatly in quality from their ME ancestors and did so at the beginning of the 17th century, to which a number of authors date the end of the GVS (cf. Tables 14.3 and 14.4 for detail); the great majority of modern speakers – including modern speakers of English varieties that descend from dialects which did not participate in all GVS-related changes between 1200 and 1800 – command variants that are somewhere on the paths given in Figure 14.1. And finally, to conclude on a utilitarian or didactic note, about half of the apparent mismatches between modern English orthography and pronunciation are related to the changes sketched in Tables 14.1 and 14.2. Once we have understood the history of the long vowels, such mismatches become more systematic and we can enhance considerably the chances for students of English to deduce the pronunciation from the spelling and vice versa.

2.2 Why a "shift"?

Hock (1991: 156) refers to chain shifts as "developments [...] in which one change within a given phonological system gives rise to other, related changes." Generally, two types of shift are distinguished: (i) "drag chain" (or "pull chain") shifts, which are motivated by the gaps resulting from a vacated space into which other, adjacent phonemes are pulled; (ii) "push chain" shifts, in which one phoneme encroaches onto an adjacent segment's phonetic space and thus causes the former occupant of this space to shift away (cf. Hock 1991: 156–157; Thomas 2006: 486; for a more detailed discussion of definitional issues involved in shifting, see also the section *Metaphors we shift by* below).

Let us start from a bird's eye perspective and briefly list aspects that have been advanced in favor of chain shifting from an early date onwards. These usually exploit the notions of symmetry (front vs. back vowels) and gap or slot filling, which explains why the label of "shift" has been particularly attractive to researchers from a structuralist background. Figure 14.1 illustrates the following points:

– The high vowels – both front and back – diphthongized, most probably via a central path involving nucleus-glide dissimilation (cf. Section 4 below).
– All non-high vowels – both front and back – raised, most probably via a peripheral path.
– Diphthongization occurred only for the two highest positions.

The question of timing is essential to determining whether the changes are interlinked and whether we are dealing with a "push chain" or a "drag chain" shift. So let us now turn to the question of when the changes shown in Table 14.2 occurred. It is, of course, impossible to pin down exact dates for historical sound changes, inter alia because (a) there exists a gap between writing and speech, (b) progressive pronunciations always coexist with conservative ones, and (c) modern sociolinguistic research into ongoing sound change has revealed that a complex network of social, stylistic, and regional factors plays a role in the distribution of the variants (as well as in the adoption of some of them in the eventual standard). Table 14.3 is a synopsis of previous scholarship (notably Stockwell 1972 and his subsequent work; Lass 1976 and his subsequent work; Faiß 1989; Görlach 1991, 1994; Barber 1997), all of which is essentially based on the interpretation of spelling evidence, rhyming conventions in poetry, dictionaries of rhyming words, as well as early modern English orthoepists' descriptions, such as those by John Hart (1551) or Alexander Gil (1619). Modern analysts generally assume that the pronunciations featured in Table 14.3 were common and stylistically unmarked in mainstream southern English speech around the dates given and that progressive dialects anticipate such pronunciations by at least fifty years.

Table 14.3 suggests an early phase of interrelated changes from about 1300 to 1500 (some authors assume that the changes started about 100 years earlier). A second phase looks likely for the time between 1500 and the second half of the 17th century, when the first merger of two long vowels occurs, which leads to the homophony of *see* and *sea*. There can be little doubt that the first phase indeed constitutes a chain shift because the ME pairs /iː/ and /eː/ as well as /uː/ and /oː/ change in lockstep, and in each pair the latter supplants the former. This makes it almost impossible to deny a causal link (be that pushing or dragging). On closer inspection, it becomes clear that we are already dealing with two chain shifts in

Table 14.3: Dating the changes of Middle English long vowels

	Middle English c.1300		c.1500		c.1600		c.1700		Modern English (RP)
(I)	iː	>	ɪi	>	əɪ	>	aɪ	≈	aɪ
(II)	uː	>	ʊu	>	əʊ	>	aʊ	≈	aʊ
(III)	eː	>	iː					≈	iː
(IV)	oː	>	uː					≈	uː
(V)	ɛː	>	e̝ː	>	eː	>	iː	≈	iː
(VI)	ɔː			>	oː			>	oʊ > əʊ
(VII)	aː			>	æː > ɛː	>	eː		eɪ

the upper half because the changes in the front and back are merely parallel, not causing each other – except if one wanted to invoke a general upward drift (the great vowel drift?) or a tendency towards parallelism. But it seems rather implausible to conceive of a reason why an upward drift in the back should trigger an upward drift in the front or vice versa. (Keeping this in mind, I will nevertheless, in line with the vast majority of researchers, continue to refer to these two parallel subshifts as one joint shift in order to avoid confusion.)

Whether or not we are dealing with one extended shift from 1300 to 1700 or with two independent subshifts in the upper and lower half of the vowel space (as, for instance, Johnston 1992 believes) depends, inter alia, on whether we see the raising of ME /ɛː/ (which would then set off the raising of ME /aː/) and the raising of /ɔː/ as interlinked with, i.e. motivated by the prior raisings from ME /eː/ to [iː] and /oː/ to [uː] respectively. This would be the most encompassing drag chain view of the Great Vowel Shift, where /ɛː/ and /ɔː/ fill the gaps left by the departure of the next higher vowels and ME /aː/ would be dragged into the position of /ɛː/. The question of "Chain shifting or not?" therefore turns out to be definitional rather than factual in nature because the label is legitimate only if we allow time gaps of about 100 years as instances of gap filling (cf. also Guzmán-González 2003). The issue becomes a bit more complicated because the gap between the two subshifts can be closed if we take raisings by about half a step – ME /ɛː/ to [e̝ː] and ME /aː/ to [æː] – into consideration.

2.3 Revisiting Dobson, reconsidering shifting

In discussions of the GVS two methodologies prevail: one type of analysis concentrates on a limited number of dialects or orthoepists; the alternative approach uses spelling evidence irrespective of the dialect area. Both approaches have their uses: the first is helpful to understand the relationships between different phonemes and the interrelatedness of ongoing changes in a given speech community. The second identifies incipient signs of changes. Both of them are thus valuable for approaching the inception problem of the GVS, although from different angles. At the same time, both approaches pose methodological questions, in particular for the dating of changes. Does early evidence suggest consistent or sporadic allophonic variation in spoken English? Is it representative of a region or just an idiolect? Do medieval and Renaissance writers pay equal attention to all vowels or focus on those that may cause misunderstandings due to their potential for mergers? A related question is whether early sources record raising or lowering of monophthongs earlier than incipient diphthongization, as Dobson (1968: 659) believes. Furthermore, to what extent does spelling or writing about pronunciations reflect the actual pronunciation of a (however specific) speech community and to what extent does it reflect an idealized model?

To address such questions, a more global perspective should complement the above approaches. In an attempt to minimize the potential of oversight and overstatement by individuals, this chapter will use Dobson's (1968) qualitative interpretations in the following quantitative way: each pronunciation in Table 14.4 is listed for a given point in time as soon as at least half of the sources cited in Dobson record a significant change, where "significant change" is defined in a pretheoretical but unbiased manner as "transcribable by IPA vowel symbols without the addition of diacritic marks" (for details, see Krug and Werner 2009). This quantitative method prevents isolated progressive or conservative dialects from entering the present discussion of the GVS. The lines below each pronunciation specify the periods during which the proportion of dialects with the respective pronunciation rises from a third to 50%. In order to avoid spurious findings, such intervals are only given for variants that have at least nine sources in Dobson. Following this method, we can chart cross-dialectal parallel changes and relative time gaps between different vocalic changes. (There exist, of course, some problematic classifications, for instance the categorization of [ʌʊ], [ʌɪ], and [ɛɪ], which are, following Dobson (1968: 660–661), classified in Table 14.4 with [əʊ] and [əɪ], respectively, but could potentially be categorized as further intermediate stages.) What a quantitative survey of Dobson's sources can serve to do, then, is essentially two things: first, identify in a principled way from what point in time onwards a certain pronunciation is common in many dialects of England;

second, identify periods during which many dialects undergo the same (or similar) change. In other words, we can identify when there was a spurt across dialects towards a new pronunciation.

This approach has its limitations, too: for one, since Dobson's sources almost all date from the late 16th and 17th centuries, it goes without saying that this methodology is not appropriate to establish a detailed account of the early phase of the GVS until 1550. It is the period between 1600 and 1650 for which we can draw our conclusions most confidently and which has thus the finest differentiation on the time axis in Table 14.4. Furthermore, this approach cannot serve to identify incipient stages of individual changes. Against this background and in view of the fact that on paths (I) and (II) [əɪ] and [əʊ] include more advanced diphthongizations, it comes as no surprise that all datings in Table 14.4 (except the uncertain ones marked by an asterisk) are later than in Table 14.3, even though the chronologies of Tables 14.3 and 14.4 are surprisingly congruent overall. Time gaps between 10 and 50 years suggest, however, that not all pronunciations of Table 14.3 were actually mainstream as early as hypothesized by previous scholarship.

Table 14.4: Majority pronunciations according to Dobson (1968)

	Middle English c.1300	1500	1550	1600	1620	1630	1640	1650	1700	Late Modern to Modern English (RP)
(I)	iː	ɪi				əɪ (or ɛɪ, ʌɪ)				aɪ/ɑɪ
(II)	uː	ʊu					əʊ (or ʌʊ)			aʊ/ɑʊ
(III)	eː	iː								iː
(IV)	oː	uː								uː
(V)	ɛː					eː			iː*	iː
(VI)	ɔː							oː		oʊ > əʊ
					ɛː				eː	eɪ
(VII)	aː				æː					

*Fewer than five sources in Dobson.

Most importantly, Table 14.4 suggests two critical cross-dialectal phases: the first is complete by 1500 and involves the four ME high and mid-high vowels /iː, uː, eː, oː/. This concurs with previous research on the early – and according to some researchers only – stage of the shift. As Dobson contains no earlier sources, 1500 is the *terminus ante quem* for the first changes affecting ME /iː, uː, eː, oː/. While his sources do not commonly report the early diphthongal pronunciations, Dobson (1968: 659) notes, with reference to Australian and Cockney English (and many other varieties and languages could be invoked), that incipient diphthongization often escapes people's notice. Such developments can therefore be integrated into a Labovian framework (e.g. Labov 1994: 78), as "changes from below vs. above the level of consciousness", and their sociolinguistic and prestige-related ramifications (on which see, e.g., Labov 2001: 76–77, 196–197, 509–518) could be investigated in modern dialects.

The second major phase suggested by Table 14.4 starts in the late 16th century and ends about 1650. During this period the remaining three ME long monophthongs /ɛː, ɔː, aː/ rise and the nucleus-glide dissimilation of /ıi/ and /ʊu/ continues. In view of such periods of overlapping change, it seems difficult to dismiss chain shift scenarios. (The stricter definition requiring the preservation of equidistance is dismissed here because this is difficult to apply in changes involving diphthongizations and difficult to put into practice in phonetic analyses.) The reanalysis of Dobson's sources thus corroborates the major interpretations of Table 14.3, *viz.* that we can either speak of two phases of a single great shift or of two smaller shifts. Another observation consistent with both Tables 14.3 and 14.4 is that the first candidate for exclusion from the GVS is path (VI), the raising of ME /ɔː/, because here the time gap since the departure of ME /oː/ is biggest (greater than 100 years), while the overlap and likelihood of interrelatedness with other contemporaneous changes is smallest. (As this reprint goes to press, the author's attention is drawn to Stenbrenden's (2016) illuminating account of long-vowel shifts in English between 1050 and 1700. The spelling evidence she discusses sheds new light on the GVS, in particular on the beginnings of each individual vowel change (as well as on the development of vowels not discussed in this handbook chapter on the GVS). Her focus on long-term and dialectal variation is related to the present account, as is her scepticism towards simple answers to many issues raised in the previous literature.)

Finally, the trajectories of ME /aː/ and /ɛː/ seem to suggest a pushing impulse from the lower vowel in the second half of the 17th century. However, there are fewer than five sources for post-1650 [iː] in path (V), so no firm conclusions can be drawn from such datings. It might nevertheless seem tempting to posit a third phase starting in the late 17th century for the second-step raising of ME /ɛː/ to [iː] and for the diphthongization of the reflexes of ME /ɔː/ and /aː/ to [oʊ > əʊ] and [eɪ], respectively, but this is not consistent with even a wide definition of chain shifting. The former development is the first merger of two long vowels under discussion here (ME /ɛː/ and /eː/) and, as late 18th and 19th century developments, the latter two seem simply too late to be part of a chain shift that started around 1300. They should therefore not be included in treatments of the shift proper except for didactic purposes, i.e. for tracing historical pronunciations from modern ones.

2.4 Metaphors we shift by: zebras, constellations, dunes, chess, and musical chairs

Let us now tackle the problem of chain shifting in a more principled manner by discussing definitional problems. Two criteria are universally advanced in definitions of shifts (cf. Martinet 1952; Stockwell and Minkova 1988; Stockwell 2002; Gordon 2002):
(i) the functional credo of preservation of phonemic contrast (i.e. avoidance of mergers) for two or more changing phonemes and
(ii) a causal connection between the changes in question, i.e. Change A must have triggered Change B (and so on).

These criteria for chain shifting are fulfilled by mainstream southern English if we consider the period from roughly 1400 to 1650 and if the ME diphthongs are excluded from consideration. Lass (1999) has famously labelled a focus on a limited period and a limited number of phonemes and changes a "constellation" or "zebra" fallacy, which implies that linguists see a zebra or constellation because they want to see a particular pattern. And yet, concentration on a limited period is methodologically unproblematic, in fact unavoidable for any discussion of a historical change. Researchers are free in their decision when the highest descriptive or explanatory potential is achieved for their model, and McMahon (2006a: 174) makes a similar point when arguing that "it is hard to see how we can discuss historical patterns at all except insofar as they are the product of hindsight on the part of linguists." On the basis of Table 14.4, it is the raising of ME /ɔː/ that seems least connected with the remaining developments and might thus be excluded from GVS accounts. We would then have to date the end of the shift to 1640 rather than 1650 – and thus incidentally exclude the second diphthongization stage of ME /uː/, but not that of /iː/, which does not increase the appeal of the account. Both approaches are equally post-hoc, and, in fact, equally justified as doubting that Dobson's sources allow such precise datings at all.

Whether or not exclusion of ME diphthongs is legitimate, however, depends on methodological perspectives which cannot easily be evaluated positively or negatively: it is a reasonable approach for those who want to study the developments of the (system of) ME long vowels only; but it is not a legitimate procedure for those who want to study the systems of and interactions between long ME vowels and diphthongs. Scholars studying mergers, on the other hand, must include former vowel-(semi-)consonant sequences such as *may, eight, sty, night, bow, know* that merge with vowels (see Stockwell 2002). On the former – let us for convenience call it the "focus-on-long-vowels-only" – approach we find no phonemic mergers until about 1650 to 1700, when ME /ɛː/ and /eː/ merge. (Individual lexical exceptions can be neglected in a discussion of phonological merger.) On the latter approach (which one might term the "focus-on-merger approach"), we find mergers from an early period onwards. Whether the GVS observes the no-merger condition, then, is a matter of perspective and methodology and thus not a matter that can be verified or falsified.

This chapter adopts the "focus-on-long-vowels-only" approach, in part because a discussion of ME diphthongs, vowel-glide, and vowel-consonant sequences would increase the complexity to a level that cannot be handled in a handbook. Readers interested in other phonological changes are therefore referred to Schlüter (Chapter 3).

Perhaps the focus on ME long monophthongs and their changes over some 250 years can be conceptualized by an alternative metaphor to Lass's star constellation: dunes (like vowels), although in a steady state of change, can be measured instrumentally and we can take synchronic snapshots of them. It seems legitimate for researchers studying the changing shape and position of dunes (or vowels) to focus on a specific type or selection of dunes, e.g. underwater dunes (or long vowels), those composed of sand (or monophthongs) vs. those composed of gravel (or vowels followed by glides) or those in a specific area (or vowel space). To be sure, the resulting picture will be incomplete, but not necessarily wrong.

In summary, if one excludes the developments of ME diphthongs from a discussion of the GVS, then the synopsis of Dobson's interpretations of orthoepistic evidence presented in Table 14.4 is consistent with the classic description of the GVS as a chain shift, during which all long ME non-high vowels raised by one step and the two high vowels diphthongized. This scenario describes fairly accurately the changes from about 1400 to 1650, i.e. very roughly from Chaucer's to Shakespeare's time. (The change from ME /aː/ via [æː] to [ɛː] is only an apparent counterexample as the intermediate step [æː] is only half-way between the low and mid-low position.) At the same time, Table 14.4 confirms that not all changes in (I) to (VII) proceeded in lockstep. ME /ɛː/, /ɔː/ and /aː/ started to change much later than /iː/, /uː/, /eː/ and /oː/. This seems to be a good reason for questioning the unitary nature of the shift or for dividing the shift into two phases.

On the other hand, the chronological progression of the changes is precisely what some adherents of both push and pull chain scenarios might interpret as supporting evidence *for* a chain shift. An important definitional problem is that in the literature on chain shifting there is no consensus on lockstep vs. sequentiality. Some authors consider as definitional for shifting, a lockstep movement of different phonemes (e.g. Stockwell 2002), while many general discussions of shifts (like Hock 1991; Bynon et al. 2003; Thomas 2006; Smith 2007: 75) assume the musical chairs analogy, where one change precedes another. The famous Saussurean chess analogy allows for both lockstep and gap interpretations, as recent discussions have thrown into relief its dynamic potential for discussions of language change (Thibault 1997: 96–98). The problem is aggravated by the fact that even among musical chairs adherents there exists no consensus on how small or big the time gap between two changes may or must be for them to be considered interrelated, a difficulty we already encountered in the interpretation of Table 14.3. In terms of the classic musical chairs analogy, we might ask: how long may it take for a chair (or a gap in the system) to be filled to still qualify as one and the same game? For those theorists who allow a gap of up to 150 years, according to Dobson's sources, the whole series of changes from (I) to (VII) can be interpreted as forming a unitary Great Vowel Shift – even though, as pointed out above, it would seem preferable to speak of one shift in the back and one in the front since the two are not interrelated. For those who require lockstep or a maximum time gap of 50 years, however, it will be two smaller shifts (affecting the upper half of the ME vowel inventory) followed by another small chain shift raising ME /aː/ and /ɛː/ in the first half of the 17th century plus an individual, but roughly contemporaneous change from ME /ɔː/ to [oː]. Both of these positions are legitimate and neither one is inherently superior from an analytic point of view.

3 On the history of Great Vowel Shift theories

In order to improve our understanding of the origin and succession of GVS theories, it is useful to briefly consider their respective intellectual backgrounds. For dominant strands in the philosophy of science – in particular empiricism, positivism, and Darwinism – have had an impact on linguists who have directly or indirectly contributed to the discussion, be they neogrammarians, traditional dialectologists, Prague school and other functionalists, or modern sociolinguists and phoneticians.

3.1 Phonemes, species, and habitats

Most of this chapter was written in 2009, which happens to be the year marking the 100th anniversary of Jespersen's coining of the term "Great Vowel Shift". The roots of early GVS theories, however, can be traced back further, as the late 19th century had seen a major paradigm shift in the history of scientific thinking: in the middle of that century, Darwin's evolutionary theory had replaced earlier theories of the evolution of species. In the development of Great Vowel Shift theories, the analogy between biology and language must have seemed particularly appealing because both evolutionary biology and GVS treatments try to describe and explain change (on issues concerning evolutionary sciences and linguistic change, see also Guzmán-González 2005).

Now 2009 also celebrates the bicentenary of Charles Darwin's birth and at the same time the 150th anniversary of his ground-breaking work *On the Origin of Species*, which saw three editions within two years and as many as six editions until 1872. Chronological order and parallelism in reasoning suggest strongly that evolutionary thinking had spread from biology to other scholarly domains by the early 20th century, notably to the domain of language and language change. It is probably no coincidence, therefore, that about half a century after Darwin's (1859) first edition of the *Origin of Species*, the two most influential push chain and drag chain theories of the GVS were developed by Luick (1896) and Jespersen (1909), respectively. It should be emphasized, however, that this was by no means a new analogy, as venerable linguistic terms like "morphology" illustrate. Nor has this analogizing come to an end since, as can be seen from more recent theories related to evolution and biology as well as mathematical models (like dynamical systems or chaos theory) with applications to both biology and language (cf. McMahon 1994: Chapter 12; Lass 1997: 291–301; Schneider 1997; Croft 2000, 2006; Mufwene 2001, 2008).

In modern terms, both push chain and drag chain theories are essentially ecological niche accounts, in which – on the push chain scenario – one species drives a former inhabitant or competitor out of its habitat or – on the drag chain scenario – one species moves into a niche vacated by another species. Such an ecological theory has considerable appeal for sound change theories because of a number of possible analogies: vowels (like species) can be seen as competitors; vowel spaces of adjacent vowels are analogous to habitats; they may overlap and the spaces into which (say, 95% of) vocalic allophones constituting a phoneme fall may shift.

After a century of GVS theories, it seems, however, also necessary to reconsider some of the tenets underlying both push and drag theories that have perhaps for too long gone unchallenged. One general difference is that long stressed vowels (unlike species) rarely become extinct. Also, vowels can merge with neighboring vowels – unlike species. The next section will discuss more concrete problems of early theories.

3.2 What's wrong with the push chain theory?

It is in particular Luick's push-chain theory which has a few serious logical flaws. Although Luick describes adequately a difference between the south (where both ME high vowels diphthongized) on the one hand and what are now conservative northern English and Scottish English dialects on the other (where the back high vowel did not diphthongize), the conclusion that the Great Vowel Shift must have been a push chain seems rash.

South		North after fronting	
(and North before fronting of /oː/)			
iː	uː	iː	uː
eː	oː	eː øː	←☐
ɛː	ɔː	ɛː	ɔː
aː		aː	

Figure 14.2: Southern and northern Middle English long vowel inventories according to Lass (1999: 76)

Adherents to push chain scenarios attribute the fact that northern varieties did not diphthongize their back high vowel to a missing back /oː/, which was fronted to /øː/ in northern dialects in the late thirteenth century (Smith 1996: 99–101; Johnston 1997: 69). Consider Luick's (1896) original formulation, which has a certain ring of circularity to it:

> [W]enn also mit einem Wort ū nur dort diphthongiert wurde, wo ō zu ū vorrückte, so ergiebt sich völlig zwingend, dass ū nur *deswegen* diphthongiert wurde, *weil* ō zu ū vorrückte und es gewissermassen aus seiner Stellung verdrängte. Wir sind also in den Stand gesetzt, eine causale Beziehung zwischen diesen zwei Lautwandlungen sicher festzustellen (Luick 1896: 78; emphasis original).

> In brief, if ū was diphthongized only in regions where ō raised to ū, then it necessarily follows that ū was diphthongized only *because* ō raised to ū and thus, as it were, pushed it out of its place. We are therefore in a position to firmly establish a causal relationship between these two sound changes [transl. MK].

Lass (1999) summarizes and refines the push chain position as follows:

> [N]o dialect has done anything to ME /eː/ like what the North did to ME /oː/, i.e. moved it 'out of position' before the GVS. And no dialect has consistent undiphthongised ME /iː/. This makes no sense except in the context of a chain shift beginning with the raising of the long mid vowels. A high vowel diphthongises only if the slot below it is filled by a raisable vowel when the shift begins. If the slot below the high vowel is empty (nothing there to push it out of position), there will be no diphthongisation (Lass 1999: 76–77).

Both quotations show that the push chain scenario is explained *ex negativo*. The argument is that /uː/ did not diphthongize in northern dialects because there was no adjacent vowel /oː/ to push it out of its place. Although this theory seems intuitively plausible and has been described as "beautiful", the causal link is underdeveloped. For one, the situation was a great deal more complex than Figure 14.2 suggests (see the detailed discussion in Smith 2007: Chapter 6), and northern varieties had in fact developed long /oː/ in words like *throat* and *hope* prior to the GVS as a reflex of Middle English open syllable lengthening (Smith 1996: 99–101). The number of /oː/ words was obviously lower than in dialects that preserve Old English ō words like *food*, which is why scholars who want to save Luick's theory can with some justification speak of lower pressures in northern dialects.

There are more serious problems in the argumentation, however. First, from a strictly logical perspective, the back high vowel space has no explanatory power for what happens in the front vowel space and vice versa. In other words, if diphthongization occurs in the front, this does not entail that it *must* occur simultaneously in the back, even if this is what we find in southern Middle English dialects. Second, long high-vowel diphthongization can happen without concomitant raising of the next lower position, as many Present-day English varieties show (see Foulkes and Docherty 1999). Third, there are modern varieties that diphthongize /iː/ much more noticeably than /uː/, which may be rather stable or centralized (cf. modern RP or standard American English). All this suggests that high-vowel diphthongization in the front and back are (a) independent of each other and (b) independent of the existence of a lower pushing vowel. After all, long (or half-long) mid-high vowels exist only in some modern English dialects as allophones of the RP phonemes /eɪ, əʊ, ɔː/ in words like *say, so,* or *force*.

A last problem for Luick's and Lass's push chain theories is that there is no *a priori* reason why only a mid-high back vowel /oː/ should be able to push /uː/. Although there may be a greater probabilistic likelihood for front vowels to raise along a front path, in principle, *any* adjacent vowel could have pushed /uː/ out of its position. Fronted northern ME /øː/ could therefore have pushed /uː/ equally well as /oː/, because no long vowel was on the trajectory between /uː/ and /øː/ in the relevant period either. Admittedly, the path from [ø] to [u] is somewhat longer than from [o] to [u], but if we consider the large phonetic space that other vowels travelled during and after the GVS, minor differences in spatial distance do not present a convincing argument for or against certain paths. This is particularly true for /ø:/ and /u:/, which are both rounded and thus rather similar from an overall articulatory point of view. In conclusion, if diphthongization of /u:/ does *not* happen in northern English varieties, the failure of this change to occur cannot be logically linked to the absence (or limited presence) of /o:/. The push chain theory in its current form is therefore to be rejected.

Notice that rejecting a causal link between /o:/-fronting and the absence of /u:/-diphthongization in the north does not entail an outright rejection of the push chain scenario. It is in principle possible for /e:/ and /o:/ to have initiated the shift in the south by pushing the higher vowels out of their habitats. But – and this is the last counterargument to Lass's justification of the push chain scenario – if two adjacent vowels change, it is not necessarily because an adjacent vowel pushes. It may be helpful to invoke the habitat analogy again: species /i:/ may prefer a new habitat for reasons independent of /e:/'s possible occasional inroads into its habitat. Other motivations for /i:/'s move may include a complex of factors like supply of water, food, and sun, all of which would be analogues to phonetic or other motivations for a vowel to change beyond a pushing neighbour. And there may finally be no apparent reasons at all for a vowel to change, not even a pulling neighbour, and yet it does change.

What, then is this chapter's conclusion regarding the inception problem? Lass (1976, 1999) finds no evidence of a clear chronological order, while Stenbrenden (2003) appears to have found evidence of very early high-vowel diphthongization and thus supports the drag chain scenario. The present author also favors the drag chain scenario for the majority of dialects, one reason being uniformitarianism: many modern English dialects diphthongize their high vowels (see the synopsis in Krug 2003a) but have not (or not yet) raised their lower vowels. A second reason is that many northern English and Scottish dialects have followed or are currently following the diphthongization path of /u:/ (see the synopsis in Stuart-Smith 2003). Such dialects can thus be interpreted as conservative rather than as true exceptions to the GVS because adaptation due to contact with southern English as the sole explanation for the diphthongization can be excluded for these varieties on phonetic grounds (see Section 4). In addition, there is a strong historical and crosslinguistic argument against an explanation in terms of contact: there are many related as well as unrelated languages that – at different stages in the past 500 years – underwent high-vowel diphthongizations similar to those of the GVS. The contact situations of these languages and of the Middle English dialects that were affected by the GVS, however, are simply too diverse for contact with southern standard English to be considered as the sole or even major explanatory force. The ultimate jury on pushing and pulling may still be out, then, but perhaps such a verdict is not necessary. "English" is not and has never been a monolithic block and it seems quite conceivable that different dialects followed different routes (see, e.g., Knappe 1997 on the development of ME [x] in syllable-coda position). If one adopts this perspective, both the "dialect problem" and the "inception problem" lose some of their poignancy.

4 Motivating the Great Vowel Shift and avenues for further research

The question of why the changes known as the GVS happened is not often asked. In other words, accounts of motivation or causation are rare in the literature, unless we include the countless contributions to the inception issue (some of which are summarized in Stockwell and Minkova 1988) and ad-hoc accounts for individual dialects under the rubric of explanations. It is in this area, therefore, that future research seems most promising and new insights can be expected from the digitization of medieval and early modern English texts. Social accounts of causation in the vein of Smith (1996, 2007), who capitalizes on the famous Mopsae argument of hyperadapting incomers (cf. Alexander Gil 1619), are also appealing but difficult to corroborate empirically in the absence of unambiguous historical sociolinguistic evidence or modern parallel cases. As long as there are no detailed sociophonetic accounts, the most realistic path to a motivation theory would be one that appeals to more general principles of phonetic and phonological change. What comes closest to such a crosslinguistic motivation are two of the recurrent tendencies identified for chain shifting and granted principle status by Labov (1994: 116, 176):

Principle I. In chain shifts, long vowels rise.
Principle IIa. In chain shifts, the nuclei of upgliding diphthongs fall.

Principle I can accommodate the raisings of all non-high vowels in the GVS, while Principle IIa captures the diphthongization paths (I) and (II) of Table 14.2, which are for convenience repeated below with the minimal addition of a moraic representation for the ME long vowel starting points:

(I) iː = ii > ɪi > əɪ > aɪ

(II) uː = uu > ʊu > əʊ > aʊ

An alternative (but compatible) phonetically driven approach is the optimality-theoretic account by Minkova and Stockwell (2003), who focus on the nucleus-glide dissimilation of the same diphthongizations, i.e. the increasing phonetic distance between the first and second element of these diphthongs. They argue convincingly that this process creates more optimal diphthongs from a hearer's perspective because the likelihood of misunderstanding decreases.

If we subscribe to the drag chain scenario, then a hearer-based economy can be invoked for the subsequent filling of the high-vowel spaces, too. This follows from the functionalist principle of maximal differentiation, which was formulated and refined by Martinet (e.g. 1952) but had implicitly been utilized by historical linguists arguing for gap filling since at least the 19th century, including the GVS chain shift advocates from both camps. According to this principle, it is useful for languages to have the extreme positions /a, u, i/ filled to maximize the distance between the distinctive vowels in the available vowel space, and indeed there are very few languages that lack one of these three vowels (Ladefoged and Maddieson 1996). Researchers therefore speak of an "unbalanced system" when the two high vowel positions are empty and assume that they are likely to be refilled soon.

Language is the constant negotiation between hearer-based and speaker-based economies, so it would be surprising if speaker-based principles did not play a role in the GVS. Elsewhere (Krug 2003a), I have presented arguments in terms of speaker economy pointing in a similar direction as the principles and optimality-theoretic accounts cited above, thus strengthening the case for the drag chain scenario. The arguments presented involve phonetic factors that exploit the tense-lax opposition, hiatus avoidance, and the sonority hierarchy with its implications for high-vowel diphthongization. In essence, I argue that the instability of long high vowels is due to their relatively high production effort: since high vowels are more tense than low vowels and since pure [i] and [u] are more peripheral, their production (in particular when they are long) involves more muscular effort than that of lower vowels. Long high vowels are therefore assumed to be intrinsically prone to diphthongization, which is well supported not only by English but also by crosslinguistic evidence (Wolfe 1972: 131–134; Krug 2003a). The first stages [ɪi, əɪ] and [ʊu, əʊ] in high vowel diphthongization along a central path are interpreted as lenition that is led by high frequency items, notably pronouns like *thou, I, my, thy*. A similar case for lenition has been made by Feagin (1994) for the monophthongization of /aɪ/ in southern American English, which seems to be led by the pronouns *I* and *my*. Such high-frequency items tend to develop progressive variants below the level of consciousness (Krug 2003b), which may be the impulse for a shift of a phoneme's prototypical realization and thus of its positional displacement.

An additional argument for early diphthongization in terms of speaker economy derives from the fact that the loss of epenthetic [ʔ] in hiatus contexts (on which see Minkova 2003) is roughly contemporaneous with the beginning of the GVS. From a usage-based perspective, then, it seems likely for the two most frequent pronoun-verb sequences of English (*I-am* and *thu-art*) to develop intrusive glides (/j/ and /w/ respectively) at the former word boundaries. The matter is more complex for *I-am* due to the history of the first person pronoun, but there is clear evidence for an increase of potential hiatus contexts from the historical *Helsinki Corpus* (on the development from ME [iç] via [ij] to [iː] see Dobson 1968: 667). Even if, as seems likely, glottal onset before potential low-stress items like *am* and *art* or between tightly bonded sequences like *thu-art* was infrequent or did not exist in early ME at all, the liaison argument remains nevertheless valid: the development of intrusive glides would merely have to be antedated. In any case, the resulting pronunciations of the pronouns *I* and *th(o)u* in these high-frequency sequences would have resembled open-syllable diphthongization of words like *my, thy* and *thou* in isolation. On that view, two independent phonetic, hence natural tendencies of high-vowel diphthongization mutually reinforced each other.

And yet, high-vowel diphthongization may not be the full answer to the issues of inception and causation. Modern phonetic research (see for instance the gamut of studies presented in Labov 1994: Chapters 6 and 8) allows for simultaneous change as it suggests that the reality is neither fully congruent with lockstep movement nor with a major time gap: synchronically, vowel spaces of adjacent phonemes overlap, especially so during ongoing change, where one phoneme encroaches on the space of an adjacent phoneme. This situation holds for a single speaker, is common within any speech community and normal for different dialects. Detailed quantitative phonetic and sociolinguistic research of conservative and progressive speech communities, e.g. northern England, Scotland, Australia, New Zealand, or London could therefore throw new light on the historical GVS.

Another area that deserves more attention in future research (and not only on GVS-related research) is the role of allophonic variation of vowels, the abundance of which has led some researchers to reject the existence of phonemes altogether (see e.g. Kretzschmar and Tamasi 2003). Without a doubt, more research is necessary on the effects of high-frequency items and sequences (cf. the studies in Bybee and Hopper 2001) as well as of syllable type (e.g. open vs. closed) and neighboring sounds in such sequences as *me/my bike* or *It was me*. And yet, it is almost surprising how regular and parallel the changes were that affected the allophones of each ME long vowel and such regularity points indeed to the cognitive reality of more abstract, phonemic representations.

In conclusion, I still tend to believe, as in 2003, that the most likely answer to the question of who triggered the GVS is: "*You* and *me*, basically; and maybe also *he* and *she*, or *us* and *we*. All of us essentially." But a lot more detailed sociophonetic research and theoretical refinement will be necessary before we can turn this hypothesis into yet another theory that students of English historical linguistics should consider for memorization. Students might consider, however, discussing the many GVS-related hypotheses and debates mentioned in this chapter as heuristics for critically evaluating and better understanding the nature of linguistic change and theory building.

5 References

Barber, Charles. 1997. *Early Modern English*. Cambridge: Cambridge University Press.
Bloch, Bernard and George L. Trager. 1942. *Outline of Linguistic Analysis*. Baltimore: Linguistic Society of America.
Bybee, Joan. 2003. Mechanisms of change in grammaticization: The role of frequency. In: Brian D. Joseph and Richard D. Janda (eds.), *The Handbook of Historical Linguistics*, 602–623. Oxford: Blackwell.
Bybee, Joan and Paul Hopper (eds.). 2001. *Frequency and the Emergence of Linguistic Structure*. Amsterdam/Philadelphia: John Benjamins.
Bynon, Theodora, Elizabeth Closs Traugott, Anthony Kroch, Rex E. Wallace, and Henry M. Hoenigswald. 2003. Language change. In: William J. Frawley (editor-in-chief), *International Encyclopedia of Linguistics*. 2nd edn. Oxford: Oxford University Press. (e-reference edition, accessed 11 November 2009).
Chomsky, Noam and Morris Halle. 1968. *The Sound Pattern of English*. New York: Harper and Row.
Christy, T. Craig. 1983. *Uniformitarianism in Linguistics*. Amsterdam/Philadelphia: John Benjamins.
Croft, William. 2000. *Explaining Language Change: An Evolutionary Approach*. Harlow: Longman.
Croft, William. 2006. Evolutionary models and functional-typological theories of language change. In: van Kemenade and Los (eds.), 68–91.
Darwin, Charles. 1859. *On the Origin of Species by Means of Natural Selection*. London: Murray.
Dobson, Eric J. 1968. *English Pronunciation 1500–1700*. 2 vols. Oxford: Oxford University Press.
Faiß, Klaus. 1989. *Englische Sprachgeschichte*. Tübingen: Franke.
Feagin, Crawford. 1994. "Long I" as a microcosm of southern states speech. Paper given at NWAV1994. Ms., Zurich University.
Foulkes, Paul and Gerard Docherty (eds.). 1999. *Urban Voices: Accent Studies in the British Isles*. London: Arnold.
Gil, Alexander. 1619. *Longonomia Anglica*. (2nd ed., 1621). London: Beale.
Gordon, Matthew J. 2002. Investigating chain shifts and mergers. In: J. K. Chambers, Peter Trudgill, and Natalie Schilling-Estes (eds.), *The Handbook of Language Variation and Change*, 244–266. Oxford: Blackwell.
Görlach, Manfred. 1991. *Introduction to Early Modern English*. Cambridge: Cambridge University Press.
Görlach, Manfred. 1994. *Einführung ins Frühneuenglische*. Heidelberg: Winter.
Guzmán-González, Trinidad. 2003. Revisiting the revisited: Could we survive without the Great Vowel Shift? *Studia Anglica Posnaniensia* 39: 121–131.

Guzmán-González, Trinidad. 2005. Out of the past: A walk with labels and concepts, raiders of the lost evidence and a vindication of the role of writing. *International Journal of English Studies* 5: 13–32.

Hart, John. 1551. *The opening of the unreasonable writing of our inglish toung*. Unpublished Ms.

Hock, Hans Heinrich. 1991. *Principles of Historical Linguistics*. 2nd edn. Berlin/New York: Mouton de Gruyter.

Jespersen, Otto. 1909. *A Modern English Grammar on Historical Principles*. Vol. I *Sounds and Spellings*. London: Allen and Unwin.

Johnston, Paul A. 1992. English vowel shifting: One great vowel shift or two small vowel shifts? *Diachronica* 9: 189–226.

Johnston, Paul A. 1997. Older Scots phonology and its regional variation. In: Charles Jones (ed.), *The Edinburgh History of the Scots Language*, 47–111. Edinburgh: Edinburgh University Press.

Jones, Daniel. 1909. *The Pronunciation of English*. Cambridge: Cambridge University Press.

Kemenade, Ans van and Bettelou Los (eds.). 2006. *The Handbook of the History of English*. Oxford: Blackwell.

Kretzschmar, William A., Jr., and Susan Tamasi. 2003. Distributional foundations for a theory of language change. *World Englishes* 22: 377–401.

Knappe, Gabriele. 1997. Though *it is tough: On regional differences in the development and substitution of the Middle English voiceless velar fricative [x] in syllable coda position. (Special issue on Language in Time and Space: Studies in Honour of Wolfgang Viereck on the Occasion of his 60th Birthday, ed. by Heinrich Ramisch and Kenneth Wynne.) Zeitschrift für Dialektologie und Linguistik* 97: 139–163.

Krug, Manfred. 2003a. (Great) vowel shifts present and past: Meeting ground for structural and natural phonologists. *Penn Working Papers in Linguistics (Selected papers from NWAVE 31 at Stanford)* 9(2): 107–122.

Krug, Manfred. 2003b. Frequency as a determinant in grammatical variation and change. In: Günter Rohdenburg and Britta Mondorf (eds.), *Determinants of Grammatical Variation in English*, 7–67. Berlin/New York: Mouton de Gruyter.

Krug, Manfred and Valentin Werner. 2009. Dobson revisited: Long vowel variation and the Great Vowel Shift. Ms. Bamberg.

Labov, William. 1994. *Principles of Linguistic Change*. I: *Internal Factors*. Oxford: Blackwell.

Labov, William. 2001. *Principles of Linguistic Change*. II: *Social Factors*. Oxford: Blackwell.

Ladefoged, Peter and Ian Maddieson. 1996. *The Sounds of the World's Languages*. Oxford: Blackwell.

Lass, Roger. 1976. Rules, metarules and the shape of the Great Vowel Shift. In: Roger Lass (ed.), *English Phonology and Phonological Theory: Synchronic and Diachronic Studies*, 51–102. Cambridge: Cambridge University Press.

Lass, Roger. 1992. Phonology and morphology. In: Norman Blake (ed.), *The Cambridge History of the English Language*. Vol. II. *1066–1476*, 23–155. Cambridge: Cambridge University Press.

Lass, Roger. 1997. *Historical Linguistics and Language Change*. Cambridge: Cambridge University Press.

Lass, Roger. 1999. Phonology and morphology. In: Roger Lass (ed.), *The Cambridge History of the English Language*. Vol. III. *1476–1776*, 56–186. Cambridge: Cambridge University Press.

Lass, Roger. 2006. Phonology and morphology. In: Richard Hogg and David Denison (eds.), *A History of the English Language*, 43–109. Cambridge: Cambridge University Press.

Luick, Karl. 1896. *Untersuchungen zur englischen Lautgeschichte*. Strassburg: Truebner.

Martinet, André. 1952. Function, structure and sound change. *Word* 8(1): 1–32.
McMahon, April. 1994. *Understanding Language Change*. Cambridge: Cambridge University Press.
McMahon, April. 2006a. Restructuring Renaissance English. In: Lynda Mugglestone (ed.), *The Oxford History of English*, 147–177. Oxford: Oxford University Press.
McMahon, April. 2006b. Change for the better? Optimality theory vs. history. In: van Kemenade and Los (eds.), 3–23.
McMahon, April. 2007. Who's afraid of the vowel shift rule? *Language Sciences (Issues in English phonology)* 29(2–3): 341–359.
Minkova, Donka. 2003. *Alliteration and Sound Change in Early English*. Cambridge: Cambridge University Press.
Minkova, Donka and Robert Stockwell. 1999. Explanations of sound change: Contradictions between dialect data and theories of chain shifting. In: Clive Upton and Katie Wales (eds.), *Dialectal Variation in English: Proceedings of the Harold Orton Centenary Conference 1998*, 83–102. Leeds: School of English.
Minkova, Donka and Robert Stockwell. 2003. English vowel shifts and "optimal" diphthongs: Is there a logical link? In: D. Eric Holt (ed.), *Optimality Theory and Language Change*, 169–190. Amsterdam: Kluwer.
Mufwene, S. Salikoko. 2001. *The Ecology of Language Evolution*. Cambridge: Cambridge University Press.
Mufwene, S. Salikoko. 2008. *Language Evolution: Contact, Competition and Change*. London: Continuum.
Ogura, Mieko. 1987. *Historical English Phonology: A Lexical Perspective*. Tokyo: Kenkyusha.
Schneider, Edgar. 1997. Chaos theory as a model for dialect variability and change? In: Alan R. Thomas (ed.), *Issues and Methods in Dialectology*, 22–36. Bangor: University of Wales, Department of Linguistics.
Schützler, Ole. 2009. Unstable close-mid vowels in Modern Scottish English. In: Carlos Prado-Alonso, Lidia Gómez-García, Iria Pastor-Gómez, and David Tizón-Couto (eds.), *New Trends and Methodologies in Applied English Language Research: Diachronic, Diatopic and Contrastive Studies*, 153–182. Bern: Peter Lang.
Smith, Jeremy. 1996. *An Historical Study of English: Function, Form and Change*. London: Routledge.
Smith, Jeremy. 2007. *Sound Change and the History of English*. Oxford: Oxford University Press.
Stenbrenden, Gjertrud F. 2003. On the interpretation of early evidence for ME vowel-change. In: Barry J. Blake and Kate Burridge (eds.), *Historical Linguistics 2001: Selected papers from the 15th International Conference on Historical Linguistics, Melbourne, 13–17 August 2001*, 403–415. Amsterdam/Philadelphia: John Benjamins.
Stenbrenden, Gjertrud F. 2016. *Long-Vowel Shifts in English, c. 1050–1700: Evidence from Spelling*. Cambridge: Cambridge University Press.
Stockwell, Robert. 1972. Problems in the interpretation of the Great Vowel Shift. In: M. Estellie Smith (ed.), *Studies in Linguistics in Honor of George L. Trager*, 344–362. The Hague: Mouton.
Stockwell, Robert. 2002. How much shifting actually occurred in the historical English vowel shift? In: Donka Minkova and Robert Stockwell (eds.), *Studies in the History of the English Language: A Millennial Perspective*, 267–281. Berlin/New York: Mouton de Gruyter.
Stockwell, Robert and Donka Minkova. 1988. The English Vowel Shift: Problems of coherence and explanation. In: Dieter Kastovsky, Gero Bauer, and Jacek Fisiak (eds.), *Luick Revisited*, 355–394. Tübingen: Gunter Narr.

Stuart-Smith, Jane. 2003. The phonology of Modern Urban Scots. In: John Corbett, J. Derrick McClure, and Jane Stuart-Smith (eds.), *The Edinburgh Companion to Scots*, 110–137. Edinburgh: Edinburgh University Press.

Thibault, Paul J. 1997. *Re-reading Saussure: The Dynamics of Signs in Social Life*. New York: Routledge.

Thomas, E. R. 2006. Vowel shifts and mergers. In: Keith Brown (ed.), *Encyclopedia of Language and Linguistics*, 484–494. 2nd edn. Amsterdam: Elsevier.

Trager, George L. and Henry Lee Smith, Jr. 1951. *An Outline of English Structure. Studies in Linguistics, Occasional Papers* 3. Norman, OK: Battenburg Press.

Wolfe, Patricia M. 1972. *Linguistic Change and the Great Vowel Shift in English*. Berkeley: University of California Press.

Christine Johansson
Chapter 15:
Relativization

1 Introduction —— 267
2 Written and speech-related Early Modern English: *that*, *wh*-forms and zero —— 269
3 The relative clause: *that*, *wh*-forms and zero —— 270
4 Personal versus nonpersonal antecedents —— 274
5 Forms and functions of the relativizers —— 281
6 Summary —— 283
7 References —— 284

Abstract: This chapter describes the use of relativizers in Early Modern English, focusing on speech-related material, i.e. Trials and Drama texts from the periods 1560–1599 and 1680–1719. What is most striking as regards the use of relativizers is the predominance of the relativizer *that*. It is used with all types of personal and nonpersonal antecedents and in restrictive and nonrestrictive relative clauses, although it is rare in nonrestrictive relative clauses. The *wh*-forms compete with *that* in restrictive clauses but *who* is not frequent except with personal names, and *which* decreases in frequency, as it is rarely used with personal antecedents. The zero construction becomes increasingly frequent, particularly in the second period (1680–1719). Thus, the variation is rather between *that* and the zero construction than between *that* and the *wh*-forms. By 1719, we recognize many of the features of Present-day usage of relativizers. These features probably appeared earlier in speech-related data than in the literary language.

1 Introduction

In the Early Modern English period (c.1500–1700), the use of relativizers and relative clauses is in many ways different from Present-day English usage. In Early Modern English, the *wh*-forms increase in frequency, particularly in restrictive relative clauses, especially when the personal (*who*) / nonpersonal (*which*) contrast becomes more explicit. Throughout the period, however, *that* is the most

---

Christine Johansson: Uppsala (Sweden)

DOI 10.1515/9783110525069-015

frequent relativizer. Moreover, individual letter writers, scientists, and educators have preferences as regards the use of *wh*-forms versus *that*. Previous studies (e.g. Rydén 1966; Dekeyser 1984) focus on the use of relativizers in EModE literary and scholarly language whereas this paper will focus on the use of relativizers in spoken language and compare the two uses.

"Adnominal relative clauses" (i.e. relative clauses as postmodifiers, see examples 1–3), will be studied to examine the frequency of the relativization strategies *that*, *wh*-forms and the zero construction. "Sentential relative clauses" will also be included in the study (see example 4). Here, the whole preceding clause or the predicate or parts of it function as antecedent (see Quirk et al. 1985: 1118–1120). Sentential relative clauses are typical of spoken language (Biber 1988: 106–107) and comment on what has been said before. "Nominal relative clauses", as in example (5), will not be examined in this paper.

(1) Nightingale. [...] *I enquired of another **who** lived in the Mews, if he knew Mrs. Baynton* (1702 Trials, Haagen Swendsen)

(2) S. G. *Pray is she a Country Lady **that** has got a good Joynture.* (1702 Trials, Haagen Swendsen)

(3) Swen. *[...] I beg it, my Lord, for 'tis the most material thing **Ø** I have to ask,* (1702 Trials, Haagen Swendsen)

(4) Att. Gen. *[...] but by proof he did not come in till Twelve, **which** was after the thing was done.* (1680 Trials, John Giles)

(5) Men. *Because she did as you do now, on **whom soeuer** she met withall, she railed, and therfore well deserued that dogged name.* (1595 Drama, Warner, Menaecmi)

The paper will concentrate on the variation between *that*, *wh*-forms and zero as regards type of relative clause, antecedent, and the function of the relativizer in the relative clause. Section 2 will present the speech-related material and frequencies of *that*, *wh*-forms, and zero in my study, as well as in previous studies on EModE relativization.

2 Written and speech-related Early Modern English: *that*, *wh*-forms and zero

The closest representatives of spoken EModE are speech-related texts, such as Trial proceedings and Drama comedy (see Culpeper and Kytö 2000: 186–193). The speech-related texts (henceforth spEModE) in my study are drawn from *A Corpus of English Dialogues 1560–1760* (CED) (see Kytö and Culpeper 2006; Kytö and Walker 2006). The Trials include 56,710 words and the Drama texts 87,460. The periods studied are 1560–1599 and 1680–1719.

In Table 15.1, the distribution of *that*, *wh*-forms, and zero is given as presented in the studies of Rydén (1966), Dekeyser (1984), and in the two spEModE periods. To show the distribution of relativizers within each period, the two spEModE periods are treated separately in Table 15.1, but are otherwise throughout the paper treated mainly as one category representing spEModE. Rydén's study describes the use of relativizers in literary and scholarly language as represented by Thomas Elyot (1490?–1546) and his contemporaries and covers the period 1520–1560. Although Rydén (1966) concentrates on the early 16th century, most of the results and comments presented there can be taken as representative of the remainder of the EModE period. Rydén's detailed study is thus the main source of written EModE but naturally the time period (i.e. the early 16th century) will be taken into account when comparison is made with the later spEModE texts studied in this paper.

Dekeyser's corpus covers the period 1600–1649 and includes literary texts, prose, and poetry, but also letters and speech-related Drama texts. In Table 15.1, Dekeyser's Drama texts have been separated from prose, poetry, and letters (wrEModE: 1600–1649) to compare with the distribution of the relativizers in the spEModE material in this paper.

Table 15.1: *That*, *wh*- forms, and zero in EModE: written and speech-related texts

That/*wh*-form/zero	That	*Wh*-form	Zero
wrEModE: 1520–1560 (Rydén 1966)	46%	52%	2%
wrEModE: 1600–1649 (Dekeyser 1984)	28%	65%	7%
EModE Drama: 1600–1649 (Dekeyser 1984)	46%	30%	24%
spEModE (Trials and Drama): 1560–1599	51%	38%	11%
spEModE (Trials and Drama): 1680–1719	47%	32%	21%

As appears from Table 15.1, *that* is the most frequent relativizer, particularly in the two periods of spEModE analysed in the study, 1560–1599 and 1680–1719 (47%–

51%), and in Dekeyser's Drama texts from 1600–1649 (46%). *That* is more common than the *wh*-forms taken together. In the Trials studied in this paper, containing recorded authentic dialogue, *that* is the preferred relativizer, both with members of the legal profession and with the defendants and witnesses. Ball (1996: 246–248), who includes a study of EModE Trials (the State Trials from 1680, 1692 and 1693, and the Salem Witchcraft Trials from 1692), reports the same result: *that* is the most frequent relativizer whatever speaker role (i.e. members of the legal profession and defendants and witnesses).

In the Drama texts included in this paper, *that* is predominant irrespective of social class. Characters representing the lower social classes could be expected to use *that* and zero even more frequently (see Barber 1997: 235–236). However, the playwrights use other means, such as spelling or vocabulary, to mirror in writing features of a dialect or of uneducated speech (cf. Culpeper 2001: 206, 209, 212). Dekeyser does not discuss the use of relativizers in terms of social class in his Drama texts from 1600–1649. The *wh*-forms increase in frequency during the EModE period, but this is only true of the written data: 52% of *wh*-forms occur in the period 1520–1560 (Rydén's study) and 65% in 1600–1649 (Dekeyser's study). In spEModE, only 32%–38% of the relative clauses are headed by a *wh*-form. In Dekeyser's Drama texts, the frequency of *wh*-forms is also low: 30% (see Table 15.1).

The most striking difference between the first and the second spEModE periods in my study is the frequency of the zero construction: it is nearly twice as frequent between 1680–1719 compared with 1560–1599 (21% versus 11%, see Table 15.1). Although the use of the zero construction is not necessarily an indication of informal style in EModE (Rissanen 1984: 430; Visser 1963: 853), a zero relativizer is apparently more typical of spEModE dialogue than of literary and formal language. Zero constructions are also frequent (24%) in Dekeyser's Drama texts. Ball (1996: 248) notes in her Trials study that zero relativizers are mainly used by speakers other than lawyers and aristocrats (see also Section 4.4). The next section will take a closer look at the relative clause in EModE; more precisely, how the two types of relative clause, restrictive and nonrestrictive, influence the use and frequency of relativizers in spEModE.

3 The relative clause: *that*, *wh*-forms and zero

Relative clauses are the most frequent type of subordinate clause in EModE literary and scholarly language (Rydén 1966: xix, 362). Relative clauses are also common in spEModE (876/100,000 words). Restrictive relative clauses restrict the reference of the antecedent, in terms of classification or identification, whereas a nonrestrictive relative clause merely gives additional information about a previously identified antecedent (cf. Quirk et al. 1985: 1239–1242; Poutsma 1926–1929: 421–430; Rydén 1974). A frequent type of nonrestrictive clause in my spEModE data is the sentential relative clause (see Section 1).

Table 15.2 shows the frequencies of *that*, the *wh*-forms and the zero relativizer in restrictive and nonrestrictive relative clauses in my spEModE material. Restrictive relative clauses are predominant in the spEModE data: 78% of the relative clauses are restrictive. Given their classifying and identifying function, restrictive relative clauses are particularly frequent in the Trials where establishing the identity of people or evidence is crucial. As in Present-day English, the zero construction appears only in restrictive relative clauses. The distribution of the relativizers in restrictive and nonrestrictive relative clauses will be discussed in the following sections.

Table 15.2: *That*, *wh-* forms, and zero in restrictive and nonrestrictive relative clauses in spEModE

That/*wh*-form/zero	Restrictive	Nonrestrictive	Total *that*/*wh*-form/zero
That	**532** (58%)	**40** (16%)	**572**
Wh-forms (total)	**188** (21%)	**217** (84%)	**405**
Who	42 (5%)	46 (18%)	88
Whom	16 (2%)	17 (6%)	33
Whose	30 (3%)	17 (6%)	47
Which	100 (11%)	137 (53%)	237
Zero	**193** (21%)	—	**193**
Total	913 (78%)	257 (22%)	1170 (100%)

3.1 Restrictive relative clauses

Most of the restrictive relative clauses are headed by *that*, both in written EModE and speech-related data (spEModE: 58%, see Table 15.2). The conjunction-like character of *that* signals, in principle, a tighter link to the antecedent and antecedent clause than a relative clause with a *wh*-form (Rydén 1974; Rissanen 1984: 420–422). This is particularly apparent when a pronoun is the antecedent, as in example (6).

(6) Bridges. *You said thus, That the Papists were the best Religion, and that those **that** were not of that Religion were Damn'd.* (1680 Trials, John Giles)

In spEModE, *who* and *which* are not very frequent in restrictive relative clauses (*who*: 5% and *which*: 11%, see Table 15.2) and do not compete with *that* to any great extent. There is no increase in the use of *who* and *which* (examples 7 and 8) during the second spEModE period (1680–1719).

(7) Mr. Att. Gen. *Then, my Lord, we have another piece of Evidence* **which** *we wou'd offer to your Lordship,* **which** *is not direct Evidence against the Prisoner,* (1696 Trials, Ambrose Rookwood)

(8) Wild. *[...] If a Woman be very handsome, and meets with a Man* **who** *has Wit enough to know and value it; the Consequence speaks it self, and needs no Corroborating Evidence.* (1696 Drama, Manley, *The Lost Lover*)

The *wh*-forms (*who, whose, whom,* and *which*) as a whole are not more frequent than the other relativization strategy in restrictive relative clauses, the zero construction. A *wh*-form or zero occurs in 21% of the cases (see Table 15.2).

3.2 Nonrestrictive relative clauses

In nonrestrictive relative clauses, the *wh*-forms predominate in spEModE (84%, see Table 15.2). *Who* is fairly common in nonrestrictive relative clauses (18%). Also the inflected forms *whom* and *whose* are more frequent in nonrestrictive relative clauses than in restrictive clauses (6%, see Table 15.2), but are still rare. However, the most frequent relativizer in nonrestrictive relative clauses in spEModE is *which*. In Drama and Trials, more than 50% of the nonrestrictive relative clauses are headed by *which* (see Table 15.2). As mentioned earlier, sentential relative clauses are typical of speech and speech-related language and they represent a frequent type of nonrestrictive relative clause in my spEModE texts. This influences the frequency of *which*, since it is the only possible relativizer in such clauses, see example (9).

(9) Mr. Slater. *[...] I took him for a* Frenchman, *he used very much to espouse the Interest of the King of* France, **which** *I used to chide him for.* (1716 Trials, Francis Francia)

Nonrestrictive *that* is infrequent in the EModE period; both in the early 16th century and in later periods. Rydén (1966: 278) reports that in Elyot and his contemporaries' works, only 10% of the nonrestrictive clauses are introduced by *that*. In Dekeyser's (1984) data, which includes prose, poetry, and letters but also speech-related drama texts from the early 17th century, only 20% of the nonrestrictive clauses are headed by *that*. In the spEModE data in this study, nonrestrictive *that* occurs in 16% of the relative clauses, but it decreases towards the end of the second spEModE period studied (1680–1719). Most of the examples of nonrestrictive *that* are to be found in the early comedies, see example (10).

(10) Hephest. *[…] You (Alexander)* **that** *would be a God, shewe your self in this worse then a man,* (1584 Drama, Lyly, *Alexander and Campaspe*)

3.3 Structural complexity of EModE relative clauses

In EModE, the relative clauses can be of considerable structural and semantic complexity, including different types of co-ordinate relative clauses (cf. Rydén 1970: 13–15, 20–27). In spEModE, co-ordinate relative clauses contribute to the complexity, as do sentential relative clauses and relative clauses which expand on the premodifiers and postmodifiers of the noun functioning as antecedent. In example (11), the first of the three relative clauses is sentential. In a sentential relative clause, an argument is summed up or commented on (*which was done* and *which I did* occur frequently in the Trials). The other two relative clauses in example (11) are co-ordinated, including a *wh*-clause (*who*) + a clause introduced by zero. *Who* refers to "Gutbert".

(11) Sollic. *This is not so, as hath well appeared. Besides this, the conveying away of* Gutbert, **which** *was done by your means, and* **who** *decyphered this Letter, and could have disclosed the Matter, proveth a great Guiltiness in you.* (1571 Trials, Thomas Howard Duke of Norfolk)

In example (12), the relative clause, which is nonrestrictive, expands on the information given in the premodification and completes the characterization of an identified antecedent, *a sorry ignorant Knave* (see Rydén 1974, 1984; Jacobsson 1994). Such relative clauses are frequent in Drama, as shown in example (12).

(12) Oliv. *Are you so silly to believe it, he seems to be a sorry ignorant Knave,* **that** *has more Will than Power to do Evil.* (1696 Drama, Manley, *The Lost Lover*)

4 Personal versus nonpersonal antecedents

The personal/nonpersonal contrast becomes increasingly explicit during the EModE period and the most important change is apparently the use of *which*. Although *which* does occur with personal nouns, it becomes more restricted to nonpersonal antecedents. Deities are a special group of antecedents in EModE texts and have a very high personal status. It is with this type of antecedent that *who* starts being used (cf. Rydén 1983). As antecedents, deities are more common in written EModE data, not only in religious writing and the Bible but also in letters (Nevalainen and Ramoulin-Brunberg 2002: 118). In spEModE, *which*, as in example (13), and *that* are used with deities but the form *who* is not found. On the other hand, with preposition + relativizer, *whom* is used.

(13) Perin. *[...] The God of trueth and perfect equitie,* **Which** *will reuenge wrong to the innocent, with thousand plagues and tortors worse than death.* (1594 Drama, Anon., *A Knacke to Know a Knave*)

Table 15.3 shows the distribution of the relativizers with personal and nonpersonal antecedents in spEModE and how the subject and (direct + prepositional) object functions are realized as *that*, a *wh*-form or as zero with the two types of antecedent. The functions of the relativizers will be discussed in more detail in Section 5.

Table 15.3: Antecedent and function of *that*, *wh*-forms and zero in spEModE

Function Antecedent	Subject		Total Subject	Object		Total Object	Total
	Personal	Non-personal		Personal	Non-personal		
That	245 (69%)	196 (62%)	441	18 (25%)	98 (31%)	116	557
Who	86 (24%)	4 (1%)	90				90
Whom	4 (1%)		4	30 (41%)		30	34
Which	8 (2%)	109 (34%)	117	2 (3%)	106 (33%)	108	225
Zero	12 (3%)	9 (3%)	21	23 (31%)	113 (36%)	136	157
Total	355	318	673	73	317	390	1063

4.1 *That*

In spEModE, the relativizer *that* is used as frequently with a personal as with a nonpersonal antecedent, particularly when *that* functions as subject in the relative clause (see Table 15.3: 62%–69%). Although *that* is frequent with most types of personal and nonpersonal antecedents, there are certain types of antecedent in spEModE with which it is particularly common. *That* is often used with *all* (as pronoun and determiner) and with pronouns such as *everything, something, any thing, one, any body*, with general nouns such as *person(s), people*, and *thing*(s) and with a superlative + noun, as in examples (14)–(16) (cf. also Johansson 2006: 154–166). With many of these types of antecedent, we also find the zero construction when functioning as direct object or as prepositional object (cf. Present-day English, and see Section 4.4).

(14) Ld. Townshend. *All* **that** *Mr. Walpole brought me were laid there, and I saw him take them back again.* (1716 Trials, Francis Francia)

(15) Smy. *[...] And, let me tell you, Mr. Wildman, I Love my Wife, and don't like People* **that** *slight her Charms,* (1696 Drama, Manley, *The Lost Lover*)

(16) Boy. *Go thy waies for the prowdest harlotrie* **that** *euer came in our house.* (1599 Drama, Chapman, *An Humerous Dayes Mirth*)

Not only indefinite pronouns (e.g. *any body, one, some*) occur as personal antecedents of *that* but also personal pronouns and demonstratives (*he, you, they, those, this,* and *who* in the combination *who that*). In example (17), *he that* is generic (= 'anyone who'; see Jespersen 1927: 98–99, 120, 154–155).

(17) Hone. *I, but he remembers not where Christ saith, hee* **that** *giveth a cup of water in my name shall be blessed. [...] He* **that** *giueth to the poore lendeth vnto the Lord,* (1594 Drama, Anon., *A Knacke to Know a Knave*)

That is used repeatedly in "cleft sentences" in spEModE, particularly in the Trials. Cleft sentences serve the purpose of emphasizing a person's identity, actions or whereabouts, or the time of a crime, for instance in the statements of witnesses. In cleft sentences (*it*-clefts, *th*-clefts and *wh*-clefts), *that* is used as frequently with personal and as with nonpersonal antecedents. Examples (18)–(19) are from the Trial of Haagen Swendsen, where cleft sentences are particularly common.

(18) Judge Powel. *How long was it from the time* **that** *you were parted after Arresting, that you saw Mrs* Rawlins *again.* (1702 Trials, Haagen Swendsen)

(19) Wakeman. *at the 5 Bells, but it was* Mr Holt **that** *gave it me.* (1702 Trials, Haagen Swendsen)

Ball (1996: 246–247) states that the crucial change in the use of *that* took place in the second half of the 17th century: *that* began to be confined to nonpersonal antecedents and *who* to personal ones. This is, however, mainly in writing, while in spEModE, *that* is as frequent with personal as with nonpersonal antecedents, as shown by the figures presented in Table 15.3.

4.2 *Who*, *whom* and *whose*

Who as a nominal relative meaning 'whoever, anyone who' is often used in Middle English (see Meier 1967: 281; Steinki 1932: 29; Poutsma 1926–1929: 985) but is not very frequent in the EModE period. *Who* as adnominal relative (i.e. in postmodifying relative clauses) first occurred with deities in the closing formulas of letters, with a personal name, and in nonrestrictive relative clauses (see Rydén 1983; Rissanen 1999: 294; Nevalainen and Raumolin-Brunberg 2002: 116–118). Not until the beginning of the 18th century, however, did *who* replace *which* with most types of personal antecedents (Rydén 1983: 132). Most examples of *who* in spEModE are with personal names, as in example (20).

(20) Wil. *I am not Beaux enough for that yet. To be short then,* Beliria **who** *you know lives with, and governs my Lady* Young-Love, (1696 Drama, Manley, *The Lost Lover*)

As subject with personal antecedents, *who* is considerably less frequent than *that* in my spEModE data (*who*: 24% and *that*: 69%, see Table 15.3 above). *Who* is common as subject with a personal antecedent only with proper names (see example 20 above) and in "progressive" (or "continuative") relative clauses. Progressive relative clauses (see Rydén 1966: xlvii; Jespersen 1927: 83) are a type of nonrestrictive relative clause where the narrative is continued and expanded introducing a new element of action or a fact about the antecedent (see Rydén 1966: xlviii; Abbott 1966 [1870]: 176). In progressive clauses, *who* can be substituted by e.g. "and he", as in examples (21)–(22).

(21) RAWLINS ANSWERS. [...] she said to me Madam I pity you, will no body Bail you? she told me I will send to my Brother **who** shall be Bail for you, (1702 Trials, Haagen Swendsen)

(22) Mask. [...] For your honest man, as I take it, is that nice, scrupolous, conscientious Person, **who** will cheat nobody but himself; such another Coxcomb, as your wise man, **who** is too hard for all the World, (1694 Drama, Congreve, *The Double-Dealer*)

When *who* appears with a nonpersonal noun or an animal in spEModE (Table 15.3: four examples or 1%), some element of personification is involved. Personification of nonpersonal antecedents is found in literary EModE texts (e.g. in Shakespeare; cf. Abbott 1966 [1870]: 179–180; Franz 1924: 295). Example (23) is from Lyly's comedy, where literary, or rather poetical, language is more frequent than in the other plays studied.

(23) Alex. *Not with* Timoclea *you meane, wherein you resemble the Lapwing,* **who** *crieth most where her neast is not.* (1584 Drama, Lyly, *Alexander and Campaspe*)

Whom and *whose* appear earlier than *who* as relativizers in Middle English and EModE. The use of the inflected forms could have favored the introduction of nominative/subjective *who*, to fill a gap in the paradigm (Steinki 1932: 30; Rydén 1983: 130). *Whom*, like *who*, is mainly used with reference to persons or human nouns but instances of *whom* with nonpersonal antecedents also occur, e.g. in Elyot's writings from the early 16th century (Rydén 1966: 34–35). In my spEModE texts, *whom* occurs only with a personal noun (see Table 15.3) as in (24).

(24) Capt. Harris, *The next night I went to look for Sir* George Barclay, **whom** *the King told me I should certainly find by such a Sign of a White Handkerchief hanging out of his Pocket,* (1696 Trials, Ambrose Rookwood)

The possessive relativizer *whose* is mostly used with a personal antecedent in spEModE, as in example (25).

(25) Host. *To be scarce, is to be rare: and therefore where as he sayes Gentles* **whose** *wits be scarce, is as much as to say, Gentles* **whose** *wits be rare.* (1599 Drama, Chapman, *An Humerous Dayes Myrth*)

When nonpersonal *whose* occurs in spEModE, some implications of personal qualities or characteristics can be discerned (the nouns referred to include *beauty* and *face*). Historically, *whose* is the genitive of both personal (*who*) and nonpersonal (*which*) antecedents (see Campbell 1983: 292; Jespersen 1927: 116, 129).

4.3 *Which*

Which could refer to both a personal and nonpersonal antecedent in EModE. With regard to written EModE and the early 16th century, Rydén (1966: 277) reports that in Elyot as many as 53% of the instances of *which* refer to a person. The works of Thomas Starkey (c.1535) and the Tyndale Bible (1525) show as much as 77% and 80% personal *which*, respectively. In the period 1600–1649, the figure for personal *which* is 10% (Dekeyser 1984: 71). The situation is different in the spEModE data used in this study: in only 5% of the examples does *which* refer to a personal antecedent (see Table 15.3: *which* as subject: 2% and as object 3%). My spEModE data does not reveal whether personal *which* decreases further. The few examples that occur are from the second period 1680–1719. Most of the examples of personal *which* are from Trials, as in example (26).

(26) Mrs Busby. *[...] I saw a man in the Coach, which was* Hartwel *the Bayliff,* (1702 Trials, Haagen Swendsen)

Personal *which* occurs in witnesses' speech as opposed to that of members of the legal profession. However, it is not possible to ascertain whether the use of *which* with persons in my spEModE data is typical of a particular social rank or speaker role (in Present-day English personal *which* occurs in nonstandard spoken language and in dialects, see Hughes et al. 2005: 29; Kjellmer 2002).

Which tends to be much less frequent than *that* with all types of antecedent: nouns, names and pronouns. In spEModE, *which* seems to be frequent only where *that* is not used or for some reason is not the preferred relativizer. *Which* is used in sentential relative clauses with a clausal antecedent (where *that* does not occur, see Section 3.2) and in non-adjacent relative clauses, i.e. relative clauses that are at some distance from their antecedent. *Which* is then felt to be a more explicit construction than *that* as regards reference (Steinki 1932: 16–17; Rissanen 1984: 424; Jespersen 1927: 122). Furthermore, *which* is found with *that* + noun to avoid repetition of *that*, in e.g. *that cloake which*, *that Matter which* and in the combination *that which* (i.e. the nominal relative *what* in Present-day English). In adverbial relative clauses with a temporal or locative noun such as *time*, *day* and *place* as antecedent, *which* is the only alternative when a preposition precedes the relativizer. See example (27).

(27) Lord Townshend. *My Lord, having receiv'd Information that there was a Treasonable Correspondence carry'd on between the late Duke of Ormond, Duke D'Aumont, Coulange and Mr.* Harvey, **in which** *the Prisoner was concern'd, and was the Channel* **in which** *the Correspondence was convey'd;* (1716 Trials, Francis Francia)

The construction *the which* is extremely rare in my spEModE material. Only three examples occur and the relativizer is preceded by the preposition *of*. Two of the three examples are found in the Trial of the Duke of Norfolk, see example (28). Individual writers between 1520 and 1560 prefer *the which* but it is not frequent generally (see Rydén 1966: 278–279).

(28) Attorney. *[...] so that there was for every Name a Cypher,* **of the which** *40 was for the Duke, and 30 for the Lord* Lumley. (1571 Trials, Thomas Howard Duke of Norfolk)

Of which as an alternative to *whose* with nonpersonal antecedents is first recorded in Middle English (see Johansson 2002; Schneider 1993). *Of which* does not replace its main rival *whereof* until the second half of the 17th century and it is not a frequent alternative to *whose* in the EModE period (Schneider 1993: 253). Only one example of *of which* occurs in my spEModE texts, see example (29). However, the emergence and use of the *of which* construction is important as an example of the desire in EModE times to mark more clearly the personal/nonpersonal contrast. *Whose* is increasingly regarded as the possessive relativizer only for a personal noun (cf. Dekeyser 1984: 70–71).

(29) Lord Townshend. *[...] was after that Letter had been deliver'd to me, the Contents* **of which** *will sufficiently justifie the Precautions used in that Warrant.* (1716 Trials, Francis Francia)

4.4 The zero construction

This construction occurs with both personal and nonpersonal antecedents in spEModE but is most frequent with the nonpersonal category. As is the case with *that*, the zero relativizer is particularly frequent with certain types of antecedent: *nothing* (as in example 30), *something*, *any thing*, *all*, the general noun *thing* and with a superlative + noun.

(30) Bell. *I have nothing Ø I can call my own; you, like a bold Invader, have born away by force what else my Faith and Love had offer'd.* (1719 Drama, Killigrew, *Chit-Chat*)

Furthermore, a zero relativizer is often used in prepositional constructions with a stranded preposition (see Section 5.2), in cleft sentences, as in example (31), and in adverbial relative clauses, mainly with time expressions, as in example (32).

(31) Flor. *But since such a one is not upon Earth, I shall insist 'tis in Resistance Ø we acquire our Fame.* (1719 Drama, Killigrew, *Chit-Chat*)

(32) Town. *[...] The Day Ø we din'd last together,* Bellamar *negligently went into the Room before* Lurcher, *sate upon his Right Hand at Table.* (1719 Drama, Killigrew, *Chit-Chat*)

In my spEModE material, the zero construction is used more frequently in the Drama texts than in the Trials. It seems as if the zero construction is one feature that individual playwrights want to include in their characters' dialogue. As mentioned earlier in this paper, there is an important difference between the two spEModE periods here: the zero relativizer is nearly twice as frequent in the period 1680–1719 (see Table 15.1 above). It is of course not possible to maintain that the increase in the use of the zero construction mirrors real dialogue at the time but the playwright may just be anxious to render EModE speech as closely as possible. Drama is more speech-related in some respects, as interruptions and lexical repetitions reveal (see Culpeper and Kytö 1999: 293–312, 2000: 179–185). In Killigrew's comedy *Chit-Chat* (1719), the zero construction is used very often by characters representing the higher social classes. In this comedy, the zero relativizer is used with most of the typical antecedents of zero (e.g. *person(s)*, *people*, *thing*, *nothing*) and in clefts and adverbial relative clauses, see examples (31)–(32) above. Individual writers and letter writers use zero, but it is rare in the early 16th century (Rydén 1966: 286, 294–295, cf. also Table 15.1 above).

When the zero relativizer functions as object (direct + prepositional) with nonpersonal antecedents in spEModE, it is slightly more frequent (36%) than both *that* (31%) and *which* (33%, see Table 15.3). When, on the other hand, the zero construction functions as subject, it is rare and mainly restricted to certain syntactic environments. This will be discussed in the next section, which deals with how the subject function of the relativizers is realized (see Section 5.1).

5 Forms and functions of the relativizers

This section will focus on the forms and functions of EModE relativizers, more precisely, *whom* and zero as subject, and preposition + relativizer as prepositional object.

5.1 *Whom* and the zero construction as subjects

In examples (33) and (34) below, *whom* is the subject of the main clause and at the same time the object of the inserted clauses *he then well knew* and *they said*. Such relative clauses are a type of blended construction (or "push-down relative clauses"; see Quirk et al. 1985: 1118–1120; Quirk 1957: 103 for Present-day English examples). As is the case in Present-day English, there was in EModE, a tendency to regard *whom* as the direct object of the verb in the main clause (see Visser 1963: 495–496). Jespersen (1927: 198–199) refers to "the speech-instinct", which does not readily accept two subjective forms in the same clause. As shown in Table 15.3, there are only four examples in my spEModE texts. Hence it is hardly possible to argue that subjective *whom* is a frequent feature of the spoken language.

(33) Serj. *[...] his Practice to join himself in marriage with the Scotish Queen, **whom** he then well knew falsely to claim and pretend Title to the present possession to the Crown of England:* (1571 Trials, Thomas Howard Duke of Norfolk)

(34) Mrs Rawlins. *There was a Minister in the House, **whom** they said had been there about a quarter of an hour but I supposed longer,* (1702 Trials, Haagen Swendsen)

As with subjective *whom*, examples of the zero construction as subject are not very frequent in my spEModE data (Table 15.3: 3% for both personal and non-personal antecedents). Zero occurs mainly in presentative constructions, such as *'tis, who is it ...* (in cleft sentences), *there is* and *here is* (Rydén 1966: 268–269; Curme 1931 235–236; Poutsma 1926-29: 995, 1001; Tottie and Johansson 2015). See examples (35) and (36). Zero as subject could be taken as a feature that is more typical of EModE speech than of literary language. The zero relativizer as subject occurs for instance in Shakespeare (cf. Abbott 1966 [1870]: 164; Barber 1997: 115–116), but is extremely rare in Elyot's works and those of his contemporaries in the early 16th century (Rydén 1966: 278, 290).

(35) L. C.J.H. *Who was it Ø came to you?* (1702 Trials, Haagen Swendsen)

(36) Scrub. *[...] There's not Day Ø goes over his Head without Dinner or Supper in this House.* (1707 Drama, Farquhar, *The Beaux Stratagem*)

Zero as subject does not, however, increase in the second spEModE period (1680–1719), as is the case with the zero construction as object and prepositional object.

5.2 Preposition + relativizer as prepositional object

As in Present-day English, prepositional objects (and adverbials) in EModE could be expressed in different ways, depending on the placement of the preposition; both preposition + *whom/which* ("pied piping") and *whom/which/that/zero* + preposition ("stranding") occur. First, it should be noted that the object function is one of the few functions where *that* is not the most frequent form in spEModE. Table 15.3 above indicates that with personal antecedents, *whom* is most frequent (41%), whereas the most common relativizer with a nonpersonal antecedent is the zero construction (36%). If only prepositional objects are considered, *that* (+ a stranded preposition) is, again, the most frequent form with both types of antecedent, 50% (see Table 15.4). When a *wh*-form is used, pied piping is the most common pattern. With *whom* it is the only pattern, whereas *which* occurs with a stranded preposition in a few examples (see Table 15.4). What is most interesting, however, is that stranding is nearly twice as common (63%) as preposition + relativizer (37%) in my spEModE material.

Table 15.4: Prepositional objects in spEModE: placement of preposition

Function	Prepositional object		
	Pied piping	Stranding	Total
That	—	26 (50%)	26
Whom	8 (26%)	—	8
Which	23 (74%)	8 (15%)	31
Zero	—	18 (35%)	18
Total	31 (37%)	52 (63%)	83 (100%)

A construction with a stranded preposition was not generally looked upon as informal style in the EModE period. It is at the beginning of the 18th century that some writers started questioning the correctness of preposition stranding (see

Visser 1963: 402–403). The fact remains, however, that stranding is the preferred pattern in spEModE and possibly it was or became associated more with spoken than with written EModE. In example (37), stranding with Ø and *that* is illustrated.

(37) Mr. Conyers. *My Lord, the first Meeting Ø Mr. Porter speaks **of**, where the Prisoner Mr. Rookwood was, is at the Globe-Tavern, where this Discourse was; the next Meeting **that** he speaks **of**, was on the Friday Night, before the first Saturday [...]* (1696 Trials, Ambrose Rookwood)

Preposition + *which* is the predominant pied piping pattern. It occurs in 74% of the pied piping constructions (see Table 15.4). Often preposition + *which* seems to be obligatory due to the complexity of the sentence structure, as in example (38). Rydén (1966: 297) states that preposition + *which* is preferred by individual writers in the early 16th century (e.g. Sir Thomas More and William Tyndale).

(38) Do. *[...] that caulfe with a white face is his faire daughter, **with which**, when your fields are richly filled, then will my race content you,* (1599 Drama, Chapman, *An Humerous Dayes Mirth*)

6 Summary

This paper describes the use of relativizers in EModE, focusing on speech-related Trials and Drama texts (spEModE). The periods studied are 1560–1599 and 1680–1719.

What is most striking as regards the use of relativizers in my spEModE material is the predominance of the relativizer *that*. Although the *wh*-forms start competing with *that* also in restrictive relative clauses (mainly in writing), *that* does not decrease in frequency to any great extent. *That* is used with all types of personal and nonpersonal antecedents, nouns, proper names, and pronouns. It occurs in both restrictive and nonrestrictive relative clauses but decreases in nonrestrictive relative clauses in the second spEModE period (1680–1719).

Who does not really threaten the position of *that* as subject with personal antecedents in spEModE: it is used in only 24% of the examples (often with proper names). Instead, it is *which* that disappears more and more with a personal antecedent. The real threat to the position of *that* in spEModE is the zero construction, which increases and is nearly twice as frequent in the second spEModE period (1680–1719). The zero construction is more common with nonpersonal antecedents than *that* but is used as frequently as *that* with antecedents such as *all*, *nothing*, and a superlative + noun. The function of direct object with non-personal antecedents is the only function where *that* is not predominant in my spEModE texts. Here, the zero construction is the most frequent relativizer.

At the end of the EModE period studied in this paper, we recognize many of the features of Present-day English usage of relativizers. These features probably appeared earlier in spEModE texts: *which* is more or less restricted to nonpersonal antecedents, *that* occurs mainly in restrictive relative clauses where it is particularly common with *all*, *nothing*, *thing* and superlatives + noun. Also, the zero construction increases in frequency. However, it is important to note that in spEModE around 1700, *who* is not yet a frequent alternative to *that* with personal antecedents.

Acknowledgments: First of all, I want to thank Mats Rydén for valuable comments on my paper and for taking a special interest in my work. I also want to thank Angela Falk, Christer Geisler, Edward Long, and Terry Walker for valuable comments, and I am grateful to Christer Geisler and Merja Kytö for their help in suggesting and providing the material from *A Corpus of English Dialogues*.

7 References

Abbott, E. A. 1966 [1870]. *A Shakespearian Grammar: An Attempt to Illustrate Some of the Differences between Elizabethan and Modern English*. New York: Dover Publications.
Ball, Catherine N. 1996. A diachronic study of relative markers in spoken and written English. *Language Variation and Change* 8: 227–258.
Barber, Charles. 1997. *Early Modern English*. 2nd edn. Edinburgh: Edinburgh University Press.
Biber, Douglas. 1988. *Variation across Speech and Writing*. Cambridge: Cambridge University Press.
Campbell, Alistair. 1983. *Old English Grammar*. Oxford: Oxford University Press.
Culpeper, Jonathan and Merja Kytö. 1999. Modifying pragmatic force: Hedges in Early Modern English dialogues. In: Andreas Jucker, Gerd Fritz, and Franz Lebsanft (eds.), *Historical Dialogue Analysis*, 293–312. Amsterdam/Philadelphia: John Benjamins.
Culpeper, Jonathan and Merja Kytö. 2000. Data in historical pragmatics: Spoken interaction (re)cast as writing. *Journal of Historical Pragmatics* 1(2): 175–199.
Culpeper, Jonathan. 2001. *Language and Characterisation. People in Plays and Other Texts*. London: Pearson Education/Longman.
Curme, George O. 1931. *Syntax*. Vol. III: *A Grammar of the English Language*. Boston: Heath.
Dekeyser, Xavier. 1984. Relativizers in Early Modern English. A dynamic quantitative study. In: Fisiak (ed.), 61–87.
Fisiak, Jacek (ed.). 1984. *Historical Syntax*. Berlin/New York: Mouton de Gruyter.
Franz, Wilhelm. 1924. *Shakespeare-Grammatik*. Heidelberg: Winter.
Hughes, Arthur, Peter Trudgill, and Dominic Watt. 2005. *English Accents and Dialects*. 4th edn. London: Hodder Arnold.

Jacobsson, Bengt. 1994. Nonrestrictive that-*clauses revisited*. *Studia Neophilogica* 66(2): 181–195.
Jespersen, Otto. 1927. *A Modern English Grammar on Historical Principles*. Part III. *Syntax (Second Volume)*. Copenhagen: Munksgaard.
Johansson, Christine. 2002. The relativizers *whose* and *of which* in Middle English. In: Poussa (ed.), 37–49.
Johansson, Christine. 2006. Relativizers in nineteenth-century English. In: Merja Kytö, Mats Rydén, and Erik Smitterberg (eds.), *Nineteenth-century English: Stability and Change*, 136–182. Cambridge: Cambridge University Press.
Kjellmer, Göran. 2002. On relative *which* with personal reference. *Studia Anglica Posnaniensia* 37: 20–38.
Kytö, Merja and Jonathan Culpeper. 2006. *A Corpus of English Dialogues 1560–1760*. With the assistance of Terry Walker and Dawn Archer. Uppsala University and Lancaster University. http://www.engelska.uu.se/Research/English_Language/Research_Areas/Electronic_Research_Projects/A_Corpus_of_English_Dialogues
Kytö, Merja and Terry Walker. 2006. *Guide to A Corpus of English Dialogues 1560–1760*. Uppsala: Acta Universitatis Upsaliensis.
Meier, H. M. 1967. The lag of relative *who* in the nominative. *Neophilologus* 51(3): 277–288.
Nevalainen, Terttu and Helena Raumolin-Brunberg. 2002. The rise of relative *who* in Early Modern English. In: Poussa (ed.), 109–121.
Poussa, Patricia (ed.). 2002. *Relativization on the North Sea Littoral*. München: Lincom Europa.
Poutsma, Hendrik. 1926–1929. *A Grammar of Late Modern English*. Groningen: Noordhof.
Quirk, Randolph. 1957. Relative clauses in educated spoken English. *English Studies* 38: 97–109.
Quirk, Randolph, Sidney Greenbaum, Geoffrey Leech, and Jan Svartvik. 1985. *A Comprehensive Grammar of the English Language*. London: Longman.
Rissanen, Matti. 1984. The choice of relative pronouns in 17th century American English. In: Fisiak (ed.), 417–435.
Rissanen, Matti. 1999. Syntax. In: Roger Lass (ed.), *The Cambridge History of the English Language*. Vol. III. *1476–1776*, 292–301. Cambridge: Cambridge University Press.
Rydén, Mats. 1966. *Relative Constructions in Early Sixteenth Century English. With Special Reference to Sir Thomas Elyot*. Uppsala: Acta Universitatis Upsaliensis.
Rydén, Mats. 1970. *Coordination of Relative Clauses in Sixteenth Century English*. Uppsala: Acta Universitatis Upsaliensis.
Rydén, Mats. 1974. On notional relations in the relative clause complex. *English Studies* 55: 542–545.
Rydén, Mats. 1983. The emergence of *who* as relativizer. *Studia Linguistica* 37: 126–130.
Rydén, Mats. 1984. När är en relativsats nödvändig? [When is a relative clause essential?]. *Moderna Språk* 78: 19–22.
Schneider, Edgar. 1993. The grammaticalization of possessive *of which* in Middle English and Early Modern English. *Folia Linguistica Historica* 14(1.2): 239–257.
Steinki, Johannes. 1932. *Die Entwicklung der Englischen Relativpronomina in Spätmittelenglischer und Frühneuenglischer Zeit*. Breslau: Die Schlesische Friedrich-Wilhelms-Universität: Dissertation.
Tottie, Gunnel and Christine Johansson. 2015. Here is an olde mastiffe bitch Ø stands barking at mee: zero subject relativizers in Early Modern English *(t)here* constructions. In: Philip Shaw,

Britt Erman, Gunnel Melchers, and Peter Sundkvist (eds.), *From Clerks to Corpora: Essays on the English Language Yesterday and Today. Essays in Honour of Nils-Lennart Johannesson*, 135–153. Stockholm: Stockholm University Press.

Visser, F. Th. 1963. *An Historical Syntax of the English Language*. Vol. I. *Syntacical Units with One Verb*. Leiden: E. J. Brill.

Colette Moore
Chapter 16:
Literary language

1   Introduction —— 287
2   The construction of literary language —— 289
3   Literary language in its communicative context —— 299
4   Summary —— 305
5   References —— 305

Abstract: Literary language between 1500 and 1700 was strongly influenced by classical models of poetic language from which it imported figures, tropes, and schemes to create a high or grand style for literary genres. Although not all literary language was written in high style, the high style shaped patterns of syntax and lexical usage in literary texts by encouraging copious, excessive, and elaborately ornamental usage. The Early Modern impulse to codify and organize English was reflected in a self-conscious approach to literary language: the period saw the publication of many rhetorics designed to develop and classify literary usage. Literary texts also contributed to English nation-building efforts during the 16th and 17th centuries; efforts to develop a language of literature sought to legitimize English as a medium for artistic expression.

1 Introduction

To define literary language in the Early Modern period – indeed, in any period – is to engage in a circular practice: on its most basic level, literary language is language characteristic of literary genres, but literary genres are identifiable as those genres that employ literary language. Moreover, as the Russian formalist Yury Tynyanov (2000[1924]: 29–49) pointed out, works themselves only resonate within genre systems, and to take a literary work out of its generic context is to change its literary function. What makes literary language literary, then, is our knowledge of its generic function and the place of the genre in a culturally-negotiated hierarchy of aesthetic value. (For further description of thorny problems in defining literary language, see Herman 1983 and Carter and Nash 1983.)

Colette Moore: Seattle (USA)

In order to describe language that is distinctly literary, we find our focus falling inevitably upon usage that is marked in some way – in other words, to describe the features that particularly constitute linguistic art, we attempt to isolate the ways that it differs from other registers. Sixteenth-century rhetorician George Puttenham, for example, describes the ways that literary figures (the tools for poetic ornamentation) depart from ordinary speech in his *Arte of English Poesie* (1589), "As figures be the instruments of ornament in every language, so be they also in a sort abuses [distorted lexis], or rather trespasses [distorted syntax], in speech, because they passe the ordinary limits of common utterance" (Puttenham 2007 [1589]: 238). Puttenham identifies figures as distortions of ordinary syntax and lexicon, and it is, in a sense, this linguistic distortion that we most often see when we examine literary language. Although it is an oversimplification to strictly reduce our understanding of literary language to a set of marked features, any description of literary language necessarily foregrounds some aspects or variables as "literary." "Literary language", in other words, is a perceptual category, and to study it is to study our perceptions of literariness.

For this reason, any examination of Early Modern literary language poses some historical dilemmas of taxonomy. The very phrase *literary language* is anachronistic when applied to the period between 1500 and 1700: the terms *literary* and *literature* do not gain their modern associations with writing in a creative, imaginative, or artistic fashion until the 18th and 19th centuries. Users of Early Modern English certainly had ideas about artistic uses of language, of course, some of which we no longer hold. When 16th-century rhetorician Alexander Gil, for instance, names the six major dialects of English as the general, the Northern, the Southern, the Eastern, the Western, and the Poetic, he nicely calls to our attention the differences between Early Modern ideas of literary language and our own (Gil 1621: 6). Apparently Gil considered poetic language to be identifiable by notable features in the same way that one might characterize a regional dialect. Few poets today, though, would consider their language to be distinct from "general" or regional English, let alone part of a separate (but communally-held) dialect. An obvious question then arises when considering 17th-century poets and theorists such as Gil: if literary language is a perceptual category (as per above), whose perceptions should we examine, theirs or ours? In this section, I attempt to negotiate between these two endeavors, examining a wider variety of uses of literary language than Puttenham and Gil perhaps had in mind, but acknowledging wherever possible Early Modern ideas about language as artistic craft.

Literary language in the early Modern period carries over many of the practices of literary composition from the late Middle Ages, certainly, but it becomes further conventionalized and further developed in the Renaissance, and it is more widespread, more self-conscious, and, as we will see, tied to the growth of English nationalism. The rise of literary language also developed through a confluence of material factors in the 16th century: a radical increase in literacy brought about by the multiplication of grammar schools, the decreasing use of French and Latin in formal settings, and the marked increase in the availability of books owing to cheap paper and the establishment of the printing industry in London. For comparison, we find 54 titles in 1500, but 214 by 1550, and 577 by 1600 (Görlach 1991: 5–7).

The Early Modern period saw the systematizing and theorizing of the words and style of literary English, and the literary register played a larger sociopragmatic role in cultural shifts in England, such as the spread of literacy and the reformulation of English literature as a nationalist project. To examine the language of literature, therefore, this chapter will look at what characterizes the construction of literary language (its syntax and lexicon), and will then discuss the importance of literary language in a larger communicative context (the function of the developing sense of national literature, the pragmatics of language play).

2 The construction of literary language

Our perspectives on literary language are often discussed in terms of registers, or levels of style. What has been called "the high style" or "the grand style" has received particular attention as being the culmination of ornate and ornamental stylings, and was the one most clearly recognized during the Early Modern period as being elevated and suitable for literary purposes (Adamson 2001). Thomas Wilson, in his *Arte of Rhetorique*, called it, "the great or mightie kinde [style], when we vse great wordes, or vehement figures" (Wilson 1909 [1560]: 169). Middle and low styles are present and important for literary writing as well, certainly, in their own right and as foils for high style. In fact, our attention to high style has been disproportionate enough to influence the way that we approach authors and works of the period. A. J. Gilbert (1979: 173) discusses the way that our emphasis on John Donne's high style, for example, has resulted in suppression of low style in editions of his works and a resulting impression of his prose as more elaborate than it actually is. Our emphasis on the high style has also affected the genres that we focus upon: the heroic style of epic and the flowery language of love poetry have been emphasized at the expense of the lyrics of pastoral poetry which are typically written in lower style. (For a contemporaneous, i.e. late 16th century, discussion of types of poetry, see Philip Sidney's *Apology for Poetry* [1970 (1595)].) Yet the spotlight of literary language study falls most prominently on high style because it is the most distinct and most artificial (in the sense of constructed artifice) form of literary language and thus most apparent to observers both in the period and afterwards. The focus on high style (both by Early Modern critics and present-day ones) occurs because it is the most marked of literary forms (as discussed above), and my discussion here will similarly concentrate on this style as being particular to and characteristic of literary language, even though literary language certainly did not use it exclusively.

High style is built around classical models, unusual constructions, involved syntax and noticeably decorative rather than mimetic style. Consider the famous sixteen-line first sentence of *Paradise Lost*, (1):

(1) OF Mans First Disobedience, and the Fruit
 Of that Forbidden Tree, whose mortal tast
 Brought Death into the World, and all our woe,
 With loss of Eden, till one greater Man
 Restore us, and regain the blissful Seat,
 Sing Heav'nly Muse, that on the secret top
 Of Oreb, or of Sinai, didst inspire
 That Shepherd, who first taught the chosen Seed,
 In the Beginning how the Heav'ns and Earth
 Rose out of Chaos: Or if Sion Hill
 Delight thee more, and Siloa's Brook that flow'd
 Fast by the Oracle of God; I thence
 Invoke thy aid to my adventrous Song,
 That with no middle flight intends to soar
 Above th' Aonian Mount, while it pursues
 Things unattempted yet in Prose or Rhime (1667 Milton, *Paradise Lost* ll. 1–16)

The inverted structure of this sentence begins with an extended prepositional phrase, and progresses through a set of extended and embedded relative clauses, yoking syntactic features for an effect that is quite distinct from spoken English. The sentence serves as a distillation of the features of high style: classical models (invocation of the muse), involved syntax, use of rhetorical figures (apostrophe), use of abbreviations (*Heav'nly*, *advent'rous*), conservative morphosyntax (*thee*, *thy*). The passage also declares as well as performs its desire to syntactically rise above the common language – no "middle flight" will do when it "pursues / Things unattempted yet in Prose or Rhime". The literary projects of the Early Modern period developed and refined this ambitious, high-flying style that Milton describes, and although it was certainly not the only form of literary language, it was one of the most noticeable and consciously constructed.

The very term *high* style points to a hierarchy that privileges particular types of language: written language, formal language, the language of the upper classes, the language of the educated. We see contemporaneous attitudes when we look at the coexistence of high and low styles in drama, in which the upper class characters often speak in blank verse and high style oratory, and the lower class characters speak in low style and in prose. Our attitudes towards high style (both the term for it and also the register itself) have shifted over time and altered the goals and construction of literary language. In the last two centuries, our ideals of literary language have grown out of regular speech (cf. Wordsworth's "language really used by men"), and our most literary of works (increasingly novels) are fed by our notions of everyday language. Present-day readers hold it up as a great virtue of literary writing that characters should speak like real people (though, of course, our ideas of what real people sound like remain cultural artifice). In the Renaissance, by contrast, the features of high style followed classical models and were determined by their distinctness from the everyday. This affected both writers who were influenced by ideals of high style and writers (especially later in the 17th century) who rejected them and defined their own styles in opposition.

2.1 Classical models

Renaissance critical practice – and thus, its models for literary composition – drew from classical templates and was primarily directed towards tropes and figures of thought and writing. As the central categories for understanding literary and rhetorical methods of discursive organization, these figures, schemes, and tropes included a broader range of stylistic features than our present-day lists of "figures of speech" take into account. It is difficult for present-day readers to inhabit the mindset required for the 16th century rhetorically inflected literary experience, and to understand the practice of the reader who read Sidney's *Arcadia* with pen in hand, labeling all of the figures and tropes in the margin. (See the frontispiece to Adamson et al.'s 2007 volume for an image of a page of Arcadia marked in this manner.) And while not every reader had equal training, critical reading entailed conversance with dozens of figures (Henry Peacham 1577, for instance, lists nearly 200). Rhetorics of the 16th and 17th century were essentially lists categorizing figures, schemes, and tropes and illustrating their use (even if the relationships between the three were differently negotiated in different sources). The classical categories were imported by Early Modern rhetoricians and adapted in different ways. Bernard Lamy (1676), for example, differentiated between figures and tropes based on functionality. He describes tropes as "an

Ornament to Discourse" (Lamy 1676: 90) and figures as attempts to express passion in language; they are *"Manners of Speaking, different and remote from the ways that are ordinary and natural*; that is to say, quite other than what we use, when we speak without passion" (Lamy 1676: 94–95). Abraham Fraunce (1588: 3) constructs a provenance for tropes in *The Arcadian Rhetorike,* asserting the tropes were invented because of lexical inadequacies, but continued "by reason of the delight and pleasant grace thereof".

Figures are the largest category, and sometimes the superordinate term for all of the techniques, but there can be no exhaustive list of Renaissance figures because rhetoricians were not in complete agreement on what would belong on such a list. I will not attempt to delineate and illustrate the use of figures here (for the clearest categorizing description see the works of Sylvia Adamson, especially Adamson 1999). But the long lists of Greek and Latin figures (from *anadiplosis* to *zeugma*) coalesce around two general categories: figures of varying and figures of amplifying, and these two divisions indicate the richness and amplitude of Early Modern literary style. Figures of varying include ways to multiply words; rhetoricians itemized examples of *paronomasia* (words that begin with the same sound, but have contrasting meanings), *polyptoton* (repetition of the same root word with varying affixes), *paraphrasis* (circumlocutory and excessive discourse), and *diaeresis* (the use of particulars to stand in for general categories). Figures of amplification were designed for elaboration and exaggeration. John Hoskyns described their function in *Directions for Speech and Style*: "To amplify and illustrate are two the chiefest ornaments of eloquence, and gain of men's minds two the chiefest advantages, admiration and belief" (Hoskyns 1935 [1599]: 17).

Although figures functioned as the dominant analytic tool for understanding literary style and rhetorical construction, they eventually began to be viewed with suspicion (as we saw in the quotation from Puttenham in Section 1). Figures and tropes, it was argued, distort ordinary language, they bend the truth, they present reality in an altered way in service of persuading and pleasing the reader, and as such they began to be regarded as potentially morally questionable. Reformers of usage in the 17th century in the cause of science called for the rejection of tropes as tools of falsification: Bacon spoke of them in *The Advancement of Learning* (1605) as "deceiving expectation" (II.V.3), and Thomas Sprat (1667) in his *History of the Royal-Society* (1667) wrote, "Who can behold without indignation how many mists and uncertainties these specious *Tropes* and *Figures* have brought on our Knowledg?" (Section 20; both cited in Partridge 1971: 20). Bernard Lamy warns of the dangers that figures, as expressions of our passions, can also work public feeling in ill ways: "They are Instruments used to shake and agitate the Minds of those to whom we speak: If these Instruments be managed by an unjust Passion, Figures in that Man's Mouth are like a Sword in the Hand of a Mad Man"

(Lamy 1676: 142). Figures and tropes, therefore, were the tools of literary language, but they created anxiety owing to the perceived possibility of abuse. If literary language has the power to inspire us, to move us, to please us, to touch our hearts, it also has the power to incite us, to enrage us, to indulge our destructive emotions. In the wrong hands, literary language seems a dangerous thing.

Striking a balance between levels of style also became more fraught as the period wore on. Navigating between extravagant and barren style has always been a point of cultural taste, and the mounting 17th-century condemnations of over-the-top style merely present a shift of the general taste, and not a complete rejection of all of the elements of Renaissance high style. Dudley North's (1645) *A Forest of Varieties* presents a typical example. He states, "The Poetry of these times abounds in wit, high conceit, figure, and proportions; thinne, light, and emptie in matter and substance; like fine colored ayery bubbles or Quelquechoses, much ostentation and little food" (North 1645: 2), but a few pages later he asserts that we must be sure to elaborate enough because otherwise we risk obscurity: "I feare wee all often unwillingly incurre the errour of it by thinking our meaning as open to others, as to our selves, when indeed the Characters of our expression are fully supplyed by our owne understanding to our selves, whilst to others they are lamely contracted and imperfect" (North 1645: 4). North asserts that we should avoid empty overwriting and sparse underwriting, but he doesn't provide a list of criteria for how we are to distinguish between the two. Ben Jonson also describes the two extremes of style in his early 17th century precepts on style; his description of the body of a language includes a description of the flesh, blood, and bones of style. Fleshy style, he describes, has more than enough and is "fat and corpulent" through, for example, *periphrasis*. The opposite is also a problem: "but where that wanteth, the Language is thinne, flagging, poore, starv'd; scarce covering the bone, and shewes like stones in a sack. Some men, to avoid Redundancy, runne into that; and while they strive to have no ill blood, or Juyce, they loose their good. There be some styles againe, that have not lesse blood, but lesse flesh, and corpulence" (Jonson 1640: 121). Striking the middle path between fleshy style and style that is "thin, flagging, poor, starved, scarce covering the bone", of course, is a point of taste, and different authors have achieved it in different ways. Modern readers find the style of 16th and 17th century literary texts to be more complex and ornate than our present tastes dictate. But many of the issues and choices of style remain the same.

2.2 Syntax and lexicon

The features of high style shaped the syntax of Early Modern literary language, pulling the sentential organization in the direction of involved syntax and encouraging particular constructions. We see in literary language, for example, an extensive use of subordination, parallelism, balanced clauses, modification, and coordination. These manifest differently in verse and in prose, of course, but the use of modifying words and clauses resulted in some of the long descriptive sentences that we find in Early Modern prose, as in (2).

(2) *Turning from the table, she discerned in the roome a bed of boughes, and on it a man lying, depriued of outward sense, as she thought, and of life, as she at first did feare, which strake her into a great amazement: yet hauing a braue spirit, though shadowed vnder a meane habit, she stept vnto him, whom she found not dead, but laid vpon his back, his head a little to her wards, his armes foulded on his brest, haire long, and beard disordered, manifesting all care; but care it selfe had left him: curiousnesse thus farre affoorded him, as to bee perfectly discerned the most exact peece of miserie; Apparrell hee had sutable to the habitation, which was a long gray robe* (1621 Wroth, *The Countesse of Mountgomeries Urania* 3)

We see, here, both coordinate and subordinate clauses, pre- and post-modifications (*great amazement, braue spirit, haire long, beard disordered*), and inverted syntax (*Apparrell hee had*). Lady Mary Wroth's *The Countess of Montgomery's Urania* is perhaps not a representative literary work in many ways, but a sentence like (2) shows how the full stop (period) organized literary prose less syntactically and more rhetorically. The punctuation indicated pauses of varying lengths – ordering the oral delivery rather than the logical structure, though the functions certainly overlap). Such sentences can therefore seem uncomfortably long to present-day readers. The desire for amplification also resulted in, for example, compounding, as in (3):

(3) a. *With **joy and jollitie** needs round must rove* (1642 More, *Psychodia platonica* 96)
 b. *Viewing Leanders face, **fell downe and fainted*** (1598 Marlowe, *Hero and Leander* sig. C4v.)

Example (3) shows syntactic doublings with the parallels emphasized through the alliteration. These were popular and sometimes formulaic (The phrase "joy and jollity" in (3a), for example, retrieves 23 hits in Early English Books Online [Chadwyck-Healey 2003–11]).

Decorative writing also used words in unusual ways for aesthetic effect. Early Modern English in general was characterized by an increase in functional shift – the conversion of a word from one functional category to another (i.e. noun to verb) – and literary writing particularly exploits the flexibility in morphosyntactic categories. The functional shift derived from the simultaneous liberation of structure from the system of inflectional case endings and the shifting of word order patterns such that synthetic constructions were declining in favor of analytic ones (Rissanen 1999: 187). This looser structure unleashed lexical items from their strict functional categories, and writers were freer to use them in other functional ways:

(4) a. *Cruell and sodaine, hast thou since*
Purpled *thy naile, in blood of innocence?* (1633 Donne, *Poems* 119)
b. *Thy saints trust in thy name,*
*Therin they **joy** them*: (1823 [c.1599] Mary [Sidney] Herbert, Countess of Pembroke, Psalm 52: 93)

In the first instance, Donne uses *purple* as a verb, and in the second Mary (Sidney) Herbert uses *joy* as a verb. These creative functional shifts were one of the hallmarks of Renaissance literary style.

Stylistic expansion happens through doublings, through functional shift, and through elaborations. Some elaborating stylistic strategies came into vogue in the 1580s in the wake of John Lyly's (1578) *Euphues*. The influence on style was so marked that the term *Euphuistic* arose for a style based on comparisons (sometimes reinforced by phonetic cues like alliteration). Here is Lyly's description of his hero:

(5) *This younge gallant, of more wit than wealth, and yet of more wealth than wisdome, seeing himselfe inferiour to none in pleasant conceits, thought himself superiour to al in honest conditions ...* (1578 Lyly, *Euphues* 1)

The syntactic parallelism and semantic patterning – the comparisons (*more wit than wealth*), the relational words (*inferiour to none, superiour to al*) – were a runaway sensation in the 1580s. Notice here, also, the use of figures: *antithesis* (*inferiour to none*) and *isocolon* (*more wit than wealth, more wealth than wisdom*). Euphuistic style had a short run, however, and quickly turned from a popular phenomenon into the object of parody. The very possibility for fads in literary style, though, shows the emerging significance of English literary language, and the readiness of the community of readers for experimentation and wide-ranging transformation in English literary style.

Examining the words of literature is also critical to understanding literary language, and important for our understanding of the Early Modern period in general. Literary texts have been one of the primary sources for our knowledge of the changing lexicon of English in the 16th and 17th centuries: they have been disproportionately represented in the OED, and they constitute a disproportionate slice of extant evidence. And yet we know that literary language is not colloquial language. So examining the words of literature reveals both contemporaneous ideas about the ways that literature may be used as a source for lexical change and about how word choice is related to high style.

James Beattie defines the "English poetic dialect" in 1762 as consisting of seven characteristics: (1) Greek and Latin idioms (*quenched of hope*), (2) words with extra syllables (*dispart*), (3) ancient words (*fealty*), (4) uncommon words (*cates*), (5) abbreviated words (*o'er*), (6) compound epithets (*rosy-finger'd*), (7) nouns transformed into verbs and participles (*cavern'd*) (cited in Sherbo 1975: 1). This analysis, though written after the period in question, was composed largely with Renaissance poetry in mind, so it gives us a fairly good idea of the features of literary (especially poetic) language that stood out for its users and readers. The list itemizes those we might expect: the out-of-the ordinary words, the fancy or elaborate ones: borrowed words, old words, dressed-up words. These are the lexical items that are particularly marked in literary usage and they correspond to (or serve as) stylistic figures.

One prominent aspect of the Renaissance literary lexicon (and an important influence upon word choice) lies in the emphasis on copiousness, an aspect of high style. Erasmus's *De Copia* (1963 [1512]) led the way in describing the abundant or copious style – providing as an example of its methods 144 different ways to say "Thank you for your letter". This verbal excess went along with the figure of *synonymia* and notions of abundance. Consider Peacham's definition and example: "*Synonimia*, when by a variation and change of words, that be of lyke sygnifycation, we iterate one thing divers tymes [...] [s]ometime with words, thus. / *Alas many woes, cares, sorrowes, troubles, calamities, vexations, and miseries doe beseige me round about* [...]" (Peacham 1577: sig. P4r). The driving philosophy seems to be that if one word would do, then two words must be better. Adamson describes the 16th-century prominence of *synonymia* and dates its decline to 1600. After this point, it begins to be considered one of the "vices of style" (Adamson 2007: 18). But through the 16th century, a superfluity of vocabulary was required for literary genres – a stylistic preference which pushed the language not to merely expand its technical and specialized vocabulary, but to expand its general lexicon as well.

A poetic lexicon was also characterized by its excess in degree: beautiful language is ornate and embellished, and so word choice is exaggerated. The use of figures of amplification previously discussed influenced literary lexical choice. *Hyperbole*, for example, is a figure that encourages lexical diversity and lexical superfluity, as Hoskyns illustrates with Sidney's *Arcadia*:

(6) *The world should sooner want occasions than he valour to go through them* (29) (cited in Hoskyns 1999 [1599]: 413)

Other amplification figures center on word opposition, or the choice of words in context, such as *synoeciosis*, a type of contradiction in terms:

(7) *A wanton modesty, and an enticing soberness* (315) (cited in Hoskyns 1999 [1599]: 415)

These excessive words were characteristic of literary language, and certain genres in particular. A passage from *Edward III* that is widely attributed to Shakespeare mocks over-the-top words in love poetry:

(8) *Better then bewtifull thou must begin,*
Deuise for faire a fairer word then faire,
And euery ornament that thou wouldest praise,
Fly it a pitch above the soare of praise,
For flattery feare thou not to be conuicted,
For were thy admiration ten tymes more,
Ten tymes ten thousand more [the] worth exceeds
Of that thou art to praise, [thy] praise's worth, (1596 Shakespeare(?), *Edward III* 13)

In this passage, Edward III wants words that are bigger, better, and more beautiful than the typical words for describing beauty. The speaker asserts that one could never overstate the beauty of the referent, a parody of the vocabulary of amplification. And the passage exemplifies the poetic ideals that it describes, in the use of *polyptoton* in *fair, fairer, fair*; in the four-fold repetition of *praise* (both as a verb and a noun), and the amplification of the numbers created by the rearranged syntax of the final clause: *ten times more,/ ten times ten thousand more*.

Marked literary words also include borrowed words, or, as they were disparagingly called, "inkhorn terms". The very existence of disparaging terms in the period for the practice of borrowing words itself shows how prevalent the practice became during the Early Modern period and also how the practice was employed: inkhorn terms were born of the inkwell, and therefore (we presume) they were more frequent in literary language than in common speech. Aureate diction (popularized in the 15th century by John Lydgate) continued in the literature of the 16th century and was characterized by its Latinate lexical stylings. Even writers who disapproved of the practice of excessive borrowing from Romance languages were obliged to take issue with it in these same borrowed words because the English lexicon was already so full of loan words. Estimating the borrowing practices using the OED electronic record shows that Latin borrowing exceeded French in the period, and that the influx of Latin loan words peaked between 1575–1675, with more than 13,000 loan words entering the lexicon during that time (Culpeper and Clapham 1996: 218; Nevalainen 2006: 53). It is more difficult to estimate, of course, the difference between bookish usage and oral usage with respect to borrowed words, but it is reasonable to assume that the large-scale Latin borrowing of the Early Modern period was much more characteristic of written, formal, restricted, and technical genres. Since the OED records disproportionately represent literary sources in the Early Modern period, the recorded 13,000 Latin borrowings in the century between 1575–1675 must also be disproportionately literary (see further Lancashire, Chapter 6).

Another aspect of literary words is the greater prevalence of compounds, as in (9). This is a long-standing technique of literary style with both classical precedent (*the wine-dark sea*) and Anglo-Saxon (kennings like *whale-road*).

(9) a. *Saphir-winged Mist* (1681 Marvell, *Upon Appleton House, to my Lord Fairfax* 100)
 b. *dewy-feather'd Sleep* (1646 Milton, *Il Penseroso* 43)

Facilitated by the diminishment of case endings and the more fluid functionality of words, compounding was one of a range of creative solutions that Early Modern English exploited to expand the lexicon. Beattie's list at the beginning of this section, moreover, suggests that readers perceived compounds to be a particularly characteristic feature of poetic language.

Beattie also focuses in his list on the use of abbreviated words. George Gascoigne similarly mentions the practice of reduction as part of poetic licence; he gives examples like "'o'ercome' for 'overcome'", "'ta'en' for 'taken'", and "'heav'n' for 'heaven'", but he also mentions additions like "'ydone' for 'done'" and substitutions like "'thews' for 'good parts'" (Gascoigne 1999 [1575]: 168). Jonathan Swift (1712) complains about this practice as well in his *Proposal for Correcting, Improving and Ascertaining the English Tongue*. He condemns the practice as "barbarous" and blames Restoration poets for it, claiming that they shorten words for metrical reasons. Yet all of the examples that he gives (*drudged, disturbed, rebuked, fledged*) have reduced final syllables in Present-day English, and this is probably not owing to the influence of poetry. Swift and Gascoigne's assessments serve to emphasize that abbreviated words and the use of apostrophes to indicate truncated syllables were a marked feature of poetry, marked to the extent that Swift attempted to blame poetry for the phonological deletion.

While "literary style" is certainly composed of elements present in the language as a whole, particular features and constructions are observed to be characteristic of literary genres. In the Early Modern period, these perceptual aspects were likely to be associated with high style or poetic language: classical figures, complex syntax, Latinate words, functional shift, compounding, abbreviation (of words), and amplification (in lexical choice, in phrases, and in discourse). Not all language in literary texts adhered to this description, of course, but the language perceived to be the most literary did.

3 Literary language in its communicative context

3.1 Literature as nationalist project

I will now move on to contextualize the ways that this register of literary language assumed a particular cultural function in Early Modern England. The proliferation of literary texts in both the classical and the vernacular languages was accompanied by the rise of literature as an English national project in the Early Modern period. Richard Mulcaster remarks in an oft-cited peroration to his *Elementarie*:

> For is it not in dede a meruellous bondage, to becom seruants to one tung for learning sake, the most of our time, with losse of most time, whereas we maie haue the verie same treasur in our own tung, with the gain of most time? our own bearing the ioyfull title of our libertie and fredom, the Latin tung remembring us, of our thraldom & bondage? I loue Rome, but London better, I fauor Italie, but England more, I honor the Latin, but I worship the English (Mulcaster 1582: 254).

Mulcaster famously describes here the way that the choice of English for learning and literature is a point of national pride, even a rejection of bondage. Mulcaster, a schoolmaster, presumably passed some of these opinions on to his students, and indeed we find that his most illustrious student, Edmund Spenser, went on to use and adapt the English tongue for his own nationalist projects (as will be discussed below).

English language historians have long noted that the developing sense of nationhood in the 16th century was accompanied by greater attention to codifying

English. And English literary historians have similarly noted that the 16th century begins a period of increased consciousness of and attention to a national literature. The two of these overlap in the increased attention to codifying literary language in the Early Modern period: the rise in production of rhetorics, studies of poetic language, and guides to figures and schemes. Developing a self-consciously national literature must involve, in part, a consideration of what constitutes literary art. And the proliferation of rhetorical and critical texts testifies to a national energy that developed in the period for classifying and cataloguing literary language. Earlier in the *Elementarie*, for example, Mulcaster (1582: 77) describes his ambitions: "therefore I will first shew, that there is in our tung great and sufficient stuf for Art: then that there is no such infirmitie in our writing, as is pretended, but that our custom is grown fit to receaue this artificiall frame [...]". Mulcaster asserts that the English language is suitable to be adapted for artistic purposes, and we find a collective initiative in that direction. Explicit attention to the analysis of rhetorical and poetic tools created a larger awareness of them among both writers and readers, making them more fundamental to the expressed characteristics of literary genres and meaning that the act of authorship became in part a dialogue with other crafters of style. The industry of literary creation becomes driven by the need to engage with and personalize figures and tropes, adapting them for the English literary tradition. Puttenham identifies expressly this as his motivation for renaming the classical figures and tropes with English names:

> But when I consider to what sort of readers I write, and how ill-faring the Greek term would sound in the English ear; then also how short the Latins come to express many of the Greek originals; finally, how well our language serveth to supply the full signification of them both, I have thought it no less lawful, yea, peradventure, under license of the learned, more laudable, to use our own natural, if they be well chosen and of proper signification, than to borrow theirs. *So shall not our English poets, though they be to seek of the Greek and Latin languages, lament for lack of knowledge sufficient to the purpose of this art.* (Puttenham 2007 [1589]: 3.9.242 [italics mine]).

Puttenham's manual makes the tools of literary analysis (figures) available to his audience and it brings these to its readers in English rather than by simply importing the Greek and Latin terms. Puttenham's anglicizations did not catch on, of course, and we now smile at his attempts to rename *hyperbole* as *the Overreacher* (3.18.276) or *micterismus* as *the Fleering Frump* (3.18.275). But the drive to improve English, to make it a language for art and for analysis was a powerful motivation, and the literary language of the Early Modern period was both a product of and an engine for this national self-improvement impulse.

One stylistic feature pressed into nationalistic service was purposefully archaic or conservative English. Archaisms represent for some a purer English, unadulterated by Latin and the romance languages. Edmund Spenser's *The Faerie Queene* is typically perceived as the foremost Early Modern example of a poet employing purposeful archaism for nationalist ends, as shown in (10).

(10) *High time it seemed then for euery wight*
Them to betake vnto their kindly rest;
Eftsoones long waxen torches weren light,
Vnto their bowres to guiden euery guest:
Tho when the Britonesse saw all the rest
Auoided quite, she gan her selfe despoile,
And safe commit to her soft fetherednest,
Where through long watch, & late dayes weary toile,
She soundly slept, & carefull thoughts did quite assoile (1596 Spenser, *The Faerie Queene* 407)

Stanzas like the above show Spenser's stylistic choice of archaic or conservative diction (*wight, eftsoones, assoile*), his use of old morphosyntactic forms (*weren, guiden, gan*), and his use of conservative semantic senses (*kindly* meaning 'natural'). The conservative forms and lexical choices evoke for the reader the early English poetic tradition (*wight*, for example, is a common word in Middle English alliterative poetry). The use of these older forms and words created a veneer of older language for readers of *The Faerie Queene*, instantiating through the style the creation of an authorizing epic for Elizabeth I, and lending it an air of solemnity and historicity. To write an English epic, then, Spenser selects what he sees as the purest "English" in the linguistic repertoire. The dedicatory epistle to his *Shepheardes Calender* (Spenser 1579) sets out the philosophy of such literary projects. This prefatory section (by an author named as "E. K.", but who may be Spenser himself) sets out Spenser's ambitions to restore older English:

> he hath laboured to restore, as to theyr rightfull heritage such good and naturall English words, as have ben long time out of use and almost cleare disherited. Which is the onely cause, that our Mother tonge, which truely of it self is both ful enough for prose and stately enough for verse, hath long time ben counted most bare and barrein of both. Which default when as some endevoured to salve and recure, they patched up the holes with peces and rages of other languages, borrowing here of the french, there of the Italian, every where of the Latine, not weighing how il, those tongues accorde with themselves, but much worse with ours: So now they have made our English tongue, a gallimaufray or hodgepodge of al other speches (1579 Spenser sig. ¶2v).

E. K. praises Spenser for reviving long-neglected English words to remedy the deficits perceived in English as a literary language. He applauds the use of archaism over large-scale borrowing. In this ideological framework, older words were commonly regarded as better and more venerable, and newer words (especially borrowed words) as suspect.

Archaism can come in the choice of Anglo-Saxon words, or in the form of older morphosyntactic variants. The inflectional ending -s for the third person present singular verb appears with more and more frequency in the 16th and 17th centuries in the place of the -th endings (*he goes* rather than *he goeth*), but the Early Modern period witnesses the coexistence of the two: the -s ending is the more progressive form and the -th ending is the more conservative (Nevalainen 2006: 89–92; see further Cowie, Chapter 4). This permits a choice between the two: a choice which could be partly syntactic. Frequency is one predictor for the use of more conservative forms (thus, the -th forms *doth*, *hath* and *saith* are more resistant than most other verbs), but so is the genre of the text: the higher the style of the writing, the more conservative the forms are likely to be. The Authorized Version of the Bible (the King James version), for example, is well-known for immortalizing some of these older morphosyntactic variables as religious-sounding language by consistently employing the conservative -th forms, as well as now-archaic plurals like *kine* and *brethren*. The desire of literary language to utilize styles that are elevated and formal has kept variants alive in poetry long after they were moribund in speech. Consider the use of the second person *thou/thee* pronouns which were utilized in poetry even through the 19th-century, and still sound vaguely poetic to our contemporary ear (see further Busse, Chapter 12). Examples like these second person singular pronouns show us how morphosyntactic features can move from functioning grammatically and referentially to functioning also as markers of a literary register.

Early Modern texts do show some overlap between the purposeful use of archaism and the literary use of dialect. It can often be difficult to distinguish dialectal forms from archaic ones; the use of Northern dialectal forms in poems like *The Shepheardes Calender* (Spenser 1579) creates confusion in many places about whether Spenser was trying to employ a dialectal form or an archaic one. The two, indeed, were viewed as related: Northern English was seen as older and less tainted by foreign borrowings (Blank 1996: 100). The dialect used in poetry was apparently usually the English of northern England, if Alexander Gil is to be believed. Northern English attained the stylistic *gravitas* of an acceptable regional dialect for poetry, in a way that the dialect of, for example, Dorset only did later.

3.2 Language play

The use of dialect also functions in this period as comic material, especially in Early Modern drama: this period begins to see more evidence of dialect comedy and playful contrasts in register. Although literary depiction of dialect does not originate in the Renaissance – we see some dialect representation in literary language in Chaucer, for example – it becomes much more developed, and there is more evidence of dialect as a stylistic tool for literary use, for characterization, realism, disguise, comedy. This includes the use of regional dialects and also some subcultural dialects, such as cant, the language of the London underworld. The specialized lexicon of thieves and other lawbreakers was apparently of great interest to the reading public – over 100 glossaries of cant and slang were published between 1567 and 1784, according to Coleman (2008). Cant had quite a developed literary presence, and a number of plays feature the use of cant: Thomas Dekker and Thomas Middleton's *The Roaring Girle* (1607–1610), Richard Brome's *A Jovial Crew or the Merry Beggars* (1641), and Francis Beaumont, John Fletcher, and Philip Massinger's *The Beggars' Bush* (1622). The literature of cant also includes other descriptions of social outliers, from Samuel Rowlands's *Slang Beggars' Songs* (1610) to Daniel Defoe's *The Complete Mendicant* (1699) (all available – with the exception of Rowlands – on Early English Books Online [Chadwyck-Healey 2003–2011]).

The Early Modern period employed language for other playful purposes: flyting (the art of insulting), political satire, punning. Some texts accomplish all of the ends at once – more than one of John Skelton's verses is devoted to ridiculing assorted public figures, as in (11).

(11) *His hed is so fat*
 He wotteth neuer what
 Nor wherof he speketh
 He cryeth and he creketh
 He pryeth and he peketh
 He chydes and he chatters
 He prates and he patters
 He clytters and he clatters
 He medles and he smatters
 He gloses and he flatters
 Or yf he speake playne
 Than he lacketh brayn (1545 Skelton, *Colyn Cloute* A2v)

This passage from *Colyn Cloute* shows a combination of alliteration, rhyme, and *onomatopoeia* that collude for the purposes of ridicule. And studying the aesthetic pleasures of language entails studying the aesthetic pleasures of mockery.

From comic plays to humorous verse, literature gives language some of its most playful genres. It even does so with literary language as the butt of the joke; to the extent that the high style provided models for elevated tones in literary writing, it also provided parallel fodder for mockery and lampoon. Characters like Holofernes in Shakespeare's *Love's Labour's Lost* serve as exaggerated users of high style features, and show the pomp and preciousness of Renaissance ornate styling. There is even a name for mock-ridiculous high style: *fustian style*. In 1599 John Hoskyns (cited in Adamson 1999: 576) spoke with pride about his "fustian speech" – a speech delivered in the Middle Temple. Adamson points out that both the terms *bombast* (the overuse of Latinisms) and *fustian* (their playful or anarchic use) develop their metalinguistic senses at the end of the 16th century – both developing out of words for clothing (Adamson 1999: 576). Making fun of the figures and tropes of elevated writing was a way of deflating some of the "height" of high style, but it also serves as evidence for how pervasive these stylistic techniques were. One kind of linguistic joke about the misuse of language came through humorous speech errors on the part of comic characters. Although this comic use of misspeaking is not named "malapropism" until Sheridan's Mrs. Malaprop lends her name to the practice in 1775, the literary exploitation of language errors is, of course, much older. Peacham (1577: sigs. G2v–G3r) calls the figure *cacozelon* and the Renaissance provides several famous examples: Shakespeare's Mistress Quickly and Dogberry among them.

The category of language play might even extend to include aspects of literary language utilized for aesthetic pleasure, such as the rise of certain metrical forms. Metrical structure is a feature of form, certainly, but it also becomes an aspect of cultural context. Communities of writers develop and popularize particular forms, and these forms attain significance within this cultural setting. I will not give here a history of the cultural significance of Early Modern metrics, but it is notable that the Renaissance saw an explosion of energies in metrical form. The period saw such major innovations, for example, as the importing of the sonnet by Sir Thomas Wyatt in the early 16th century, a form that quickly established itself as central to English poetry. As English poets explored the capability of English as a language for poetry, they also attempted to adapt foreign metrical forms to suit English. Some ambitious attempts were ultimately regarded as unsuccessful (see Attridge's 1974 book about the many poets who tried to make the classical dactylic hexameter line work in English), but the shift in poetic meter, the development of the Spenserian stanza, and the development of the blank verse form were radical transformations for the literary tradition. Blank verse, in particular, demonstrated a breadth and flexibility that have made it one of the predominant poetic forms in English. Developments and fads in poetic form are revealing about the ideologies and influences of literary language: how poetry is made English and how the English made poetry.

4 Summary

Literary language is language with a specialized pragmatic purpose, and to examine the literary language of the Early Modern period is to provide perspective on the English that pleased and amused 16th- and 17th-century speakers. It is also the medium for the narratives that people construct about their lives. This is seen in the Early Modern period, for example, in the nationalist pursuit of a particularly English literary tradition. Literary language functions pragmatically in such ways as a culture has defined its notions of literature. In the Renaissance, literary texts – and by extension literary language – were taken as didactic, entertaining, beautiful, morally edifying, and culturally unifying. The stylistic elements that heightened or marked these effects include the decorative elaborations, the stylized comparisons, the elegant repetitions, the passionate metaphors, the comic manglings, and the meticulous figures. All indicate how speakers and writers crafted their language for aesthetic purposes. Certainly it is a testament to their success that we still read and appreciate Early Modern literary texts from many centuries' remove.

5 References

Adamson, Sylvia. 1999. The literary language. In: Lass (ed.), 539–653.
Adamson, Sylvia. 2001. The grand style. In: Sylvia Adamson, Lynette Hunter, Lynne Magnusson, Ann Thompson, and Katie Wales (eds.), *Reading Shakespeare's Dramatic Language: A Guide*, 31–50. London: Arden Shakespeare.
Adamson, Sylvia. 2007. Synonymia: or, in other words. In: Adamson (eds.), 17–36.
Adamson, Sylvia, Gavin Alexander, and Katrin Ettenhuber (eds.). 2007. *Renaissance Figures of Speech*. Cambridge: Cambridge University Press.
Attridge, Derek. 1974. *Well-Weigh'd Syllables: Elizabethan Verse in Classical Metres*. Cambridge: Cambridge University Press.
Blank, Paula. 1996. *Broken English: Dialects and the Politics of Language in Renaissance Writings*. London: Routledge.
Carter, Ronald and Walter Nash. 1983. Language and literariness. *Prose Studies* 6(2): 123–141.
Chadwyck-Healey. 2003–11. *Early English Books Online, 1475–1700 (EEBO)*. Ann Arbor: ProQuest. http://eebo.chadwyck.com/home; last accessed 14 April 2017.
Coleman, Julie. 2008. *A History of Cant and Slang Dictionaries*. Oxford: Oxford University Press.

Culpeper, Jonathan and Phoebe Clapham. 1996. The borrowing of Classical and Romance words into English: A study based on the electronic Oxford English Dictionary. *International Journal of Corpus Linguistics* 1(2): 199–218.

Donne, John. 1633. *Poems by J.D. With elegies on the authors death*. Early English Books Online.

Erasmus, Desiderius 1963 [1512]. *On Copia of Words and Ideas*. Trans. by Donald B. King and H. David Rix. Milwaukee: Marquette University Press.

Fraunce, Abraham. 1588. *The Arcadian rhetorike, or The praecepts of rhetorike made plaine by examples Greeke, Latin, English, Italian, French, Spanish …* London: Printed by Thomas Orwin. Early English Books Online.

Gascoigne, George. 1999 [1575]. A primer of English poetry. In: Vickers (ed.), 162–171.

Gil, Alexander. 1621. *Logonomia Anglica*. Series Logonomia Anglica. (*English Linguistics 1500–1800*, ed. by R. C. Alston, 68.) Menston: The Scolar Press, 1968.

Gilbert, A. J. 1979. *Literary Language from Chaucer to Dryden*. London: Macmillan.

Görlach, Manfred. 1991. *Introduction to Early Modern English*. Cambridge: Cambridge University Press.

Herbert, Mary (Sidney), Countess of Pembroke 1823 [c.1599]. Psalm 52. In: Philip Sidney and Mary (Sidney) Herbert, Pembroke, *The Psalmes of David translated into Divers and Sundry Kindes of Verse, more rare and excellent for the method and varietie than ever yet hath been done in English. Now first printed from a copy of the Original Manuscript, transcribed by John Davies of Hereford in the reign of James the First*, 91–93. London: Chiswick Press.

Herman, Vimala. 1983. Introduction: Special issue on literariness and linguistics. *Prose Studies* 6(2): 99–122.

Hoskins, John. 1935 [1599]. *Directions for Speech and Style*. Ed. by Hoyt Hudson. Princeton: Princeton University Press.

Hoskyns, John. 1999 [1599]. Sidney's Arcadia and the rhetoric of English prose. In: Vickers (ed.), 398–427.

Jonson, Ben. 1640. Timber: or Discoveries; Made Vpon Men and Matter: As they have flow'd out of his daily Readings; or had their refluxe to his peculiar Notion of the Times. In: *The workes of Benjamin Jonson. The Second Volume. Containing These Playes viz. 1. Bartholomew Fayre. 2. The Staple of Newes. 3. The Divell is an Asse*, 410–435. London: Printed for Richard Meighew. Early English Books Online.

Jonson, Ben. 1999 [1615–35]. Notes on Literature. In: Vickers (ed.), 558–589.

Lamy, Bernard. 1676. *The art of speaking written in French by Messieurs du Port Royal in pursuance of a former treatise intituled, The art of thinking*. London: Printed by W. Godbid to be sold by M. Pitt. Early English Books Online.

Lass, Roger (ed.). 1999. *Cambridge History of the English Language*. Vol. III. 1476–1776. Cambridge: Cambridge University Press.

Lyly, John. 1578. *Euphues. The anatomy of vvyt Very pleasant for all gentlemen to reade, and most necessary to remember: wherin are contained the delights that wyt followeth in his youth, by the pleasauntnesse of loue, and the happynesse he reapeth in age, by the perfectnesse of wisedome*. London: T. East for Gabriel Cawood. Early English Books Online.

Marlowe, Christopher. 1598. *Hero and Leander: begun by Christopher Marloe; and finished by George Chapman*. 2nd edn. London: Printed by Felix Kingston, for Paule Linley. Early English Books Online.

Marvell, Andrew. 1681. Upon Appleton House, to my Lord Fairfax. In: *Miscellaneous Poems*. London: Printed for Robert Boulter. Early English Books Online.

Milton, John. 1646. *Il Penseroso*. In: *Poems of Mr. John Milton, both English and Latin, compos'd at several times. Printed by his true copies. / The songs were set in musick by Mr. Henry Lawes Gentleman of the Kings Chappel, and one of His Maiesties private musick. Printed and publish'd according to order*. London: Printed by Ruth Raworth for Humphrey Moseley. Early English Books Online.

Milton, John. 1667. *Paradise Lost. A poem written in ten books*. London: Printed and are to be sold by Peter Parker.., and Robert Boulter..., and Matthias Walker. Early English Books Online.

More, Henry. 1642. *Psychodia platonica, or, A platonicall song of the soul consisting of foure severall poems ... : hereto is added a paraphrasticall interpretation of the answer of Apollo consulted by Amelius, about Plotinus soul departed this life*. Cambridge: Printed by Roger Daniel, printer to the Universitie. Early English Books Online.

Mulcaster, Richard. 1582. *The First Part of the Elementary*. (*English Linguistics 1500–1800*, ed. by R. C. Alston, 219.) Menston: The Scolar Press, 1970.

Nevalainen, Terttu. 2006. *An Introduction to Early Modern English*. Oxford: Oxford University Press.

North, Dudley. 1645. *A Forest of Varieties*. London: Printed by Richard Cotes. Early English Books Online.

Partridge, A. C. 1971. *The Language of Renaissance Poetry: Spenser, Shakespeare, Donne, Milton*. London: Andre Deutsch.

Peacham, Henry. 1577. *The garden of eloquence conteyning the figures of grammer and rhetorick, from whence maye bee gathered all manner of flowers, coulors, ornaments, exornations, formes and fashions of speech, very profitable for all those that be studious of eloquence, and that reade most eloquent poets and orators, and also helpeth much for the better vnderstanding of the holy Scriptures*. London: H. Iackson. Early English Books Online.

Puttenham, George. 2007 [1589]. *The Art of English Poesy*. Ed. by Frank Whigham and Wayne A. Rebhorn. Ithaca: Cornell University Press.

Rissanen, Matti. 1999. Syntax. In: Lass (ed.), 187–326.

Shakespeare, William(?). 1596. *The Raigne of King Edvvard the third: As it hath bin sundrie times plaied about the Citie of London*. London: Printed for Cuthbert Burby. Early English Books Online.

Sherbo, Arthur. 1975. *English Poetic Diction from Chaucer to Wordsworth*. East Lansing: Michigan State University Press.

Sidney, Philip. 1970 [1595]. *An Apology for Poetry*. Indianapolis: Bobbs-Merrill.

Skelton, John. 1545. *Here after foloweth a litel boke called Colyn Cloute compyled by mayster Skelton poete Laureate*. 2nd edn. Early English Books Online.

Spenser, Edmund. 1579. *The shepheardes calender conteyning twelue aeglogues proportionable to the twelue monethes. Entitled to the noble and vertuous gentleman most worthy of all titles both of learning and cheualrie M. Philip Sidney*. London: Printed by Hugh Singleton. Early English Books Online.

Spenser, Edmund. 1596. *The Faerie Queene Disposed into twelue bookes, fashioning XII. morall vertues*. 2nd edn. London: printed by Richard Field for VVilliam Ponsonbie. Early English Books Online.

Swift, Jonathan. 1712. *Proposal for Correcting, Improving and Ascertaining the English Tongue*. (*English Linguistics 1500–1800*, ed. by R.C. Alston, 213.) Menston: The Scolar Press, 1969.

Tynyanov, Yury. 2000 [1924]. The literary fact. In: David Duff (ed.), *Modern Genre Theory*, 29–49. Harlow: Pearson Education.

Vickers, Brian (ed.). 1999. *English Renaissance Literary Criticism*. Oxford: Clarendon Press.
Wilson, Thomas. 1909 [1560]. *Arte of Rhetorique*. Ed. by G. H. Mair. Oxford: Clarendon Press.
Wroth, Lady Mary. 1621. *The Countesse of Mountgomeries Urania*. London: Printed for Iohn Marriott and Iohn Grismand. Early English Books Online.

Ulrich Busse and Beatrix Busse
Chapter 17:
The language of Shakespeare

1 Introduction —— 309
2 General considerations —— 313
3 Phonology —— 314
4 Vocabulary —— 316
5 Grammar —— 320
6 Pragmatics and discourse —— 323
7 Recent trends and further directions —— 326
8 References —— 327

Abstract: The present chapter provides a brief outline of Shakespeare's linguistic contribution to EModE. As a starting point, important reference works and tools for further research are introduced. Then some general considerations on Shakespeare's language are presented, because Shakespeare's language, or rather his use of language, can, and in fact has been defined in broader or narrower terms. The description and illustration of Shakespeare's language begins with a section on pronunciation, then moves on to vocabulary and grammar and ends with pragmatic and sociolinguistic studies and other relatively recent trends. Each section begins by listing basic works on a topic and then presents more detailed or more advanced studies, usually in chronological order. Where necessary, illustrative examples are provided.

1 Introduction

For the final decades of the Renaissance the works of William Shakespeare (1564–1616) and the King James Bible (the *Authorized Version*) of 1611 are the dominating influences: "Dominate, that is, from a linguistic point of view. The question of their literary brilliance and significance is not an issue for this book. Our question is much simpler yet more far-reaching: what was their effect on the language?" (Crystal 1988: 196).

Ulrich Busse: Halle/Saale (Germany)
Beatrix Busse: Heidelberg (Germany)

Shakespeare's linguistic quality can be seen on many levels of language. Insightful observations have turned proverbial, one among those is that *love is blind*. Some Shakespearean words, such as *powerfully* or *obscenely*, are still used today, others, such as *indirection* or *incarnadine*, are no longer used, but they seem to have a particularly challenging contextual quality. Generally speaking, the number of words Shakespeare invented is impressive (see Section 4). His word-stock is equally striking. Depending upon one's definition of *word*, different results concerning the total size of the Shakespeare corpus may be obtained. If the word count of the Spevack concordances (1968–80) is taken as a reliable basis, the sum total of words used in the 38 plays and his non-dramatic works amounts to 884,647 (see Spevack 1968–80 IV [1969]: 1).

Spevack also supports the importance of Shakespeare's English when he states that "indeed, our picture of English as a whole will be improved by a detailed study of all of Shakespeare's language not only because Shakespeare, we will agree, may be the greatest practitioner of English but certainly because he accounts for about 40 per cent of the recorded English of his time" (Spevack 1972: 108).

1.1 Reference works and research tools

Linguistic contributions to Shakespeare's English date back at least to the tradition of late 19th-century scholarship. There we find grammars and dictionaries that list and describe linguistic peculiarities of Shakespeare's language use. The first comprehensive account is Abbott's (1966 [1870]) *Shakespearian Grammar*; Franz (1986 [1898/99, 1939]) follows in this tradition.

In 1990, Blake (1990: 61) deplored that "we still badly need a grammar on modern principles and a new comprehensive dictionary of Shakespeare's language". With two new Shakespeare grammars, one written by Blake (2002) himself, and another one by Hope (2003), this wish finally came true, at least for grammars. It is perhaps not so incidental that the two grammars came out at this very point in time, because both reflect a revived interest of modern linguistics in historical language studies. In the introductory chapters of their books, both Hope and Blake point out that for more than 130 years the grammar by Abbott has been the standard work for the English-speaking world, although those scholars familiar with German could resort to Wilhelm Franz's 1986 [1898/99, 1939] *Shakespeare-Grammatik*. Blake argues that "there have been no substantial grammars of Shakespeare's language since Franz's, and that the grammars that have appeared are altogether slimmer volumes with relatively little detail. In addition, most of them have built upon the work of Franz and Abbott (e.g. Brook 1976 and Scheler 1982)" (Blake 2002: 10).

Both modern grammars take a descriptive approach, but the scope of Blake's book is wider than that of Hope's. While Hope covers grammatical ground up to the clause and sentence level, Blake in addition to this includes two chapters on discourse and register and on pragmatics. For a detailed review of both grammars see U. Busse (2007).

The oldest Shakespeare dictionaries also date from the late 19th century. Schmidt and Sarrazin (1971 [1874/75]) still provide valuable insights, as all of the entries are amply illustrated by quotations. Less comprehensive in that they concentrate on difficult words are the dictionaries by Cunliffe (1910), Onions (1911), and Kellner (1922).

In contrast to grammar writing, we still lack a modern comprehensive Shakespeare dictionary, but we have got a number of modern specialized dictionaries, thesauri, and glossaries. Most importantly, there is Spevack's (1993) *Shakespeare Thesaurus*. Based on a historically informed semantic categorization of the Shakespeare lexicon this glossary contains 15 semantic categories ranging from *animal terms* to *body* and *bodily functions* to *plants, religion,* and *time*. Crystal and Crystal (2002) is in parts close to Spevack (1993). Leisi (1997) deals with difficult or problematic words and passages in Shakespeare's plays. There are also specialized dictionaries, such as those that focus on Shakespeare's use of sexual language (Partridge 1955; Rubinstein 1984; Williams 1997), or on legal language (Sokol and Sokol 2000).

The nine volumes of Spevack's (1968–80) *A Complete and Systematic Concordance to the Works of Shakespeare* are based on Evans's (1972) *Riverside Shakespeare*. This concordance supersedes the older one by Bartlett (1894). The nine volumes are an unprecedented achievement that goes beyond the usual requirements of a concordance in that they provide the frequencies and words used by each character in the respective plays. Volumes 1–3 focus on words used in the comedies, histories and tragedies and follow the generic distinction of the First Folio (F1) from 1623. Volumes 4 and 5 provide the words of all the plays and poems in alphabetical order. Volume 6 contains the appendices and special cases, such as hyphenated words, hapax legomena, and so on, and Volume 7 is a concordance to the stage directions and speech prefixes. Volume 8 is a concordance to the bad quartos, and Volume 9 is a concordance to the substantive variants.

Perhaps the most comprehensive current investigation into Shakespeare's language is the *Shakespeare Database* carried out at the University of Münster in Germany under the direction of H. Joachim Neuhaus (forthc.). The database constitutes a full lemmatization of Shakespeare's work, which is organized into a relational database and follows Evans's (1997 [1972]) *Riverside Shakespeare*. Unfortunately, this database is still not publicly available.

Wordhoard (Parod 2004–2010), which is a joint project of the Perseus Project at Tufts University and The Northwestern University Library, presents among other texts like Homer's *The Odyssey*, Chaucer's *The Canterbury Tales* and Edmund Spenser's works, a lemmatized and morphosyntactically tagged database of Shakespeare's language. It also uses a modern edition of Shakespeare.

Regarding bibliographies, there are Bradbrook's (1954) retrospect "Fifty years of the criticism of Shakespeare's style" and Partridge's (1979) "Shakespeare's English: A bibliographical survey" as older works. Adamson et al. (2001: 302–315) provide an annotated bibliography of the most important monographs and collections of Shakespeare's English, ranging from Kökeritz (1953) to the new millennium, and concentrating on works that appeared in the 1980s and 1990s. The comprehensive bibliography in Blake's (2002: 346–361) grammar lists titles ranging from 1870 (Abbott) to 2000 (Kermode).

Apart from the reference works and research tools above, a number of book-length accounts on Shakespeare's English appeared from the 1960s to the early 1980s, as, for instance, Hulme (1962, 1972), Brook (1976), Hussey (1982), Scheler (1982), and Blake (1983). In addition to these monographs, there are the collections by Muir and Schoenbaum (1971) and by Salmon and Burness (1987), which contains thirty-three essays published between 1951 and 1983. The studies cover the following subject areas: "Shakespeare and the English language", "Aspects of colloquial Elizabethan English", "Studies in vocabulary", "Shakespeare and Elizabethan grammar", "Studies in rhetoric and metre", "Punctuation", and "The linguistic context of Shakespearean drama".

After many years during which linguistic descriptions of Shakespeare were not high on the agenda of historical linguists, the two grammars together with other recent publications such as Crystal (2008) show a renewed interest in the subject. Some of these, e.g. Adamson et al. (2001), Kermode (2000), Magnusson (1999), and McDonald (2001), combine linguistic investigations with aspects of rhetoric and style. For example, Adamson et al. (2001) is directed both at an academic readership and at teachers and students. Therefore, the collection takes on an interdisciplinary perspective and the chapters range from those that focus on rhetoric and style, to Shakespeare's word-formation and his use of puns to techniques of persuasion.

2 General considerations

In a classical article, Quirk makes the following observations: "It should be superfluous to point out that the language of Shakespeare is an amalgam of the language that Shakespeare found around him – together with what he made of it. [...] It is necessary, therefore, to study the language of Shakespeare's time and then to distinguish Shakespeare's language within it" (Quirk 1987: 3, 4). In order to do so, Quirk proposes a threefold distinction:
1. English as it was about 1600
2. Shakespeare's interest in his language
3. Shakespeare's unique use of English (Quirk 1987: 4).

However, the 400 years of linguistic change on all levels of the language system and in language use, will leave a "discrepancy between Shakespeare's intuitions about language and our own" (Crystal 2003: 67). Although we have to be aware of the fact that our modern intuitions may lead us astray, a "modern historical linguistics" (Mair 2006) approach, encompassing socio-historical, pragmatic, cognitive, and corpus-linguistic aspects, makes it possible to reconstruct the past and to study the language of Shakespeare from new angles.

Methodologically, a number of different approaches with different objectives or foci are possible. Salmon (1987: xiii) lists four different approaches to Shakespeare's English, which are exemplified by the essays collected in Salmon and Burness (1987). The four groups of essays pursue the following purposes:
1. to enable the speaker of Present-day English to share as far as possible in the responses of the original audience;
2. to draw attention to the manner in which Shakespeare handles the language of his time for artistic purposes;
3. to use the language of Shakespearean drama as data on which to base conclusions about Elizabethan English in general; and
4. to provide illuminating information about various aspects of Shakespeare's linguistic background, in particular, the attitude to the language of his time.

To any of these ends, the object of investigation – Shakespeare's language – can be defined in narrower or broader terms. For instance, Blake (1990: 63) argues that "the language of Shakespeare has received little attention in the twentieth century – at least in so far as language is concerned with the grammatical system of expression". In this context, he comments on Evans's (1952) *The Language of Shakespeare's Plays*, arguing that "[t]his book says nothing about the grammar and little about the vocabulary of the plays. The *Language* in the title means either style or comments by the characters on language" (Blake 1990: 63).

However, at present, the formerly distinct research traditions of linguistics and stylistic or literary studies are coming into closer contact also within Shakespeare studies under what one could label "the new philology" (see Taavitsainen and Fitzmaurice 2007: 22–25). As recent examples for this direction of research, one could take the work by Magnusson (1999, 2007), Adamson et al. (2001), Spevack (2002), or B. Busse (2006b).

Regardless of the purpose or scope of a given study, investigating Shakespeare's language always demands attention to those issues that are generally relevant to the analysis of historical data. These mainly revolve around the questions of how historical linguists (need to) validate their data and analyses. It also includes a consideration of such issues as the edition on which an investigation is based (e.g. modern edition or early printings). Diachronic investigations of Shakespeare's language that focus on language change and stability or a linguistic analysis that takes account of the respective genres need to meticulously consider the specifically Shakespearean textual and editorial conditions and the ways some modern categorizations deviate from historical ones. For example, the First Folio from 1623 only distinguishes between comedies, histories, and tragedies and does not contain the genre label "romance," because it is a modern category. Also, it does not contain any act, scene, or line divisions.

The extent to which Shakespeare's language can or cannot be regarded as a true representation of authentic spoken EModE has been frequently discussed (Salmon 1987 [1965]). Within this discussion the fictional character as well as the verse and prose distinction needs to be observed, on the one hand, while, on the other, it can be assumed that Shakespeare made use of the language around him and exploited it creatively for his dramatic purposes (see also Moore, Chapter 16).

3 Phonology

Brook (1976: 140–159) and Scheler (1982: 17–32) provide short and practical introductions to Shakespeare's pronunciation, spelling, and punctuation, and Lass (2001) offers a recent and short chapter on "Shakespeare's sounds". He points out that "[m]odern readers or playgoers are auditorily misled by their experience of Shakespeare". This can be attributed to the fact that we "read Shakespeare in editions with modern spelling and punctuation, and hear him performed with modern English pronunciation" (Lass 2001: 256). Thus, changes in vowel quantity or quality can obscure rhymes, and word stress may occur at unexpected positions. For instance, in order to work out puns, it is essential to know about the homophony of the words and their differing sense. To illustrate the major differences between EModE pronunciation and that of standard PDE, Lass provides the following passage, (1), from *A Midsummer Night's Dream*:

(1) Through the forest have **I gone**;
     But Athenian found **I none**
     On whose **eyes** I mi(gh)t **approve**
     This fl**ow**er's fo(r)ce in stirring **love**.
     Ni(gh)t and silence – Who is **here**?
     Weeds of Athens he d**o**th **wear**:
     This is he my m**a**ster **said**
     Despis(e)d the Athenian **maid**;
     And he(r)e the maiden, sleeping s**ou**nd,
     On the dank and di(r)ty gr**ou**nd.
     (*Midsummer Night's Dream* II.ii.65–74; Lass 2001: 267)

In this passage "[v]owels that have undergone major change in pronunciation are in **bold** [straight characters]; rhymes which were possible in Shakespeare's time but are no longer so are in ***bold italics***". Vowels or consonants that are no longer pronounced are in round brackets. The *r*s are marked as well, because many dialects do not now pronounce them in these positions (Lass 2001: 267). In addition to this, EModE pronunciation was not yet codified, and therefore much more variable, implying also a greater availability of dialect forms.

Lass (2001: 268) deplores that "[t]here is unfortunately no comprehensive, elementary introduction to Shakespeare's pronunciation", but he recommends Kökeritz (1953) and his own chapter in the *Cambridge History of the English Language* (Lass 1999: 56–186), which, he himself describes as "fairly technical, and not devoted to Shakespeare" (Lass 2001: 268), but covering the period as a whole.

The assessment of EModE pronunciation can be controversial. While Cercignani (1981), Scheler (1982: 31), and Barber (1997: 140–141) are critical about Kökeritz from a scholarly point of view, Adamson et al. (2001: 306–307) stress its usefulness for the purpose of students. According to Barber (1997: 140), the two volumes of Dobson (1968) can be considered as "[t]he standard work on English phonology in the period" in a "very conservative" representation (see Schlüter, Chapter 3).

Recently, two books dealing with EModE and Shakespearean sound appeared, namely Smith (1999) and Folkerth (2002). The Globe Theatre now offers selected performances of Shakespeare's plays in EModE pronunciation. Crystal (2005) reports on this project (audio extracts are available at *The Shakespeare*

Portal [Crystal 2005]). The success of the project calls into question an earlier position, as pronounced by Quirk in 1971:

> Now that we have the technical ability to put on a play in roughly the pronunciation of 1600, the desirability of so doing has become less apparent. Since so many of the features of Elizabethan pronunciation have remained in twentieth-century use with utterly different sociological connotations, it is exceedingly difficult to avoid farcical overtones (Quirk 1987: 5 [1971: 69, 1974: 48]).

4 Vocabulary

In the introduction to his Shakespeare grammar, Blake (2002: 7) says that "[t]he language of Shakespeare has been studied and his texts edited almost from the moment he died in 1616" and that two features have remained constant factors of scholarship and criticism: vocabulary and grammar.

It has been claimed that the EMod period, and in particular the time span from 1530 until 1660 saw an unprecedented growth in vocabulary (see Lancashire, Chapter 6). For example, on the basis of the *Chronological English Dictionary* (Finkenstaedt et al. 1970), 3,300 neologisms are attested for the year 1600 alone (see Görlach 1994: 109). As concerns the means of expanding the lexicon, "substantial use was made both of borrowing (especially from Latin) and of word-formation (especially by affixation)" (Barber 1997: 219). The so-called "inkhorn controversy" discussed the desirability of vocabulary growth and its appropriate methods. These topics are also reflected in Shakespeare's English.

> People talk a lot about Shakespeare's "linguistic legacy", saying that he was a major influence on the present-day English language, and citing as evidence his coining of new words (such as *assassination* and *courtship*) and idiomatic phrases (such as *salad days* and *cold comfort*). But when we add all of the coinages up, we do not get very large numbers. No-one has carried out a precise calculation (Crystal 2003: 77).

This statement is not quite true, as a number of estimations have been made. Scheler (1982: 89–90) lists the following approaches. As concerns the overall size of Shakespeare's vocabulary, Brook (1976: 26) estimates it to be "of the order of twenty thousand words". Spevack (1968–80 [1969], IV: 1) counts 29,066 different words (i.e. lemmas). His count is based on the *New Riverside Shakespeare* and counts different word forms (tokens) such as *cried, criedst, cries*, and not types or lexemes. Scheler, on the other hand, carries out a type-based count and uses the *Shakespeare-Lexicon* of Schmidt and Sarrazin (1971 [1874/1875]) as a basis, coming to a total of 17,750 words. However, these statistics do not tell us anything about the number of words that are coined by Shakespeare. The *Shakespeare*

Database (see Section 1.1) lists 3,179 lemmata (4,512 word forms) coined by Shakespeare (B. Busse 2006b). Despite the difficulty that a word first attested in Shakespeare's work need not necessarily be an original coinage, Schäfer (1973: 204–220) lists 1,630 words by year. His list of 308 hyphenated words is far from complete. For the methodological difficulties in tracking first quotations with the help of the OED see Schäfer (1980).

In terms of etymology (meaning the immediate donor language and not the ultimate source language), Shakespeare's word stock consists of 43% Germanic words and 54% non-Germanic words (mostly Romance-Latin), if only types are counted, another 3% are difficult to classify (see Scheler 1982: 90). On "Shakespeare's Latinate Neologisms" and on "Latin-Saxon Hybrids in Shakespeare and the Bible" see the two articles by Garner (1987a, b). For a more recent comprehensive study of the etymology of Shakespeare's vocabulary see Franken (1995).

Shakespeare systematically exploits the stylistic difference between Germanic and Romance vocabulary. According to Romaine (1982: 122) "the working principle of sociolinguistic reconstruction must be the 'uniformitarian principle'", which implies that, as in PDE, the Germanic word is the ordinary word, often being more personal, more lively, or more affectionate. By contrast, the Romance loanword is more unpersonal, sought-after, or more dignified. This distinction, both then and now, presupposes from the language users a kind of implicit etymological knowledge, language awareness, or at least a feel for the language.

Elizabethans were keenly aware of linguistic decorum and appropriate style (see Adamson 2001a, which includes annotated references for further reading). Apart from decorum, "copia", which could be expressed by Germanic-Romance synonym pairs, was another important stylistic device. Schäfer (1973: 184–203 [appendix II]) lists 529 of these synonym pairs. In order to highlight the stylistic potential of such pairs, Scheler discusses the following example from *Macbeth*, (2):

(2) *Will all great Neptunes Ocean wash this blood*
     Cleane from my Hand? no: this my Hand will rather
     *The multitudinous Seas **incarnardine** [sic!],*
     ***Making** the Green one, **Red** (Macbcth II.ii.60–63; Scheler 1982: 93)*

The atrocity of Duncan's murder, and Macbeth's guilt is expressed in a hyperbole, whose force is amplified by the contrast between the Romance *incarnadine* and the plain Germanic *make red*.

Inappropriate use of difficult Romance vocabulary by uneducated speakers is a constant source of linguistic humor in the Elizabethan theater. Especially the idiolect of speakers representing the lower social orders has attracted some scholarly attention. See, for instance, Schäfer (1973: 97–115), Brook (1976: Chapter 9, which includes dialects, registers and idiolects), Scheler (1982: 97–100), or Blake (1983: Chapter 2 varieties, Chapter 3 vocabulary, 2002: Chapter 8, 300–302). Schlauch (1987 [1965]) reports on Shakespeare's characters' use of malapropisms.

With idiolectal language use, the author slips into a character, and his or her linguistic peculiarities can serve the purpose of characterization. This does not only go for uneducated characters such as Mistress Quickly, who, for example, mixes up *honeysuckle* for 'homicidal', *honey-seed* for 'homicide' (*2 Henry IV*, II.i.47, see Quirk (1987: 14) for this and further examples), but also for characters such as Polonius (in *Hamlet*) making use of affected, verbose, and bombastic language. In *Love's Labors Lost*, Holofernes and Nathaniel are laughed at for having "been at a great feast of languages and stol'n the scraps" (V.i.34). Examples such as these do however not imply that Shakespeare was against augmentation of vocabulary and scorned inkhorn terms, but that he wanted to draw attention to the fact that "the uneducated would make ridiculous errors" and others would be ridiculous because of their "use of learned language for obscurity's sake" (Quirk 1987: 14).

Since dialogue is the most important constitutive device of drama, the playwright pays particular attention to mark socio-regional variants (see Meurman-Solin, Chapter 8) marking the language as spoken. Among other things, this requires the use of colloquial lexical expressions (see the papers by Salmon 1987 [1967], Replogle 1987 [1973]) and also sentence structures (see Salmon (1987 [1965]).

As social dialects, the language of thieves and vagabonds ("cant") and sexual slang ("bawdy") play a particular role (see Scheler 1982: 108–111 with many examples, the dictionary by Partridge 1955 and Musgrove 1987 [1981]). In the 19th century, Shakespeare's linguistic permissiveness led to the publication of a purified *Family Shakespeare*, published by Thomas Bowdler (1807), in which "those words and expressions are omitted which cannot with propriety be read in the family".

> The influence of regional dialects is to be found in Shakespeare's plays in vocabulary and pronunciation, and to a much less extent in syntax and semantics. The features of the conventional stage dialect that he used are today found chiefly in the South-West, but they were originally found in most of the dialects south of the Thames. They included such characteristics as the voicing of initial [f] and [s], the change of initial [θr] to [dr], and the use of *ich* for the pronoun *I*, with the consequent use of the contracted forms *cham* 'I am' and *chill* 'I will' (Brook 1976: 177)

The best-known examples of a stage representation of regional dialect are the exchanges between Edgar and Oswald in *King Lear*, (3):

(3) Edgar: *Chill not let go, zir, without vurther [cagion].*
     Oswald: *Let go, slave, or thou di'st!*
     Edgar: *Good gentleman, go your gait, and let poor*
     voke pass. And chud ha' bin zwagger'd out of my life,
     'twould not ha' bin zo long as 'tis by a vortnight. Nay,
     come not near th' old man; keep out, che vor' ye,
     or Ice try whither your costard or my ballow be the
     harder. Chill be plain with you.
     Oswald: *Out dunghill!* [They fight.]
     Edgar: *Chill pick your teeth, zir. Come, no matter*
     vor your foins. (King Lear IV.vi.235–245)

Apart from borrowing, word-formation proved to be a very important means in EModE of enriching the vocabulary. Thus, Barber in his analysis of "a 2 per cent sample of the OED" consisting of "1,848 words of reasonably certain etymology" (1997: 219; 220) comes to the conclusion that while 625 words (33.8%) are borrowings, 1,223 words (66.2%) can be attributed to word-formation processes. Out of these processes, affixation, and in particular suffixation with 607 words is the most productive process, followed at some distance by compounding with 217 words (Barber 1997: 221). By and large, the same holds true for Shakespeare, even though it looks as if in the OED more compounds are ascribed to Shakespeare than affixes. Scheler (1982: 115–128) reports in detail on a number of older German studies from the 1950s which sought to quantify Shakespeare's compounds, prefix- and suffix-formations and conversions. All of these studies are of course limited by the reliability of the OED in correctly attributing neologisms to Shakespeare. The article by Salmon illustrates "some functions of Shakespearian word-formation" by discussing a number of examples in order "to illustrate one aspect of Shakespeare's craftsmanship as a poet and dramatist – and assist in a more precise characterization of his style" (Salmon 1987: 194 [1970: 14]). Nevalainen (2001) provides a chapter on "Shakespeare's new words" and deals with compounding, conversion, and affixation.

5 Grammar

Apart from the two modern grammars introduced in Section 1.1, the classic monographs by Brook (1976: Chapters 3 and 4) and Hussey (1982: Chapter 4) provide general overviews of morphology and syntax (see Cowie, Chapter 4; Seoane, Chapter 5). The books by Wikberg, *Yes-No Questions and Answers in Shakespeare's Plays* (1975), Burton, *Shakespeare's Grammatical Style* (1973), and Houston, *Shakespearean Sentences* (1988) deal with more specific syntactic aspects of Shakespeare's language. The collection of papers by Salmon and Burness (1987) offers articles on sentence structures in colloquial Shakespearean English, on auxiliaries, on multiple negation, and on the use of *-eth* and *-es* as verb endings in the First Folio. The short overview by Adamson (2001b) studies "small words" such as *his* or *it*, the auxiliaries *may* and *shall*, deictics such as *this* and *that*, etc.

With regard to grammar, the language of Shakespeare shows no marked differences to that of his contemporaries. Scheler (1982: 87) is of the opinion that there is no single construction that occurs exclusively in the Shakespeare corpus. For instance, we do not find split infinitives in Shakespeare's works, but they cannot be found in the works of his contemporaries Spenser and Kyd either. Thus, the differences between Shakespeare and other dramatists are differences in style and degree but not in kind, so that in comparison to Spenser's old-fashioned, formal, and learned mode of expression, Shakespeare's use of language appears to be more modern and popular.

However, when we read a play by Shakespeare, we automatically compare his language use to the standards of Modern English grammar. Against this linguistic background, two features of Shakespeare's and EModE morpho-syntax in general stick out:

On the one hand, the language sounds old-fashioned and quaintly German, especially in terms of the use of inversion in questions, the use of pronouns in imperatives, and the use of modals as main verbs as shown in the following citations, (4)–(6):

(4) *What makes he heere* (*Othello* I.ii.49)

(5) *go we* (*Much Ado about Nothing* III.i.32)

(6) *I can no more* (*Hamlet* V.ii.312; Scheler 1982: 84–85)

On the other hand, these and other constructions have counterparts and show a good deal of variation, often within a single play. Quirk (1987: 9) shows that in imperatives "[t]he pronoun may have subject form or object form or it may be absent, and in some cases [...] all three possibilities can occur with the same verb", (7)–(9):

(7) *Come thou on my side.* (*Richard III* I.iv.263)

(8) *Come thee on.* (*Antony and Cleopatra* IV.vii.16)

(9) *Come on my right hand.* (*Julius Caesar* I.ii.213)

Quirk (1987: 9) concludes: "While it would be idle to pretend that these three forms of imperative were always carefully distinguished in meaning at this time, we must not assume that they were usually synonymous".

Variation within a single play or even a scene can be highlighted by the use of *do*. Barber (1997: 193–194) illustrates the use of *do* in negative, interrogative, and affirmative sentences by resorting to the scene of Clarence's murder in *Richard III*. Among others, he cites the following examples. In (10) and (11) we find questions formed with *do*, but (12) and (13) illustrate questions in which the subject is placed after the lexical verb. Similarly, negative sentences can be formed with *do*, as in (14), or without, as in (15) and (16):

(10) *How do'st thou feele thy selfe now?* (*Richard III* I.iv.120)

(11) *Wherefore do you come?* (I.iv.171)

(12) *Why lookes your Grace so heauily to day?* (I.iv.1)

(13) *how cam'st thou hither?* (I.iv.85)

(14) *O do not slander him.* (I.iv.241)

(15) *He sends you not to murther me for this* (I.iv.213)

(16) *beleeue him not.* (I.iv.147)

With regard to affirmative declarative sentences in this scene, Barber concludes that these "are mostly formed without *do*. [...] There is however a substantial minority of cases where *do* is inserted. [...] In these cases, it is highly improbable that *do* is inserted to give emphasis: Clarence is not saying 'Your eyes DO menace me'. His sentence is just an alternative way of saying 'Your eyes menace me', and the *do* is probably quite unstressed" (Barber 1997: 194).

In the case of *do*, particular findings for a Shakespearean play or the entire corpus (see Stein 1990: Chapter 7) can now be linked to the work on the development of *do* in EModE at large, which is outlined by Nevalainen (2006: 108) as follows: "During the Early Modern period, *do* first spreads to negative questions, then to affirmative questions and most negative statements as well as, to a certain extent, to affirmative statements" (see Warner, Chapter 13). In this case, another long-standing complaint that much linguistic work on Shakespeare is isolated and fragmented is fortunately no longer true.

Methodologically, the treatment of functional variants needs careful consideration, because the Shakespeare corpus also shows differences over time. Therefore, "we have to bear in mind that Shakespeare's plays were written over a period of at least twenty years in a time of extremely rapid language change, so that we cannot always assume that all the instances of a particular feature were used according to identical principles" (Grannis 1990: 106).

The morphological variation between the verb endings *-(e)s* and *-(e)th* of the third-person singular of the present tense is a good case in point to show such changes over time in the Shakespeare corpus. When we take a look at language histories or introductory textbooks to EModE, the general development is well known and can be summarized in just one sentence. "Of northern origin, *-(e)s* had largely replaced the southern *-(e)th* in the General dialect by the seventeenth century, although *-(e)th* prevailed in some regional dialects and formal genres much longer" (Nevalainen 2006: 90). However, in a number of detailed works on the Shakespeare corpus, Stein has found out that the corpus shows a systematic internal divide at around 1600 because "[b]etween 1590 and 1610 the morphology of the Shakespeare corpus changes in such a systematic way that the effect of textual history in creating these patterns can be ruled out" (Stein 1987: 413–414).

As a third example showing differences between PDE and EModE, modal auxiliaries were mentioned at the beginning of this section. Unlike Modern English, an EModE auxiliary could be followed by a past participle, as in the following example, (17):

(17) *her death was doubtfull,*
And but that great commaund oreswayes the order,
She **should** *in ground vnsanctified* **been** *lodg'd (Hamlet V.i.227–229; Barber 1997: 197)*

Barber (1997: 197) points out that the text "is taken from the good Quarto of 1604: the First Folio of 1623 reads 'She should in ground vnsanctified haue lodg'd'". He further mentions that this construction was not frequent, but that it did occur often enough not to be mistaken as a mistake or misprint. This example shows that the evaluation or interpretation of language forms is laden with difficulties that can be attributed to the authenticity of the text and the different publication histories of individual plays. *Hamlet* exists in two Quarto editions (Q1 from 1603 and Q2 from 1604) and in the Folio version from 1623. Q1 is not regarded as a reliable text.

Another syntactic peculiarity is the possibility that the lexical verb, normally following a modal auxiliary, could "be dispensed with in sentences indicating motion" (Barber 1997: 197) as in

(18) *I **must** to Couentree* (*Richard II* I.ii.56)

While these peculiarities may just seem odd from the point of view of PDE, they do not pose major stumbling blocks for the understanding of an utterance. However, with regard to this, the modals are situated at the crossroads between syntax, semantics, and pragmatics. Nakayasu (2009: Chapter 2) provides an overview of these different strands of earlier research on modals in EModE. For instance, Kakietek (1972) examines their use in ten Shakespeare plays by means of componential analysis, pointing out the following: "By paying attention to the context in which the modals happen to appear, the grammarian manages to avoid the common mistake of confusing the semantics of the modals with what pertains strictly to the context" (Kakietek 1972: 17). The comprehensive study by Nakayasu (2009: 243) analyzes the modals *shall/should*, *will/would* and their contracted forms for *Antony and Cleopatra*, *Julius Caesar*, and *Love's Labors Lost* by subjecting them first to "a variationist analysis of syntactic, semantic, and pragmatic aspects" and then to micro- and macro-pragmatic analyses in terms of the relationships that hold between modals and speech acts, between modals and politeness, and among dialogue, discourse, and modals.

6 Pragmatics and discourse

Historical pragmatic investigations of Shakespeare's language are more recent (for a more general view of EModE pragmatics, see Archer, Chapter 7). Excepting early studies such as Fish (1976) and Porter (1979), the approach (see Rudanko 1993) came into being in the 1990s. Blake's (2002) grammar has a chapter on "Discourse and Register" (Blake 2002: 271–303) and on "Pragmatics" (Blake 2002: 304–325). Pragmatic features studied in Shakespeare's language mainly cover the investigation of forms of address, politeness strategies, discourse markers, or speech acts. For a more detailed overview Busse and Busse (2010).

Pragmatic studies of Shakespeare's language cannot clearly be separated into pragmaphilological studies and those that use a function-to-form or a form-to-function mapping of diachronic pragmatics (see Jacobs and Jucker 1995). Often these approaches are combined. Some of the classic studies have also focussed on linguistic features with discourse function in context. The collection of papers in Salmon and Burness (1987) contains a number of classic studies on forms of address, e.g. Barber (1987 [1981]) and Mulholland (1987 [1967]), and on ritual utterances, such as greeting or parting formulae, e.g. Salmon (1987 [1967]).

Generally speaking, the point of the social and pragmatic relevance of address behavior in Shakespeare's plays has been frequently researched and commented on, and within this framework many studies have concentrated on pronouns since the 19th century until the present. In particular, one focus is on the use of the distinction between *you* and *thou* forms, or what is often called a T (*tu*) and V (*vous*) distinction (see U. Busse, Chapter 12, Section 2.5; for critical reports see U. Busse 2002: Chapter 2; Mazzon 2003; Stein 2003; Freedman 2007). The investigation of nominal forms of address or vocative constructions has been influenced by established models for explaining pronoun usage, although only rarely has the interplay between nominal and pronominal forms of address been explored comprehensively as one interlinked phenomenon (Barber 1987 [1981]; U. Busse 2002: Chapter 6; B. Busse 2006a).

B. Busse (2006a) investigates the functions, meanings, and variety of forms of address in a corpus of seventeen Shakespeare plays, which are selected according to editorial, thematic, generic, synchronic, and diachronic considerations. Contrary to Brown and Gilman's (1960) and Brown and Ford's (1961) parameters of power and solidarity and the rigid social structure allegedly existent in Shakespeare's time (Breuer 1983; Stoll 1989), B. Busse (2006a) claims that nominal forms of address in Shakespeare are experiential, interpersonal, and textual markers which reflect and create relationships, identity, and attitude as well as messages and habitus. They also structure the discourse, and are meaning-making within a performative context. Drawing on a new categorization of vocative forms, which includes labels like "conventional terms" or "terms referring to natural phenomena", B. Busse (2006a) establishes the functional potential of vocative forms also from a quantitative perspective and according to synchronic, diachronic, and generic parameters and with regard to the use of vocative forms by the characters of the plays.

Politeness studies of Shakespeare's language are most frequently based on Brown and Levinson's (1987 [1978]) theory. Blake (2002: 320–325) is a non-technical introduction to their model. He uses several pertinent examples to illustrate how politeness works. Brown and Gilman (1989) investigate four Shakespearean tragedies (*Hamlet*, *King Lear*, *Macbeth*, and *Othello*) and apply Brown and Levinson's (1987 [1978]) three variables of power, distance and ranked extremity to discourse between two characters, which only differs in one of the three variables. Kopytko (1993, 1995) applies Brown and Levinson's framework but explicitly excludes forms of address. He finds that in his sample of Shakespearean comedies and tragedies positive politeness strategies prevail over strategies of negative politeness. Rudanko (1993) uses Brown and Levinson's (1987 [1978]) framework as a base but stresses the need to enlarge their framework for the historical analysis of Shakespeare's *Timon of Athens*. Because "acting in a way other than politely [is not] necessarily the same as the absence of politeness" (Rudanko 1993: 167). He also develops an inventory of substrategies for nastiness (Rudanko 1993: 168–171). Culpeper (1996, 1998) applies his theory of impoliteness to Shakespeare's dramatic dialogue in the banquet scene of *Macbeth*. He highlights the functional potential of impoliteness, which goes beyond entertaining the audience. Impoliteness is seen as a "symptom or as a cause of social disharmony" (Culpeper 1998: 86) and as a means of characterization. Magnusson's (1999) historically situated comparison of politeness in Early Modern letter writing and Shakespeare's plays uses an interdisciplinary approach that emphasizes the social exchange in Shakespeare's language.

Discourse markers are less frequently investigated for Shakespeare's English than they are within historical pragmatics in general. Salmon (1987 [1967]) investigates colloquial English in the Falstaff plays. Blake (2002) studies interjections like *o/oh, alas, 'sblood/zblood* ('God's blood'), and *why*, interrogative pronouns like *why, what,* and *well*, shorter clauses or phrases like *I say, for upon my life*, and forms which derive from imperatives like the doubling of *come*. Discourse markers stress an emotional overtone and the speaker's attitude and serve as a means of characterization. He also draws our attention to the complex interplay between editorial considerations and pragmatic interpretation. For example, F1 and quarto editions of respective plays are likely to be deviating from one another due to editorial decision-making. Variants occur and the syntactic as well as pragmatic function of words like *well* can be interpreted differently. U. Busse's (2002: Chapter 7) case study of *prithee* and *pray you* analyzes the functions of these discourse markers from both a quantitative and a qualitative point of view. *Pray you* is identified to be most frequently used as a discourse marker and most frequently collocating with the form of address *sir*. Also, he stresses a complex interplay between the communicative functions of *prithee* and *pray you*, which no longer sees *(I) pray you* as deferential and *prithee* as an in-group identity marker (Brown and Gilman 1989: 183–184).

Although it can be assumed that what Romaine (1982: 122) called "the uniformitarian principle" is also valid for the realization of speech acts in the past history of English, the analyses of speech acts in Shakespeare have revealed a number of methodological challenges, which also generally occur when older stages of the English language are analyzed. As early as 1993, in his study of speech acts in *Coriolanus*, Rudanko (1993) drew our attention to the fact that two approaches need to be distinguished when studying speech acts in Shakespeare: the lexical properties of illocutionary verbs and their classification, on the one hand, and the "direction of fit" between words and the world, on the other.

From a historical-pragmatic point of view, it can be said that a form-to-function mapping might not include all relevant syntactic realizations of speech acts, even if a comprehensive electronic text corpus is used. Then there is also the challenge of assigning the right communicative function to the respective form. A function-to-form mapping partly cannot immediately assume that, for example, a directive speech act is only realized by one or two syntactic forms. On the basis of an analysis of *King Lear*, U. Busse (2008) explains the relationships which hold between grammatical sentence types such as imperatives, on the one hand, and their communicative function on the other.

In addition, as modern linguists we can only reconstruct the past and we have to be aware that the choice of available forms also depends on the period of observation. Furthermore, speech acts are fuzzy and it seems appropriate to introduce the concept of a "pragmatic space" (Jucker and Taavitsainen 2000: 73, 84) to explain their functions in context. Nonetheless, Jucker and Taavitsainen (2000) and others have illustrated that diachronic speech analysis is possible and that different realizations may in part also reflect differences in function.

7 Recent trends and further directions

Recent trends in studies of Shakespeare's language show the same dominance of corpus linguistics that is also generally visible in (English) historical linguistics. Some are highly interesting contributions to Shakespeare's language and to the field of "modern historical linguistics" in general. These focus, for example, on key words, which are retrieved by complex statistical procedures (Culpeper 2002), and relate these characterizations to the fact that Shakespeare's language is constructed dialogue. Others use a historical corpus-linguistic approach as a method and combine it with historical-pragmatic, historical sociolinguistic, stylistic, and literary critical considerations (B. Busse 2006a, b). Those studies that focus on EModE features of the English language or take on a diachronic perspective (including a function-to-form or a form-to-function mapping) also frequently draw on Shakespeare's language, because it is a closed set of data. For example B. Busse (2010) uses the Shakespeare corpus to discover the syntactic realizations of stance adverbials in Shakespeare and to establish their functional import. The informed interplay between linguistics and literary criticism can be seen in Munkelt and B. Busse (2007) and Biewer (2009).

Recently there has also been an interest in using a multimodal approach between text and performance (B. Busse 2006a) and film adaptations of Shakespeare's plays (McInytre 2008).

Generally speaking, it can be said that some areas of Shakespeare's language are still rather unexplored. For example, a syntactic investigation of Shakespeare's language using modern corpus-based approaches and methodology and leading to a comprehensive grammar would be desirable. Also, pragmatic features, such as speech acts, are less well charted, or still unexplored, as, for instance, the investigation of discourse markers or modality in the entire Shakespeare corpus. Those features will hopefully be studied in the Shakespeare corpus by including socio-historical and also cognitive aspects and by relating them to pragmatic considerations.

8 References

Abbott, Edwin A. 1966 [³1870]. *A Shakespearian Grammar: An Attempt to Illustrate Some of the Differences Between Elizabethan and Modern English*. London: Macmillan [Repr. New York: Dover, 1966].
Adamson, Sylvia. 2001a. The grand style. In: Adamson (eds.), 31–50.
Adamson, Sylvia. 2001b. Understanding Shakespeare's grammar: Studies in small words. In: Adamson (eds.), 210–236.
Adamson, Sylvia, Lynette Hunter, Lynne Magnusson, Ann Thompson, and Katie Wales (eds.). 2001. *Reading Shakespeare's Dramatic Language: A Guide*. London: The Arden Shakespeare [Cengage Learning].
Barber, Charles. 1987 [1981]. *You* and *thou* in Shakespeare's *Richard III*. In: Salmon and Burness (eds.), 163–179. (First published in *Leeds Studies in English*, New Series 12 [1981]: 273–289.)
Barber, Charles. 1997. *Early Modern English*. 2nd edn. Edinburgh: Edinburgh University Press.
Bartlett, John. 1894. *A New and Complete Concordance or Verbal Index to Words, Phrases, and Passages in the Dramatic Works of Shakespeare*. London: Macmillan.
Biewer, Carolin. 2009. Dietetics as a key to language and character in Shakespeare's comedy. *English Studies: A Journal of English Language and Literature* 90(1): 17–33.
Blake, Norman F. 1983. *Shakespeare's Language: An Introduction*. Basingstoke: Macmillan.
Blake, Norman F. 1990. Shakespeare's language: Some recent studies and future directions. *Deutsche Shakespeare-Gesellschaft West. Jahrbuch 1990*, 61–77.
Blake, Norman F. 2002. *A Grammar of Shakespeare's Language*. Houndmills: Palgrave.
Bowdler, Thomas. 1807. *The Family Shakespeare*. London: Longman.
Bradbrook, Muriel C. 1954. Fifty years of the criticism of Shakespeare's style: A retrospect. *Shakespeare Survey* 7: 1–11.
Breuer, Horst. 1983. Titel und Anreden bei Shakespeare und in der Shakespearezeit. *Anglia* 101: 49–77.

Brewer, Charlotte. 2013. Shakespeare, word coining and the OED. In: *Shakespeare Survey* Volume 65: 345–357.

Brook, George L. 1976. *The Language of Shakespeare*. London: Deutsch.

Brown, Penelope and Stephen C. Levinson. 1987 [1978]. *Politeness: Some Universals in Language Usage*. Cambridge: Cambridge University Press.

Brown, Roger W. and Albert Gilman. 1960. The pronouns of power and solidarity. In: Thomas A. Sebeok (ed.), *Style in Language*. Cambridge, MA: MIT Press.

Brown, Roger W. and Albert Gilman. 1989. Politeness theory and Shakespeare's four major tragedies. *Language in Society* 18: 159–212.

Brown, Roger W. and Marguerite Ford. 1961. Address in American English. *Journal of Abnormal and Social Psychology* 62: 375–385.

Burton, Dolores M. 1973. *Shakespeare's Grammatical Style: A Computer-assisted Analysis of Richard II and Antony and Cleopatra*. Austin: University of Texas Press.

Busse, Beatrix. 2006a. *Vocative Constructions in the Language of Shakespeare*. Amsterdam/Philadelphia: John Benjamins.

Busse, Beatrix. 2006b. Linguistic aspects of sensuality: A corpus-based approach to will-construing contexts in Shakespeare's works. In: Christoph Houswitschka, Gabriele Knappe, and Anja Müller (eds.), *Anglistentag 2005 Bamberg: Proceedings*, 125–143. Trier: WVT.

Busse, Beatrix. 2010. Adverbial expressions of stance in Early Modern "Spoken English". In: Jörg Helbig (ed.), *Anglistentag 2009 Klagenfurt: Proceedings*, 47–64. Trier: WVT.

Busse, Ulrich. 2002. *Linguistic Variation in the Shakespeare Corpus: Morpho-syntactic Variability of Second Person Pronouns*. Amsterdam/Philadelphia: John Benjamins.

Busse, Ulrich. 2007. Review of Blake (2002) and Hope (2003). *Journal of Historical Pragmatics* 8(1): 127–137.

Busse, Ulrich. 2008. An inventory of directives in Shakespeare's King Lear. In: Andreas H. Jucker and Irma Taavitsainen (eds.), *Speech Acts in the History of English*, 85–114. Amsterdam/Philadelphia: John Benjamins.

Busse, Ulrich and Beatrix Busse. 2010. Shakespeare. In: Andreas H. Jucker and Irma Taavitsainen (eds.), *Historical Pragmatics*, 247–281. (*Handbooks of Pragmatics*, 8.) Berlin/New York: Mouton de Gruyter,

Cercignani, Fausto. 1981. *Shakespeare's Works and Elizabethan Pronunciation*. Oxford: Clarendon Press.

Crystal, David. 1988. *The English Language*. Harmondsworth: Penguin.

Crystal, David. 2003. The language of Shakespeare. In: Stanley Wells and Linda Cowen Orlin (eds.), *Shakespeare: An Oxford Guide*, 67–78. Oxford: Oxford University Press.

Crystal, David. 2005. *Pronouncing Shakespeare: The Globe Experiment*. Cambridge: Cambridge University Press.

Crystal, David. 2008. *Think on My Words: Exploring Shakespeare's Language*. Cambridge: Cambridge University Press.

Crystal, David and Ben Crystal. 2002. *Shakespeare's Words: A Glossary and Language Companion*. Harmondsworth: Penguin.

Culpeper, Jonathan. 1996. Towards an anatomy of impoliteness. *Journal of Pragmatics* 25: 349–367.

Culpeper, Jonathan. 1998. (Im)politeness in dramatic dialogue. In: Jonathan Culpeper, Mick Short, and Peter Verdonk (eds.), *Exploring the Language of Drama: From Text to Context*, 83–95. London: Routledge.

Culpeper, Jonathan. 2002. Computers, language and characterisation: An analysis of six characters in Romeo and Juliet. In: Ulla Melander-Marttala, Carin Ostman, and Merja Kytö (eds.), *Conversation in Life and in Literature: Papers from the ASLA Symposium*, 11–30. Uppsala: Association Suédoise de Linguistique Appliquée.
Cunliffe, Richard John. 1910. *A New Shakespearean Dictionary*. London: Blackie.
Dobson, E. J. 1968. *English Pronunciation 1500–1700*. 2 vols. Oxford: Clarendon Press.
Evans, Ifor. 1952. *The Language of Shakespeare's Plays*. London: Methuen.
Evans, G. Blakemore with the assistance of J. J. M. Tobin (ed.). 1997 [1972]. *The Riverside Shakespeare*. 2nd edn. Boston: Houghton Mifflin.
Finkenstaedt, Thomas, Erst Leisi, and Dieter Wolff (eds.). 1970. *A Chronological English Dictionary*. Heidelberg: Winter.
Fish, Stanley E. 1976. How to do things with Austin and Searle: Speech act theory and literary criticism. *Modern Language Notes* 91: 983–1025.
Fitzmaurice, Susan M. and Irma Taavitsainen (eds.). 2007. *Methods in Historical Pragmatics*. Berlin/New York: Mouton de Gruyter.
Folkerth, Wes. 2002. *The Sound of Shakespeare*. London: Routledge.
Franken, Gereon. 1995. *Systematische Etymologie: Untersuchung einer 'Mischsprache' am Beispiel des Shakespeare-Wortschatzes*. Heidelberg: Winter.
Franz, Wilhelm. 1986 [1898/99, 1939]. *Die Sprache Shakespeares in Vers und Prosa unter Berücksichtigung des Amerikanischen entwicklungsgeschichtlich dargestellt: Shakespeare Grammatik*. 4th edn. Tübingen: Niemeyer.
Freedman, Penelope. 2007. *Power and Passion in Shakespeare's Pronouns: Interrogating 'you' and 'thou'*. Aldershot: Ashgate.
Garner, Bryan A. 1987a [1982]. Shakespeare's Latinate neologisms. In: Salmon and Burness (eds.), 207–228. (First published in *Shakespeare Studies* 15 [1982]: 149–170.)
Garner, Bryan A. 1987b [1983]. Latin-Saxon hybrids in Shakespeare and the Bible. In: Salmon and Burness (eds.), 229–234. (First published in *Studies in the Humanities* 10 [1983]: 39–44.)
Görlach, Manfred. 1994. *Einführung ins Frühneuenglische*. 2nd edn. Heidelberg: Winter.
Grannis, Oliver. 1990. The social relevance of grammatical choice in Shakespeare. *Deutsche Shakespeare-Gesellschaft West, Jahrbuch 1990*, 105–118.
Hope, Jonathan. 2003. *Shakespeare's Grammar*. London. The Arden Shakespeare [Thomson Learning].
Houston, John Porter. 1988. *Shakespearean Sentences: A Study in Style and Syntax*. Baton Rouge: Louisiana State University Press.
Hulme, Hilda M. 1962. *Explorations in Shakespeare's Language: Some Problems of Word Meaning in the Dramatic Text*. London: Longman.
Hulme, Hilda M. 1972. *Yours that Read Him: An Introduction to Shakespeare's Language*. London: Ginn.
Hussey, Stanley S. 1982. *The Literary Language of Shakespeare*. London: Longman.
Jacobs, Andreas and Andreas H. Jucker. 1995. The historical perspective in pragmatics. In: Jucker (ed.), 3–33.
Jucker, Andreas H. (ed.). 1995. *Historical Pragmatics: Pragmatic Developments in the History of English*. Amsterdam/Philadelphia: John Benjamins.
Jucker, Andreas H. and Irma Taavitsainen. 2013. *English Historical Pragmatics*. Edinburgh: Edinburgh University Press.
Jucker, Andreas H. and Irma Taavitsainen. 2000. Diachronic speech act analysis: insults from flyting to flaming. *Journal of Historical Pragmatics* 1(1): 67–95.

Kakietek, Piotr. 1972. *Modal Verbs in Shakespeare's English*. Poznań: Adam Mickiewicz University Press.
Kellner, Leon. 1922. *Shakespeare-Wörterbuch*. Leipzig: Tauchnitz.
Kermode, Frank. 2000. *Shakespeare's Language*. London: Allen Lane.
Kökeritz, Helge. 1953. *Shakespeare's Pronunciation*. New Haven, CT: Yale University Press.
Kopytko, Roman. 1993. *Polite Discourse in Shakespeare's English*. Poznań: Adam Mickiewicz University Press.
Kopytko, Roman. 1995. Linguistic politeness strategies in Shakespeare's plays. In: Jucker (ed.), 515–540.
Lass, Roger. 1999. Phonology and morphology. In: Roger Lass (ed.) *The Cambridge History of the English Language*. Vol. III. *1476–1776*, 56–186. Cambridge: Cambridge University Press.
Lass, Roger. 2001. Shakespeare's sounds. In: Adamson (eds.), 256–268.
Leisi, Ernst. 1997. *Problemwörter und Problemstellen in Shakespeares Dramen*. Tübingen: Stauffenburg.
Magnusson, Lynne. 1999. *Shakespeare and Social Dialogue: Dramatic Language and Elizabethan Letters*. Cambridge: Cambridge University Press.
Magnusson, Lynne. 2007. A pragmatics for interpreting Shakespeare's sonnets 1 to 20: Dialogue scripts and Erasmian intertexts. In: Fitzmaurice and Taavitsainen (eds.), 167–184.
Mair, Christian. 2006. *Twentieth-century English: History, Variation, and Standardization*. Cambridge: Cambridge University Press.
Markus, Manfred. 2015. "Sirrah, What's Thy Name?": The Genesis of Shakespeare's Sirrah in Relation to Sir and Sire in Late Middle and Early Modern English. In: *English Studies* 96 (2), 191–203.
Mazzon, Gabriella. 2003. Pronouns and nominal address in Shakespearean English: A socio-affective marking system in transition. In: Taavitsainen and Jucker (eds.), 223–249.
McDonald, Russ. 2001. *Shakespeare and the Arts of Language*. Oxford: Oxford University Press.
McIntyre, Dan. 2008. Integrating multimodal analysis and the stylistics of drama: A multimodal perspective on Ian McKellen's Richard III. *Language and Literature* 17(4): 309–334.
Muir, Kenneth and S. Schoenbaum (eds.). 1971. *A New Companion to Shakespeare Studies*. London: Cambridge University Press.
Mulholland, Joan. 1987 [1967]. *Thou* and *you* in Shakespeare: A study in the second person pronoun. In: Salmon and Burness (eds.), 153–161. (First published in *English Studies* 48 [1967]: 34–43.)
Munkelt, Marga and Beatrix Busse. 2007. Aspects of governance in Shakespeare's Edward III: The quest for personal and political identity. In: Sonja Fielitz (ed.), *Literature as History. History as Literature*, 103–121. Frankfurt am Main: Peter Lang.
Murphy, Sean. 2015. I will proclaim myself what I am. Corpus stylistics and the language of Shakespeares soliloquies. In: *Language and Literature* 24 (4), 338–354.
Musgrove, S. 1987 [1981]. Thieves' cant in King Lear. In: Salmon and Burness (eds.), 245–253. (First published in *English Studies* 62 [1981]: 5–13.)
Nakayasu, Minako. 2009. *The Pragmatics of Modals in Shakespeare*. Frankfurt am Main: Peter Lang.
Neuhaus, H. Joachim forthc. *Shakespeare Database*. http://www.shkspr.uni-muenster.de/; last accessed 14 April 2017.
Nevalainen, Terttu. 2001. Shakespeare's new words. In: Adamson (eds.), 237–255.
Nevalainen, Terttu. 2006. *An Introduction to Early Modern English*. Edinburgh: Edinburgh University Press.

Onions, Charles T. 1911. *A Shakespeare Glossary*. 3rd edn., enlarged and revised throughout by Robert D. Eagleston. Oxford: Clarendon Press.

Parod, William. 2004–10. *WordHoard*. Northwestern University and Nu-IT Academic Technologies. http://wordhoard.northwestern.edu/userman/whatiswordhoard.html; last accessed 14 April 2017

Partridge, Astley Cooper. 1955. *Shakespeare's Bawdy*. London: Routledge.

Partridge, Astley Cooper. 1979. Shakespeare's English: A bibliographical survey. *Poetica* 11: 46–79.

Porter, Joseph A. 1979. *The Drama of Speech Acts: Shakespeare's Lancastrian Trilogy*. Berkeley: University of California Press.

Quirk, Randolph. 1987 [1971, 1974]. Shakespeare and the English Language. In: Salmon and Burness (eds.), 1987: 3–21. (First published in Kenneth Muir and S. Schoenbaum (eds.), *A New Companion to Shakespeare Studies*, 67–82. London: Cambridge University Press, 1971. Repr. with minor alterations in Randolph Quirk, *The Linguist and the English Language*, 46–64. London: Arnold, 1974.)

Replogle, Carol A. H. 1987 [1973]. Shakespeare's salutations: A study in stylistic etiquette. In: Salmon and Burness (eds.), 101–115. (First published in *Studies in Philology* 70 [1973]: 172–186.)

Romaine, Suzanne. 1982. *Socio-historical Linguistics: Its Status and Methodology*. Cambridge: Cambridge University Press.

Rubinstein, Frankie. 1984. *A Dictionary of Shakespeare's Sexual Puns and Their Significance*. London: Macmillan.

Rudanko, Juhani M. 1993. *Pragmatic Approaches to Shakespeare: Essays on Othello, Coriolanus and Timon of Athens*. Lanham: University Press of America.

Sairio, Anni. 2013. Elizabeth Montagu's Shakespeare essay (1769): The final draft and the first edition as evidence of two communities of practice. In: Joanna Kopaczyk and Andreas H. (eds.), *Communities of Practice in the History of English*, 177–97. Amsterdam/Philadelphia: John Benjamins.

Salmon, Vivian. 1987 [1965]. Sentence structures in colloquial Shakespearian English. In: Salmon and Burness (eds.), 265–300. (First published in *Transactions of the Philological Society* 1965: 105–140.)

Salmon, Vivian. 1987 [1967]. Elizabethan colloquial English in the Falstaff Plays. In: Salmon and Burness (eds.) 37–70. (First published in *Leeds Studies in English* 1 [1967]: 37–70.)

Salmon, Vivian. 1987 [1970]. Some functions of Shakespearian word-formation. In: Salmon and Burness (eds.), 193–206. (First published in *Shakespeare Survey* 23 [1970]: 13–26.)

Salmon, Vivian. 1987. Introduction. In: Salmon and Burness (eds.), xii–xxii.

Salmon, Vivian and Edwina Burness (eds.). 1987. *A Reader in the Language of Shakespearean Drama*. Amsterdam/Philadelphia: John Benjamins.

Schäfer, Jürgen. 1973. *Shakespeares Stil: Germanisches und romanisches Vokabular*. Frankfurt am Main: Athenäum.

Schäfer, Jürgen. 1980. *Documentation in the O.E.D. Shakespeare and Nashe as Test Cases*. Oxford: Clarendon Press.

Scheler, Manfred. 1982. *Shakespeares Englisch: Eine sprachwissenschaftliche Einführung*. Berlin: Schmidt.

Schlauch, Margaret. 1987 [1965]. The social background of Shakespeare's malapropisms. In: Salmon and Burness (eds.), 71–99. (First published in *Poland's Homage to Shakespeare* 1965, 203–231.)

Schmidt, Alexander and Gregor Sarrazin. 1971 [1874/1875]. *Shakespeare-Lexicon: A Complete Dictionary of all the English Words, Phrases and Constructions in the Works of the Poet.* 2 vols., 6th unchanged edn. Berlin/New York: de Gruyter.

Smith, Bruce R. 1999. *The Acoustic World of Early Modern England.* Chicago: Chicago University Press.

Sokol, B. J. and Mary Sokol. 2000. *Shakespeare's Legal Language: A Dictionary.* London: Athlone Press.

Spevack, Marvin. 1968–80. *A Complete and Systematic Concordance to the Works of Shakespeare.* 9 vols. Hildesheim: Olms.

Spevack, Marvin. 1972. Shakespeare's English: The core vocabulary. *Review of National Literatures* 3: 106–122.

Spevack, Marvin. 1993. *A Shakespeare Thesaurus.* Hildesheim: Olms.

Spevack, Marvin. 2002. Shakespeare@Computer.Horizons. *The Shakespeare Newsletter* 254 (Fall 2002) (1): 82–86.

Stein, Dieter. 1987. At the crossroads of philology, linguistics and semiotics: Notes on the replacement of *th* by *s* in the third person singular in English. *English Studies* 68: 406–432.

Stein, Dieter. 1990. *The Semantics of Syntactic Change: Aspects of the Evolution of do in English.* Berlin/New York: Mouton de Gruyter.

Stein, Dieter. 2003. Pronominal usage in Shakespeare: Between sociolinguistics and conversational analysis. In: Taavitsainen and Jucker (eds.), 251–307.

Stoll, Rita. 1989. *Die nicht-pronominale Anrede bei Shakespeare.* Frankfurt am Main: Peter Lang.

Taavitsainen, Irma and Susan Fitzmaurice. 2007. Historical pragmatics: What it is and how to do it. In: Fitzmaurice and Taavitsainen (eds.), 11–36.

Taavitsainen, Irma and Andreas H. Jucker (eds.). 2003. *Diachronic Perspectives on Address Term Systems.* Amsterdam/Philadelphia: John Benjamins.

Wikberg, Kay. 1975. *Yes-No Questions and Answers in Shakespeare's Plays: A Study in Text Linguistics.* Åbo: Åbo Academi.

Williams, Gordon. 1997. *A Glossary of Shakespeare's Sexual Language.* London: Athlone Press.

Index

address term 5, 16, 50, 198, 199
– in EmodE 113–116
– *thou/you* 50, 198, 199, 218–221
– in Shakespeare 323–326
adjective 23, 34, 54, 65, 151, 173, 217
– comparison of 50, 176, 177, 184
– prefixation of 56–58
– suffixation of 62–64
adverb 23, 24, 65, 81, 83, 84, 119, 120, 232
– loss of verb-adverb order 234–236
adverbial 72–74, 83, 84, 118, 278, 280, 282, 326
alliteration 294, 295, 304
allophonic variation 32–34, 42–45, 250, 256, 258, 262
analogy 52, 57, 59, 61, 63, 170, 216, 217, 231
Anglo-Saxon (language) 100, 167, 211, 298, 302, *see also* Old English
auxiliary 23, 31, 52, 53, 73–77, 81, 84, 175, 195, 196, 234, 322, 323, *see also* periphrasis *do*

borrowing
– lexical 5, 22, 23, 152, 180, 181, 211, 297–302, 315, 319
– morphological 23, 54, 56, 65

Celtic 19, 152, 153, 228
collocation 31, 230, 231
consonant inventory
– changes in 31–34, 44, 315
contact, language 10–13, 131, 145, 150–163, 199–201, 211, 228, 259
corpus/corpora 2, 20, 21, 38, 50, 51, 69, 75, 93, 109–112, 117, 129–145, 146, 167, 173, 175, 179, 190, 197–202, 214, 229, 230, 236, 238, 262, 269, 322, 324, 326, 327

determiner 29, 49, 70, 174–176, 184, 209, 210, 212, 213
dialect(s) 12, 22, 24, 28, 32, 33, 34, 36–39, 100, 128–147, 150–166, 192, 199–201, 211, 243–260

– in literary language 288, 296, 302
– in Shakespeare 315, 318, 319, 322
dictionary 2, 55, 65, 90, 91, 93–96, 99, 134, 182, 316
– OED 91, 92, 100–102
discourse 108, 117–121, 135, 146, 216, 218, 229, 230, 233, 323–327
– markers 117–121
do, auxiliary, *see* periphrasis *do*
Dutch 154–157, 161

education 9, 11, 13–16, 18–20, 101, 182, 188, 192, 193, 196, 198

French 17, 19, 28–33, 37, 49, 91, 95, 96, 132, 170, 218, 289, 298
– affixes from 54–65
– contact with 150, 154–157, 161

gender
– as sociolinguistic variable 14, 122, 188–196, 230
– grammatical 48, 175, 212, 213
genre 11, 13, 16, 18, 19, 130, 132–133, 202, 236
– and language change 189, 193, 219, 220, 237, 322
– in corpora 20, 21, 190
– letters 9, 16, 17, 50, 51, 114–116, 122, 131, 132, 135–138, 143, 144, 158, 189, 193–197, 202, 203
– literary 287, 289, 296–298, 300, 302, 304
Germanic 1, 29, 31, 32, 42, 44, 55, 60, 217, 221, 228, 317
grammars 1, 22, 28, 90, 91, 169, 170–173, 310
– prescriptive 8, 22, 50, 81, 130
grammaticalization 53, 72, 74–77, 82, 121, 228, 236
grapheme 40, 170–172
Great Vowel Shift 24, 27, 35–44, 241–263
Greek 64, 163, 292, 296, 300

idiom/idiomaticity/idiomaticization 120, 189, 296, 316

DOI 10.1515/9783110525069-018

Indo-European 150, 221
inkhorn
– terms 64, 65, 297, 298, 318
– controversy 182, 316
impoliteness 116, 117, 325

Late Modern English 20, 37, 75–77, 159, 168, 179, 184
Latin 11, 17, 19, 20, 22–24, 54–70, 90, 91, 99, 150–152, 169–172, 176, 177, 181, 289, 298, 299, 316, 317
Latin Stress Rule 29, 44
literacy 9, 11, 14–16, 95, 192, 289
lexicon 9, 20, 22, 90–97, 245, 294–299, 316

Middle English 2, 8, 28–39, 41, 44, 47–54, 59, 64, 70–72, 78, 83–85, 133, 151, 158, 163, 211, 212, 228, 242–255
modal 23, 52, 53, 116, 320–323
morphology 5, 47–65, 173–177
– inflectional 5, 23, 47–54, 173–177, 322
– derivational 5, 54–65
– typology 47, 68–70, 85, 155

names 48, 59, 63, 89, 98–100, 151, 152, 267, 276–278
negation 23, 56, 57, 80–82, 162, 173, 177–179, 183, 194–196, 198, 199, 202, 224–228, 230–232, 234, 321, 322
Norman Conquest 19, 28
noun 47, 48, 56–65, 78, 89, 98, 274, 275, 277–279, 284, 295, 296

Old English 2, 22, 31, 39, 48, 52, 53, 69, 74, 75, 78, 80–84, 167, 211
Old Norse 150, 155, 157, 211, 221
orthography 31, 274
– standardization 22
orthoepists 22, 35, 242, 248, 250, 254

periphrasis 5, 23, 50, 53, 54, 73–77, 176, 177
– *do-* 4, 6, 23, 153, 179, 196, 224–240
phoneme 31, 33, 40, 42–45, 170–173, 241–263
phonotactics 29–34, 44, 231–234
phraseological unit, see idioms

politeness, *see also* impoliteness 49, 113–118, 131, 218–221, 324–325
pragmatics 108–122, 218–221, 323–327
Present-day English 23, 28–31, 34, 41, 45, 73–77, 82, 110, 128, 168, 210, 243, 267, 278, 281, 282
printing (press) 8, 9, 11, 16–19, 22, 89, 90, 93, 94, 130, 135, 172
pronouns 23, 48–50, 72, 144, 145, 159, 174, 175, 193, 209–223, 261, 302, 324, 325
– relative, *see* relativizer

reanalysis 38, 72, 78, 80, 228
register 17, 19, 20, 57, 75, 76, 99, 131, 202, 288–291, 299, 302, 303
– legal 19, 176, 184
relativizer 158, 180, 267–284
rhyme 93, 229, 304, 314, 315

semantic change, lexical 90, 97, 100–103, 227
Shakespeare 48, 50, 51, 54, 68, 71–76, 81, 83, 90, 91, 94, 95, 98, 109, 113, 116, 117, 120, 121, 153, 177, 178, 211–221, 297, 304, 309–327
Spanish 90, 96, 154, 155
speaker(s) 6, 17, 28–31, 54–56, 72, 77, 89, 90, 96–103, 109, 112, 115, 118–120, 153–166, 174, 183, 188, 203–205, 212, 215, 226, 227, 243–247, 261, 262, 270, 278, 317, 325
– individual 99, 102, 157, 158, 203, 205, 245
– "Ego documents" 9, 17, 50, 75, 131, 157, 158, 202
speech act 108–113, 323–327
sociolect 96, 129, 134, 135, 146
– social rank 14–16, 51, 114, 129, 134, 174, 178, 188, 191–198, 206, 216, 218, 220, 278
social network 11, 135, 156–158, 188, 189, 204–206, 248
sound change(s) 28–45, 203, 231, 245, 248, 257
spelling, norms of 16, 22, 28, 52, 90–93, 169–173, 192, *see also* standardization
spoken language 16–19, 22–24, 135, 190, 214, 230, 237, 268, 278, 281

standard, English
– Late Modern English 37, 77, 167, 168, 179, 184, 251, 252
– Middle English 27, 29, 33, 34, 37–39, 47–50, 70, 71, 81–85, 158, 163, 173, 174, 235, 236, 243–251
– Old English 53, 211, 212, 258
standardization 22, 28, 167–184
– spelling 22–28, 90, 170–173, 183, 192
– pronunciation 29, 33, 36, 37, 171, 172, 183
– grammar 28, 170–172, 175–180, 192
stress 29–35, 44, 45, 212, 217, 245
style 10, 20, 131, 229, 230, 270, 282, 289–299
– oral vs. literate 19, 20, 28, 29, 51, 120, 298–305
– plain vs. clergial 16, 19, 20, 23, 101–103, 302
subject, category of 23, 24, 49, 71, 72, 77–85, 141–144, 174, 193, 194, 198, 200–202, 209, 210, 216, 217, 221, 231–234, 274–284

superlative, *see adjective*
syllable structure 28–45

Tudor English 89–96, 101

verb 23, 51–65, 71–77, 83, 84, 141–143, 174, 175, 201, 224–236, 320–323
vernacular 91, 180–183
vernacularization 16–20

word formation
– changes in 22, 23, 54–58, 61–63, 184, 316–319
– processes of 59–65, 93–101, 181
word order, changes in 24, 83–85, 217, 295
writing system
– classification of 16–19, 170–173
– English 20–22, *see also* standardization, spelling

www.ingramcontent.com/pod-product-compliance
Lightning Source LLC
Chambersburg PA
CBHW030105010526
44116CB00005B/111